Lighthouses of Hope

Prayer, Healing and the Body-Mind Matrix
By Ronald Rehrer

Dedication

To my four granddaughters:
Raelle and Rivven,
Emily and Audrey

and to the unknown little boy, the street violinist and woman on Rue Cler, Paris, France, a few days after 9/11. They gave me a glimpse of hope for healing a broken world.

A Page of Reflection

Peter, Paul and Mary (from their album "Reunion")
"...and somehow with the magic of music the message comes through... music speaks louder than words... it's the only thing that the whole world listens to... "

Chris de Burgh (from his album "Into The Light"):
"As we walked along the beaches of Normandy,
We came to Juno, Omaha and Gold,
And whispered a prayer for the boys,
Who said goodbye to it all."

Isaiah 53:5:
"...by His stripes we are healed."

John 10:10:
"I came that they might have life and have it abundantly"

Copyright 2013-17 Ronald Rehrer
All Rights Reserved
www.RonRehrer.com

Cover Photo by Charles Jackson
www.NightBeacons.net

Kindle Version 1.1 (Nov 2014)

Paperback Version 1.2 (Jan. 2017)

Table of Contents

- Preface
- Section I - The Sabbatical Begins
    - 1. A Spy and a Nurse: The Seeds Are Sown
    - 2. Toronto, Canada: The Study Begins
    - 3. After Canada: A Healing Story
    - 4. A Man From Jacksonville
    - 5. Signs and Wonders in Toronto
    - 6. Richmond Hill Healing Traumas
    - 7. Rufus Womble and the Order of St. Luke
    - 8. Andrew Weaver Opens the Doors
    - 9. In Person with Dr. Harold Koenig
    - 10. In Person with Dr. David Larson
    - 11. In person with Dr. Robert Ader
    - 12. A Place of Prayer: Abbey of the Genesee
    - 13. Glastonbury Tor
    - 14. Chalice Well and the "Waters of Healing"
    - 15. "Blessed Be, Ron!"
    - 16. Burrswood, England
    - 17. The Midlands: Healing in the Parish
    - 18. Notre Dame Cathedral, Music and Prayer
    - 19. Chartres Cathedral and the Labyrinth
    - 20. Paris to Munich
    - 21. Salzburg and a Night at the Castle
    - 22. September 11, 2001
    - 23. Venice - The Day After 9/11
    - 24. Taize, France: Prayer as Music
    - 25. Rue Cler, Paris, France
    - 26. Amsterdam to Prague
    - 27. The Infant Jesus of Prague

- - 28. Prague to Paris
- Section II - Beyond the Sabbatical
  - 29. Walking a Prayer
  - 30. In Memorium: David Larson
  - 31. The Blumhardts at Bad Boll, Germany
  - 32. The 14 Helpers and Healing
  - 33. "Little Switzerland" Germany
  - 34. Augsburg and a Healing Priest
  - 35. Chimayo, the Lourdes of North America
  - 36. Rev. Bill Dasch and Prayer for Healing
  - 37. My Personal Story of Healing Prayer
- Photographs
- Section III - Authors, Ideas and Research
  - 38. Morton Kelsey - On Healing and Christianity
  - 39. Luther's Role in the Healing Tradition
  - 40. Dr Garth Ludwig - Order Restored
  - 41. Reclaim! The Healing Ministry of Jesus Christ
  - 42. Arthur Umbach and The Many Forms of Prayer
  - 43. Dale Matthews - The Role of Faith in Healing
  - 44. The Byrd Study - Does Prayer Make A Difference?
  - 45. Dr. Nemeh on the Oz Show
- Section IV - Other Voices of Healing
  - 46. Guided Imagery and the Healing Mind
  - 47. Molecules of Emotion
  - 48. Non-Religious Forms of Healing
  - 49. Psychoneuroimmunology Revisited

- Section V - Where Do We Go From Here?
  - 50. The Starting Place Matters
  - 51. What is this force?
  - 52. Lighthouse of Hope
  - 53. Postscript 2017
- Appendices
  - A. List of Biblical Healings
  - B. How To Set Up A Healing Ministry
  - C. Preaching on Healing: A Sermon by Garth Ludwig
  - D. Additional Healing Stories and Poems
  - E. Rev. Paul Teske - Healed and Healing
- Acknowledgments

Preface
Why This Book?

I've written this book at the request of friends and colleagues who urged me to report what I saw and heard on a sabbatical journey I did in 2000-2001. When I returned from my travels, many people asked me to describe what I learned from the field. They asked me about the books I read, the music I heard, the people I visited.

What you hold in your hands is the result of their requests. I think of myself as a 'chronicler' who is reporting to you much like a reporter might offer on Nightline or CNN. I'm like a chronicler who writes a newspaper column about some places I visited, what happened there, and what people shared with me about what they believe and practice. As a chronicler or reporter, I try to capture the exact words spoken, the sounds and smells of the environment, and the tone of the events I witnessed. Privately, I may not agree with the viewpoints of all those I met or read, but as I bear witness to what I saw, I try to bring to you, dear reader, the essence and importance of each encounter.

In the years 2000-2001, I went on a study sabbatical to learn about prayer, healing and the new field of mind-body medicine called psychoneuroimmunology. During the three months of my study, carried out one month at a time over an 18 month period, I was fortunate to meet some of the leading pioneers and practitioners in prayer, healing and mind/body medicine. My travels took me to the east and west coasts of America, on into Canada, and across the ocean to Europe (England, France, Germany, Austria, Italy, Switzerland, and Czechoslovakia.) I also read many books on prayer, attended conferences on healing, and rubbed shoulders with some of the brightest and the best in interrelated fields (such as psychoneuroimmunology). When I returned from my studies, I shared some of what I had learned with friends and colleagues. I watched them listen intently and with excitement to the stories I told. Then one of them said, "Please write a book about all of this: I will never meet the people you met or read all of those books. I want to know more about where you went. I really want to experience through your writing what your experience was like." Another colleague said, "Ron, you've got to write a book about all that you saw and heard," Then a third colleague I deeply respect said, "The Church needs a book like this. It will help us focus again on what really matters."

So I began to seriously consider writing this book. The purpose would be to inform, educate, and share my sabbatical journey. It also gave me an opportunity to offer some hope and help to those suffering illness and in need of healing. Perhaps they would find something here that would help them in the midst of stress and pain. Perhaps they would deepen their prayer life and grow closer to God. For those who are non-believers in God, perhaps they would learn more about natural healing systems, which I have come to believe are part of God's good creation.

But as I was to discover, while there were many books on healing, and prayer, and a few books on psychoneuroimmunology (mind-body medicine which looked at how one's mind interacts with the body's immune system), I couldn't find any books that wrote across all three disciplines. While many books have been published from the 1980's to the present describing healing and the mind, very few have related to religious concerns, and none included a journey such as mine.

So why this book? To share something unique and interesting with many and to whet the appetite to go deeper.

So the book you hold in your hands is about my travels, about some of the people I met along the way, and about some of the things I learned as a result of my study. Instead of this being a scholarly book that argues a particular point of view, this will be more autobiographical and travelogue. It will include vignettes of people and places. This is not a theological or psychological book.

Instead it is a personal report from a sabbatical that began simply as an area of interest and grew to become something I want to share with others.

I have tried to describe people and places as I experienced them, so you will hear people speaking in their own words. You will also have my personal interpretations of some of the places I visited. From time to time I will share with you my thoughts about spirituality and health, as well as the efficacy of prayer in healing. One thing I want the reader to know is that I am not endorsing all points of view in my book, nor have I censured any offering. The purpose here is to share with you where I went and what I heard. You, the reader, must decide for yourself if there are things you agree or disagree with as you visit with me the people and places of my study.

I am grateful that you have chosen to read my book. I hope you will find it interesting as you meet new people here and visit new places. Some of those I was blessed to meet are true visionaries and pioneers in the prayer and healing field. When considered with psychoneuroimmunology, or what I am calling the body-mind matrix (a term borrowed from Candace Pert), we are drawn into a very exciting interface of healing.

What you will be introduced to within these pages are what I am calling "Lighthouses of Hope." These are the people and places which offer the hope for healing. From people like Francis and Judith MacNutt to Chumaya, the Lourdes of North America, from the labyrinths in San Francisco, to the spa town of Bad Boll, Germany, you will see and hear about many of these "Lighthouses of Hope." For Christians who read this book, you will learn more about the healing ministry of Jesus Christ, and how that healing continues even to this day. From Chartres, France to Mansfield, Texas you will hear how the Church continues to reclaim its historic healing ministry.

A Word about Lighthouses

Perhaps a word is in order as to why I have chosen the lighthouse as my metaphor of hope.

Lighthouses are very special places. They do very important work. The dedication and commitment of those lighthouse keepers of yesteryear, who manned lighthouses alone in the dead of night, has always been fascinating to me. I have friends who collect lighthouses of all kinds. What all of these lighthouses of various shapes and sizes and colors symbolize is the constant beacon of hope and strobe light for safety in a world of darkness or storm. Lighthouses off shore, on rock pilings, on shoals, or high on hills, give mariners the relentless warning of danger so that sailors can steer away from destruction (prevention). Lighthouses near safe harbors flash their "welcome home" messages in sweeps of light that calm the heart and lift the spirit. The lighthouse keepers kept those lights shining 24 hours a day, all year round. Their tireless dedication and commitment to providing hope reminds me of the researchers and healers I met on my sabbatical.

I've seen many lighthouses over the past few years. Some were up along the Pacific Northwest shores, some were along the Great Lakes near Canada, some were along the East Coast and in the Southeastern United States, and some were in Southern California. I've also seen dozens of replicas of them in shops and stores, on t-shirts and sweaters, on the backs of playing cards, and matchboxes, and many photographs of them on postcards, on calendars and in paintings. I even purchased from my local Post Office, a matted, underglass, enlarged postage stamp of the Marblehead Lighthouse, across the water from where I wrote a substantial amount of this book in Ohio. There is a great love for the lighthouse these days.

Why? I think there are many reasons. Here are some I think of. The steady blink of the lighthouse light is a welcome point for navigation for those on the water. It reminds sailors that there is a sign of hope out there in the darkness. It warns of danger but is a sign of safety, for the lighthouse beacon reassures that there is someone "out there" that knows you are there in that darkness. There are dark times for patients who are told they have a catastrophic disease or find themselves in failing health. People seek out places of hope and comfort when their lives are about to be turned upside down.

As one close friend said, "Lighthouses are like churches. They welcome people. They shine with light. People find safety in them."

The Church has always been a place of shelter and support for weary travelers or for those who have lost their way or find themselves in darkness. Churches can be lighthouses of hope for those who are ill, stricken by grief, or have fallen on difficult times.

Today I believe there are human "lighthouses" beckoning people to the shores of healing. On my sabbatical I met some of these modern day "lighthouses," who are lights to people in darkness. Some of these men and women are people of prayer. Some of them are in healing ministries while others are in religion and health research. Others come from fields of mind/body research and scientific investigations. Some are physicians and nurses, while others are energy healers and Reiki masters. Some find Jesus Christ at the very heart and center of all healing, while others have taken a different belief pathway. From churches to research labs, from the National Institutes of Health to the government's Office for Alternative Medicine, there are many visionaries in prayer, healing and health, who stand like sentinels on the edges of life, pointing the way for us to find safe harbors of healing.

It is a gift to us that these people have shared so much with us. I will be eternally grateful for the opportunity to have met some of them in person and to have read their writings. They opened their offices, their homes and their hearts so that I would be the recipient of their wisdom. Unfortunately, some have passed away since I began writing this book. But they live on in my memory and in the writings, research and teachings they shared with so many.

So, come with me into a journey of discovery. There are many Lighthouses of Hope ahead. I hope you enjoy the journey.

Section 1 Chapter 1
A Spy and a Nurse: The Seeds Are Sown

The Spy

It was a Tuesday evening and my plane was landing at Sky Harbor Airport in Phoenix. The sky in the west was all pinks and blues as the wheels of my plane touched down. I made my way quickly to the car rental counter, signed the paperwork, and stepped outside into the Arizona heat. I found my rental car, checked the map, and drove north out into the Arizona desert towards a place called Cave Creek, near Carefree. Elleston had warned me that after awhile I would be driving in a semi-remote area with very few lights along the road. Was he ever right! It wasn't long before I found myself driving in the dark, with the night sky clear above me with twinkling stars, and very few lights along the road. Today if you were to make this drive you would be surrounded by lights because Phoenix has expanded northwards all the way to Carefree and Cave Creek. But back then, in the mid-1980's, it was dark and remote. I was concerned I would miss the dirt road turnoff that would lead to Elleston's home.

I had to look very carefully so as to not miss the road marker. I was fascinated with the idea that someone from England would now live in this remote, secluded area of Arizona. What would he be like? What would we talk about? Why had he not written a Quiller novel in three years? Was he writing one now? So many thoughts swirled in my head.

There it was! The road marker to my left was there. Turn left... scenes from the Quiller novels flowed through my mind. Quiller behind the wheel. Quiller in a red sector. Quiller in a remote area. Quiller in the shadows. And now as I drove in the darkness I had the thought: this is metaphor. The writer of Quiller the spy lives in a remote, secluded, very private, hard to find place.

I was looking for Christmas lights - in August. He had said there were some Christmas lights strung up so I would see the house. Suddenly, there it was.

My headlights split the darkness, and I could hear the crunch of my tires on tiny stones as I made my way onto the property. I parked, left my car, and approached the large double doors to the home. I took a breath, feeling nervous, raised my hand, hesitated, then knocked.

What had brought me to this moment in time? Those who know me well, know that I love mystery and spy novels. I'm often at the Mystery Book Store in Westwood, near UCLA, on at least one weekend per month meeting favorite authors, buying first editions and getting signed copies of the author's works.

The roots to this hobby of reading spy and mystery novels can be traced back to my years as a college student in Oakland and Berkeley. In the mid 1960's, my college buddies and I had gone to see a new movie entitled "The Spy Who Came In From the Cold," based on John LeCarre's novel of the same title. The film starred Richard Burton as the spy coming in from 'the cold,' which was a reference to the Cold War. I loved the film and not long after there was another spy movie released. It was called the Quiller Memorandum, based on a novel of the same title by Adam Hall. This film featured George Segal and Max Von Sydow, and while the film was rather bland, I loved the soundtrack which featured the song, "Wednesday's Child." One line from the song went, "Wednesday's child is a child of woe." It seemed to fit the cold war bleakness of spy novels. I decided to read the novel because I had discovered that very often books were much better than the films based on them.

I found the novel, The Spy Who Came In From The Cold, quite easily, but I could not find The Quiller Memorandum anywhere. But I did manage to find a different Quiller novel from the same author. This book was called the Tango Briefing. After reading it, the Quiller character became my favorite spy character and I set out to read every one of Adam Hall's novels.

As the years went by, I looked for new Quiller titles but they were very difficult to find. Perhaps I would find one in a drug store by accident, or I would pass by a rack of novels at a book store and find one. Sometimes I would be on vacation and would discover a Quiller book in a remote or second-hand book shop. Regular bookstores did not seem to carry Adam Hall "Quiller" novels but somehow I did manage to find six or seven of these novels. Then one day while reading the L.A. Times newspaper I discovered a book review section that said this author had moved from Europe to the United States. The notice specifically mentioned that he had moved to Arizona.

I continued to find Quiller books as the years passed, sometimes even in hardback. I still knew no one who had ever read a Quiller spy book. I felt as if I was the only one in the world who liked these books. No one I knew had ever heard of the writer, Adam Hall, much less the Quiller character.

At the same time I was also reading detective fiction. I had seen another film entitled "Harper" starring Paul Newman. I loved Newman's portrayal of a Southern California detective named Lew Harper, a kind of updated version of the famous Raymond Chandler character, Philip Marlowe. As the credits rolled by at the end of the film Harper, I noticed that this movie was based on a book entitled "Moving Target" by Ross MacDonald. The next day I went out and found this book and discovered the best writer of the mystery novel of all time.

MacDonald's character in the Newman film is called Lew Harper but in the novels he is known as Lew Archer. I absolutely loved the Archer character and over the years I purchased all of the Lew Archer novels.

So now I had two favorite authors, one who wrote of a spy character (Quiller) and the other who wrote of a detective character (Archer). As the years went by, from the mid-1960's until the mid-1980's, I read each of these novels with great relish. Then one day I came upon an article that said Ross McDonald had died. The literature world was mourning his passing for he was the kind of writer who could have written equally well in any genre. Many held that his works were like fine wines or fine literature. Unlike Adam Hall who was basically unknown in the United States, Ross McDonald was very well known. His passing was written about from coast to coast. I felt sad that he had died. It was like losing a friend. I believe the article said he had died of cancer, but years later I learned from his biographer, Tom Nolan, that Kenneth Millar (MacDonald's real name) had died of Alzheimer's complications.

The thing is, I had actually thought about trying to visit Ross McDonald a year or two earlier. I had no idea if famous writers ever met their reading public, and I had no idea where Ross MacDonald lived at the time, or even how one would go about trying to connect with an author. But now it was too late. He was gone.

Then a thought occurred to me. Perhaps I had better see if I could visit Adam Hall before it was too late. Then another thought occurred! It had been over three years since I had seen any new Quiller novel. I wondered if perhaps Adam Hall may have also passed.

So I got my last Quiller book off my shelf and looked at the publishing date. It HAD been three years! What if Adam Hall had died? Could I have somehow missed that notice in the paper? If he was still living in Arizona I must try to make contact.

And so I did. I wrote a letter to Adam Hall in care of the Berkeley Publishing Group, the publishers of the last Quiller book I had on my bookshelf. Several months passed by after I sent that letter, and I heard nothing.

It was in August of that year that my family and I had gone on vacation, and when we returned there were several messages on our answering machine. This was in 1988. My wife began to play these messages back while I took the suitcases into the bedroom to unpack. A few moments later I heard her call out, "Do you have a client named Elleston Trevor who is trying to reach you?" "No," I replied, "I've never heard of anyone by that name." "Well, come and listen to this... he sounds British" she said.

So I went into the kitchen and stood by the phone answering machine and pressed the "listen" button again. What I heard was a deep baritone voice, a much better sounding "James Bond" type voice than that of Sean Connery.

"Hello, Ron, this is <u>Elleston Trevor</u>. You probably know me as Adam Hall, and I got your lovely letter, and yes, the next time you come into the Phoenix area, I would love to visit with you. Here is my phone number and why don't you call me and I'll give you directions out to my home. Goodbye for now." *click*

I stood there stunned! Shocked! I had just heard the voice of my favorite author. He was alive and inviting me to his home! I was feeling like a kid in a candy store, or like the boy who hits the grand slam home run to win the game in the bottom of the ninth inning!

I was going to get to meet Adam Hall, or rather <u>Elleston Trevor</u>. I couldn't wait to make the plans! I had no idea what to expect. I was excited and nervous. I was grinning from ear to ear!

It was too late to call that evening, so I called the next day and got his answer machine. Later on in the week he left another message on our machine. This time he said, "Hello, Ron, I'm on my way to the vet with my dog, so I thought I'd call again. Let me know when you think you might come over for a visit. I look forward to meeting you and talking with you. Have a great day." I returned the call and he answered! It really was thrilling to be speaking with Elleston. Our conversation was brief, we made a date for dinner at his home, and I called some close friends in Arizona, Larry and Linda Stoterau, to see if I could stay the night with them after my visit with Adam Hall. I booked a flight and a rental car. A dream was about to come true. What I didn't know was that a seed was about to be planted which would later sprout into my sabbatical study on prayer, healing and body-mind medicine.

* * *

I knocked. A few moments later the door opened, and a trim, fit man, wearing a black karate style robe opened the door, and said, "You must be Ron. Come in. Welcome to my home." He extended his hand and his handshake was firm and inviting.

As I walked into his living room I saw beautiful horse saddles mounted on display, and looking up I saw the front covers of the Quiller novels greatly enlarged and beautifully framed, hanging around the room. To my left was the dining area. A young, beautiful woman was just lighting the candles on the dinner table, which was elegant and well set. Elleston said, "This is my wife, Chaille," and I said hello and commented about how lovely her home was. Elleston then asked me if I would like to see where he worked, where he wrote his books. I said a very enthusiastic yes, and he led me out into his converted garage.

To my right was a desk with a standard Underwood typewriter. On the desk were papers and several books, and I saw dozens of books stacked in piles on the floor around the room. Over the desk was a long Samurai sword... a scene from a Quiller novel flashed in my mind. To my left was a book cabinet with books by Elleston under several pen names. He told me these were first editions. I noticed that some of the books were translated into numerous foreign languages.

Here I stood, in the writing room, of an internationally famous writer. It was an awesome moment for me. At some point I asked him who he liked to read, who was his favorite author. He said he was partial to the works of Martin Cruz Smith, and asked if I had ever read him. I quickly said yes, and told him that I had read Gorky Park and thought it was an excellent book. He replied that he felt that Smith was a wordsmith and that he wished he had the craft that Smith had. I replied that I felt he was a far better writer than Smith, and that no one could touch him in the spy genre of fiction. He asked me why I thought that. I told him that the techniques he used in bringing his characters to life were unusual and superb. I mentioned how the Quiller novels are written in first person, how many of the chapters end with Quiller in harm's way, in a cliff hanger, like in the old Saturday afternoon matinee movie serials, and that the following chapter would begin somewhere else, as if nothing had happened to Quiller and that in the telling, one would learn how Quiller escaped his predicament. I also spoke about how Quiller is so in touch with his inner self, understanding alpha brain waves and the like, how to slow down his consciousness, how he is self reflective, and how the intricacies of martial arts was explained. I spoke about how each of Quiller's "Controls" (the agents running the spies in the field) was interesting, especially my favorite one, Ferris, and how I was intrigued with Ferris' habit of squashing bugs with his fingers.

At that, Elleston chuckled and then with a half-serious tone, he asked me why I thought he had invited me to his home. I replied, "Because I am a loyal fan who has read every one of your books I suppose." He said, "Yes that's true, but I was taken by a few things in the letter you wrote to me."

I asked, "What did I write that interested you in inviting me?"
He paused, then he said, "There were a couple of things. First, you noticed that I have not written anything in the past couple of years. There's a reason for that. My wife of many years got cancer. I took her all over the world trying to save her life. Money was no object. I just wanted her to live. I loved her so much. And during this time I stopped writing. I could not write. And after she died I had no will to write. In fact I decided not to write anymore. In your letter you saw I was not writing and you mentioned that you are a mental health counselor with a religious background. Tonight if it's alright with you I'd like to talk about metaphysical things, existential things, about death and dying. About healing and the afterlife. Would that be alright with you?"
I was stunned. Here I had come to stand "star struck" in the presence of my favorite writer. Instead he was opening up an area of his pain and suffering. He was wanting to talk about life and death, and the profound loss of his wife.
I said, "Of course, I'd be willing to talk with you about anything you would like to talk about."
He replied, "Thank you." Then he told me how devastated he was after losing Jonquille, his wife. They had met during World War II during the Blitz. (To see into this profound love of his life, read A Bridge Across the Years at the Quiller website. My good friend Jon Peralez made this such a wonderful website in tribute to Elleston Trevor.)
Elleston spoke about how he could not save his wife. Then he spoke about becoming a widower, a single man who was older. He spoke about how he could not do the bar scene, and how he thought he would never remarry. Then a long-time friend, a woman, introduced him to her daughter. He said he felt he was old enough to be her father, but they met anyway, and talked, and shared meals together. He learned that she was also struggling with a painful loss. Her boyfriend enjoyed flying planes. One morning he flew off in a World War II refurbished fighter plane and never returned. His plane crashed somewhere in the Arizona desert.
They continued to get to know each other better, and eventually their friendship turned into love and Elleston married Chaille. He began to write again. As he told me about his first wife I could

tell how profoundly he loved her. And I could tell how deeply he loved his new wife, Chaille, and how life had given him a second chance. He then said, "So now I have a new Quiller book pending a publishing company, and I'll be showing this book to potential publishers at an upcoming trade show. I'm writing another Quiller story, so are there any elements you would like for me to include in a future Quiller story?" I smiled and said, "Sure, of course! I would like to see Ferris return. He's my favorite "Control" over Quiller when Quiller is in the field." Elleson laughed and said, "I'll see what I can do for you." Little did I know that Elleston would bring Ferris back in that very next novel he was writing. Ferris would also return in a poignant encounter with Quiller in what would be Elleston's final book years later, a book that he finished just two days before his own death of cancer. In fact, he dictated the last few paragraphs over a single day, just a few words at a time, trying to complete the book before he passed away. He dictated these final words to his son, which his son writes about in the Epilogue in the final Quiller novel entitled "Quiller Balalaika." His son and Chaille were at his bedside in those last moments. That final Quiller book became a rarity in that it was only published in England because Elleston missed the publishing deadline with an American publisher because of his illness. In 2001, on e-Bay, a hardcover copy of Quiller Balalaika sold for over $500. In the back of that book, in the epilogue, his son carefully describes his father's home, including the Underwood typewriter and the Samurai sword over the desk. Reading it brought tears to my eyes because I can still picture it all in my mind, having stood in these very places in his father's home. (Later the final Quiller book was published in America by Elleston's friend, publisher and bookseller, Otto Pensler).

* * *

But on this magical night for me, Elleston said "Shall we have supper?"

So we joined Chaille at supper, enjoying wine and delightful ambience. We spoke about many things. Elleston eventually asked me if I knew of the book Quantum Healing. I told him I'd never heard of the book. He told me I must read it since it deals with healing. He described the writer to me, a physician from

New York named Deepak Chopra, and that this was one of the first books he read during his first wife's struggle with cancer. He talked about how much he had learned about the body, about disease and health, and about dying. I told him I would definitely read the book, simply based on his recommendation. I told him that given all that he had been through recently, I appreciated him recommending Quantum Healing to me. Little did I know that this would be the first seed towards my study sabbatical eleven years later.

We spoke about many other things that night in his home. He and Chaille spoke about grief, about how painful it is to lose someone you deeply love. They spoke about how their love blossomed, and Chaille described how romantic Elleston was. It was apparent the way they looked at each other across the table that I was in the presence of a profound love story. Elleston was always the romantic, the lover, the giver. He was completely dedicated and loyal to his wives. Chaille deeply understood Elleston and his love for his first wife. What then blossomed between she and Elleston seemed even more profound. Years later, when my friend Jon Peralez and I met with Chaille during a celebration of Elleston's great writing career (much of his collection is at ASU, Arizona State University library archives), Chaille brought along their wedding album to share with us what it was like marrying Elleston, and to share what a deep and wonderful love story they truly shared. She also brought along a tape for us to listen to so that Jon could hear Elleston's voice. He was lecturing at ASU in a writer's class.

That night, at Elleston's home, I was privileged to be allowed a brief glimpse into the hearts of two people who had suffered profound loss, and deep grief. They shared with me the need for healing wounds, and the need to find a cure for cancer. They spoke of prolonged pain and suffering, and the awfulness of sudden death. Elleston's intensity around healing moved me deeply. I wanted to learn what he had learned. I decided that I had to read the book he had read, Quantum Healing.

After supper, as we approached his door to say goodbye, I noticed a very large stem glass, a few feet tall, standing near the front door, filled with dozens of wine corks in it. Then I noticed Elleston writing my name and date on the side of the wine cork from our evening together. "This is how we remember the guests to our home." He put the cork into the large glass and picked up another one. "Here's one from when another friend visited." Then he showed me a few more. He invited me to return. We shook hands and I stepped out into the night air. It had been a magical night.

The Nurse

Her name was Betty, wife to Pastor Jim Lareva. We had been good friends and it was a Monday night at a conference when I saw Jim escorting Betty towards a table near the pool of this large hotel where we were attending the conference, She was walking slowly, and looked pale, even though she wore her ever ready smile. I had heard she was battling cancer, but I hadn't seen her in awhile.

Jim saw me and came over and said, "Hi, Ron. Betty would like to talk with you if that's ok." I broke away from the friends I was with, and walked over to where Betty was sitting. I sat next to her and she took my hand between her two hands and said, "It's good to see you, how have you been?" We caught up with each others' lives and then she said, "You know I've been battling cancer?" "Yes, I had heard that," I replied. "Well," she said, "I've been going to see someone who practices alternative medicine. It's called guided imagery. Do you know what that is?" I said no that I had never heard about it. She told me that her imagery counselor helped her form images of her cancer and other things that were helping her a lot. She said she was in remission now and that she believed she would be getting better. As I looked at her I could see how much weight she had lost. It saddened my heart to see her this way. I had lost other friends to cancer and had watched them slowly waste away. Now I was seeing another friend heroically fighting for her life.

As Betty shared more details of her "guided imagery" therapy, her eyes sparkled with hope and confidence. At one point, as she continued to hold my hands in her hands across the small table where we sat, she looked me straight in the eye and said, "I want you to promise me something. Many people count on you and trust you with their hearts when they see you in counseling. I

want you to promise me you will learn guided imagery. It can make a huge difference for the people you work with."
Something stirred me by her request. I promised her I would do it for her. Somehow this felt right to me. Betty was a nurse, an excellent caregiver for others. She understood what she was facing and had confidence in this guided imagery process. She spoke of how it addressed mind, body and spirit. She told me how it could be used with a variety of mental and physical conditions. The more I listened, the more I was intrigued and genuinely curious about this procedure. She smiled and said, "I want to hear later on what you think of it." I said I'd let her know at next year's conference. She said, "I'll meet you right here." We then talked about other things, and then her husband, Jim, rejoined us. After talking for awhile, we said goodnight and it would be another year before I saw them again.

A few weeks later, a brochure came across my office desk. It was an invitation from the Academy for Guided Imagery! I couldn't believe it. I had just promised Betty I would study imagery, but I had no idea who taught it, where it was taught, or anything about it. Suddenly, here was a brochure on Guided Imagery. It was as if I was "being led" by God. I was to have this thought many more times in the years ahead.

A.G.I, the Academy for Guided Imagery was offering a one-day introduction to Interactive Guided Imagery at a low price. So I decided now was the time to discover for myself what this was all about. Betty had gotten me started on this search, and I vowed I would complete my promise. I wont go into details here, but I want to share one personal experience I had during the introductory workshop.

Dr. Martin L. Rossman, M.D. (whom I would later call "Marty" as I continued on in my training with A.G.I.) was leading this portion of the workshop. He led everyone through an imagery experience in which we were to "allow an image" to come to our imagination of some physical symptom we had now or in our past. Since I had recently recovered from major knee surgery to replace my ACL, I still had swelling and pain in my right knee where the surgery had been done. So the image that came to me was of a Nazi Panzer tank grinding through the blazing, hot desert sands of North Africa. In this image, the tank was moving across my field of vision, moving to the left, with its massive track digging deeply into the sand. It was at the place where the track of the tank dug into the sand that corresponded to the pain in my right knee. I could hear Dr. Rossman's voice as my eyes remained closed during this exercise. Marty then said something about allowing the image to modify in some way that changes the image in a positive way. My image slowly changed. The Panzer tank now turned into a water balloon in the shape of a Panzer tank. The water balloon tank was filled with water and still moved across my field of vision. But instead of the tank having metal tracks that dug into the sand, it now slid across the sand as if moved by an invisible hand. It had a smooth bottom now like a water balloon would have. As it slid through the sand smoothly, filled with water, I seemed to become aware that the pain in my right knee was lessening.

Marty then invited us to allow the image to change again. Suddenly my tank transformed into a helium balloon! It now began to bounce gently up into the air, then float back down to the desert floor, as if pulled gently back down to earth by gravity. It was sort of like watching astronauts on the surface of the moon leaping into the air only to be brought back down by gravity in a soft landing. I watched the image of my "balloon tank" bounce up... then back down... up... then back down. I could now barely sense the discomfort in my knee. As if far away I heard Marty's voice now, once again as he invited us to let the image change again in any way it wished to bring us even greater comfort or peace. Now my helium balloon image, still in the shape of a tank, began to rise higher into the air with each bounce. It was as if there was greater helium inside the form now. Then, a strange thing happened. The tank turned to the right so that I now saw its rear end moving away from me. Then the tank began to bounce high into the sky, moving further away from me, moving towards the horizon. With each new bounce it took, it became smaller and smaller as it moved towards that far distant horizon. It continued to move away from me. It bounced... became smaller as it grew further and further away from me.

It bounced again... smaller... bounced... diminished in size... almost a small dot now, so far away from me... bounced... and disappeared over the horizon, like a very tiny pink head... then... it was completely gone. So was my pain.

Marty invited us to open our eyes and share our experiences with a partner in the room.

A woman to my right agreed to listen as my partner. I told her my imagery experience. When I had finished she asked me how my knee felt. I reached down to my pant leg covering my knee. The swelling had completely gone away. I flexed my knee–absolutely no pain. I was amazed. It would be another 72 hours before I felt any discomfort in my knee. Even then it was only with slight discomfort.

No wonder my friend Betty wanted me to experience guided imagery. I had experienced first hand the salutary effect of imagery. I made the decision then and there to learn guided imagery.

I went through the basic course in Guided Imagery. Later on I would be invited to become one of the Mentors for AGI training. Eventually I would be invited to become part of the AGI "faculty around the country." At one point in the early 1990's Roxanne Whitelight (the chief trainer and mentor with AGI) and I co-led a wonderful all day training for fellow faculty members and AGI students called "Imagery and the Christian client."

During the debriefing of the opening sequences of imagery exercises, there was a healing of old wounds for some of the attendees as they shared about hurts they had experienced in the name of the Church. I was beginning to understand the deep need for healing on all sorts of levels.

Today in my counseling practice I still use interactive guided imagery to help people in their healing processes.

Later, Betty would succumb to her disease, but that following year after we had spoken about guided imagery, she did return with Jim to the conference. She looked beautiful, young and vibrant, as if she had never been ill a day in her life. She eventually did die from the cancer. But she fought the good fight and not only taught me about guided imagery but sowed a seed for me to later grow an interest in healing.

* * *

Elleston also would later succumb to cancer. I read about it on an America West airplane as it rose out of the Arizona desert. A guy across from me was reading the Arizona newspaper and there was a picture of Elleston. I asked for the newspaper when the man was finished with it. He gave it to me and I sat with tears reading about him.

Later on, years later, my friend Jon Parelez and I would work with the archivist at ASU to have a week to honor Elleston's great writing history. His Quiller novels are at Arizona State University in Tempe, Arizona.

These two, Elleston, writer of the spy, Quiller, and my good friend, Betty, the nurse, were the seeds that took root for my study sabbatical in prayer, healing and body-mind matrix.

A spy and a nurse, the beginnings...

Chapter 2
Toronto, Canada: The Study Begins
Canon Linda Nicholls, Canon Lynne Calhoun and "The Power Within" Video

My plane was now descending out of the clouds at 30,000 feet, and I would soon be landing at Buffalo International Airport, Buffalo, New York. My mind was filled with thoughts about how I had decided to make this the first step of my sabbatical. One night, weeks before, I had sat at my computer, used a search engine, and began a search on religion and healing. To my surprise, one of the first websites that came up described a new video entitled "The Power Within" (<https://vimeo.com/10941191>) which dealt with the healing power of prayer. The website had wonderful scenes from this video, created by the Anglican Church of Canada. Little did I know that finding this website that night would be such a trigger event for the way I would be led throughout my sabbatical journey. But it is like that sometimes. Only in retrospect do we see it.

Before laying out my itinerary for the three month sabbatical, I put onto paper the key questions I wanted to have answered, if they could be answered.

Does God still heal today? That was the central question at the heart of my proposed study. I wanted to know if God still heals today, how does it happen?

Does one approach God through prayer? If so, how does one pray for healing?

What happens when one prays? Does God listen? Does my very praying somehow effect my mind and my body? What is the relationship between prayer, healing and mind/body health?

Those were some of the questions I posed for myself as I began my study sabbatical in 2000-2001. I gave my study sabbatical a working title: "Prayer, Healing and Psychoneuroimmunology." What I wanted to learn was more about prayer, and healing and their connection to mind/body medicine.

So the night I did that search on religion and health, I had no idea how important this event would become and how it would lead me to new people and new places. I simply printed out some things from the website, and the next day I made a few phone calls to set up some appointments.

The people at the Anglican Church House were wonderful on the phone. The receptionist in the resource center said she would preview the video for me when I came to Toronto. She also said she would have some time for me to answer any questions I had about the making of the video. She gave me the contact phone number for Canon Linda Nicholls who was chairperson of the Bishop's Commission on Healing. She also suggested I contact Canon Lynne Calhoun who she explained was involved with the healing Order of St. Luke's. She also told me to plan some time for their bookstore because they had a very large section on healing and prayer.

Somehow going to Toronto felt like the right "first step" as my mentor and friend Roxanne Whitelight would say. Roxanne was the phenomenal lead mentor, teacher and guide at the Academy for Guided Imagery during the early 1990's. A deeply spiritual person, her focus is on helping people take "the right size bite" for themselves for whatever "work" they are doing. She had invited me to attend her ordination service in the Order of Glastonbury, and during this service she lay face down before the altar of the Lord, committing herself to her work in the service of others. She invited me to her home to sit in on a small house church gathering of people from various religious backgrounds who had been wounded by the Church. Gathered around a small altar in the center of the circle, I listened to people sharing their pain from their emotional and spiritual wounds. Some had come from traditional churches that held no life for them anymore. Some had journeyed through eastern spirituality on quests for meaning, value and wholeness. There in Roxanne's home they were finally finding a safe, healing place. They were taking those important small steps to spiritual recovery. Somehow I could sense that being with Roxanne in Spokane that one evening, with those seeking a deeper relationship to God, had opened up in me the admission of my own spiritual desert, and my own need for a new rain for my parched soul. I could see Roxanne's face, gently smiling, and her voice of encouragement asking "does this feel like the right step?"

For me the Spirit of God leads us in many ways. One of those is through the comforting and guiding words of good friends. So as I finished with my phone calls to the Anglican house, to Canon Nicholls, and to Canon Calhoun, I felt a calm warmth come to me. I really cannot explain this. It just felt "right" in the direction I was going.

As mentioned earlier, I had designed my Sabbatical study very simply. I created a working title for it, calling it "Prayer, Healing and Psychoneuroimmunology." The term "psychoneuroimmunology" is another word for mind/body study. It is the exploration of the interrelationship and interactions of the "psyche" (or mind), the "neuro" system (from the field of neurology), and the "immunological" systems of the body (dealing with the body's natural inner defense mechanisms and defense against diseases and disorders). It is often abbreviated as PNI. I didn't know if anyone had ever written a book or article on prayer, healing and mind/body medicine in relationship to each other. I only knew that there were books on prayer, and that, while prayer has always been practiced for thousands of years, only recently had prayer once again come to the forefront for growing numbers of people for whom prayer had only been tangential and rarely practiced. I also knew that healing was also being "reclaimed" by the church-at-large. I was also aware that medical schools had been doing research since the late 1970's into the relatively new field of mind/body studies. Somehow, going to Toronto seemed like the right thing to do.

For some reason what popped into my mind were other famous journeys, especially Biblical stories. Abraham was called out of Ur to follow the Lord's lead. The Israelite's journey through the wilderness came to mind as well. Then I thought of Jonah being summoned to Nineveh, and what happened to him as he became disobedient. Then it came to me. Each of those journeys became transformational for those on the journey. So then I thought, "would something happen to me with this first step in Toronto?" What would I learn? What did God want me to learn? What would He want me to "see"? I had no idea. I only knew that my Sabbatical was to listen, study and learn. I had no idea where it would lead. But like with all journeys, it began with a first step, "the right size bite."

* * *

My plane landed in Buffalo safely, and I rented a car, and drove across the border into Canada. After leaving American soil, you drive across the bridge that leads to Niagara Falls. To my left, looking through the driver's side window, I could see the mighty spray lifting up from the great Niagara Falls, which plunges from the Saint Lawrence seaway into the depths below. While I couldn't see it I knew that somewhere down there was the Maid of the Mist boat, loaded with people in raincoats, standing at the front of the ship, covered in the rainy mist kicking up from the great spray of water where the Falls crash on the grand rock piles below. I thought back to other times when I had been to the Falls: with my parents (now deceased) when we were on vacation as they took me to college; another time with Pastor Bob Spillman, clinical pastoral education supervisor from Buffalo, New York; with friends from the Internet on-line club that likes the music of Chris de Burgh.

I drove up through St. Catherines, on up to a Motel 6 in Burlington. That first night, I had an appointment to meet with Brian Morton, another friend from the Chris de Burgh group. Brian is an excellent musician and we scheduled a night in a small sound studio to make a cut of the song "Say Goodbye To It All" which is my favorite song by Chris de Burgh. We were doing this cover version for a Tribute album being made by the Friends of Chris de Burgh. We began our work on the song around 7 p.m. that evening with Brian Morton laying tracks using various instruments. I did the vocal at midnight, and we finished up with Brian's voiceovers around 2 a.m. At 3 a.m. the sound mixer guy was done with the mixing and sent my version of the song over the Internet to Montreal where it would be gathered together with all of the other cover versions of songs coming from around the world.

I slept soundly that night, exhausted from the plane ride and the recording event.

The next morning I drove to a northwest suburb of Toronto called Thornhill where I was to meet with Canon Linda Nicholls, chairperson of the Anglican Bishop's Commission on Healing. I pulled into the parking lot of her old, beautiful church. A large complex of meeting rooms and hallways is part of this old village church, called the Holy Trinity Anglican Church. The day I visited, the Disney company was making a film on the property, so there was a great deal of activity going on inside and outside the facility. I walked down a long corridor and then a staff person came from somewhere and asked if she could help me. I said I had an appointment with Canon Linda Nicholls. She replied that Canon Nicholls was expecting me. Within moments, I was escorted into Canon Nicholls' office where she had been waiting for me. She stood up from her chair, welcomed me to Canada, and offered me, coffee, tea or water. I took the water, sat in a chair opposite her, and introduced myself and told her why I had come to see her.

Linda is a trim, very neat looking minister. Her eyes are bright and her pleasant smile makes you feel immediately at ease. She is intelligent, articulate and well educated. She invited me to share more about the purpose of my Sabbatical and very quickly honed in on what was essential for her to offer me. She was excited to know that Lutherans were beginning to explore more about health and healing, and that we wanted to know more about healing service in the Church.

She described the history of her congregation, outlining that it was an old church with very traditional Anglican liturgical worship and values. When she first came to serve in this parish, there were no healing services. The notion of healing was simply unknown. After a time, she decided to slowly introduce leaders of her parish to the concepts of health and healing within the context of the Church. At that time, as there is in any parish, beloved members were ill, and this notion of healing, while greeted with some skepticism, was embraced initially by key members. She described how she spent about six months preparing the congregation through sermons and other conversations. When the time came for the first public expression of a healing component during the Sunday eucharistic meal, it was decided to have anyone who wished for a prayer of healing, to move off to the side of the altar area, to receive prayer from one of the healing teams, before joining the majority of the worshipers who were coming for the bread and wine of the eucharist.

At first, she said, only a few came for the healing prayer. Prayers were requested for more than physical healing. People came with concerns about life circumstances, their relationship with God, and other issues. But within a few short weeks, the vast number of the congregation were going first for a prayer of healing before kneeling before the Lord at the altar to receive the body and blood of Christ. Over time her parish has become a place of healing prayer and she shared some of the stories of healing within her parish. Some people have been healed in their emotions. Some have been healed in their relationships. Some have been healed of spiritual wounds. Almost all have grown closer to their Lord.

There have even been a few of her members who have shared their experiences of healing that we might call "a miracle." This kind of healing is not the primary focus of her church's ministry of healing, but she believes that God does sometimes meet us in an extraordinary way.

She then shared that one of her member's story is recounted in the new video entitled "The Power Within" produced by the Anglican Church of Canada. I smiled and told her that the next day I was scheduled to go into downtown Toronto to see the film. She hadn't known that, and she said, "Well why make another trip up from Burlington? You really aren't that far from the Church House. Let me see if I can reach someone there and set it up for you later this afternoon."

She made a call, told the resources center person I had spoken to weeks before that I was now in town. After a brief conversation she laughed and said, "Yes he'll be there by 4 p.m."

"It's all set for you," she said after hanging up the phone. "You will want to notice the first story in the film. The man is a member of our church, and what he experienced was extraordinary." She said that this man's wife had a heart attack and that her situation became critical. The man is on his way back to the hospital and hears a voice behind him as he makes his way across a crosswalk. The voice reassures him that his wife will be OK. He turns around to see who has spoken to him. There is no one there. He knows this is the voice of Jesus. His wife recovers and he believes he has encountered his Lord. (This would not be the first time I would hear this kind of testimony during my sabbatical.)

She then went on to share that another part of the film was videotaped during one of her church's worship services, featuring the healing service portion. (Later on I would see Canon Linda Nicholls in the video as she and her healing team laid on hands during prayer.)

Then she asked me if I knew about Burrswood. I told her I'd never heard of it and she shared that it is a Christian healing place outside of London, England. She said that it was also featured in a segment of "The Power Within." She said that she had the opportunity to visit there and that it was a key element in their understanding of God's healing. She described it as a serene place, surrounded with beautiful woods and foliage. Its purpose is to minister to the entire person.

She said it had a hospital wing, an outpatient wing and had a medical staff, Chaplain's office, a hydrotherapy pool and bookstore. She added that Christian healing services were held weekly there for patients and staff and that they also welcomed anyone from the surrounding area and greater London to join with them in these healing services.

I was very impressed with her description and said, "This sounds like a place I should add to my sabbatical." "Yes," she replied, "It is unique in all the world. There is nothing like it anywhere. You'll see when you watch the video."

She then went on to share how the Commission on Healing, and members of her own church, were in the process of considering having a Burrswood-like facility in Ontario, Canada. She described some of the enthusiasm as well as some of the setbacks they were encountering. But she continued to be optimistic about the project getting off the ground. (In fact they did finally start a healing center which I visited in 2004 and met its first director over lunch with Canon Linda Nicholls.)

As our conversation continued on to a wide variety of matters related to healing, what became crystal clear to me was how gentle and calmly Linda spoke about the healing power of prayer. Within the traditional Anglican prayer book style of worship, members of her parish were being healed in a variety of ways. Some were healed physically, not necessarily cured, but many had significant physical health improvements. Many were experiencing profound changes in their inner self as well as in matters in their external living. Her belief in ministry to the whole person was quite evident and prayer was clearly the "centerpiece" for her in the newly begun healing ministries. She also shared with me some writers who had influenced her thinking about the ministry of Jesus and the ongoing power of the Spirit. As I said my farewell and thanked her for everything, she invited me to return. I was to do just that, nearly three years later, for an update in which I joined her and her members in a healing prayer service. (That day she preached to about 50 senior citizens in a midweek, midday worship service. Her message that day was one of the finest sermons I had ever heard.)

* * *

I made my way through traffic in the downtown area of Toronto and drove past the Anglican Church House. After parking I entered the building and made my way to the resource center. The staff person at the resource center who had set up my appointment was so gracious to me. She arranged for me to go to the floor housing the foreign missions area of ministry where they set up a monitor for me to watch "The Power Within" video.

Little did I know how important this video would become for the progress of my sabbatical.

The Power Within Video

I had no idea what to expect as I sat in the small cubicle in the Anglican Church House starting to watch the Power Within Video. I had made this trip primarily to see this film, which as I have already said, I had discovered during a web search on healing and religion. The images on the website had inspired me to believe that perhaps this might be a very important film. I had no idea how important it would become for me.

The film opens with Peter Downey, Jr. narrating. He speaks about the power of prayer to heal and the power of belief in prayer. He shares that this film will be an investigation into prayer. Indeed it is.

One of the first stories which is recreated is the one Canon Linda Nicholls had already alerted me to for it involved one of her members. He tells his own personal story about his wife's heart attack and how she was stabilized at the hospital and he was told he could go on home. On his way back to the hospital, what he didn't know, is that she had gone into cardiac arrest and was probably going to die. Doctors and nurses were frantically trying to save her life. This is dramatically portrayed in the video. He tells how he is making his way through a crosswalk when he hears this voice behind him telling him not to worry that his wife is going to be fine. He turns to see who has spoken to him and there is no one behind him. He doesn't understand until he gets to the hospital and learns that the physicians are fighting for his wife's life. He prays and believes Jesus has spoken to him and he trusts this voice. The doctors come out and tell him that she is safe now and that she will improve. As the camera moves into a close-up of his storytelling you can see the tears in his eyes and he shares that this was a miracle.

Later on in the film there is another miracle story. This one is about a father who is carrying his little boy down a staircase when he suddenly steps on what look like books on the stairs, he falls and his little boy suffers head injuries. Just a week earlier the father had organized a prayer chain and as he says in the video, little did he know that he would be the first to use it. His little boy was rushed to a hospital in London, where, to his surprise he is met by his pastor. His pastor was contacted by someone on the prayer chain and hearing of the tragedy, rushed to London. The pastor immediately went into prayer and the father joined him in prayer. The doctors told them that there was only a 30% chance for his little boy to survive. They prayed and prayed. The prayer chain prayed. In the video the camera focuses on the father and he tells how his son recovered fully (there is a photograph of his son now as a smiling teenager). He goes on to say that some might say it's just a matter of percentages, but that he considers it a miracle. (I would later learn that this was the Executive Director at Burrswood in England at the time.)

Also featured early on in the film is an interview with Dr. Herbert Benson, author of the wonderful book, Timeless Healing. Dr. Benson of Harvard University describes his three-legged stool concept in the film (which is expanded upon in his great book). He says that there are three legs to health. One is surgery and other medical procedures. Another is pharmaceuticals (drugs). The third is selfcare. The interviewer in the film makes the statement that the first two are "do it to me, do it for me." Dr. Benson agrees. The third leg is the one that says "do it for yourself." There are many ways to self care and self improvement, and one of those is the use of the power of prayer. I highly recommend Dr. Benson's book on Timeless Healing. Along with Candace Pert's book, Molecules of Emotion, these were two of the best works I read during my sabbatical. (More on Molecules of Emotion later.)

One of the great books I read prior to my trip to Toronto was Dr. Larry Dossey's seminal book entitled Healing Words. This work is now being used in medical schools and elsewhere as a valuable teaching tool for medical students to learn that power of prayer. It is in this book that I first encountered Dr. William Bryd's study in San Francisco of the power of prayer to heal remotely. Dr. Dossey tells how this study was done. A group of cardiac patients are divided into two groups. One will not be prayed for. The other will be prayed for by people of prayer in the greater San Francisco area. These people of prayer were given only the first name of the person for whom they prayed. They were given only a little about the patient's medical condition. They never met these patients, but simply prayed for them for healing.

The results from this double-blind study are remarkable. As Dr. Dossey points out in his book (and I've now read other accounts of the Bryd study that substantiate Larry Dossey's report), the group "prayed for" had less complications and symptoms following bypass surgeries and other procedures. In other words, the results were astounding! (More on the Byrd study later.)

The reason I share this with you is not only because it is a remarkable study, but also because in the film, The Power Within, there is a similar study created by Dr. Elizabeth Targ, with very similar results. Those being prayed for did better in almost every area of measurement.

It was perhaps a year or so later that, while previewing a website, I found an "in memorium" tribute to Dr. Targ. Apparently she died of a rare form of breast cancer, one that she had been studying. The research community lost a brilliant young

researcher. It would have been wonderful to see what further results she might have had with this and other future studies.
A year or so later I was to discover through a website that a controversy arose around the Power Within film. Apparently some of the more traditional Anglicans were upset that part of the video shows non-Christian healing. I can understand how this might upset some people. But all in all I thought it was a tremendous film, documenting real physical healing and showing how healing prayer might be incorporated into a Sunday morning religious service. It also featured Burrswood which I will share about in another chapter.

The film clearly demonstrated that healing prayer can be used with real results. It showed a glimpse into the research now being conducted by the Church and other institutions on how prayer works. The small piece featuring Dr. Larry Dossey was excellent as he described the future of prayer and how the Church should not be afraid of that future.

I appreciate the pioneering work of the Anglican Church of Canada and their boldness in trying to present a difficult topic on film. I also greatly love their Anglican bookstore in downtown Toronto. It has the largest selection of prayer and healing material I've ever seen gathered in one place.

Before leaving Toronto, I called Canon Lynne Calhoun. We were not able to see each other in person, but she proved enormously helpful in explaining the Order of St. Luke and her position in the organization. She offered to send me an application to join this important organization in prayer and healing. This introduction was very helpful and would come into play when I met an important person in Richmond, Virginia later on.

It was now time to go back to California and see if I could find anyone who had a healing story to tell. There was indeed.

Chapter 3
After Canada: A Healing Story

I no sooner returned from Canada than a friend of mine informed me about a friend of hers that she thought I should interview for my book. The interview was to take place in a private home. I made contact, set a date for the interview, and traveled to the town where the interview was to take place. (For confidential reasons the name of the person interviewed will not be revealed.) I pulled my car to the curbside, got out and scanned the neighborhood. Typical of so many residential areas in this town, the street was lined on both sides by small homes, with lots of foliage and trees. This street was quiet and reserved, and seemed far away from the hustle and noise of so much of what makes up the downtown area of this town. I checked the addresses on the homes around me, and made my way to the front door of the home where lunch awaited. I raised my hand, knocked on the door and waited. Within moments the door opened, and a very pleasant woman smiled at me and said, "Ron?" "Yes," I replied. "Welcome to my home. Come in."

She ushered me in through her living room and directly into the small dining area just off her kitchen. She offered me something cool to drink and had me take my seat. Lunch was already prepared and on the table. I immediately liked this lady. Her home was neat and tidy, and she seemed to be the kind of person who likes things to start and end on time, in a very gentle way. While she brought final things to the luncheon table, I noticed the many tapes and music CDs she had nearby. I smiled because music is such a large part of my life. I felt warm inside and welcome. Her voice had a calming effect as well, so that I immediately relaxed and slipped into my chair, wondering what might have happened in this woman's life. I was about to discover something deep and profoundly meaningful.

Over lunch she told me a little about her background, some of her history and how she came to live in this town. She described her religious background and how she served her community. It was clear that she was a woman of deep spirituality. She spoke of her professional life and about some of her friendships. We discussed various disease processes and in particular, breast cancer as both she and I knew women struggling with this disease.

Without telling her story in great detail, she shared with me that when she was diagnosed with her own cancer, she sought out support from another who also had struggled with cancer. It was a devastating diagnosis for her, and she found a spiritual mentor in the other woman, and felt loved and supported as she discussed her thoughts and feelings about what she faced. As it turns out, her friend knew something about guided imagery. (I write more about guided imagery later in this book.) Through this process she was able to better understand her condition.

One of the images which came to her through her guided imagery was imagining cancer cells leaving her body. These cancer cells left in a particular way, and she did this image many times and each time she came away feeling more and more hopeful.

Very often when an imagery practitioner guides a patient or client through some imagery process, the practitioner asks the one who has experienced the image to do a drawing, or painting of this experience. This is a way to anchor and remember the image. In a similar way, the woman I was speaking to did something similar. She found a way of expressing her experience in a medium that was very familiar to her. Using her talent in this medium, she was able to "see" the cancer cells clearly leaving her body.

At her next medical appointment she was to learn that there was no longer any indication of the cancer. She had been healed. It appeared that imagery was crucial to her healing.

As she described what this entire process was like for her, it was obvious to me how deeply grateful she is for her healing. Just as her friend supported her, she in turn has supported others who struggle with cancer. Her care for others is a part of who she is, and she can identify with a range of feelings others have when they first hear a devastating diagnosis.

When I visited her it had already been several years since her recovery. I was deeply moved by her story and thanked her for sharing it with me.

There would be others I would learn had used guided imagery for healing. I also would meet others who had "seen" a wise, loving figure who spoke words of healing. I was reminded of my friend, Betty, who had gone into remission after the use of guided imagery. I also thought of the man in the Power Within video who had heard a voice behind him telling him that his wife would be alright. I thought about the medical literature on spontaneous healing. I also thought about the healing power of prayer and the research on gratitude being such a key concept in recovery.

I had spent a couple of hours with a woman who was living proof of healing. I was eager to continue on my sabbatical study, wondering what other stories I would hear, and what else I would learn about healing. I would not be disappointed in the weeks and months ahead.

Chapter 4
A Man From Jacksonville
Francis MacNutt and Christian Healing Ministries

"Who is Francis MacNutt?" I asked. My good friend, Leland Meyer said, "He's someone you should really meet if you can. I dont know where he is, but he's been a healer for many years." "How do you know about him?" I asked. "Well, Joannie went through some things some years ago and discovered his healing work. I think he's a Catholic priest." "Do you think he would take time for me?" I replied. "Oh I'm sure he would. Given your topic I think he would be very interested." I will be forever grateful to Lee for leading me to Francis MacNutt.

"Hello, this is Francis MacNutt," the warm, soft, inviting voice said. I responded, "Hello, my name is Ron Rehrer. I'm from California. I'm doing a study sabbatical on prayer, healing and psychoneuroimmunology. I was wondering if you might have some time for me if I came to visit you." "What a wonderful topic!" he said, his voice sounding genuinely interested. I could hear the smile behind his tone. "Of course I would have time for you. Why don't you come out to Jacksonville, Florida and I'll give you most of a day, how does that sound?" I'm sure he could hear the smile in my voice when I said, "That's very generous of you. Thank you!"

He then asked me to tell him a little about myself. I told him I was a licensed Marriage, Family, Child Counselor in California and was also counselor for professional church workers in the Lutheran church, I told him a little about how I became interested in prayer, healing and mind-body medicine. He responded by saying, "Well you know, I've always believed that Luther was right about the Grace of God and justification by faith. Catholics have been slow to understand that. I've always believed that Lutherans and particularly those in the Missouri Synod have the best understanding of this doctrine. But what I also find is that they very often lack heart. At least that is my experience. They have a weak understanding of the work of the Holy Spirit. But you know, there are quite a number of

Lutherans involved in the ministry of prayer and healing. When you come I'll give you some of their names and phone numbers so you can expand your sabbatical."

So we settled on a date for our Florida meeting. I thanked him again for his gracious time, hung up the phone, logged onto the Internet and purchased my airline ticket to Jacksonville. Little did I know that God was about to change my life forever. Little did I know that Francis MacNutt would become the key force of my sabbatical and the doorway to my own personal spiritual renewal.

A few days after a conversation with Francis, one of my favorite clients, Cathy, came in for an appointment. She began the session by asking in her upbeat, bubbly way, "So what's new with you?" Knowing her interest in how my sabbatical was shaping up, I told her about my phone call to Francis MacNutt and I asked her if she knew of him. (Cathy is a former clergy spouse and is a very strong spiritual person with an interest in healing.)

Her eyes lit up and she said, "Oh, Ron, this is wonderful! Of course I know about Francis McNutt. I heard him speak at the annual meeting of the Association of Christian Therapists. He and his wife Judith are so loving and kind. You will love him! He just sort of surrounds you with the love of God. So are you making a trip to see him?" "Yes," I said, adding "I was very impressed with him on the phone. He is so well educated, has a good clinical understanding, and has a real pastoral heart." Cathy smiled her brighter smile and said, "I just have a hunch that meeting him is going to somehow be transformational for you. And he's going to like you a lot too." "Well, I'm really looking forward to it," I replied. Then I paused and said, "So what do you want to work on tonight?" and we went on with her session.

When I landed in Jacksonville, I rented a car and headed out towards my meeting with Francis. <u>Christian Healing Ministries</u>, which is the organization that Francis and his wife, Judith, co-direct, is located on the grounds of a former Episcopal church seminary in a residential part of Jacksonville. I found a parking space, got out of my car and began to look around a bit before my meeting time with Francis. The physical plant is quite large, with a chapel near the two story office buildings. Nothing about this rather ordinary set of buildings gave any hint of the extraordinary ministry which it houses.

I found the office door, and as soon as I stepped inside, I was warmly welcomed by one of the staff members. I introduced myself and shared that I was from California and was here for a meeting with Francis MacNutt. I was told that he was waiting for me and was anxious to meet me. This gave me a very good feeling and I knew that somehow this conversation was going to be important. The staff person ushered me into a large room where Father MacNutt sat and he immediately rose and greeted me with a great warm smile and generous handshake. "Hi, Ron, I've been looking forward to meeting you." "Thank you," I replied, "I have really been looking forward to meeting you too." He pointed to a chair and he took his seat as well.

What transpired over the next several hours was a fascinating close up look at Christian Healing Ministries, inspired by my host's deeply held beliefs in the power of prayer and the work of the Holy Spirit. Francis told me how he came to a new understanding of healing and how he was baptized into the power of the Holy Spirit early on in his ministry as a priest. This experience changed him forever and he was led to join other healing ministers during the 1970's, as they humbly took this message of healing and hope to other places throughout the world. He described some of the times when he stood on platforms with other ministers, surrounded by hundreds and sometimes thousands of people who came forward seeking healing. Along the way he met the woman who would become his wife and lifelong partner in sharing this transformational message of God's love for people and the rich outpouring of God's Spirit which brought inner healing.

Francis was opening a door for me into a new world. As he spoke of some of his colleagues in America and elsewhere, I began to catch a glimpse of the growing number of ministers from all parts of the world who were praying with people for healing of their minds and bodies, strengthening their very spiritual selves. He spoke of the healing power of God's Word and how the Spirit of God was ever increasing in blessings to many.

What was amazing to me was the humble, soft spoken spirit of this man. I learned of his excellent clinical training in mental health, and the depth and breadth of his reading in psychology, theology and healing literature. Yet his style was warm, gentle, without any sense of "ego" in his words or his spirit. He spoke about the mystery of healing and how in his own experience of laying on hands and praying for the ill, he was certain that it was nothing he himself was doing that healed persons, but that he was only a kind of conduit for God's healing Spirit. Later on, when Francis had to take a phone call, and I was perusing their extensive library of training tapes and books, another staff person happened to come by and introduced herself. She asked me, "Well what do you think of him?" I replied, "He's wonderful. I don't think I have ever met a servant of God who is so humble and warm and soft spoken who makes things so simple and clear." She replied, "Exactly... and he does things that no one knows about. For example, a woman came in yesterday with a huge goiter on the side of her neck. Francis placed his hands on her goiter and prayed... for nearly two hours... and that goiter actually shrunk. I know that that sounds incredible, but I saw her come in and saw her come out and it really was a kind of miracle."

When Francis was done with his call, he apologized for having to interrupt our meeting and I told him that I had just heard about the woman with a goiter from the day before. He replied, "Yes, sometimes people will come here just for prayer, for something troubling in their life and in this case, it was a physical disorder, so I prayed with her, not only for a healing of the goiter, but also a healing of her troubled spirit which may have something to do with it, although it isn't for certain."

I asked Francis if he could estimate how many people actually had a physical healing from his praying for them. Once again his humbleness was evident. He said, "I really don't know, but I suppose... I suppose that perhaps 50% of the people for whom I pray have some kind of healing experience... it may not always be a physical healing, or perhaps later on, something physical that needs healing may improve after I am gone. And I would say that perhaps 50% of those for whom I pray have no obvious change. That doesn't mean that there is no change, only that I am not aware of it."

I shared with him that this reminded me of something Dr. Larry Dossey says in his book Healing Words, that not all medicine works all of the time and that perhaps, prayer, like a medicine, doesn't always appear to have immediate or direct effect all of the time. I don't know if he agreed with that, but he once again reiterated that he didn't see himself as having any kind of power in himself that made a difference. He simply saw himself as someone God used for the purpose of healing.

This reminded me very much of the healing ministry of Kathyrn Kuhlman who also made it very clear that there was nothing about herself that was special in her healing ministry. She saw herself as just one more person whom God was using to bring about healing of the soul first, and perhaps healing of the physical self as well.

As we spoke I noticed that Francis had a red sore of some kind on his nose. I didn't comment on it, but later on in the afternoon he asked if he could show me a film of some of the healing work that had been done in Orlando with severe arthritis patients. He said that he had a doctor's appointment to remove a small cancer on the end of his nose (what I had noticed) and would be gone for about an hour, so that I could view the video while he was gone. Again, like some other Christian healers who have great respect for the medical community, Francis was going to have this infirmity taken care of. I mention this because sometimes we hear about Christian healers who say that one should avoid medical help from competent physicians or surgeons because it is faith alone that we should rely on for healing. Healers such as Francis MacNutt or Kathryn Kuhlmann strongly disagree with this viewpoint. We need to use both... competent medical help as well as the power of prayer. He needed to see a doctor to have this growth removed. This was not simply a matter for prayer. It was something that needed outpatient surgery. I didn't say anything about this to Francis. So he took me into another room and set up the video, then excused himself to go see his doctor. The video I watched was absolutely fascinating! The video began with a narrator introducing himself as Dr. Dale Matthews. This is the Dale Matthews whose name was on my list of persons to interview. I had previously contacted Dr. Matthews, author of the excellent book, The Faith Factor and had hoped that I would be able to meet him while I was on the east coast meeting with Francis MacNutt. In our exchange of email, Dr. Matthews told me that during the weeks that I would be in the Washington, DC area (where he has his medical practice), he would unfortunately be out of town. He regretted that we would not have an opportunity to meet. So here he was on video! It was great for me to see what he looked like and to hear his voice.

To my knowledge the video I watched has not yet been released. However, it showed Francis and Judith MacNutt working with perhaps a dozen or more patients who had severe arthritis. Francis has written about the results of this study and I believe Dr. Matthews published a report in a medical journal. In this video, you actually see results from the four day period of praying and teaching. People who four days earlier could not move their arthritic joints now found themselves pain free and having new motion in joints and limbs. One person whose hands were folded over in severe arthritic pain actually was able to move her hands and fingers without discomfort. Another person confined to a wheelchair was able to not only get out of the chair and stand, but was actually able to dance! Others had significant movement in their joints and the level of new mobility was actually awesome to see.

The power of prayer was quite remarkable. When Francis returned from the doctors we discussed the video. I could clearly see that he was proud of this research and was eager to have other people know about it. Once again, it was clear that this had nothing to do with one's ego, but was another example of the healing power that comes through God's Holy Spirit in the name of Jesus. I read the research document that reported the pre-event and post-event prayer weekend with these patients. The power of prayer was clearly in evidence. While not every arthritis patient in the study had remarkable healing, all of them had some reduction in discomfort and movement.

Was this simply mind over matter as some would say? Would the reduction in discomfort last and would the increased range of motion be sustained? I suppose different people might draw different conclusions or even be skeptical of this study. But I clearly saw a range of changes in these patients. While some had only minor changes (which for them, any change is actually major!), others had very dramatic results from having hands laid upon them and having received a great deal of concentrated prayer. I was to learn later on that there is something that is called "soaking prayer" which is a longer period of intensified prayer for the person in need. The video clearly demonstrates the power of 'soaking prayer."

Our conversation turned to other places or people Francis might recommend for me to meet. He keeps a list of such persons and places that he has accumulated over the years. He had one of his staff retrieve some of these names. While she was doing this, he said, "One place you should really visit is the Toronto Airport Christian Fellowship church, in Toronto, Canada." I told him that I had heard of it and that I had heard it called the "Laughing Church." He smiled and said, "Yes there are some who think this is a controversial church, but I think you should visit it and form an opinion of it for yourself. You might find it a little unusual or maybe even a little uncomfortable, but it is a place where the power of the Spirit is strong. They are having a week long pastors' conference with ministers coming from around the world to pray together, sing together, and it is a healing conference. This will be the church's seventh anniversary and I think you would gain a great deal from it." He gave me the contact number and the dates.

He then added, "I think there is something else you would find useful in your research, too. At Richmond Hill, Richmond, Virginia, we are gathering together counselors and psychotherapists like yourself, along with healers from various places, to talk with each other about healing and the demonic. I would like to give you another contact person for this conference. I will vouch for you, and Judith and I will be leading this gathering along with the director of Richmond Hill. I really would like to see you there."

These two events, the Toronto Airport Christian Fellowship and the Conference at Richmond Hill were to be two of the most powerful learning events during my sabbatical. I share about each of them elsewhere in this book.

My time with Francis was invaluable and I will be forever grateful for all that he shared with me. I have gone on to read his writings and listened to many of his educational tapes produced by Christian Healing Ministries. Before I left him that day, he introduced me to his wife Judith. I was later to learn more about her special gifts in healing ministries through several teaching tapes she has made and also at the Richmond Hill conference. I am certain that Francis MacNutt has influenced more people in Christian healing ministries than any other teacher of healing. His books are well balanced, sophisticated, measured and deeply speak to the heart. Everything he says or writes is deeply rooted in the Spirit. He has thought long and hard about difficult questions and he brings forth clear and insightful answers for anyone seeking to understand the ministry of healing. One of his recent books, <u>Deliverance from Evil Spirits</u>, gives keen insight and practical suggestions for discerning the demonic. His book on <u>Healing</u> is still the classical Christian writing in the field. Today Francis and Judith MacNutt are still actively teaching and doing equipping seminars around the country. Everyone who meets he and Judith and spends time with them will be enlightened as well as challenged in their spiritual understanding of healing. They are a remarkable couple who have learned much over the many years of their work.

Chapter 5
Signs and Wonders in Toronto
The Toronto Airport Christian Fellowship and the ministry of John Arnott

I first heard about the <u>Toronto Airport Christian Fellowship Church</u> from a pastor friend in Canada many years ago. I was told that it was called the "Laughing Church" and that there was considerable controversy about it. But Francis MacNutt had suggested I experience it. Before I had left his office, Francis had given me the phone number and location of the Toronto Airport Christian Fellowship Church in Toronto. I phoned the contact person that Francis gave me and registered to attend, booked a room at the suggested hotel and wondered what I was getting myself into.

Not long after that, I had a pastor friend tell me that he was concerned about me if I was going to attend this church and the pastors' conference. He had been reading a great deal about it and said that the Bible Answer Man on national Christian radio was highly critical of it. He suggested that if I was going to attend then by all means I must read the book entitled <u>Counterfeit Revival</u> by Hank Hannegraf, the Bible Answer Man. I agreed to do so in preparation for my trip to the Toronto Airport Christian Fellowship, known as TACF.

I must admit that I was curious yet a bit frightened of what this was all about. Hearing about the laughing church and hearing that sometimes people barked like dogs during the worship services or that some people spontaneously "fell out," left me with a bit of foreboding. So I decided to read Counterfeit Revival and that was exactly what I was doing as I boarded a plane for Toronto once again.

Hannegraf in his book, Counterfeit Revival, has absolutely nothing positive to say about John Arnott, the pastor of the Toronto Airport Christian Fellowship church. He tells about where he believes it's roots are and how he attended a worship service himself in Anaheim, California only to decide that what is really going on during the worship service is actually the use of mass hypnotism and mesmerism practices.

So as I flew to Toronto reading Hannegraf's book, I thought about my own clinical training in formal hypnotism as well as my training in guided imagery. I was confident that unless I wanted to become hypnotized, I was not going to fall under anyone's spell. However, I did have serious wonderings about how wise it might be for my own mental health to go to such a pastors' conference if what Hannegraf was describing was actually true.

My plane landed in Toronto and I caught the shuttle to the church's designated hotel not far from TACF. The weather was bitter cold since this was in January. Everyone was bundled up as they boarded the shuttle for the hotel. At the hotel, the lobby was filled with laughing, smiling people. The check in counter was crowded but people were very patient and I caught snatches of conversation.

"Is this your first time to attend the church?"

"Oh no, this is my fourth time and I wouldn't miss it. it strengthens me every time I come."

"The last time I was here John gave such a wonderful message. I was filled with the Spirit and it transformed my ministry.."

"My wife and I are here from England. This is our second time. We were greatly moved last time and have started a revival of our own in our small village and it has been amazing how the Spirit has changed our church."

"Have you read John Arnott's recent book? It's fabulous. Don't forget to order the videotapes after each session."

The above snippets of conversation from different parts of the lobby was what I heard as I walked through the lobby towards the elevator leading to my room. Whatever misgivings I had from reading Hannegraf's book were melting away as I listened in to people's eager anticipation of worshipping together. These people did not look like they would bark like dogs or "fall out." They looked like you or me and they were all looking forward to a high spirited week. So I began to relax somewhat, not fully coming off guard, but feeling more comfortable.

The opening session was about to begin as we cued up to be shuttled over to the church. I caught the shuttle and everyone on board was introducing themselves to each other. "Is this the first time for you?" someone asked me. "Yes," I replied. "Where are you from?" someone asked. "From California," I said. "Well welcome. You are in for a treat. This is my third time and this is the highlight of my year each year."

There it was again... "The highlight of my year" type of language. In the space of a few hours I had heard words like "highlight," "transformed," "wouldn't miss it," "strengthens me," etc. Something was definitely happening here. What could it be? I was about to find out. The enthusiasm among all of these people reminded me of the enthusiasm people have when they attend a baseball World Series or a Super Bowl event or some exciting rock concert.

The shuttle deposited us in front of the church. I noticed that this church seemed rather humble. I had anticipated something huge on the outside, like one of those famous mega-churches where thousands of people worship with huge praise bands or pipe organs. But as I approached the outside of the church, it looked almost as if the building had been lowered into the ground and just the top part of the building was visible at ground level. It was not impressive. The sign outside announcing this as the Toronto Airport Christian Fellowship was also rather ordinary. Could it be that this was an extraordinary, ordinary place? Walking along icy sidewalks, hearing the crunch of ice beneath my feet, I joined the dozens of persons filing through the doors. Once inside the lobby, I found literature and maps about cell groups scattered throughout the Toronto area. There was a counter very much like a hotel counter where representatives of the church welcomed all of us and handed out literature to those who requested it. We continued to file to the right through tall doors into a huge hall. My first impression was that I was entering into a large warehouse type structure or a huge oversized concert hall with plain pews everywhere. There was a large stage off to my right and people were already seated or standing as they listened to music being broadcast from a central console like one sees at a concert hall with words projected up onto huge screens on either side of the hall. In this case, it was like any other contemporary church that projects words of the songs that will be used in the worship. What was different was how huge these screens were on either side of the stage. Up on stage a band was beginning to set up and to my left, there was a staircase leading up to rooms and other observation areas. To my extreme left was an open air bookstore filled with people. I decided to visit that first.

Upon entering the bookstore which is only protected by panels linked together, standing about six feet high, I immediately saw to my left dozens of music CDs. These CDs were arranged by Christian artist or type of Christian music. I asked people what they felt was the best music. There were, of course, various opinions from salespeople and conference attendees, but nearly everyone agreed that if I were to purchase just one CD then it should be "<u>Revival in Belfast</u>." So I bought it and continued to walk around long counters of books and tapes, some which spoke of the history of the charismatic renewal in America and Europe. I found reproductions of videos and tapes of previous presentations by Pastor John Arnott and others. I found some audio tapes of Francis MacNutt's presentations from a year earlier. Whatever happened during this pastors' conference I felt confident that I would learn much. That was the point of my sabbatical, after all... to listen and to learn from those in prayer and healing ministries.

I went back into the main hall, thoroughly enjoying the music radiating out from large speakers mounted over the stage. Pockets of people were beginning to sing the words up on the screens. The conference had not officially begun but already there were people kneeling on the floor in prayer or standing with hands held up in praise. I had seen this before all the way back to my early childhood when I attended a tent revival near my home in California. My mother had been raised in what was known as a Shouting Methodist Church in which people sometimes stood and raised their hands towards heaven. Most people were still talking with old or new friends or quietly sitting in the pews or reading. Before long the entire place was packed. Then the band came out and began to play wonderful songs, all of them with the words up on the screens.

We sang for over an hour and I found myself seated next to a couple of pastors and their wives from the Church of England. They were very welcoming. It was interesting to hear their British accents. But behind me were people from Africa and to my left were people in from South America. I looked up and noticed that flags from every country were mounted overhead. Clearly this church was international in its invitation and pastors by the hundreds were flying in from literally every corner of the world. Why? What was happening here? Why was everyone in such a good mood?

Finally after great singing, the band stopped and a man came out and walked up to the microphone and said... "Whoooosh... did you feel it?" as he waved his hand across his body as if pushing someone along in front of himself... "the Spirit just passed by!" And immediately there was thunderous applause and loud shouts of pleasure! "Yes Lord!" "Amen!" "Praise God" "Come on Spirit!" I grinned. "These people are already primed," I thought. Francis MacNutt had warned me that this all may be a little out of my comfort zone. Well, this definitely was different from a liturgical service so common in my Lutheran tradition. But I was not uncomfortable. People were genuinely happy and upbeat and welcoming. How could anyone feel uncomfortable? They were singing praise music and giving honor to God.

The speaker up on the stage spoke about what was to come and a little history of the church. Then he invited some people up on stage to give testimonies of what they had experienced over the years here at the church. This would be an ongoing ritual at each service. Each time a speaker would come out, greet everyone, share something about the church and then invite at least two people up to give a testimony. Testimonials were very important messages to all in attendance.

Each of the three persons who gave the first testimonials were pastors. Each got to laughing or smiling during their testimonies about what had happened to them. I noticed that as each one spoke, someone would come up and stand behind them or off to the side. It wasn't long before I knew why. At some point during their testimonial they would begin to sway a bit and then... they would fall backwards into the waiting arms of the person behind them. One of the pastors just could not stop laughing. This must be why they call it the laughing church I thought. The only odd thing to me was that the actual content of what some of these clergy were sharing was not actually humorous, but as they testified about what God was doing in their ministries or in their personal lives, they would begin to laugh.

This emotional energy was infectious. One of the clergy wives near me began to jump up and down and praise God, as did others around the hall. When this happened, sometimes people nearby would clap or shout, or sometimes even get up and join in. Clearly there was excitement for what the Spirit was doing in those pastors on stage. The energy level in the hall went up exponentially. There was great joy and wonderful bubbly enthusiasm. The testimonies were good. They were honest, from the heart and each pastor told how his life and ministry had been transformed. I found nothing offensive at all. I thought the phenomenon of "falling out" was somewhat interesting. Every testimonial was followed by the presenter falling backwards and being laid upon the stage. While the joy in the church was genuine and "catching," it was a little unbelievable to me that every single presenter would fall backwards and be laid upon the stage. But I decided not to be very critical of this. Perhaps it was expected or perhaps people were actually experiencing something foreign to me.

Finally it came time to introduce the pastor of the church, Pastor John Arnott. I don't know exactly what I was expecting, but I think I was expecting a big, expansive, bombastic televangelist type of person, charismatic (as in personality) and perhaps even a huckster, charlatan type of communicator. I could not have been further form the truth.

Pastor John Arnott is a quiet, soft spoken man. In fact, I would describe him as rather plain and uneventful. He doesn't preach or raise his voice. In fact he is so ordinary in his speaking that I would never go to church to hear him preaching. He is not a preacher. He is a speaker, a quiet almost folksy speaker, or at least he was during my visit to the TACF.

He simply walked casually across the stage, picked up a microphone and said hello and welcomed everyone. It was such a contrast to the high spirited cacophony of voice and song and testimonial that I had just experienced. Now everyone was calm and attentive. John Arnott did not look or sound like some guru or snake oil salesman or a devil without horns, as some would have you believe. Somewhat overweight with a slight belly and some grey in his hair, dressed in a simple shirt and blue Levis, he could have been your Uncle Lewis or your next door neighbor.

Everyone was listening as he said that tonight's talk was going to be about getting into the "river" and how it's not always easy to get into the river and that's OK because there is no pressure to receive the gifts of the Holy Spirit. As his talk went on he said that he himself does not fall backwards slain in the spirit and that he has never fallen backwards. He did share that his wife, Carol, frequently had this experience as many have. He told how his wife was first overcome by the Spirit, but that perhaps as many as half of those in the hall tonight would not have that kind of experience and that that was OK, perfectly fine. He explained that the Spirit of God had many ways of touching hearts and lives. When he said that I smiled because it was through the music that I was being touched. What also crossed my mind was a not very nice thought, a technique actually, that does come out of counseling practices and that is giving someone permission to not experience something which in fact creates the experiencing of that very thing. I didn't want to think that Pastor Arnott was somehow trying to "trick" us into falling out. Actually, he sounded very genuine to me, that he was honestly sharing that he doesn't ever fall backwards and that it was perfectly normal not to do that. There was no "should" or "ought to" in his tone.

He continued his message on getting into the "river" and he concluded simply by inviting everyone to enjoy their week and to drink deeply of the Spirit. He did speak about God's grace and said a few things about Jesus' love for us, but it was very clear that the emphasis at the TACF was on the third person of the Trinity, the Holy Spirit and its power. At the conclusion of his message, everyone got back on the busses and headed back to the hotel. I slept well that night wondering what would happen during the rest of the week.

As the week progressed I noticed that each session began pretty much the same way with the band leading us in singing music, followed by testimonies with speakers falling backwards and usually quite giddy with emotion at the conclusion of their testimony. Then a speaker would come onto the stage and make the presentation for that session. Sometimes the session would conclude with music but usually the sessions just ended.

One thing I absolutely loved about the TCAF experience was all of the music. I love music and the band that lead the singing was pretty good.

One song in particular grabbed me... a song entitled "Revival." I would later find that it was on the Live in Belfast CD that I had just purchased in their bookstore. Since then, I've played it for groups of clergy and for various other church leaders and with very few exceptions, people have loved it and often ask where I got it.

Music is infectious and can move us emotionally and spiritually. There really wasn't anything that Pastor Arnott was saying that was moving me like the music played earlier. And as the Pastors' Conference continued during the week, I found myself drawn to the music, relishing the experience of joining with hundreds of pastors from all over the world, singing praise and worship songs. Some of those songs were petitions while some were about forgiveness. Some were about living the life of faith while others were about grace and mercy and love. I found myself looking forward to the beginning of each session where the band would lead us in praising God and generating enthusiastic response from the clergy.

It was absolutely amazing to see pastors from what I usually think of as the formal, stiff Church of England, calling out the name of Jesus or Holy Spirit. It was moving to see them with tears in their eyes when overcome by emotion.

Emotion. That is the main ingredient at TACF. There is no formal liturgy or creeds or even doctrine. This is not a cerebral church. It is a church that freely welcomes the expression of emotions.

During one of Pastor Arnott's talks, he spoke of the pastor's heart and its need for confession and absolution of personal failures and shortcomings. He revealed his own shortcomings in his simple straightforward manner and as he did so, pastors were moved to tears.

What I experienced was profound permission to open up and be yourself. My friend and colleague, Roxanne Whitelight, likes to speak about the need to create "a safe container" for clients in counseling to have a place from which they feel free to express their deepest pain or deepest self.

In a sense that is what I was witnessing at TACF. TACF was creating a safe container for the clergy gathered from all over the world. The closest analogy I could think of is the openness and freedom many people have experienced at AA (Alcoholics Anonymous) meetings. In the best of the 12 Step programs there is an honesty and non-judgmental framework in which to safely reveal who you really are. To be fully accepted in the spirit of who you are is what TACF is all about. In religious terms we may speak of Grace - unconditional love. People attending TACF were experiencing unconditional love.

When Pastor Arnott invited all of the pastors to sit or kneel in prayer, to confess their deepest sin and shortcomings, nearly 2,000 clergy from every denomination or non-denomination went to their knees. As they prayed, Pastor Arnott would say an encouraging word once in awhile. I opened my eyes and looked around and saw pastors with tears on their cheeks or hunched over in confession.

At some point either Pastor Arnott or one of the other leaders invited us into deeper prayer, describing that behind the stage was a place for "soaking prayer." I had never heard of this term before but I learned it is a time of prolonged prayer for someone in need, hence it is called "soaking prayer." Later I would hear Francis MacNutt speak of this soaking prayer. A session on this would later be given at the "Reclaim" conference described later in this book.

I made some new friends during the conference (you will meet them in a later chapter), and I came away from the week refreshed by the music and the friendship of new acquaintances. Much of what was experienced there was traced back to the revival roots of Azusa Street Revival at the turn of the 20th century in Los Angeles, California when it is said that the power of the Spirit fell down from heaven onto Azusa street. I would learn later on that many who came from the charismatic renewal background had experienced this kind of phenomenon many times previously. For me, not coming from a charismatic background, this was a new kind of experience. I think of it as another form of "healing" that is "out there" for people to partake of. In this case it is within the Christian healing community. I was to go deeper into this phenomena from a psychological perspective in how other reality is seen and encountered - the reality of the devil, demons, ghosts and other disruptive evil entities. I had not anticipated that this would be part of my learning during this sabbatical. But it was.

Looking back at my time at TACF, I'm glad that Francis MacNutt suggested I attend. It offered me a look inside a type of Christian fellowship that is quite unique. Later I was to learn about the phenomenal growth of the international charismatic renewal world wide, especially in Africa and Latin America. The estimated number of charismatic Christians around the world is a staggering 400 million according to the book by Dr. Harvey Cox, Fire From Heaven: The Rise of Pentecostal Spirituality and the Reshaping of Religion in the 21st Century. Some of the most powerful healing stories and testimonials are coming from these areas. What exactly was going on here? How did music, emotion, praise, belief and the Spirit relate to each other? How did healing arise from this? Or was it something else bringing about healing? I left Toronto with more burning questions. There were more surprises in store for me.

Reference Video: Toronto Airport Christian Fellowship

Chapter 6
Richmond Hill Healing Traumas
Ben Campbell and The Centrality of Prayer

My friend, Art Umbach, who lives in Virginia, said, "You've got to visit Richmond Hill." I asked, "What's Richmond Hill?" He replied, "It's a very special place of prayer and its director, Ben Campbell, has been my spiritual director. He is an incredibly gifted man of God. You will like him. They have all kinds of trainings and conferences there, almost all of them focused on prayer and healing. In fact, they pray three times each day for the City of Richmond, Va., and each month they focus their prayers on specific persons like a government official, a councilman, a police chief, fire captain, school board member. They interrupt anything they are doing when it comes time for prayer. They absolutely believe in the power of prayer."

Web Article: Bridge Work, Economic segregation, social disintegration and the regional divide: How the Rev. Ben Campbell's healing ministry could save Richmond.

I then told Art that I had met Francis MacNutt and that he had invited me to attend a conference on "Healing and the Demonic" to be held at Richmond Hill. Art said, "Fantastic! That's just what I'm talking about. You really need to go because I know you will learn a lot. Who is attending?" I told him that it would be a conference of healers, psychotherapists and others concerned about the demonic and the importance of healing those who have been involved in that somehow. He nodded and said, "Well I think this is very important. And if Francis MacNutt is leading it and Ben Campbell is involved, you will be in for something special." He was right.

I called Richmond Hill and spoke with Sandi Kerner, Coordinator of Healing Ministries at Richmond Hill and formerly on the staff of Christian Healing Ministries in Jacksonville, Florida. Richmond Hill was described as an ecumenical Christian fellowship and residential community in an urban setting, near the historic old St. John's Church where Patrick Henry, on 23 March, 1775, gave his famous, "give me liberty or give me death" speech, calling for American independence during the second Virginia revolutionary convention which included George Washington and Thomas Jefferson among others.

The mission of Richmond Hill is "to advance God's healing of Metropolitan Richmond through prayer, hospitality, racial reconciliation and spiritual development." Ben Campbell, an Episcopalian, is its pastoral director.

Reference Website: "[Richmond Hill Healing Prayer](#)" and "[SOZO School of Christian Healing Prayer](#)."

Sandi invited me to attend the conference for psychotherapists between March 26 and March 29th, 2001. I was sent brochures outlining the conference and made my air reservations and travel plans. My friend, Art, picked me up at the airport and took me over to Richmond Hill. He wanted to introduce me to Ben Campbell and show me some of the buildings there. Art had served for six years on the board of directors of Richmond Hill. We pulled into the parking lot and it was raining lightly. We went inside the building and I noticed right away the many printed flyers pinned onto walls and doors, announcing many different events happening at Richmond Hill. One in particular caught my eye. It was a sign that read: TAIZE at Richmond Hill, 7:30 P.M., First Monday Each Month. There were a few sentences below that spoke of this form of meditative common prayer that comes from a tradition of sung prayer. Since I had Taize on my itinerary for the Europe portion of my sabbatical, I was pleased to see that Taize seemed to be everywhere.

Art brought me into the office and I met Ben Campbell for the first time. He had a very alert countenance, was very friendly and welcoming and I immediately felt I was in the presence of someone of a deep spirituality as well as the gift of getting things done. I would later learn from Art that Richmond Hill had embarked on a six million dollar renovation (which they have now completed) and that Ben was at the heart of that effort. Ben told me to make myself at home, introduced me to some other staff, then he went off to his other duties. Art showed me around the facility and in the dining area I was struck by this beautiful woven tapestry in gold and green and mauve colors. It is a drawing of the outside of the Richmond Hill complex with shadow like sky scrapers hovering over the background. It is very impressive. At the top of the banner are the words in mauve color: Richmond Hill. Below at the bottom of the tapestry also in mauve color are the words, simple yet powerful: Pray For Our City. It was a banner that certainly proclaimed the mission of Richmond Hill. In another area of the building is a pretty little chapel. It was there that we would experience the healing power of prayer with Francis MacNutt several days later.

I found my room, a very simple almost monastic type of accommodation. A simple single bed was against the wall on the right hand side of the room. Next to it was a very small table with a simple lamp. A small window lets in the sunlight. Indeed it was a very simple, austere room.

I put my suitcase down and unpacked. Art had to leave and wished me well on the conference. I put several books on the small table. One of those I had read in preparation for the conference was Counseling and the Demonic by Rodger K. Bufford, Ph.D. It is one of the pastoral counseling books in the Resources for Christian Counseling series published by Word Publishers in Waco, Texas. Next to it I put the brochure announcement for the conference. It read: Healing and Deliverance Prayer to support Trauma Therapy, March 26-29, 2001, Dr. Francis MacNutt and Mrs. Judith MacNutt. Another brochure read Richmond Christian Healing Conference with Francis and Judith MacNutt. A third announcement read: Healing and Deliverance Prayer in support of Trauma Therapy: A consultation for therapists and healing prayer ministers.

When the conference finally began the next day I was very impressed with the quality of the people who had come. There were a larger number of prayer ministers than psychotherapists, but they came from around the country, and each had some level of encounter with trauma and what they called the presence of the demonic. The first thing that happened was that Francis MacNutt prayed for our protection during the conference. In his prayer he asked God to protect not only us, but also our families apart from us. He asked that no demonic force or power be able to disrupt or penetrate our meetings and he prayed that the Holy Spirit would come with power and protection and that this conference be a blessing on everyone. He prayed in a solemn, direct and unencumbered manner. I noticed that most people in the room were nodding in agreement with his words. Later on as I heard various stories and heard the issues that these prayer partners were facing, I was appreciative of Francis' prayer for protection. Following his prayer, he reminded everyone of how important it is that we pray for protection of ourselves, our ministries, and our families every single day. He reminded us that we battle not against flesh alone but against powers and principalities, drawing on the imagery of St. Paul's in the New Testament of the Bible where St. Paul in the book of Romans, the 13th chapter writes how neither powers nor principalities, nor anything can separate us from the Love of God in Christ Jesus. I am not permitted to share very much about the actual conference as we were asked to keep everything confidential for the safety of each other and those beyond the conference who may be in harm's way. I can share that at one point during the conference, Francis asked the group, "Is there anyone else we should pray for?" One person replied, telling about two persons we should pray for. When she named these people, I felt goosebumps up and down my arms and spine. I knew both of these people! I had studied with them or had been involved with them in some other ways. I knew their stories but had not heard any updates on them for some years. Now in this room, I was hearing the terrible things that had occurred in their lives. I was stunned to hear how the power of the demonic was destroying some of the most talented persons in the field who had themselves helped so many traumatized persons. It made me angry and also made me feel profound grief at what was happening. After that person spoke, Francis commented on the cases and led us into a very powerful time of prayer, praying for these persons and others encountering similar things.

Sometimes just before I attend a conference, especially one like this, I wonder if I will learn things which might apply in my own work back home. At this moment in the conference I was jolted by the fact that I was being brought home very quickly by someone speaking about very real and very ugly things. No longer was this conference theoretical but it had all become very real, all in an instant. I've never forgotten what I heard during this conference. The conference taught me many new things about how trauma works from a spiritual point of view and what the demonic is and how it appears in the real world when some people are traumatized. I am pleased to let you know that later on, Francis MacNutt wrote a book that covered many of the things shared during the conference. It's called <u>Deliverance from Evil Spirits, A Practical Manual</u>.

The cover is the famous scene of St. George slaying the dragon. A small box on the front of the work reads: "Francis continues to give us the teaching and inspiration for doing the work of the kingdom!" The statement comes from John Wimber, who was a good and close friend of Francis. The book covers topics such as the existence and kinds of evil spirits, curses and ties that bind, how to prepare and how to pray for deliverance, how to deal with satanic ritual abuse, how to set places free and how all of this relates to sin. What I like and appreciate about Francis' approach in nearly everything he does, is his intellectual honesty and humbleness when he is not sure about something.
During the conference one of the most startling things I heard him say is that he has never seen a demon. He says that a few of his staff claim to have seen one. He does pray for deliverance and has been involved in exorcism, and he understands the relationship of these to mental illness and psychological problems. But when he feels that someone he trusts claims to have seen one and asks him to pray against it, he does just that. Now for some this may stretch the imagination since many do not believe that these spirits exist and are skeptical that spirits could somehow be embodied. But Francis, good to his word, will take this seriously and pray for deliverance even if he cannot see the spirit.
What distinguishes Francis MacNutt is his prayer style. He is very calm and confident as he approaches this important task. He makes it clear that he is not healing anyone. It is only God who can heal. As more than one person has observed, Francis not only has a long history in the practice of healing prayer but he is credible. In fact, when I visited the father of the term "psychoneuroimmunology" he told me that Francis MacNutt was the only Christian man of prayer that he trusted. Also what distinguishes Francis is the way he differentiates between multiple personality disorder (now called Dissociative Identity

Disorder) and demonization, which is itself distinguished from "demon possession" which in Francis' opinion is extremely rare. So I would recommend this book as the starting place for understanding the concept of evil spirits and demonization. The examples sited in the book of how to pray are important.

I came back from the conference deeply enriched and interested to learn more about evil in the world. My deepening appreciation for the power of prayer was growing. I had started out on this study of prayer and healing not knowing what I might encounter. My childhood sense of praying had been kneeling at my bed, folding my hands and praying the child's prayer of "Now I lay me down to sleep, I pray the Lord my soul to keep; if I should die before I wake, I pray thee Lord my soul to take." From those simple prayer beginnings I had just come from a conference in which prayers for protection had been done each session and where prayers were seen as serious tools against the Evil One.

A few days later after the conference in Richmond Hill, I was back in California, up in Santa Barbara attending a different conference where I spoke to a large gathering of clergy on Stress and Burnout. My presentation had gone quite well and those in attendance sought me out after my sessions to ask questions and go deeper. When the conference ended, I decided to take a leisurely drive along the coast, down famous Highway 1, so that I could look at the sparkling blue Pacific Ocean on my way back home. As I drove along the coast my thoughts were on how beautiful the water glistened under the cloudless blue sky and bright sunshine above. It was one of those glorious days when you don't have a care in the world and driving is such a pleasure because of the scenic views everywhere. Highway 1 is such a pleasure to drive because of all of the outstanding vistas.

Suddenly my cell phone rang in the car. I picked up and said "Hello" and the caller identified himself as a pastor along the coast. He said he knew I did counseling and that he didn't know who else to turn to with a problem he was having. He said that the gardeners at his church had just brought a woman into his office whom they said was possessed by a demon. The pastor sounded anxious and worried as he said "I have no experience in this... I know you did a study sabbatical on this topic, so tell me, what should I do?"

I had never had a phone call like this before. My immediate inner thought was "I don't know what to say or do, how can I possibly help this caller. I've just returned from Richmond Hill and what is this? How strange that I would get a phone call like this after just attending a conference on this very topic!"
So I explained to the caller that I am not an expert in this field, and that I had attended a conference recently on healing and the demonic and had read several books on it, but for him to not think of me as having any expertise in this. As I glanced out my windshield I saw a beautiful white sailboat in the ocean. Here I was driving down Highway 1 with not a care in the world when suddenly this phone call breaks into that idyllic sense of peace and calm. So while driving, I focused on what I needed to say and do to help this pastor in the midst of a crisis.
Remembering some of the prayers I learned in the conference and some from the book <u>Deliverance from Evil Spirits,</u> I advised him how to pray over the woman. I told him to pray for protection and to pray for a deliverance and to praise God for his power and healing. I told the pastor to call me back in fifteen minutes. I clicked off my cell phone and waited. About ten minutes later the pastor called me back much calmer and he said, "It worked!" I said "What do you mean?" He said, "That's exactly how I prayed, and about two minutes into the prayer the woman shook, then she coughed and then she opened her eyes and smiled up at me and propped herself up and asked where she was. I told her about why the gardeners brought her in and that I was praying for her all this time. She smiled and said thank you, that this is the second time she has been possessed and that prayers seem to cast the demon out." Then the pastor added, "The gardeners all knelt around us as we prayed and some of them joined in, some spoke in Spanish, but I felt a really different Spirit here. She seems absolutely fine now. She went back outside and spoke with the gardeners for awhile and then got into her car and drove off. Thank you so much for your help." I said "You are very welcome," and he asked where he could learn more about this and I pointed him to Francis' book. My mind drifted back to the conference at Richmond Hill and I remembered different things those prayer warriors in healing trauma had said. Because I had attended the conference and had

absorbed the depth and breadth of the speakers and responders, I felt a new sense of confidence in working in an area I still had much to learn about. But in this crisis with the caller, I had taken a humble approach, patterned after Francis MacNutt's own style, not pretending to know something I didn't know, but trusting in God and the power of prayer in a different set of circumstances. I had no idea how it would turn out, but that was nothing I had any control over. I simply trusted what I had learned at Richmond Hill and this time it had a very wonderful outcome.

Then my thoughts returned to something the spiritual director of Richmond Hill spoke about during the conference. Ben Campbell, the spiritual director, told us a little of the history surrounding Richmond Hill. See the book: <u>Richmond's Unhealed History</u>. He said Richmond, Va. was the heart and the center of the slave trade in the United States. All of the railways came to Richmond, and nearly 2 out of every 3 slaves were brought here for processing. He said it was a terrible, dark and evil time when families were split apart, slaves were bought and sold and very often never saw their loved ones again. It was a harsh time as slaves were beaten and whipped, some of the women raped, and some slaves even murdered. As he spoke I was thinking that Richmond back then must have been the darkest city in the country, with all those terrible sufferings going on. Then Ben said that immediately after the civil war, a group of nuns came and established Richmond Hill as a place of prayer to cast out the darkness of the city and to promote healing for the city and its inhabitants. That group of nuns prayed every single day for Richmond and for a spirit of renewal, from the Civil War times until they sold the property (I think it was in the 1980's), and turned it over to the Episcopalians and that they have never missed a day of prayer either. I began to think about this. Christians here at Richmond Hill have been praying for healing and restoration every single day, often three times a day, since the end of the Civil War. Prayer at Richmond Hill is not only their core value but it is the tool for healing and deliverance. It is in the DNA of those who live and work there to pray without ceasing over the city of Richmond and its surrounding communities. They take the power of evil seriously. They know the darkness that came to Richmond during the Civil

War and they believe that whatever remnants of that evil remain, it is their task to do all within their human power to bring light into that darkness through the power of prayer.

I've never seen anything like it. They do not skip prayer time, no matter what is happening at the moment. I had experienced this myself when I tried to book a room for the conference. When I called Richmond Hill to book a room, I had not been on the phone but two minutes when the receptionist said, "I'm sorry I have to leave you now. It is time for prayer here. Call me back in an hour or give me your number and I'll call you back." So I gave her my number. She said "Thank you. I will call you. I must get to prayer." And then she was gone.

Richmond Hill is serious about prayer and spiritual renewal and reconciliation and many spiritual things. Ben Campbell and his staff are phenomenal. His wife is very active in the ministry there as well. I had such a delightful conversation with her one night while she tossed a gigantic bowl of salad for the evening communal meal in the kitchen.

Since my sabbatical I understand that I would not recognize Richmond Hill since the restoration of the complex has been completed. But what does not change is the commitment to prayer, to open up conversations with God and to invoke His healing presence and grace for individuals, places, and regions. Three times each day, rain or shine, people group together for prayer, every day. Everyday since around 1865 someone has been in prayer over the city of Richmond.

Richmond Hill is a very special place indeed. And the conference I attended on Healing Trauma was a profoundly moving experience in the importance of prayer.

Chapter 7
Rufus Womble and the Order of St. Luke

My friend, Art, sat across from me scratching the top of his head. We were seated in his kitchen. He said, "There must be someone else you can interview here in Richmond. I'm sure there is. I've attended healing services over the years here, but I just can't seem to remember some of the people I've met." Then he paused. He looked beyond me, as if memorizing the kitchen cupboards behind me. Suddenly his eyes lit up, and he looked at me. "I know! Rufus Womble." "Who?" I asked. "Rufus Womble," he repeated, quickly adding, "He is an Episcopalian minister who has been involved in healing ministries for years. I've attended a few of his services and I was really impressed with him." "Do you think he is still in town?" I asked. "I don't know and I'm not even sure if I could find out where he is. Let me get a phone book and check." He got up from the table, disappeared into another room for several moments and then reappeared carrying the phone book. He opened it up and scanned the pages. "He's in here!" he exclaimed. "I'm going to give him a call. Maybe he could see you this afternoon."

Art reached for the phone, dialed in the number and I listened as he said, "Hello, I'm Rev. Art Umbach and I'm trying to reach Rufus Womble."

He paused... listening to the person on the other end of the line. "This is Rufus? Hi, I have attended some of your healing services over the years and I have a friend in town who is doing a sabbatical study on prayer and healing and I am wondering if you might have some time to meet with him this afternoon or tomorrow." Again a pause. Art continued, "That's great. Four thirty will be fine... yes... ok... let me write it down." Then Art wrote down the address. "Thank you. You are very kind." Then Art hung up.

He turned to me and smiled, "He has agreed to see you this afternoon." "Us," I replied. "You want me to come along?" Art asked. "Of course I want you to come along," I grinned, continuing, "I wouldn't go without you."

We pulled to the side of the street in front of the home of Rufus Womble. I had no idea what to expect but I was excited about meeting a minister who had been involved in healing ministries for a long time. We got out of Art's vehicle and went to the door. Art knocked and the door opened almost immediately. An older kindly looking gentleman with a broad smile offered his hand to Art. "Hello, I'm Rufus Womble," he said. Art introduced himself then introduced me. Rufus said, "Come in, come in. Just follow me."

He led us through a hallway into his large office area. I scanned the room and found that it was full of books on prayer and healing and religious artifacts of various kinds. Rufus eased himself into his chair. He was wearing black clothing and a cross hung around his neck, resting gently on his chest. He looked very comfortable and relaxed. "How can I assist you," he asked in a kind voice. Art explained a little more about my study sabbatical and why I was on the East Coast. Rufus softly said, "I think it is great that someone is studying this area of life." Art continued by giving Rufus a history of Art's attendance over the years at Rufus' healing services. "I remember you," said Rufus. Then Rufus began to tell his own story of how he became involved in healing ministries.

Website Article: <u>Called to Heal in the Name of Christ</u>

He told of how when he was a young minister he went to visit a woman in the hospital. She was gravely ill and was likely to die. He simply did what any pastor would do. He prayed for her, but she asked him where his oil was and why didn't he lay hands on her. He replied that he didn't receive any training at the seminary on this. She asked him what kind of pastor he was since the book of James in the New Testament made it clear how to do this. So he excused himself and went to a market and purchased some ordinary cooking oil. He returned to the hospital, anointed the woman with oil and laid hands on her as he prayed. Later he left her bed hoping that somehow God would hear his prayer. Not long thereafter, he learned that she began to recover from her dreaded illness. In fact, she eventually healed completely. Rufus was glad that God had answered his prayer. But he didn't think anything special about himself. He just felt that in this case God was gracious.

Not long after this another person contacted him with a similar situation in which someone was very ill. Once again he went to this person's beside, anointed her with oil, laid on hands and sincerely prayed for this person. He believed that if God could heal the previous person He could help this person too. The results of this prayer were similar. This person was also healed from their disease.

Now Rufus began to wonder if God was using him in a special way. Rufus didn't feel there was anything special about himself. In fact, in over 50 years of ministry never once has Rufus believed that there was anything special about himself. And not everyone that Rufus has prayed for has had a physical healing. Rufus is humble about his praying for people. He said to Art and me, "This isn't about Rufus. I'm just a conduit of God's gracious love and healing." Listening to him you know he is telling you the truth. There is no ego whatsoever in him. He is quiet, unassuming and gentle. He also has a great sense of humor. He told us that before every healing service that he does, he always begins with some jokes. He likes to make people feel at ease, comfortable. He believes that when people laugh they make a space for the Lord. They somehow enter into His presence in a different way. Art later told me that each time he's attended a healing service led by Rufus, Rufus always tells two or three jokes. Sometimes they are silly, and sometimes they are cute. But they always make people laugh and smile. Art says that the first time he attended a healing service where Rufus was leading it, Art loved the way Rufus began with the humor. It make me think of the line "laughter is the best medicine."

Rufus answered all of our questions about healing and healing services. He shared that he believes that God selected him a long time ago for healing ministry. He believes that there are other ministers and lay people that God has appointed for this work. He mentioned the same fact that author Morton Kelsey points out in his book <u>Healing and Christianity</u>, that one fifth of the Gospels in the New Testament are the healing stories of Jesus. When you add in the healing stories of Jesus' disciples in the New Testament, the Holy Scriptures point to a significant emphasis on healing. (See <u>Appendix A</u> for a list of New Testament healings.)

As he spoke my eyes wandered to a book near me entitled "<u>Yes Virginia, There Is A God That Heals</u>." Rufus noticed me looking at it (he is very keen for his 84 years). "Would you like to borrow that book?" he asked me. "Yes, may I?" I asked. "Certainly" he said, "Just mail it back to me when you are finished with it." I handed it to him so he could put his name and address inside the book. He wrote out his name and address and then added, "I think you will find it a good book. There are a lot of good books out today on healing ministries."

We concluded our brief visit and I left with the impression that I had met a man very humble yet very committed to healing. At 84 years old he was strong and vibrant and keenly aware of his 50 years of ministry. He was a blessing to me in so many ways.

I returned his book after awhile, through the mail, along with a letter thanking him for his gracious time and gentle spirit of love for God's people. I told him I was keeping him in my prayers. I also ordered my own copy of "<u>Yes, Virginia, There is a God Who Heals Today</u>!" With the subtitle: "E-mail conversations presenting the Biblical basis for Spiritual Healing, Repentance, Being Born Again, the Power of Prayer and Helping the Poor" by Donald W. Bartow.

It wasn't until some time later that I discovered that Rufus was a founder of the <u>Order of St. Luke</u> and a key figure through all of its many years. The Order of St. Luke began many years ago as a gathering of ministers and laity from many difference church bodies who were interested in healing ministries. It became the gathering place for supporting and encouraging one another and learning more about how to go about healing ministries in mainline denominations. I think it is fair to say that many of the early members of the Order of St. Luke were charismatic or "Spirit led" Christians, but today the Order of St. Luke is broadly represented by many spiritual points of reference within Christendom.

I have mentioned earlier my conversation with Canon Lynne Calhoun, a warden with the Order of St. Luke in Ontario, Canada. There are Order of St. Luke chapters throughout the United States and Canada and perhaps elsewhere too. Its purpose is to spread the good news about prayer and healing in the name of Jesus. There are several membership levels and on the <u>Order</u>

of St. Luke website, you can fill out an application and begin receiving their excellent booklet entitled Sharing. If you look carefully at the website you will find a number of different writings by Rufus Womble. If you are at all interested in healing and prayer, it is one of the best organizations you can become a member of. When Pastor Bill Dasch and I put together the "Does God Still Heal Today?" training workshops, we used a number of references to writings found within the pages of the Order of St. Luke's magazine.

I recently went to the Order of St. Luke website, only to discover that Rufus Womble died in the Fall of 2006. There is an "in memoriam" tribute to him on the website. The eulogy sermon posted there is a tender and accurate picture that reflects my own experience of this true giant in prayer and healing ministries. It was an honor to meet him in person, and his words still echo in my mind and heart.

Rufus is gone from us now, but all whose lives he touched carry within them the spark of love, humor and the healing presence of God because of who he was, how he was and what healing spirit he brought to the world. He was a true 'lighthouse of hope' for so many over his rich 50 plus years of ministry.

Rest in Peace, Rufus. And thank you for taking the time for me. (Many of Rufus Womble's writings and talks are now available at the Order of St. Luke website)

Chapter 8
Andrew Weaver Opens the Doors

It was a pretty summer night and I was gathered with my psychotherapist friends and colleagues high in the hills of Hollywood, overlooking the sparkling lights of the Los Angeles basin. Downtown Los Angeles looked like a sparkling jewel in the night and looking south you could see the airplanes on approach to LAX. My therapist friends and I had been gathering for dinners and case discussions like this on a monthly or bi-monthly basis for more than 23 years. We rotated homes each time and shared meals together and then after the meal, we would meet to discuss conferences we had attended or consider cases we had which could use some peer review.

On this night we were at the home of my friend and colleague, Pieter Noomen. Many years ago he purchased one of the homes originally owned by the famous movie screen star, Charlie Chaplin. The outside patio looks down into a large canyon that leads to the basin below. We were sharing some wine and I was excited to share with them the plans I was making as my study sabbatical continued. I turned to my friends and asked them if they had any ideas or suggestions that might enhance my sabbatical on prayer, healing and mind/body medicine.

The newest member of our group, Dr. Richard Binggeli, a Presbyterian psychologist and former teacher at USC (the University of Southern California) said, "You know, you ought to visit Harold Koenig and David Larson." I said, "Who are they?" Richard replied, "Well, those are the two guys who are the top researchers in the country on your sabbatical topic." "Really!" I replied. I hadn't even heard of them. I asked, "How could I possibly meet such researchers and do you even know where they are?" Richard replied, "Yes, I think Harold Koenig is at Duke University and I think David Larson used to be with the National Institutes of Health and he is somewhere up in Maryland I think. You know who could set this up for you? Andrew could." I didn't know who Andrew was so I had to ask a second time. "Who is that?" Richard chuckled, "Oh that's right, you had moved on from the counseling center at First

Congregational before Andrew came to be the director. Pieter and Leila both know him and he happens to be my best friend. He has published research papers with both Harold Koenig and David Larson and knows them both on a personal level and I'm quite sure he would help you get to meet them." I was astonished! Throughout the entire sabbatical I would have the sense of being led time and time again and now it was happening again.

"So, Richard, where is Andrew now?" asked my colleague, Leila. "Well," said Richard, "He was living in Hawaii but has moved to New York City. I believe he is in charge of the research for the hospital chaplaincies throughout all of New York City. I think there may be 16 hospitals with chaplains and that's who Andrew now works for. I bet he even has research on some of your topics. I'll get you his phone number. I would suggest you fly to Manhattan and meet him in person. That's the best way so he can get to know you a little and then set up your contacts with Koenig and Larson." I remember my father once saying it's not what you know but who you know. I was feeling quite excited that Richard knew Andrew who knew Koenig and Larson, people I had never heard of before, but who are giants in the field of religion and health research, the spirit-body-mind connection.

So I called the number Dr. Binggeli gave me and spoke with Andrew Weaver. He explained that he was now working in a new research position with the New York City Chaplain's Office in Manhattan. I explained to him the nature of my sabbatical and that I understood from Dr. Binggeli that he might be able to assist me in meeting the top two people who were now on my list of those I wanted to interview.

Andrew Weaver agreed to meet me for lunch in Manhattan, not far from his office. So I booked a ticket and flew into New York, got a rental car and eventually found myself standing in the lobby of the building that houses the research wing of the New York City Chaplain's office. There were some lovely brochures in racks and on a table that spoke about grief and dealing with pain. There was a writing on coping with death. There was a list of all the hospitals in the city and the contact numbers for all of the chaplaincy offices. I was very impressed.

Looking up I saw a man approach and he immediately stuck out his hand and in a friendly voice said, "Ron, I'm Andrew Weaver. How about some lunch?" And off we went out the door and down several blocks to a fine restaurant that served excellent spaghetti. On the way to the restaurant, Andrew explained about his job and about the chaplaincy's offices in the city. He also told me he was highly interested in my study sabbatical and would do everything he could to help me out with it.

Once inside the restaurant, we were escorted to a booth and were each handed a menu. Andrew made some suggestions indicating that the food here was excellent. After we told our waitress our selections, he seemed to relax more, settling in across from me. He asked me to outline my reasons for wanting to meet Koenig, Larson and Matthews. I told him that I was at the beginning of my study on prayer and healing and that I had heard he had published research monographs with them on a variety of topics, and that since I had heard that these were among the top researchers on religion and health, they would be critical to my sabbatical study.

Weaver then gave me a brief history of his publications with them. He shared with me a little about how each of them, Harold Koenig and David Larson, had come to be the top researchers in their fields. He explained to me about "peer-reviewed" journals and a little about how the research being done by Koenig at Duke University and the work of Dave Larson at the National Institute of Religion and Health were pioneering efforts based on solid research methodologies. He shared how each time a new research finding came out from either place, Duke or NIRH, it was usually picked up by the print and broadcast media and was carried in nearly every major newspaper in the country. Needless to say, I sat in awe and wonder.

Our meals arrived and between mouthfuls of pasta and delicious bread, Andrew continued to fill me in. I experienced Andrew Weaver as a wonderfully warm and sensitive man. I was impressed with his intelligence and great knowledge. He has an air of humility yet underneath I could tell that he was proud of his own work based on solid research. As the meal progressed, I could tell that I was meeting his approval as someone who was taking seriously my subject matter. He later was to give me the phone numbers of his colleagues along with email addresses. He told me the best way to approach each man.

"Harold Koenig is a very busy man, in great demand. I don't think he will have much time for you, but I think he will see you. But don't expect him to give you much more than a half hour of his time. He has a very quick mind, so have your list of questions ready for him. He will answer them fast and accurately. Have you ever heard him speak?" I told him I had heard one tape of his given to me by one of my colleagues who had heard him at a conference. I said, "He spoke rapidly but was very interesting and dynamic." "That's Harold," Andrew replied. He went on, "Tell him that I have sent you to him. Be concise with him. He is a brilliant researcher and has several books in print. He will be the highlight of your sabbatical if you get to see him."

Andrew continued, "David Larson on the other hand is soft spoken and laid back, not as intense as Harold. He comes out of the government's National Institutes of Health, and is a solid researcher. He is a psychiatrist and is a cutting-edge thinker. He will probably give you a couple of hours. He is up in Maryland, and here's how to reach him. Again, tell him I am sending you." I liked the way Andrew was prepping me to meet his colleagues. He was very professional and a keen observer of these men.

"I think Dale Matthews has now left the medical school he's worked at and gone into private practice somewhere in the Washington area. I think he will probably be the most difficult to get in to see. His patients come first. He may have to work you in between patient sessions or perhaps give you some time after work. He is very busy, so don't be discouraged if you can't get in to see him."

"I've got something else for you as well," Andrew continued. Then he produced a file folder and handed it to me across our plates of pasta. "Here are some summaries of some of my research." He then briefly described each of them as I looked through the copies he had given me. "This is one of the most interesting ones," he said, pointing to the page I held.

"Everybody prays in E.R." he said. The research study was of fathers in waiting rooms in the emergency rooms of New York City hospitals. The research was based on interviews held with these fathers who were under great stress as a loved one lay near death or was in trauma in the E.R. The research showed that 99% of these fathers prayed while in the E.R. It didn't matter if they were religious or not, they prayed. "This is an important study," said Andrew. "We know that there is a great need for chaplaincy services for families, especially fathers, who find themselves in hospital emergency rooms." Later, I would read the research brief in detail. I was amazed at how this kind of research was done. I also asked Andrew about his published books available through Internet bookstores. He summarized these for me and made recommendations for further reading.

While I only spent a little more than an hour with Andrew, he was the one who opened up the door for me for the heart of my sabbatical. I am greatly indebted to him for this gift. Later on I would contact Koenig, Larson and Matthews, and simply saying, "Andrew Weaver sent me to you," opened the door for each of them to graciously receive me. Later still, I thanked my friend, Richard, for referring me to Andrew, for without it, my sabbatical would have been for the poorer.

I paid our bill, thanking Andrew for his valuable time. He said he had to get back to the research he was doing and that he had a publishing deadline to meet or he would gladly spend more time with me. I told him that I was extremely grateful for all he had done, and that I looked forward to reading the research briefs which he had given to me. We made our way out of the restaurant back to his office building. He went upstairs to his room while I spent more time studying the chaplaincy programs of the New York City hospitals through their pamphlets and writings. I was duly impressed.

As I look back on my time with Andrew, I ponder what he said over lunch. He had said, "The research done right here in New York suggests to me that prayer is a universal reality when it comes to life threatening issues and severe trauma. I think it calls upon something deep, almost primordial within us, and we reach out to a power, to an infinite source of love and wisdom." With those words and the research papers he handed me, I knew he had come prepared to help me learn more on my sabbatical topics.

Later on I would once again meet Andrew Weaver at a national spirituality and health conference in memory of David Larson, and I would meet him back in Los Angeles when he had supper with my therapist support group at Richard's home. Each time I met him I was amazed at the breadth and depth of his knowledge on so many things.

One of the things I would learn later is that Andrew Weaver has probably done more research on ministerial health than anyone in the country. I was to learn that just a few years ago, he was doing some work for Dr. David Larson which had been requested by Dr. Bruce Hartung, who was then the Director of Ministerial Health, Health and Healing Ministries of the Lutheran Church - Missouri Synod. He has done work for many denominations and brought true expertise to understanding health and healing ministries. I am indebted to him for all he did to make my sabbatical successful.

It is with regret that prior to the publication of this book, Andrew Weaver died. He will be greatly missed by his best friend, Richard, and also by so many researchers across the country. I am most fortunate that I met him and learned from him. He was a great lighthouse of hope.

Chapter 9
In Person with Dr. Harold Koenig
Dean of Research on Prayer, Health and Healing

I had made a list of 15 persons I hoped I might meet in person during my study sabbatical. The number one name on my list was Dr. Harold Koenig. Since learning about him from my colleague Richard Binggeli, I began to read his books and articles on religion and health. I used the phone number Andrew Weaver had given to me and I reached Dr. Koenig. He told me he had an extremely busy schedule and he gave me a few dates and times. He told me he would only have a half hour for me and did I think it was worth my time. I assured him that it was, and we settled on a time and date. I then coordinated my trip to Durham with a visit the next day with Dr. David Larson, in Maryland. I knew this was going to be a very fulfilling and challenging part of the study.

I once again flew into Richmond and stayed with my friend Art. The next day I drove down from Richmond towards Duke University in Durham. During my three hour ride I made up a list of 19 questions I wanted to ask Dr. Koenig. In his email to me he had said he could grant me about a half-hour of his time since he was very busy on some projects. I figured that I would ask him these 19 questions and that we could get them answered in a half hour's time.

Dr. Koenig had invited me to his home. He sent directions, so it was easy for me to find. I walked along the side of his home to his rear office as he had directed. He greeted me warmly with a huge smile, motioned for me to sit in the large easy chair and asked me how he could help me. I replied that I was very grateful for this time to meet with him. I reminded him that he had said we could take a half hour together and that I had written down 19 questions I wanted to ask him. He chuckled and said, "Good, so begin." So I went down my list of questions. He was impressed with some of them. When we were done with the questions he said he had a little more time and was there anything else I wanted to ask. I looked around the room and asked him what he was most proud of. He got up from the couch he sat on and walked over to a stand. "This is what I am most proud of," he said. I went over to where he stood. He lifted up a framed drawing of what looked like a person with a butterfly net catching butterflies. He then shared his story of how he came to work in the same camp as Dr. Jane Goodall when she was studying gorillas.

Koenig was a young university student at the time and studying butterflies. This had come about because all of the placements had been filled and he was asked if he would be willing to go to Africa to gather information on butterflies. He agreed. Unknown to him, his assignment was a placement near the camp of Jane Goodall, the famous British anthropologist and primatologist. Also unknown to him was that she was keenly observing him, watching how he collected butterflies, recorded findings and cataloged them. She observed him sometimes taking risks on rock formations so that he could capture that one important elusive butterfly. He did not know it but Dr. Goodall had begun drawing a sketch of this young man in pursuit of research.

When the time came for Dr. Koenig to go back to America, Dr. Goodall surprised Harold by presenting him with the drawing she had made of him. It is a remarkable drawing. It shows this young man with his butterfly net pursuing butterflies. Nearby is a woman with gorillas near her. Looking into Harold's eyes you could tell how proud he was of the work he did there and his association with Dr. Goodall and her associates.

I asked Dr. Koenig if I could take a few digital photographs of him. He readily agreed. After shooting a few of him seated on his couch in his household office, he asked me if I would like one with the both of us together. I said "Absolutely! Thank you." He rose from the couch and went through his home looking for any member of his family that might take the photo. They were all out at the time, so I told him that perhaps one of the neighbors I had seen working on their front lawns when I drove up, might be willing to take the picture. So I went outside, with Dr. Koenig following me. We got about half way down his sidewalk and he announced he had to sit down. I did not ask why, I just said, "Sure, I'll go on out and look."

Looking up and down his street I saw no one in sight. Just then a garbage truck came down the street. An idea struck me. I went out and hailed the driver. I asked him if he would be willing to take the photo of the professor and me. He agreed to do it. I showed him how to focus and shoot the camera. He took a couple of pictures of me with Dr. Koenig. Then Dr. Koenig and I went back into his home for some more conversation.

I think I spent about an hour and a half with Dr. Koenig. While I was there I bought a copy of <u>The Healing Connection</u> which had just been published. It is a book about Harold Koenig and his life's work. But I was still curious about why he stopped half way down the side of his home and had to sit down.

I found out the answer in "The Healing Connection." Dr. Koenig is suffering from a degenerative ankle ailment and is often in great pain. He describes in his book how he has to take a wheelchair when he travels so he can get to lectures he is delivering. At no time while I was with him did he share this with me nor complain of pain. He simply said, as we walked down his driveway, that he had to sit down.

I am very impressed with this. Here is the chief researcher in our country, a Christian psychiatrist of great faith, who does not complain of his pain and suffering. He simply goes about his life's work, on ankles that barely hold him up. At one time he was a very powerful man. He once hiked to the top of Mt. Kilimanjaro, and he was a good athlete. But now he cannot move about so easily. Yet he goes on working, doing the research that contributes so much to other people's health and well being, and strengthening of their faith.

After taking the pictures, I gave the garbage truck driver a tip for taking the photos, and Dr. Koenig and I went back into his home. There, he asked me if I had yet seen the new large volume called <u>Handbook of Religion and Health</u> (2001) written by Koenig, Larson and McCullough. I said, "No" and he reached into a box and extricated this very large one volume summary of all of the research studies on religion and health spanning the previous 20 years. (It is now affectionately known as "the Bible" in the field of religion and health. It is a "must have" book if you are interested in this field.) I bought a copy of this compendium of research and was astounded to learn how much religion and health has been studied. Among the findings are that people who attend religious services regularly live longer and healthier lives.

Other studies have shown that regular church attenders suffer from less depression and other mental health issues. There are hundreds of studies in the enormous volume and it is quite remarkable how health is so positively impacted by religion. (Note: Since the time of this writing, a second edition of the Handbook of Religion and Health (2012) has appeared, published in February, 2012 by Harold Koenig, Dana King and Verna B. Carson. In the book description online, it says this new volume completely revises and updates the first edition. Its authors are a psychiatrist and geriatrician, a primary care physician, and a professor of nursing and specialist in mental health nursing.)

I had come to the end of my time with Dr. Koenig. I thanked him greatly for his hospitality and invitation to join him. I then shook hands with him and went out and got back into my rental car and began making my way back up the eastern seaboard to Maryland for my next interview, this time, with Dr. David Larson.

If you do a web search on Harold Koenig, you will come upon dozens of references to his books and articles. One of Harold Koenig's most important books for my study was a work entitled, The Healing Power of Faith published in 1999. His chapter titles invite the reader to delve deeper into the research literature. His book is very worthwhile reading. Look at some of his chapter titles:

Religious people have healthy lifestyles
Religious people cope well with stress
Religion offers protection from depression and helps those afflicted to recover quickly
Religious people live longer, healthier lives
Religious people may have stronger immune systems
Religion may protect people from serious cardiovascular disease
Religious people use fewer expensive hospital services

The final chapter of the book has the intriguing title of: Helping yourself and your loved ones benefit from the power of faith.

All of Koenig's books are excellent reading and are grounded in solid research. In fact, most of the time when you read in Time, Newsweek, Reader's Digest or in your local newspaper about outcomes from studies on religion and medicine, or spirituality and health, or religious faith on outcomes of illness, most of the time you are reading something Dr. Koenig has reported from his research.

Here is an example of what I mean.

Someone mailed to me a newspaper clipping from August 8, 2001, written by Nigel Hawkes, Health Editor of the Times (I'm not sure in which Times this article appeared but I'm trying to find out). The title of the article is Loss of Faith "increases risk of dying".

Nigel writes: "Christians whose faith is shaken when they fall ill are at greater risk of dying, according to a study in two American hospitals."

He goes on to write that earlier research has shown that regular church attendance can lengthen life. This is the first study to show that there are consequences from a loss of faith.

The study was of 595 people who were 55 years old or older. They had various illnesses and were hospitalized in two hospitals in the Durham, North Carolina area. The study found that those people who died were people who felt abandoned or punished by God, as compared with those persons who survived their illness condition.

The study says that those Christians who reported feeling alienated from God, or attributed their illness to the Devil, or felt abandoned by their church community, were up to 28 percent more likely to die within the next two years than those who had no religious doubts.

This study was done by Dr. Harold Koenig (see, I told you these kind of reports often are) and his colleague Dr. Kenneth Pargemant, a psychologist at Bowling Green State University in Ohio. According to Koenig, "Whenever anyone becomes suddenly ill with a disease that threatens life, or a way of life, they ask 'why?' or 'why me?'" He goes on to say, "Some people experience anger at God for not protecting them or not answering their prayers for healing. Some feel as though God is punishing them and they question God's love for them, and sometimes they feel like others have deserted them as well."

I know of many pastors who have heard these kinds of words from their parishioners, or family members of parishioners. These words and feelings reflect the deep-seated thoughts and fears that come to many people when diagnosed with a serious disease.

Koenig addresses this by saying that these feelings are normal and expected during the stage of grief people go through. He says that most people come through this stage and do get reconnected to God and their spiritual communities, using their belief as a source of strength.

But there are others who somehow get stuck, remaining in this state of feeling alienated or abandoned by God or others. Somehow they block anything spiritual from getting in.

What is clear from a report like this is that both pastors and physicians need to tune into people who have been shaken in their faith and are in big trouble. More and more medical schools are training physicians on how to take a patient's "spiritual history" but I wonder if any physician has the time to do such a history, especially if they are in an HMO (Health Maintenance Organization) or other such system.

Yet this is a serious issue that now is being surfaced from studies such as those done by Koenig, Pargemant, Larson or others.

What Koenig brings out so crucially in his writing is that in the four years of his medical school education or during the first two years of his residency, there was never a hint that religious faith could "break the grip of addiction, shield people from depression, or calm them at times of emotional trauma."

He says that in the mid-1980's the connection between health and spirituality or other "mind-body" research was embryonic and had not achieved widespread acceptance.

I remember when Joan Borysenko's book, "Minding the Body, Mending the Mind" first came out in 1987 that it was one of those ground-breaking books that told the story about the kinds of treatments that were used at the Mind-Body Clinic first established by herself and Dr. Klan Kutz in 1981. On page ten of her book, she introduces the concept of the power of faith and hope, and how science was just beginning to unlock the mystery of healing by beginning to understand the mechanisms of faith, belief and imagination. When one stops to think about it, this entire field of inquiry, with serious research on the role of faith in healing, and the mind-body connection is only 35 years old. In some ways, perhaps, this field is just now beginning to leave its youthful adolescence, and is like a young adult, beginning to grow up more.

On the Christian faith side of the equation, people such as Dr. Harold Koenig, the late Dr. David Larson, Dr. Dale Matthews and other Christian researchers are trying to present good, solid research that demonstrates the importance of the "faith factor," regular church attendance, a deepening spirituality, the powerful role of prayer and the importance of religious faith.

There are so many health benefits to religious faith that I strongly encourage you to read Koenig. Koenig, for example, points out that religion is a significant factor in preventing suicide. He demonstrates that frequent attendance at church when accompanied by a faith that is important to one's life, consistently lowers blood pressure. People who have a deepening of faith and have a frequent attendance at religious services are shown to have a lower risk of heart attack.

I am sure that there may be some person reading this book who might say, "Well, for heaven's sake, I already knew that there is a healing power of faith, or a healing power of prayer. Why in the world do I need some scientist or researcher to tell me this?" I think that from within the faith-based, religious community, it is easy to believe in the power of prayer and the power of faith. But research is enormously helpful in expanding our awareness of the benefits of prayer and faith. Research such as that of Dr. Koenig's demonstrates how the strengthening of our faith or increasing our worship attendance and our connection to God, has greater health benefits than we may have guessed.

I absolutely love chapter 12 of Koenig's book in which he gives prescriptive suggestions of how you can help yourself or a loved one benefit from the power of prayer. He makes suggestions on attending religious services, of when and where to pray, how to take time to read religious scriptures, and about how to speak to your clergy person about your thoughts about God.

If you are not a religious person already, he recommends that you keep an open mind to the existence of God, noting that 96% of Americans believe in the existence of God or a higher power. He gives a sample list of famous people who were "inspired people of great faith" who are worth reading, such as Mother

Teresa, Dr. Albert Schweitzer, Harold Kushner, Martin Luther King, C.S. Lewis and others.

And for those not ready to consider religion, he even has some suggestions for them, including trying nonreligious meditation which may help you relax and help you receive other health benefits. He is aware that there are persons who have had negative religious experiences or have been exposed to negative or frightening negative religious ideas. He suggests talking this over with a loved one or trusted friend who will take the time to seriously listen to you. He suggests that spiritually healthy people accentuate the positive and not the negative. These healthy religious people "focus on God's love, kindness, generosity and forgiveness-seeing all of us as imperfect and dependent on God's mercy."

I would later meet Dr. Koenig again at a major spirituality and health conference some years later. But he is one of the great "lighthouses of hope" for those interested in the many aspects of religion and health. Everything he has written is well worth reading. God has gifted him with a keen mind, tireless energy and a visionary perspective grounded in research excellence.

I am blessed to have met Dr. Koenig and I thank him for his time and wisdom.

For those interested in the writings of Dr. Koenig, here are some of his most important works. Some he has authored alone and some he has co-authored (with Andrew Weaver, David Larson and others). I have divided them up by topics, with those dealing with healing, faith, religion and spirituality first followed by topics such as aging listed next. The most recent publications are listed first. If I were to recommend to you, the reader, a good starting place for reading Dr. Koenig, I would suggest first reading The Healing Connection (revised 2004) and the Healing Power of Prayer.

For those of you looking for the data showing the power of religion upon health (both physical and mental), the Bible in this field is "The Handbook of Religion and Health" by Koenig, Larson and McCullough listed below or its 2012 second edition by Koenig, King and Carson.

On Healing, Faith, Religion and Spirituality:
In the Wake of Disaster: Religious Responses to Terrorism and Catastrophe (2006)
Faith and Mental Health: Religious Resources for Healing (2005)
Spiritual Dimensions of Health Care, 2nd edition (2005)
Faith, Medicine, and Science: A Festschrift in Honor of Dr. David B. Larson (2004)
The Healing Connection (2001 with new edition in 2004)
Spiritual Caregiving: Healthcare as a Ministry (2004)
Faith in the Future: Religion, Aging, and Healthcare in the 21st Century (2004)
New Light on Depression: Help and Hope for the Depressed and Those Who Love Them (2004)
The Healing Power of Prayer (2003)
Healing Bodies, Minds and Souls: A Practical Guide for Congregations (2003)
Chronic Pain: Biomedical and Spiritual Approaches (2003)
The Link between Religion and Health: Psychoneuroimmunology and the Faith Factor (2002)
Spirituality in Patient Care: Why, How, When, and What (2013)
Counseling Families Across the Stages of Life: A Handbook for Pastors and other Helping Professionals (2002)
Parish Nursing: Stories of Service and Care (2002)
The Healing Power of Faith: How Belief and Prayer Can Help You Triumph Over Disease (2001)
Handbook of Religion and Health (2001)
Handbook of Religion and Health (2012)
Handbook of Religion and Mental Health (1998)
Is Religion Good for Your Health?: The Effects of Religion on Physical and Mental Health (1997)
On Aging and Retirement:
Faith in the Future: Religion, Aging, and Healthcare in the 21st Century (2004)
Purpose and Power in Retirement: New Opportunities for Meaning and Significance (2002)
Reflections on Aging and Spiritual Growth (1998)
Pastoral Care of Older Adults (1998)

A Gospel for the Mature Years: Finding Fulfillment by Knowing and Using Gifts (1997)
Counseling Troubled Older Adults: A Handbook for Pastors and Religious Caregivers (1997)
Aging and God: Spiritual Pathways to Mental Health in Midlife and Later Years (1994)
Religion, Health, and Aging: A Review and Theoretical Integration (Contributions to the Study of Aging) (1988)
On the Web:
What Religion Can Do for Your Health
Dr. Harold Keonig on The Health of Pastors
Dr. Harold Keonig on Medical Mysteries

Chapter 10
In Person with Dr. David Larson
National Institute of Religion and Health

After visiting Dr. Koenig, I left Durham, North Carolina, for Baltimore, Maryland. My next stop would be to visit Dr. David Larson at the National Institute of Religion and Health (NIRH). After a good night's sleep, I drove to Rockport, Maryland, to the large office building that houses NIRH. Dr. Larson was delayed and so I met with Dr.Tom Smith, Dr. Larson's associate. Dr. Smith welcomed me warmly, apologized that Dr. Larson was delayed with a meeting, and that Dr. Larson had called to ask Dr. Smith if he could go ahead and start and Larson would join us soon.

This was a wonderful encounter with Tom Smith as he began to tell me about his own background and how he came to work with David Larson. What was surprising is that Tom Smith and I graduated from the same counseling program in California and knew many of the same people in the field.

Dr. Smith had been a student of the American Institute of Family Relations (AIFR) in Hollywood, which was founded by Dr. Paul Popenoe and Dr. Clint Phillips, and was the first marriage and family study institute in the United States (established I believe in the late 1930's). Later on Dr. Clint Phillips would leave AIFR, and create the California Family Study Center in Burbank, where I did my master's program. I discovered that Tom was also a graduate of the California Family Study Center ten years earlier. When I attended there in 1978-80, Clint Phillips was already an elderly man. Tom had experienced Dr. Philips in his prime and shared some wonderful stories with me. My colleague, Leila Shohet, had also studied at the American Institute of Family Relations in Hollywood in the 1950's. So here on the east coast I was meeting Dr. Larson's colleague who had studied at the same West Coast training center of my colleague and myself. I was thinking what a small world it is.

After a half hour or so, Dr. Larson came in, and we went into his office. What was to have been two hours he had allotted for me ended up as a five and a half hour visit! I learned that Dr. Larson was a psychiatrist who began to question what some of his psychiatric professors were teaching about the role of religion and mental health. While his teachers downplayed the role of religion in mental health, or were outright hostile to religion, Dr. Larson began to do research on religion and health, and began to discover that religion and faith made tremendous differences in people's lives, unlike what was being taught at major medical schools in psychiatry. Later on, he would be joined by Dr. Dale Matthews (then at Georgetown University, author of The Faith Factor: Proof of the Healing Power of Prayer). Together Dr. Larson and Dr. Matthews and others of their staff began reviewing research studies that had been done in past years but had been overlooked or neglected. Larson and his associates began reporting on these research findings to his peers. In time they began to also begin doing some of their own research.

One of the wonderful things that Dr. Larson gave to me to be shared with you, is the top ten health research studies of the last few years. These studies are but hundreds now in peer review journals and other publications. But they are indicative of the strong research evidence that faith does make a difference! For example, people who attend church weekly are not as likely to be hospitalized, and if they are hospitalized, they are not as likely to be in the hospital for as many days as non church goers. Another report indicates that attending religious services more than once a week is likely to result in a person's living seven years longer than those who do not. In the "Handbook on Religion and Health" written and compiled by Dr. Larson, Dr. Koenig and Dr. McCullough, nearly every major health issue has been researched with regard to religion and faith.

Dr. Larson made me feel easy and relaxed while he reviewed the past twenty years of research into religion and health. When Dr. Larson was finished with one aspect of this growing field, Dr. Smith would pick up the story by telling of a different research project and its results. I was clearly in the presence of two extremely bright men who had come to the same conclusions about the bias in American psychiatry against religion and its benefits. The National Institute of Religion and Health was clearly pioneering a very exciting new field in which hard research was bearing fruit as to the very positive role of religion and its impact on health. If you search the internet you will see dozens of research results from the work of Dr. David Larson. At one point he received an important phone call and excused himself, asking me to please go into their research book shelf and take a look at the titles of the works they had collected to date, which were along the lines of my research project on health and healing. They also gave me sample copies of their NIRH newsletter that kept abreast of all the latest research and findings. At the end of my visit, I joined the National Institute of Religion and Health which, among its many benefits, was getting their outstanding newsletter and invitations to other religion and health conferences. One of the sample copies of their newsletter was completely dedicated to the topic of psychoneuroimmunology. I had hit "gold" with this visit with David Larson and Tom Smith.

They were incredibly gracious with their time, were genuinely interested in sharing everything they knew about health and religion, and they encouraged me to continue in my research project. They asked me to send them a report of what I learned from my study. David Larson really made you feel you were the most important person of the hour, and pointed me in some new directions of research I had not considered. At one point he asked me who else I wanted to meet during my sabbatical. I told him I would love to spend some time with Dr. Larry Dossey. He said that he knew him well, had his private phone number and would set it up sometime over the next few months. I thanked him deeply for this, and shook hands with both David and Tom, carrying a stack of new literature and a couple of books I purchased from them. I looked forward to the next steps in my project.

But I was never to see David Larson again, and he didn't get the opportunity to set up my meeting with Larry Dossey.

The tragic news came in an email a few months later. I was visiting with friends in Sacramento and was checking my e-mails when I received the terrible news. The e-mail was sent by Lori Aveni, his administrative assistant, and read:

Dear Friends,

It is with tremendous sadness that I am writing to let you know of the sudden death of our President and founder, Dr. David B.

Larson. Dr. Larson collapsed suddenly Tuesday afternoon while exercising and was not able to be resuscitated. He is survived by his wife and professional collaborator, Susan, and their two children, Chad and Kristen.

Dr. Larson's contributions to the field of health and spirituality are simply too great to mention in this short email. His work has forever changed the landscape of health care today. Those of us who had the privilege of knowing him and working with him will be forever changed by his unbridled passion for life and his work. The International Center for the Integration of Health and Spirituality (ICIHS) plans to continue his legacy through the work of our organization.

ICIHS has established the David B. Larson Memorial Fund, contributions to which may be sent to the address shown below. The Larson family has also suggested that memorial contributions be sent to St. James' Episcopal Church or World Vision or to the charity of one's choice.

I sat stunned in my chair. My eyes welled up with tears. My friend came in and asked if I was alright and I said "No, someone very important has just died," and I explained it to my friends. I was not able to attend the services but the next year a national conference on spirituality and health was held in Maryland in David Larson's honor. The keynote speaker was to be Harold Koenig. (I attended this conference; more on this later on).

I thought back to the sparkle in his eyes when he spoke to me about the work he so loved. I would later learn at the conference the next year in his honor that he impacted hundreds of researchers, and each one of them spoke of how he always had time for them... just as he had for me. He encouraged everyone around him and inspired them to good work. He didn't like sloppy research and would sometimes push colleagues or peers to a higher plain of excellence. Everyone who encountered him met a gentle giant who was not afraid to take on the negative view of religion and health in psychiatry. Researchers around the country and indeed around the world listened when he spoke, and were inspired by him to greater heights.

I was very fortunate to have some hours with him. That he would take time out from his busy schedule to listen intently to my questions and to point out some new twist on an idea I presented was indeed remarkable. That he asked me to stay in touch and come back anytime was truly a blessing. That his death would end the research institute that he founded was unforeseeable at the time. Dr. Tom Smith tried to keep it afloat during the next year or two, and would sponsor a great conference of "Who's Who" in the world of religion and health to be held at Bethesda, Maryland. It was a tremendous conference. Dr. Larson's research partner, his wife, would do much to preserve the lifetime work of her husband.

But it really was a deep tragedy to lose this wonderful researcher and man of God in the prime time of his years.

David Larson was indeed a "lighthouse of hope" to so many people. So much so that the Library of Congress has opened a wing dedicated to his memory.

He is deeply missed but his legacy goes on.

Chapter 11
In person with Dr. Robert Ader
Father of "psychoneuroimmunology" (PNI)

One of the most influential books that I read during my sabbatical was by Larry Dossey, entitled "Healing Words." Dr. Dossey is easily the leading proponent of the value of prayer within medical circles in North America. In fact, when I mentioned to Dr. David Larson that I had read Larry Dossey's work, David said that in his opinion Dr. Dossey is a genius and knows far more than anyone about the power of prayer. I was hoping that I would meet Dr. Dossey, and Dr. Larson was going to help me make that connection but unfortunately he passed away before he was able to do that.

It was in Dr. Dossey's book, Healing Words, that I first learned that the term "psychoneuroimmunology" came out of the University of Rochester Medical School somewhere around 1980. Dr. Dossey doesn't say how that term came to be or who first coined it, but I tucked that little piece of information away just in case I ever got near the University of Rochester.

The opportunity for that visit came quite unexpectedly while I was in Buffalo, New York. A friend of mine had suggested I visit the Abbey of the Genesee, in upstate New York. To get to the Abbey one can fly into Buffalo as I did and drive east on the interstate before making one's way down to the Abbey in Piffard, New York. The Abbey is well known for its spiritual depth and is famous in part because of its association with Thomas Merton and Henri Nouwen, both well-known and popular monks who have had a wide influence within the Roman Catholic church as well as upon other people of faith. (See Chapter 12 for my visit to the Abbey).

My plan was to spend three days at the Abbey. But when I arrived in Buffalo, the snow began to fall heavily and the forecast was for heavy snow for that day and on into the next day as well. Within a short time the Interstate was closed to eastbound traffic, and I had to hunker down in a motel in Buffalo. I had a rental car and found a map that indicated that the University of Buffalo Medical School was not far, so I decided to take a chance and drive up to the north campus. It had been awhile since I had driven in snow conditions so I took my time and drove very carefully. By the time I reached the north campus, the snowflakes were becoming larger and more numerous. I saw a student walking along the snow-covered sidewalk, pulled my rental car over, and rolled down my window and inquired about the Medical School, only to learn that it was located on the south campus The student pointed to a bus that he said would take me there if I followed it. So I pulled in behind this bus and followed it south, through the falling snow, until I reached the south campus.

I found a parking lot and began walking towards some buildings. I stumbled upon the sports medicine building, stepped inside, and was met by athletes in casts and on crutches, and doctors and nurses moving about quickly in what seemed like a frenzy of activity. I stood patiently at a counter until one of the receptionists asked if she could help me. I told her I was looking for the Medical School, and she smiled and told me how to make my way through the maze of buildings. After writing down her instructions I made my way back out into the cold. The snow had lightened up, and I heard the sound of my crunching feet as I walked towards more buildings.

After a good five minute walk, I found myself standing in front of the University of Buffalo Medical School. I walked in, talked with another receptionist, who pointed me to the top floor of the building and to the stacks that would have psychoneuroimmunology books. I went up the stairs and finally found the area she spoke about. Here there were long corridors of books on shelves many stacks high. Hundreds of medical books on all kinds of diseases surrounded me as I picked my way down the aisle. Then I found what I was looking for. There were several books here on PNI (psychoneuroimmunology) and health. One of the books was about stress and the immune system while another one was a collection of articles on PNI. I took them both to a table and began reading. It was in the collection of articles book that I first came upon the name Robert Ader. This article called him the father of psychoneuroimmunology, and indicated that he was from the University of Rochester Medical School. Could this be the reference Larry Dossey was making in his Healing Words book? I became very excited because now I had a name to go with the term PNI.

I read some more and took notes and then photographed the covers of these two books with my digital camera. I replaced the books and found several others. Back and forth it went for several hours, reading more and more about PNI. I found several more references to Robert Ader and just knew that somehow, if he was still at the University of Rochester Medical School, I wanted to meet him.

It was now late in the day when I finished up with the stacks, and I went downstairs to go to the parking lot. When I stepped outside I was aghast! The entire place had turned into a white Christmas scene! Snow was everywhere and still falling. A very bitter harsh cold wind was also blowing and as I made my way along the snow covered sidewalk the wind stung my eyes, blinding me. I tucked my head down and just plowed straight forward through the snow, nearly slipping several times.

When I finally made it to the parking lot, I could not tell which car was mine because they were all covered with snow. I kept my head down and walked into the freezing cold snow. I heard something behind me, and found that someone was using my footsteps to follow me. I chuckled... thinking of myself as a pioneer for whoever was following me. I had put up my umbrella to try to break the stinging wind, and the person behind me was doing the same thing. I finally found my car, and after what seemed like an eternity of scraping off ice and snow, I finally got into the car. I started the engine and after several minutes of freezing and shivering, I put the heater on. It wasn't long before I was starting to feel comfortable.

The roads were now treacherous. The wheels of my rental car slid several times as I made my way back to my motel. When I finally got to the motel, after walking through the ice and snow, I went into my room and turned on the heater in the room. I also took out my laptop and located a local Internet dial up number and went online. I searched the web for the University of Rochester Medical School. The medical school had a website and I looked on it until I found the list of faculty members.

Scanning down the list, I looked for a Robert Ader. Finally, I found his name! An email address was printed just beneath it. I had brought a map in from the car and spread it in front of me. I located the University of Rochester Medical School off the interstate east of my location. I knew the Interstate was closed but I also had heard that New York State does an excellent job of plowing their interstates, and that perhaps in the morning, on my drive down to the Abbey, I might meet Dr. Ader for a few moments.

By now it was nearly 7 PM, as I composed my brief email to Robert Ader, introducing myself to him, and asking him if I could simply have five minutes with him for a photograph. I just wanted to meet him and thank him for all of his research. I wrote the email note and sent it, not knowing if he might get it that night or not.

At 8 PM, my email pinged. Someone had sent something to me. Could it be Dr. Ader? I rushed to the laptop, and looked at the e-mail. I was astounded!! Dr. Robert Ader had emailed me. He was online that night! I had asked him for five minutes and in his return email he was telling me to be at his office at 9 AM sharp and that he would have an hour or more for me. I could not believe it! I was now about to meet the man who coined the very phrase that is part of my sabbatical study-psychoneuroimmunology.

I slept well that night and the next morning I awoke feeling excited, as I anticipated my time with Dr. Robert Ader. I went downstairs, got into my rental car, and headed for Rochester, NY. It was turning out to be a very pretty morning with no clouds on the horizon. The temperature of course was still freezing cold. Snow was piled up by snowplows all along the interstate. But I anticipated a smooth drive on the interstate with all of the bright sunshine around.

Dr. Ader in his email had told me how to get to the campus and where to park. I found my way into the parking lot but had to park in the very last row of cars where there was only one space available. I got out of my car, looked north, and saw an enormous red brick building, which is actually several buildings woven together. I crossed the street, and entered over to the right of the center of the building, which took me through the emergency psychiatric care center. I got onto the elevator and proceeded to get lost in the maze of corridors. I found someone to help me, and managed to find myself standing outside of Dr. Ader's door at the precise time he indicated he would meet with me. His door was open. Actually it was the door that leads to his secretary's office that was open. I knocked softly on the door, she turned, stood, and welcomed me. "Are you Ron?" she asked. "Yes," I replied. "Dr. Ader is looking forward to meeting you and will be with you in just a minute."

She turned around and went back to her chair, then turned right, and entered another door. I could hear muffled voices beyond the door. She came back out and said, "Dr. Ader will see you now," as she motioned for me to come in and go through that door.

As soon as I stepped into the next room, I was met by a smiling Dr. Robert Ader. He promptly shook my hand and welcomed me to the University of Rochester Medical School. After offering me coffee or a soda, he motioned me to have a seat at a table that was actually across from his huge desk. As I passed his desk I noticed many items on this desk, but the one that caught my eyes was a two-toned bumper sticker laying under glass, flat on his desk. The upper part was white with black lettering and the bottom was black with white lettering. The bumper sticker read on the top: "Question Authority". That made me smile because I wondered if this was a man who questioned authority and was someone who thought "outside the box" as some call it. The bottom part of the bumper sticker read: "Ask Me Anything." That made me chuckle out loud, and Dr. Ader said, "Yes, that's what you have to do. You have to question authority because authorities have their biases and they are not always right... and I'm humble enough," he said with a twinkle in his eye, "that I have become the authority and people can ask me anything!" And he began to chuckle too.

I immediately liked this man! There was no pretense about him, and as my interview with him continued, I would grow to like him even better.

He sat comfortably across from me and asked me to explain to him exactly what I was studying and how I became interested in this topic. I explained about prayer and healing and told him I wanted to learn more about PNI "psychoneuroimmunology."

He listened intently and said, "I don't meet many folks from the religious community interested in this and I think your topic is intriguing. How did you come upon my name?" So I explained about what I had read in Larry Dossey's book, "Healing Words," and then about the article I had found at the University of Buffalo Medical School. He laughed at this. He said, "So you have just been following the trail to wherever it leads." I laughed and said, "Yes," and told him about meeting Andrew Weaver and how he had put me in touch with Harold Koenig and David Larson. Hearing this he sat back in his chair, his eyes narrowing, as he began to speak.

"I know of Koenig and Larson, and you have to be careful about what some people say when they make claims about healing from a religious point of view. I am not saying that people are not healed by faith, but in these peer-reviewed journals, it's like preaching to the choir. You just have to make sure they are not overstating their case." He then asked me what I had learned. I showed him an article from one of the editions of the National Institute of Religion and Health (Larson's place) periodic papers. In it was an article by Harold Koenig (from Duke University) describing a certain natural body chemical that was playing a prominent role in healing. Dr. Ader looked at the article and said, "Now this is exactly what I mean. This article overstates the case in my opinion. I think there needs to be more research before this is a foregone conclusion."

I said to him, "So you really are a true scientist; you want research solidly behind anything that is stated to the public about body chemistry and healing." He replied, "There are so many variables that it is, in my opinion, difficult to say with much certitude, exactly what cures people chemically speaking. There are so many other variables and I'm not sure we can control for all of them."

I thought as he said this, that here is a healthy skeptic who is a master in the field, who does not want to overstate anything. I had already encountered some from within the religion and faith community that were a bit like zealots. Now here in this man's presence I was hearing a cautionary note. It wasn't that he was debunking anything, but it was that he wanted to make sure, in true scientific fashion, that something for the record had to be clear, concise, duplicated by others, and that other variables were ruled out.

I asked him how the term psychoneuroimmunology came about and was he the one that coined the phrase. He smiled, not minding at all that he was probably telling this story for the hundredth or thousandth time. He said it was 1980 and he was a presenter at the national (or it could have been international) conference on psychosomatic medicine. Speaking to me he said, "In those days, back in 1980, nobody was talking to anybody. The endocrinologists were not speaking to the cardiologists, who were not talking to the immunologists. Everyone had their own specialty and everyone acted as if their system were a closed system. But I was convinced that these were co-influencing systems, and that everyone should be talking with each other in the field of psychosomatic medicine. So I tried to come up with a term, or a phrase that would try to communicate what I wanted them to understand. So I came up with that phrase. I thought of the mind, the psyche, and so I called the first part, 'psycho' referring to the mind. Then I thought of the brain, and that's the 'neuro' part of the phrase. And of course, I immediately considered the body's autoimmune reaction to things, so that's the 'immunology' part. Hence the phrase 'psycho-neuro-immunology' which means to me that the mind and the brain and the body's immune system are all part of a oneness, a wholeness if you will, and that all of the body's systems talk with each other and are influenced by each other."

I asked him, "So you used this phrase for the first time in your presentation?" He replied, "Yes, I think I used it twice in that talk, and introduced to my colleagues in the field of psychosomatic medicine the concept that no one's discipline was isolated from anybody else's. In the late 70's and early 80's this was radical thinking. But I wanted them to clearly understand my point of view. The body is many systems, all part of one great system. The mind and the body are one. Everything influences everything else."

So there it was... the key thought in PNI... everything influences everything else. This immediately brought to mind the phrase that my friend and mentor/colleague Dr. Peter L. Steinke, creator of Healthy Congregations, says in his talks, "Everything co-influences everything else." Murray Bowen and Edwin Friedman, two giants in the field of family systems thinking, developed this notion in the late 50's and early 60's as family systems and family of origin work was coming about. I knew that Joan Borysenko's book "Minding the Body, Mending the Mind" was in this early 80's era too following her work at Harvard.

Ader went on to say that the media picked up his phrase and within weeks and months the term was beginning to be used everywhere in the field of psychosomatic medicine and early mind-body studies. If you read Candace Pert's book entitled, "Molecules of Emotion," which is a book that describes how psychoneuroimmunology works, you will find her tribute to Dr Ader's work in those early pioneering days of the early 80's. Here I was, sitting with the father of "psychoneuroimmunology" and hanging onto his every word. He went on to describe some of the early experiments he and his colleagues did to prove the reality of PNI. While I did not fully comprehend one of the earliest, it was clear to me that PNI was a demonstrated reality. Later on I would read more about Dr. Ader's research which put him in the forefront of mind-body researchers and PNI studies. At one point I asked him to tell me the best book in the field. He laughed a hearty laugh and said, "Mine." Then he said, "But you won't understand any of it because it's very medical and full of special terms," as he pointed to the three volume work to his right on the bookshelf. "Those three volumes are full of research findings but it wasn't written for the lay public," he added. I looked up at the three volumes and then re-asked, "Well, is there a single good book for the lay person to read?" He smiled and said, "Well, my colleague just came across one recently, but I cannot remember the title of it. I'll have to find out."

Our conversation came back around to religion as Dr. Ader once again began to speak about research on prayer and healing. He said he was convinced that faith probably had a role to play in healing but to say so with certitude was a stretch for him. So I asked him if there was anyone within the religious or faith community for whom he had respect. Again with a twinkle in his eye he said, "Well, yes there is one fellow down in Jacksonville,

Florida who I think highly of... His name is Francis MacNutt, have you heard of him?"

You could have bowled me over! Never would I have thought that this scientist, Robert Ader, would think highly of Francis MacNutt, let alone have heard of him.

"Yes, I know him... in fact... he invited me to his Christian Healing Center a few months back and spent half a day with me. He was marvelous, quiet spoken, highly educated, and very knowledgeable about all aspects of healing, including the scientific literature," I said.

"Yes," continued Ader, "I heard him speak some years ago and was very impressed. If there is one man of faith and religion for whom I have respect it would be MacNutt."

I replied that some folks within the religious community would have a difficult time with him because of his charismatic leanings. Dr. Ader didn't bat an eye at that. He simply said, "Well, I can understand that, but he is a man rooted in research as well, and he doesn't overstate the case as others do. I find my own leaning towards research very compatible with someone like that."

I responded, "Well, I think that one question which is often asked is, 'how is God involved in this process of healing' and 'how does God function with relationship to the body's immune functioning?'"

Ader smiled and simply said, "There are no angels here." That caught me off guard. "What do you mean?" I asked. He repeated, "There are no angels here, just physical processes and chemicals and neurotransmitters and the like. We cannot see the hand of God in the process. But I am sure that there are those who believe there are angels somewhere in this, but as a scientist, all I have is the laboratory and hard science. But I listen carefully to the MacNutt's from the religious community because they have something important to say."

That phrase stuck with me throughout the rest of my sabbatical. "There are no angels here." As Ader saw it, the body is a cellular, chemical processing unit and PNI involved the mind and the body and immune system functioning. He is a scientist and stayed with scientific method and a multi-variable model. To ask him to speak outside of his science would be to ask him to raise questions, to question authority, even of religious zealots. So there would be "no angels here" for Bob Ader. Yet he listened to someone like Francis MacNutt who would and does speak of the hand of the Spirit in healing. He would be among the first to say that one's beliefs profoundly effected physical outcomes where healing was involved. For MacNutt, angels could easily be involved somehow even while Ader would not hold this to be true because it lay outside scientific proof.

Here were two different worldviews with two leaders tolerant of each other. Ader on one hand and MacNutt on the other. Body and Spirit. Body and Mind. Each man open to hearing about the other's experiences and perceived outcomes, while both very much staying within the boundaries of their own expertise.

Ader got up and got me some more coffee, and then went on to share a little of the history of PNI studies as they have grown at universities and medical schools across the country. He informed me of significant PNI work being done at UCLA and also at the University of San Diego. He mentioned several other significant places as well. I said that I had heard that perhaps as many as one hundred universities and medical schools were involved in some form of PNI studies. He readily agreed that could be true but that the most significant research being done was, in his opinion, being done at a half dozen places.

I absolutely was taken by this man... by his infectious grin, and his twinkle in his eye. I could imagine him being a mischievous little boy when he was young. What impressed me the most was how he did not take himself or his field too seriously. Obviously his work is serious work with many implications for people's health and well-being. But Bob Ader said that he is now a 75 year old, old man, and that he could look back and laugh at life and find ways of staying healthy, much of it through laughter and joy.

His office certainly evidenced this. I think I only saw one plaque announcing his degrees. His walls certainly were chock full of text books and important volumes. But later on after agreeing to have his photograph taken with me, he went around to the back of his desk, leaned back with his hands behind his head, and told a few wonderful stories about events in his field that made me smile and laugh. He had found joy in his life and in his work. At 75, he was still sharp in his mind, but had come to a kind of relaxed place inside of himself, at least that was my initial impression.

He had, in a sense, come to embody "mind-brain-immune system." As I sat with him and drank coffee and talked at length, I thought of him as a metaphor (I think he would laugh at this description!). He is a metaphor of psychoneuroimmunology. Sharp mind, a super brain, and laughter functioning as his own private immunization, perhaps not unlike Norman Cousins in his work Anatomy of an Illness, in which he used laughter to cure himself of a deadly disease.

My time with Dr. Ader had come to a close. He wished me well in my further sabbatical studies and told me he found it a pleasure and an honor to meet someone like me doing this kind of research in the name of the church. I took this as a very great compliment from someone as important as he is and of his stature in his field of scientific endeavor. Then he said to me, "If you see Francis MacNutt again, tell him I appreciate his work." With that, he escorted me out of his office and gave me a little wave as he smiled standing alongside his very nice assistant.

As I walked down one of the corridors on my way out of the medical school, I saw a long line of photographs of psychiatrists and other physicians who had graduated from there. One of the names and photographs caught my eyes. It read Simon Budman. I wondered if that was the same Simon Budman with whom I had studied Brief Therapy a few years earlier at the beginning of the HMO movement. I later learned that it was not the same Simon Budman. But it was still an interesting coincidence.

And later on I would meet Dr. Ader again, at the National Spirituality and Health Conference.

I walked out of the building into a bright sky full of sunshine and promise. I got into my car and got onto the interstate, heading for the Abbey of the Genessee. Dr. Robert Ader was another lighthouse of hope for understanding health and healing.

My sabbatical continued on...

Chapter 12
A Place of Prayer: Abbey of the Genesee

One of the things I wanted to do while on my sabbatical was to strengthen my own personal prayer life. When a friend of mine told me about the Abbey of the Genesee, having found it online, I decided to go there for a time of prayer and a time for personal retreat. When I called the Abbey to make arrangements, the monk with whom I spoke was very warm and inviting, and booked a reservation for me in their Retreat House.

In the previous chapter I described how the snowstorm delayed me in Buffalo which led to my meeting with Dr. Robert Ader at the University of Rochester Medical School. Now as I left that wonderful time with him, I looked forward to my visit to the Abbey. It was a spectacular day for driving, with the white snow from the night before glistening in the sunlight. I listened to music on the radio, and carefully navigated some of the icy patches on Interstate 90, the New York State Thruway east out of Rochester.

The Abbey of the Genessee is in Piffard, New York, near Geneseo. I drove Interstate 90 until I reached Route 63. From there I followed Route 63 south through the towns of Batavia and Pavillion. I continued on until I arrived at River Road, where I turned north into a wide valley of farmland with hillsides off in the distance, part of Livingston County

There was no sign of the Abbey as I continued through the snow covered land. Finally after several miles I could see a plain wooden sign off to the right side of the road. As I got closer to it I could see that the following words were printed on it: Abbey of the Genesee. I took a picture of the sign *(see Photography section)*, and turned left up a side road.

In the distance I could see a pointed peak of a building. I wondered what these two days might have in store for me. It was to be a very important part of my journey.

I drove up to the entrance of the Abbey. The most prominent building that can be seen from River Road is the Chapel. It is a building with a pointed roof with another smaller point below.

The roofs were covered with pure snow from the day before. I got out of my car, entered into the front door and found myself immediately in a medium sized room, surrounded by bookshelves to the left, and a small bakery room filled with Monk's bread for sale, while to my right was a door with an open panel above, and various materials and tracts in view. There was only silence. No one was here to greet me. It was, after all, a monastery. So I quietly took a seat next to the bookshelf and began to see what was there. The Abbey of the Genesee is a Trappist Monastery and my first surprise was to discover an entire bookshelf of Thomas Merton's writings and writings about him. Here it was that I discovered that Merton had been a Trappist monk and that he was part of a Trappist monastery in Kentucky. As I continued to read I discovered that he had a very warm relationship with this Abbey of the Genesee and had often come here to teach as well as to have time for his own spiritual time with the Lord.

I continued to look at more of the books and soon discovered that one of my favorite writers, Henri Nouwen, had also come to this Abbey and that he had written about his nine month stay in a work called the "Genesee Diary."

I had this strange thought: that I had been led to this place. It was no coincidence that my friend had found this abbey on the Internet. Now I was learning of the deep spiritual connection it had to Merton and Nouwen. I softly chuckled inside and said, "OK Lord... you wanted me here... so what do you want me to learn? What do you want me to see?"

As I waited, I was drawn to the books of Thomas Merton. There is no doubt that Thomas Merton is easily the most read monk in the twentieth century. There are many who consider him the most famous Catholic of the twentieth century, too. The Seven Story Mountain may be his most famous work, and his story is well known as a worldly kind of man who finds himself transformed by God through his monastic lifestyle. He became widely read and sought after because of his rich wisdom and creative way of sharing his thoughts.

I found his work entitled, "The Rebel," and was reading it when I heard a voice say, "Hello, welcome to the Abbey. I'm Brother Jerome. Are you just passing through?" I got up and offered my hand and told him I was booked for two nights in the Retreat House. He nodded and said, "Very good, and where are you from?" I told him. He then said, "What brings you to the Abbey?" I shared that I had wanted to deepen my prayer life and wanted to develop a stronger spiritual life. He smiled and said, "Then you have come to the right place. You should come and spend a month with us sometime." I replied, "Well, I deeply appreciate the invitation. Perhaps I shall do that. Would you be willing to show me around and tell me a little about the Abbey?" "Why of course," said Brother Jerome. He told me about the room we were standing in, about the books and pamphlets around us, and he took me into the room where the Monk's Bread was piled up. He explained to me that Monk's Bread comes in various types, and that it is a best selling bread in the Buffalo/Rochester area. He shared how this was the primary way that the Abbey supported itself: through the sale of bread.

He then walked me over to a recent picture of all the monks in residence. I think there were 39 monks in the picture. He also shared with me that Thomas Merton came here many times and shared with the Brothers. He also asked me if I knew of Henri Nouwen. I told him I did and named the books I had read by him. Brother Jerome replied, "Have you read his Genesee Diary?" I said I had not. He walked me over to another set of books, scanned them, and then pulled out a copy. "Here is a copy, you really should read it. It is very good in telling the reader what it is like here in the Abbey." So I purchased a copy for my further study.

Then he gave me a brief history of the Trappist order, and then when he finished he said, "Here let me show you to the Retreat House." He escorted me back outside and there in the distance across the road stood a large house where guests of the Abbey stayed.

Next he said, "Please come and join us for prayer and worship at any time. Our first prayer and worship time is about 2:10 AM. Feel free to join us then. If you see where I am pointing you will see a trail there in the snow. That's the walking trail from the Retreat Center to us here. We do several prayer times each day, and the final one is around 5 PM. Most of the Brothers are in bed sleeping by 6 or 6:30 PM." I was astonished that they would be up so early in prayer and that they went to bed so early.

We spoke some more and then he excused himself for other duties. I then left the room, and walked down the corridor that leads to the huge rounded chapel inside. Once inside my eyes adjusted to the dim light. I found a place to kneel, and I knelt in prayer, thanking God for my safe journey, and asking Him to teach me what He wanted me to learn. After some time had passed, I left the chapel and went back to the parking lot to pick up my car.

I drove off the Abbey property and went less than a quarter mile to the Retreat House. Once there I found my room with my name pinned on the outside of the door. After putting my things away I began to explore this large retreat house. I discovered two large library rooms with bookshelves filled with some of the finest religious writers over nearly 2,000 years. It was very impressive. Having finished my exploration, I drove back over to the Abbey to join the monks in prayer. They take prayer very seriously. The central piece of their prayer life is the Psalter, the Psalms.

Sometime in the past, one of the monks wrote the entire Psalter in a kind of calligraphy. It is beautiful, and at every chair and kneeling place in the chapel, there is one of these volumes. Later on I was to ask if it was for sale and found out that it was. I would bring one home with me before I left the Abbey.

Opening this beautiful volume of Psalms *(see Photography section)*, one discovers that the first page is a quotation from St. Augustine. It reads:

This Psalm is spoken in the person of our Lord Jesus Christ, both head and members. He is the head, we are the members. Not without good reason then, his voice is ours and our voice is also his.

Let us therefore listen to the Psalm and recognize in it the voice of Christ.

During this final prayer time of the day, the monks and people from the community prayed aloud various psalms. One of the monks lead the singing while another monk delivered a brief message based on a psalm. I felt very calm and relaxed through this service. I felt closer to God and more at ease within. It was spiritually moving in its simplicity. It lasts with me even to this day.

Following the service I returned to my room, set my alarm clock so that I would get up for the 2 AM service. The weather was bitter cold but it didn't matter to me. I wanted to soak in as much as I could, and it just seemed to me that the 2 AM service would be important to me.

I read for most of the time leading up to 2 AM. I dozed a couple of times, but the alarm clock woke me up. I dressed in my warmest clothing and then proceeded out the front door.

The temperature hovered down around the zero Fahrenheit mark. I was wearing several layers of clothing plus my snow jacket. I wore a scarf around my face, protecting my nose and mouth. Still I could feel the cold air trying to bite through my clothing. The night sky was completely dark with diamonds in the sky everywhere. The stars never shined brighter. I stood on the porch of the retreat center marveling at all of them. I wondered how cold I would be by the time I reached the Chapel, walking through that snow-lined trail. I went down the three steps of the porch and took a step onto the sidewalk.

Suddenly, in a heartbeat, my feet came out from under me, and I crashed hard onto my back. I think I hit my head on the frozen cement, but I couldn't remember. It had happened so fast that I really had no memory of coming off my feet. I just knew that it had happened because I was staring up into the darkness, where the stars were shining in the cold heavens above. I wondered how long I had laid there. I wondered if I had passed out. I had no sense of time. I tried to move my body but it wouldn't move. Was I paralyzed? Had I broken something? I felt dazed. I was alone. Flat on my back.

Then I remembered what Brother Jerome had told me when I first arrived. He told me I was alone in the Retreat House the first night of my stay. "Great," I now thought to myself. Here I am, all alone, on my back, 1:30 AM in the morning, or maybe it was now even later, and I was feeling numb. I noticed my breathing. Then a thought came into my head. This would be a heck of a way to end my sabbatical... right here... on my back... somewhere in the darkness... near an Abbey.

I spoke to God. "Well, here I am. I can't tell what is wrong. Maybe I've just had the wind knocked out of me. The back of my head hurts and my arms hurt, but I can't feel much of anything else. Will You help me please?"

I lay there for perhaps five or ten minutes afraid to move. Then I moved my right arm. It moved OK. I moved my left arm. It moved too. "Thank you, God." Then I tried to roll myself over... and I didn't think I had broken anything and I didn't feel any pain. It was as if my body was waking up. (I believe that God designed the body with the capacity to "wake up" naturally. That may have been what was happening here, and it wasn't God "directly" healing me. Either way, I was thanking God for making it possible for me to get up.)

As I rolled over... my gloved hands contacted... black ice. So that's what it was. I hadn't seen it, couldn't have seen it. I took that one step and whooosh... flat on my back, hard. I raised my knees up and pushed upwards... and stood up. I felt wobbly. Maybe I had hit the back of my head on the cement. I carefully walked, very slowly, back up those three steps, and unlocked the front door of the Retreat House. Inside it was warm again, and I sat and took off my gloves, and felt the back of my head.

Yes, I had a lump. A small one. I didn't think there was any bleeding underneath because it didn't feel soft or squishy. But I decided that I was not going to risk walking outside again to make the 2 AM worship.

I thought about those Trappist monks... starting their days at 2 AM... and ending them around 6 PM. They baked bread during the day. Read in their enormous library for study and personal growth. They came together for prayer in the round chapel several times each day, praying the Psalter (the book of Psalms). In their prayers they pray for the world, for their guests, and for themselves.

And I noticed how quiet everything was out in that valley. Yet I felt God's presence with me. I thought back to Canon Linda Nicholls there in Thornhill, praying for her people, laying hands on them, bringing them the peace of God. I was thinking about that, where my study had begun, and now where it had led to.

I thought about the Power Within video, and I closed my eyes, and imagined the Holy Spirit moving into my body like a warm wind. After a time, those aches and pains from my fall began to ease up. A little more time later and they were completely gone. I was able to get up from the chair and walk back down the hallway to my room without any pain or stiffness, for which I was grateful. I thought of Bob Ader's phrase, "There are no angels here," and I thought "No, Bob, you are wrong. You can not see them, nor hear them, but they are here." And I thought of how Jesus was ministered to in the dessert, and that famous story of his temptations in the wilderness.

I smiled and had a thought. I could think that I had just been very lucky not getting seriously injured with that hard fall. Or I could think that God protected me. I could have hit my head much harder or broken a bone.

I decided to think that God had been with me there. I had prayed for protection throughout my journey. I had been protected by my many layers of clothing. I felt the gentle warm wind of the Holy Spirit flowing through me. I peeled off my clothing, and crawled back under the warm blankets, and whispering a prayer of gratitude, went fast asleep.

The next day I drove back down to the Abbey. I joined the Monks again in prayer. This time a different Monk led the prayers and readings and spoke a message. All of the monks sat or knelt on the west side of the rounded worship space. Guests and others sat on the east side of the rounded space. The lighting is rather dim so it is not easy to see distinctly anyone's face. That fuzzy soft light tends to make one focus on the words of the text being read and the psalms being spoken together.

The psalms are prayers, a dialogue of the heart of man with the heart of God. The psalms deal with virtually every condition mankind experiences while on this earth. The 23rd Psalm is perhaps the best known and is used frequently at the bedside of the terminally ill, and at memorials and funerals. "The Lord is my shepherd... I shall not want... yea though I walk through the valley of the shadow of death... I shall fear no evil... thy rod and thy staff comfort me..." etc. You can find all of the psalms in the Old Testament portion of the Bible.

The time of worship with the Trappist monks ended, and I went back into that small room I first found upon my arrival. I read more of Thomas Merton. The corpus of Merton's writing is large. He was a man of deep faith and profound thinking. Some have compared him to St. Augustine. Both were "worldly" men in many ways, who were turned around by God, and who became exceptional religious leaders of their time. Their influence is still felt greatly, and their writings are among the most cherished of Christian literature. I also began reading Henri Nouwen's, "Genesee Diary." He describes coming to the Abbey, his desire to join the routine of the Abbey, and his openness to the transformations that God might bring to him while among his other Brothers.

One of the things that comes through powerfully in this Genesee Diary is the daily routine of monastic life, and how that very routine is part of the fabric of growth in God. The routine of meals, prayer, study, reflection, conversations, early to sleep, early to rise... and the prayers for the world, all coming together to deepen one's soul in God. If you have not read any of Nouwen or Merton, it is a very worthwhile read. These two men are spiritual "giants" in our lifetime. Their struggles, their inner thoughts, are our thoughts rethought. They give us things to ponder deeply. They bring us closer to a spiritual depth that is often lacking in urban society and secular society in general. Taking some time apart to read a page or two of these two "religious" men is a way of deepening one's own personal dialogue with the Creator. Their words open us up more to prayer and healing. They take us out of ourselves and our egocentricity, and place our mind back on the One who loves and cares for us.

When my time came to leave the Abbey I left feeling much calmer, more spiritually attuned, and filled with peace. The silence that I had experienced a number of times while at the Abbey and at the Retreat House was so important to me. My life is usually very hectic, driving freeways to my counseling offices, and then listening to persons talk about their troubles, and then listening to the radio for news, or music, and then at night watching the late news on TV. Each day this routine is played out over and over. But here at the Abbey, silence is part of that routine. Silence is that special place where we are met by God. The silence of the Abbey. The silence during the worship. The silence of the countryside. The silence of the sky above, so dark and beautiful as I lay on my back that cold early morning, wondering if I was injured. The silence of the Retreat House. In the Retreat House I found this writing by an earlier Abbot (leader) of the Abbey, Abbot John Eudes Bamberger. He wrote: "The truth of the matter is that we can find lasting satisfaction only in the service of that Person who alone can fill the measure of our radical solitude and who is accessible only in silence." Those words seemed so fitting here in this world of the Abbey, a world of prayer and scripture and the deepening conversation between men's hearts and minds, and the heart and mind of God. I put my Psalter which I had purchased at the Abbey bookstore, identical to the one I used in the Chapel, into the trunk of my car, and got back into my cold car. I turned on the engine, and let it idle until the car heater warmed me. As I looked out my windshield I could see across miles of farmland... all the way to the up sloping hills far away. "The snow lay on the ground... the stars shone bright..." hymn tune popped into my head. It had been good to have come here, very good. I hated to leave. I promised myself I would return someday. I saw that I was protected by God. I learned that silence is powerful and necessary for my connection with God.

I continued to look out the windshield, out at the landscape of beauty and snow of this truly wonderful valley. The phrase which ends many Lutheran worship services came to me at that moment... "and may the peace of God which passes all understanding, keep your hearts and minds in Christ Jesus." Looking at the Madonna and Child, the snow-covered statue in front of the Abbey Chapel, and the blanket of snow everywhere the eye could see, and listening to the silence that snow brings when covering everything, just made my heart burst with joy. The Trappist Monks are about keeping their hearts and minds right there... right with God, in prayer. I smiled. Thanked God for this time away.

Then I drove out onto the country road again. Moving towards the next part of my sabbatical study on prayer and healing and body-mind medicine, I knew that I had met many "lighthouses of hope" among the Trappist monks of upstate New York. Their beacons of light had fallen on another pilgrim along the way... me.

(editors note: if you would like to support the ministry of this Abbey, go to the Monks Bread website and order some of their famous, delicious breads which can be shipped directly to you)

Chapter 13
Glastonbury Tor
Healers From Around the World

One of the places associated with healing is Glastonbury Tor. (Tor means "hill" and Glastonbury is a rural town in England; *see Photography section)*. It was one of the top sites I wanted to visit during my sabbatical journey as it now turned towards Europe.

Glastonbury was first brought to my attention by my friend and mentor, Roxanne Whitelight. I first met Roxanne when she was the primary trainer for the Academy for Guided Imagery. I completed my clinical training under her supervision and went on to become a Mentor in the program, also under her tutelage. On one of the annual conferences held in Hawaii, Roxanne did a workshop that included references to spirituality and her own awakening in the Spirit. After the conference I approached her and thanked her for her outstanding presentation. There was an immediate "connection" between us. With her warm, infections smile, and wonderful laughter she said, "I think that somewhere along the line you and I are going to team up together to do something around spirituality for the Academy."

Her words came true as a year later she and I did an in-service educational workshop on "Imagery and Religion" which focused on clinician's own prejudicial images of religious clients. Many of the Academy clinicians were unfamiliar with traditional religious imagery in mainline denominations. This was not surprising since we live in an increasing post-Christian era. Some of the clinicians had been injured themselves by religion or religious persons, so we designed our workshop as a way to uncover hidden blocks to working with religious clients, as well as some ways to heal the clinician's own psychic wounds from religious experiences in their pasts. As we discovered, the workshop was both supportive and enlightening for participants. Through my continued relationship with Roxanne, I followed Roxanne's spiritual journey as she eventually became ordained in the Order of Glastonbury, a religious order dedicated to the support of spiritual growth and healing. I was honored when she invited me to attend her ordination service. I met her parents and many of her friends. It was a beautiful ceremony and a tremendous event in Roxanne's life. Later I was able to attend a small house church gathering in her home where I witnessed first hand the healing words from Roxanne to those who were struggling along their own spiritual pilgrimage.

It was first through Roxanne that I learned more about Glastonbury and its Tor. It is said that Merlin the Magician may be buried there, and that King Arthur and Lady Guinevere may also be buried there. I visited the grave sites of King Arthur and his Lady while in Glastonbury. (Of course, since King Arthur's very existence is debated, so also is his adviser, the famous magician, Merlin. Even if they were not just mere legend, there are many places throughout England that claim to be the burial grounds of these 5th century "heroes.")

The Tor is a very tall mound with a single bell tower on top. The bell tower on top is all that remains of an ancient abbey, the last monastery destroyed by King Henry the VIII when he went on his rampage throughout England, destroying monasteries everywhere.

It is reported that during a much earlier century, St. Patrick stopped here on his pilgrimage. A plaque inside the bell tower shares this claim with the visitor. It is also said that beneath this great mound may be hidden treasures and famous burial grounds. Excavation was halted years ago so it may never be known what is beneath this great earthworks.

Today Glastonbury Tor is a magnet for mostly "new-age" healers from all over the world. I had made the long difficult hike up the side of the Tor, and had spent some time in the tower that sits on top of the hill. *(see Photography section)*

The 360 degree vision from the top of the Tor gives you the vantage point of seeing in all directions across the English countryside, and down into the town of Glastonbury itself. It is well worth the hike to the top of the Tor for this beautiful view. On my long descent down from the abbey tower, down the south slope of the hill, I stopped to chat with two women who were seated in the flowers along the path. One of them was a healer from Czechoslovakia. She shared that she came to the Tor because it is one of the premiere healing energy sites in England and all of Europe. We spoke for quite awhile. I learned that she had wanted to be a healer from a very young age. She spoke of miracles of healing that she had witnessed in and around her small village. She spoke of the growing number of healers practicing ancient healing arts. She believed herself to be a channel of a healing energy given by God. Her female companion shared about what she had seen and heard. They asked me why I was here. I told them that I also had heard about the power of the Tor, and that I was studying prayer and healing. They then spoke about how important prayer is to them. They asked me to stay longer and share more but I had to hasten on. Earlier I had walked around the top of the Tor, having climbed its very steep northern trail. As I neared the top of the small mountain I saw many people sitting around the top. Some were in meditative positions. Some were talking with each other about healing practices. Others looked as if they were in prayer. Some just looked out across the great expansive plains surrounding the Tor. Others walked around reverently and quietly. There seemed to be great awe and respect for these grounds. At one point, I quietly approached someone, a young man, standing alone by himself. I said, "Hello... what is it that brings you here?" He smiled and said... "God."

Standing on such an ancient hill, one cannot help but be moved by the presence of the Sacred. How many centuries had religion been associated with this place? What were the roots of spirituality before the beginnings of Christianity here? How many people had stood where I stood now and opened their hearts to something greater than themselves, some higher Source. I sat down and absorbed in thought, I prayed to God, lifting up my friends and family to my Lord.

I now stood at the bottom of the long trail that descends from the top of the Tor down to the village below. Looking up I could clearly see the one remaining tower from centuries ago. I could no longer see the group of praying people on top of the Tor, nor the healers that were gathered there. The thought occurred to me that all over the earth there are invisible praying and healing people who even as I stood there are involved in saying and doing those things that care for people and their families.

I recalled one monk from St. Andrew's Priory, a Benedictine Monestary in the hills near Little Rock, California, telling me that somewhere in the world, every second of every day, there is a Benedictine Father in prayer. The Benedictine order has as its "work", prayer. That's what they do. They pray... all of the time somewhere in the world. As I stood at the base of the Tor, I thought of those monks in prayer, joined in prayer by dozens, hundreds, perhaps millions of others in prayer in the world. Petitioning for healing and wholeness, for wisdom or courage, or a hundred other requests.

Of course, many who gather on the Tor are energy healers and followers of the New Age movement's beliefs and practices. They would not claim to be "religious" in any traditional sense of the word, but rather they would describe themselves as spiritual, or spiritual seekers. They would not be followers of Jesus Christ or the Holy Spirit as you find in Christian healing ministries. On the other hand, many of them are "seekers" and would enter into conversation about God and about healing. Pagan gatherings are common in the countryside of England at such sites like Glastonbury Tor, Stonehenge, and other energy centers as some believe them to be.

I turned back from looking up the trail to the top of the Tor and I descended down the trail until it reached a small gate. I unlatched it and walked several dozen feet, only to find myself standing in the middle of a small alley-like street. What caught my eye were two places about fifty yards up the small roadway, one on either side of the street, where water was gushing out from the walls. At one site there were people lining up to cup their hands beneath the pouring waters. I wondered what it was, so I decided to walk up the slight incline of the tree-lined alley to learn what this was all about. Then I noticed a sign along the wall about a foot above my head. It simply said:
Chalice Well.

Chapter 14
Chalice Well and the "Waters of Healing"

I had just walked down the long narrow pathway that leads from Glastonbury Tor, to where I found myself on a narrow street. I had been told that a tour bus would be waiting to pick me up to take me back to the carpark (the British term for parking lot). I must have missed the tour bus or it had not come yet, for there were no buses up this very narrow road.

There, in front of me, was a very high and long wall. On the wall was a simple plaque that read, "Chalice Well." Nothing more. *(see Photography section)*

I had no idea what that meant. Did these walls hide some kind of water well? And why was it named "Chalice"? I conjured up a King Arthur chalice in my mind filled with cool, pure, water, or deep red wine, and of knights drinking deeply from this chalice. I laughed out loud. Well, I was in England wasn't I, home of King Arthur and Merlin, and the Knights of the Round Table, and Stonehenge?

Then as I turned to my right, I saw something astonishing! I had just thought of a chalice with water in it, and there... just up the road that inclined beneath shade trees, was water pouring out from both sides of the alleyway, from walls on either side of the narrow roadway. And lined up on both sides of the roadway were a few lads cupping their hands and drinking deeply of the water!! How was this connected to this Chalice Well if it was indeed?

I watched as the young men lifted their hands to their mouths to drink the water. A few other people on the other side of the narrow road were doing the same thing: cupping their hands and drinking water that was shooting out from the wall on the other side. Scanning back and forth I watched as people drank from water on both sides of the road. It was a very bizarre sight. I was fascinated by what I was watching, and decided to see what it was all about.

I approached the young men on the left side of the road to ask them about these two streams of water on opposite sides of the narrow street.

"Hello, I'm from America. Can you tell me what this is? I see you are drinking water from the wall, like those people over there. Are these special waters?" I asked.

The young man in the rear of the queue turned and said, "From America? You have never heard of this place?"

He explained that these waters come down from the hillsides nearby, and that they were part of the Chalice Well.

"What is Chalice Well," I asked. From behind me a voice said, "Come, let me show you."

I turned and saw an old man, wearing a kind of day-pack on his back, leaning on a walking stick. The shade from the trees whose limbs were overhanging us gave a kind of mysterious look with shadows and light playing off of his face.

"What is Chalice Well?" I again asked. He smiled and said, "It is a healing place."

"I'm here on a study sabbatical on healing," I replied. "Then it is destiny," he replied, speaking in a soft voice, adding, "Come, I will show you."

We walked a hundred yards or so, with me following single file behind the old man. He said not a word. The thought flickered in my mind that it was like following Gandalf the Wizard from the Trilogy of the Ring (by Tolkien). We turned the corner at the end of the wall, and followed along the next line of wall to the entrance of Chalice Well.

Chalice Well opened into beautiful lush trees tucked behind the small building where you had to purchase a ticket to enter. The man looked at me, asking if I would pay for him. I smiled and said, "Of course," and turning to the teller said, "Two, please." Taking my money, the teller handed me two tickets. I handed the old man his ticket and said, "You will be my personal tour guide." He smiled back and nodded. He spoke softly again, "I can lead you in there, but something else will be your Guide."

There was something mysterious about this stranger, and once again I had that unusual sense of being "led" somehow. What were the odds that I would stumble on a healing place, and then meet an old mysterious man who would lead me into a place of healing waters while on a study sabbatical on prayer and healing? I had this warm feeling in my chest thinking that it felt like a luminous moment in time.

The old man led the way as we wound along a narrow pathway beneath beautiful shade trees. As far as the eye could see there were trees everywhere, and green grass, and lush flowers, and as we went deeper into Chalice Well we began to pass small tiered water falls, and beautiful pools of blue and green waters. *(see Photography section)*

He turned and said, "Come, I shall show you Chalice Well." As we walked along we passed a shallow pool that had children splashing in it as their parents sat dangling their feet in the pool, laughing with their playful kids. Then we passed a woman meditating beneath a shade tree, seated in the lotus position. Her breathing was slow and even as we quietly passed her by. We then passed another tiered pathway of water, and here two young men sat speaking in very low tones. Across the gardens were other people, either seated on the grass, or sitting on wooden benches. Tucked into one grotto was a woman seated on a swing-type structure. She was as still as a statute, almost as if in trance. I could tell that people had come here to meditate and perhaps pray. Others seemed to just be here to enjoy the park-like atmosphere.

We continued up the pathway. The old man led me into another secluded garden area and then stopped. He hovered over a circle, which reminded me of an ancient shield from antiquity. He looked down then back up at me. "This is it," he said. "This is the Chalice Well."

He told me that here was where the Holy Grail had been buried long ago, deep in this well. He said that the waters here have never stopped flowing, not ever. He said it was a miracle, that dated back to Christ's holy cup, the Grail.

He then stood straighter, and motioned with his hand. "Everywhere you look there are healing waters here. Everywhere. People come from all over to drink of these waters, on the other side of the wall where you saw the waters coming from the walls. And there, where those people are seated is another drinking place. You can bathe in these waters, or sit beside them, or run them over your face or body. This is a very special place you have come to. I will leave you now so that you may drink of this place. Thank you for buying my ticket. I am very glad to have met you." With that, he turned around and started back down the pathway. I never saw him again.

The story is that this is where Joseph of Arimathea buried the Holy Grail, the cup of the Last Supper, so that robbers would not find it. It is said that the waters here have never stopped flowing, not since pre-Celtic times. The "red" water that I drank in the alley and which also flows inside the pool areas of Chalice Well are said to have healing properties. Apparently these waters have a high mineral content, and iron is one of the vital parts in the water. The water is great tasting. You can also buy a small plastic souvenir bottle to take some water home with you. I would do that later before departing Chalice Well.

I spent several hours just sitting beneath trees, meditating, praying, and enjoying the gurgle of streams nearby.

This wonderful place that I "stumbled upon" is one of the most ancient healing sites in all of Britain. It probably has a pre-Christian history as well. But today the associations with Chalice Well are Christian. They have to do with Joseph of Arimathea and the Holy Grail. There is a very nice bookstore on the grounds of Chalice Well, and when you walk out of the bookstore, you immediately see a lone tree off in the distance, standing by itself. I was told by another visitor that this is the very tree planted by Joseph of Arimathea about 2000 years ago. Today the Chalice Well area is well protected by walls. The pools, gardens, trees, and grass all blend into an extremely calm and welcoming place to relax, pray, meditate and commune with nature. The laughter of children blending with the sounds of the water flowing over rocks and small tiered waterfalls brings a very deep and lasting, calm reverie.

I didn't want to leave Chalice Well. My birth sign is a water sign, that of the fish, Pisces. I felt that familiar deep calm that I had once experienced while scuba diving off the coast of Maui, Hawaii. Something about water just soothes me. I believe that my heart and soul were bathed in waves of endorphins that coursed gently through my body during my visit. I breathed in deeply the aura of this beautiful place. There are all kinds of healing.

When I was done meditating and praying at Chalice Well, I followed the pathway back out onto the street. My steps were slower now, unhurried. I reflected on how my sabbatical was bringing me all kinds of surprises. Perhaps the man was right. It was destiny. In thinking about the Grail, and the Last Supper, where Jesus drank from the cup with His disciples, I was once again connected to the Healing Presence of the Christ, from 2,000 years ago.

Little did I know that several years later after my sabbatical had ended, I would look at the Last Supper painted by Leonardo Da Vinci. This famous painting shows Jesus and His disciples sharing the cup during the Last Supper. I would see this painting in Milan, Italy and think back to Chalice Well. I would also see a similar painting by one of Da Vinci's students, high up in an Italian hillside village church.

As I left Chalice Well I was thinking about the New Testament passage where Jesus says In the Gospel of John, chapter 4, verse 14;

"...but whosoever drinketh of the water that I shall give him, shall never thirst; but the water that I shall give him, shall be in him, a well of water, springing up into everlasting life." (King James Version)

Chapter 15
"Blessed Be, Ron!"
The Tree of Healing

While at Chalice Well, I visited the wonderful bookstore there, and spoke with various people about Chalice Well and other interesting aspects of this part of England. Then I overheard a woman in the bookstore talking to someone else. I heard her say that the largest crop circle to date had been seen near Avebury west of Stonehenge. A couple of other people in the shop also had heard about this, and as I listened in, two people excitedly described what it looked like. Each person in the shop had a different theory as to what was creating these crop circles. Some thought it was a man-made phenomena, others thought perhaps it was some messages from aliens, while others said that perhaps it was created by strange weather patterns. But since I had seen photos of crop circles on the Internet, and I had an extra day free, I asked them for directions to the crop circle. This would lead me into another strange encounter, in fact, two strange encounters that would forward my discoveries in healing.

Traveling out on the A344 highway, I passed Stonehenge to my left. I had visited Stonehenge twice in the past so I didn't take the time to stop. This ancient prehistoric place attracts thousands each year and is said to be Britain's greatest prehistoric monument. I have read books and seen many television specials on its suspected origin, purpose, and importance. As I passed the site, I smiled knowing that I was headed towards what some consider the most impressive of all remaining pre-historic earthworks in Europe: Avebury.

I followed my map closely and managed to find my way to Avebury. As soon as I saw the first gigantic stone along the roadway, my breath caught. This was an amazing site! I found parking and began to make my way through the village, discovering gigantic stones everywhere. It is impossible to grasp the scope of this site from the ground. But from the air, one can clearly see how huge this giant ring of stones is, and how they encompass the entire village. So what was I looking at? What is this place? I had heard from various people that Avebury is a magical place, and also a place of healing energy. As I walked along the village streets, past shops and houses, I would catch a glimpse of a huge stone here or there, and then at one point I walked out onto a gigantic plain filled with these incredibly large stones. I immediately understood why some people are drawn here.

Today, Avebury is a huge circle of giant stones peppered around and through the ancient village of Windmill Hill. It is believed that originally there were 400 standing stones here. The largest standing today is Swindon Stone, at the north end of the village. It is said to weigh 65 tons. There are actually several stone circles in the English county of Wiltshire which surround the village of Avebury. This particular one that I was standing at dates back to around 3,000 B.C., and is part of the Neolithic or "New" Stone Age. Stonehenge is about 32 km (20 miles) to the south of Avebury.

There are actually three rings of great stones here. There is the Outer Circle which has a diameter of 1,100 feet. This is nearly the width of four football fields. Many of these stones weigh more than 40 tons. The Outer Circle originally had 98 of these huge "beasts" of stones. There is also a northern and southern inner ring, both of which are difficult to detect because one only has a couple of stones still standing and the other's stones are mostly buried beneath the village buildings today.

As I stood among the great stones of the Outer Circle I was amazed at how ancient and impressive these great rocks appear. They easily dwarf people who stand next to them *(see Photography section)*. I would later discover that while it is believed that Stonehenge was for ceremonies celebrating the solstices and heavenly bodies, Avebury was more about celebrating the life circle from birth to death.

One can easily see this in the phallic nature of some of the stones as well as the way some stones appear to be crossed as if they are wombs.

Today only 27 stones survive in the Outer Circle. Many of the original stones were destroyed to make building materials, and many of the stones were also destroyed, presumably by Christians, who did not want pagan celebrations or experiences to continue on this ground. The site has been excavated a number of times, dating back into the 18th century and into the 20th century.

Today the village of Avebury is enclosed by these great stones. The theories about the stones suggest that there may have been ancestor worship here in prehistoric times. They may have been part of a larger life-cycle belief system, which included the larger stones representing "males" and the smaller stones representing "females". Whatever the case, it is an impressive place!

Again, I stopped in one of the bookshops, and asked if anyone knew about a large crop circle that had appeared a day or so before. The shopkeeper knew exactly where it was. He drew me a map to get to it. Unfortunately it was a map that I thought I understood, which led me to my next surprise.

Driving south from Avebury, I followed the hand-drawn map, traveling a few kilometers to a junction in the road. The map didn't show road numbers, just approximate mileage to the junction. Thinking this was the right place to turn left, I turned onto a road that had no vehicles. The sun was about an hour and a half from going down, and I was hoping that I could find where this crop circle had been discovered.

About 3 kilometers down this road, I knew I was lost. I had already gone too far and instead of seeing the hills that the shopkeeper had described, I was in an open plain. Just ahead and off to the right was a vehicle parked alongside the road. I slowed, hoping I might see someone who might help me. To my surprise, seated at a picnic table nearby was an entire family. I parked behind their car, got out, and made my way over to the picnic table. Before I reached it, the older woman at the table, stood up, and approached me. I put on my friendliest smile and said, "Hi, I'm lost, and I was wondering if you could help me." The woman was short and stocky, wearing a plain dress, and sandals. She spoke saying, "Where are you going?"

I now stood a few feet from her and said, "I am just coming over from Avebury where I heard about a new large crop circle, and they gave me handwritten directions, and somehow I think I'm lost." I showed her my hand-drawn map. She took it and looked at it a few moments. "Oh yes," she replied. "My husband over there passed by there just this morning. The problem with your map is that the road you are on now, isn't on this map. The road you want to take to the left, back there (she pointed) and is still two more highways south of here. You are going to have to turn around, go back to the junction and take the second road you come to after that."

I thanked her and was about to leave when she said, "Where are you from?" I told her I was visiting from America, from California, and I heard about this crop circle and was hoping I might see it before heading back to London later tonight. She said that there was not a lot of light left. Then she asked me what brought me out here. I told her I was on a study sabbatical. She asked what I was studying, and I told her that I was looking into prayer and healing.

At that she brightened up. She said that she knew about healing. Not knowing what she meant, I asked her if she was a healer. She replied that she was! I was really surprised.

I then noticed she wore a small necklace around her neck, and the charm in the center of it was a pentagram, which is an upside down five pointed cross. I had seen one in an exorcism film, and also on the cover of a book on Satan.

"What kind of healing do you do?" I asked. She replied, "Have you ever heard of Wicca?" I said that I had but didn't know much about it. She said that it was a much misunderstood spiritual belief. She touched her necklace, probably knowing I had noticed it, and explained that sometimes people misunderstand the Wicca religion.

"For example," she continued, "This upside down star is often associated with Satanism in movies about the occult and Satan. But we do not believe in Satan nor do we worship Satan. We believe in nature and are a very old religion. There are many people here in England who are part of Wicca." Then she asked, "Are you a religious person?" I said that I was. "A Christian," she asked? "Yes," I replied, "but I am looking into all kinds of prayer and healing practices." "What is your name," she asked. "Ron," I said. "Blessed Be, Ron!" she said.

Her eyes shone brightly and she held out her hand, and I took it, and she firmly gripped my hand shaking it repeating, "Blessed Be, Ron." She told me her name and I then said "Blessed Be" to her as well. She then took me over to the picnic table and introduced me to her family. They were very friendly and asked me a few questions about my trip so far.

Then she said, "Do you see that tree way out there?" as she pointed south along a fenceline. "Yes," I said. "What is it?" She continued, "If you follow along that pathway right there next to the fence, it will lead you all the way out to where the tree is. When you get there, I want you to look into the tree. Be sure to look up into it and around it. It is a tree of healing. You will see various notes attached to the tree in different colors. When one of our people become ill, we come out here and write their name on the pieces of paper or foil and what their disease or medical condition is, and we hang it on that tree. We believe that the tree has healing powers. It is part of Mother Earth, and She can bring about healing. Did you know this, Ron?"

I said that I did not know it, and that this was the first time I had heard of this. "Oh yes, this is very much a part of what we believe. It will only take you about fifteen minutes to go out there. Take a few minutes to study this tree. It fits right into what you are studying. When you are finished, go a little further on. You will find a cave a few yards from the tree. It is the entrance to an old burial ground than runs for a long ways south. You can sort of see where the ground is built up there. Healing services for the ill have been held in those caves for centuries."

Then she said I must hurry so that I would still have time to see the crop-circle. She explained that there would still be daylight after the sun set behind the hills to the west. I thanked her and she called out as I started along the pathway, "Blessed Be, Ron, God be with you." I waved back and yelled out, "Thank you!"

The pathway was rough, not really a pathway at all, but more like a line where a plow had dug up the soft earth along the fence line that must have marked off someone else's property. The path finally ended and the tree was off to my left. I made may way along a real pathway this time, which led me to beneath the tree. On the tree hung dozens of various colored pieces of what looked like foil and paper. Some were in green, others in blue, some in multicolors. It was difficult to make out the names and medical conditions because most were placed high in the tree. But a few were closer and I could see the name of someone who was ill, and next to the name it said, "cancer." On another paper, was another name, with the single word, "heart" on it which I took to mean some kind of heart problem.

I had never seen anything like this. Each of these persons were believed to be receiving healing energy from this tree and Mother Earth. She had also told me that when members of their Coven came out here, they also prayed. I had asked her if she prayed to a Higher Power or to what I thought of as a God. She had said no, that they prayed that the healing energy of the earth would fill the tissues of those who were ill, and that the healing energy of the universe would cleanse and heal the bodies and minds of the ill ones. I had not expected to discover this kind of healing along a remote road in England. But here I was, standing beneath a tree with those for whom dozens were praying for healing energy to work miracles.

I stood for a few moments and also prayed for these who were ill. I was thinking of how Jesus, out of His compassion, laid hands on strangers or said healing things to them. I didn't know any of these persons, nor anything about them, but still I prayed for their healing. Then I turned around and went further south until I came to the caves. I entered one, and found a place on the ground deep in the cave, where people had made a fire. Partially burned out wood lay strewn around. I was only in the cave a few minutes when I heard children's laughter. Turning around I saw a small boy, followed by a small girl, come out of the sunlight outside, into the darkness of the cave. Behind them came a young dad, who saw me and called out a cheery hello. I said hello back to him. I told him why I was there, and he said that this was a real treat for me, because most people didn't know about this cave.

He gave me some history of the burial ground and the healing work done in the countryside. I asked him if he was local. He said yes, that he was a farmer nearby and was taking his children out for the evening. I then asked him about the crop circle sighting. He grinned, "Oh yes... I know exactly where it is... you are not far from it, but you must hurry to see it before you lose the light." I showed him my handmade map, and taking a pen from his pocket, he revised it, showing me exactly where to go. Then he warned me, "But when you go back in off the road, you will want to watch your wallet carefully. There will be police signs warning you that this is a place of gypsies and thieves so you don't want to get close to anybody or allow anyone to get close to you. If anyone approaches you or speaks to you just smile and keep moving. The crop circle is best seen at the top of the hill. It is a strenuous hike up the hill, and there is no pathway. But when you get to the top you will look down into the valley where the farmland is, and you will see the crop circle. It is the largest one ever seen. I personally don't know who or what makes it, but it is magnificent."

At that moment the boy and girl were coming back out of the cave, running and laughing. The farmer father turned and said, "We must go now but good luck. I think you will get there in time."

I followed them out of the cave, back down the pathway, until I reached my car. I turned around on the highway, went back to the junction, turned left, and found myself winding through a very narrow lane, almost a one lane road, with trees, and shrubbery that at times brushed against the side of my rental car. I passed the first road, crossed over it, then came to the second road. By now the sun had set in the West and the light was becoming very dim. I turned left into the dirt road the farmer father had told me about. I immediately saw two police signs warning aboutharold and thieves and pick pockets. As I went further I passed several vehicles with no one in them. I found a place on the grass to park, turned off the engine, and crawled out of the driver's side. There were no signs posted that told where to climb, and I saw that on either side of this small dirt road were two hills, nearly identical, and very high. I walked towards the tents and ground fires that I saw where the gypsies were cooking evening meals. I crossed beneath a wooden cattle barrier and began to climb the hill on my left, hoping it was the right hill. By now the evening mist and slight fog began to surround the hill as I hiked up the steep incline.. The light was fading fast and within minutes I could barely see much at all. Then I got the shock of the day! There, up ahead about a hundred feet, on the very edge of this hill, stood a lone solitary figure of a woman, facing south. She wore a very long flowing black gown, much like I have seen on the covers of Victorian novels. The wind had come up, and her hair was blowing out behind her. I continued on up the hill towards her. She didn't move a muscle. She looked exactly like a statue. When I was only a few feet from her, I saw that the black dress was tight around her waist and reached into the grass at her feet. I wondered what she was doing here. I turned my head to look down into the farmland below and out into the distance. That's when I saw them: three small crop circles.

I went and stood about three feet from her, and posed as she was. Then I said softly, "Hello." "Hello," she said without turning towards me. I thought that was strange. Then she said, "Do you see them? There in the distance?" "Yes, you mean the crop circles." "Yes, they are not as large as the one you can see from the other hill, the biggest ever seen, but these are quite nice." My heart sank a little, knowing I had gone up the wrong hill. I said, "I've never seen one before but have seen many pictures of them on the internet." Then she turned her head towards me. "Where are you from?" I told her I was from America. I also asked her if she came up here often. She laughed and said, "No not at all. I brought my nephews with me and I'm just waiting for them."

I had not seen anyone else, so for a moment I thought perhaps she was a little looney. Then I heard screams of laughter and giggling, and looking up the hill, I saw two small boys rolling down the hill in the very dim light. I could barely see them and knew within minutes that I would not be able to see anything. As if reading my mind she said, "We must hurry off this hill now. It will be pitch dark soon."

I turned to go down the hill at about the same time the two boys rolled to her feet, got up, and laughing told her what a great time they were having. As we all made our way down the hillside, she spoke again, "Would you like to see the Crop Circle Cafe?" I asked her what that was, and she explained that it was along one of the canals that go up and down England, and that it has a room in it with a listing and picture of every crop circle discovered over many years. I said, "You're kidding? Now that you say that, I actually have heard of this cafe on something in America called the Art Bell show." She asked me about Art Bell and I told her he was a late night talk show host who often interviewed people about strange occurances and unusual sightings of things. She replied, "Well then you must see this. I will lead the way in my car. When we get there you can have a beer, and I'll get the children something to eat and drink. It's actually a pub next to the canals. You will see beautiful boats there. People come down the canals and dock their boats at these pubs. You will have a grand time there seeing all the crop circle pictures."

We got into our cars, and I followed her closely as she wound through narrow lanes, and various turns until she finally turned right onto an unmarked road in the dark. A few hundred yards ahead was a brightly lit up pub. We parked, and she led us all into the loud, noisy pub. The place was filled with young and old people drinking and having a grand time. She took me back to the huge room that held all of the crop circle pictures. She went and got me a beer as I looked closely at newspaper reports, photographs, and eye-witness accounts. It was an amazing room. Then the boys came in with their sodas. She explained that it was later than she thought, and that she had to get the children back to their mother. She then told me how to get back to London after I was done. I thanked her profusely, and got her address to later send her a thank you note. It was much later that I would send her a note. But I never heard back from her.

I finished my beer, and headed back out into the dark night. Finding the highway back was easy and it took me quite a while to drive back into London for the night. I pondered seeing the Avebury stones, meeting the Wicca woman and the healing tree, and the crop circle sighting. This part of England is full of mystery and ancient secrets. It is a place of prehistory as well as rumors of aliens. In the midst of it is a healing energy believed in by many people. For them, a healing tree is a lighthouse of hope. So is the energy center in the circle of stones at Avebury. I had thought mostly about persons who do healings. But here, I encountered people who looked to energy fields and inanimate objects for sources of healing. I had been unprepared to find this during my trip. I wondered about it all. I still do.

Chapter 16
Burrswood, England
Holistic Healing at Its Very Best

The trees were lush with life, surrounded by deep green foliage, as my car slowly drove through the grove. I had remembered seeing a glimpse of this idyllic setting on the video months ago when I had sat in Toronto, viewing the film on prayer and healing. Now I was overwhelmed with not only the beauty of this place, but of the serenity and holiness it inspired. As I looked either to the left or right I could see how deep these grounds went. I wondered if there might be small hiking trails somewhere hidden beneath the canopy of these trees. I was to learn later on that there indeed are such pathways for inner reflection and prayers for healing.

I slowly made my way passing acre after acre of beauty. My heart began to lift as I wondered what might lay in store for me. What would God offer to me through the staff and perhaps even the patients here at Burrswood, southeast of London. The echo of a friend's words reminded me that it was here that she found healing, and in fact, a place that saved her life. I also remembered Canon Nicholls' words that it was this place above all that she and others in Ontario, Canada hoped to somehow duplicate for the healing and welfare of those she loved and cared about.

In a matter of minutes I drove into the small area near the Burrswood buildings. I was immediately awed by the beauty and stature of these few buildings, reminding me of old castles of my childhood imagination. It wasn't that they actually looked like a castle, but rather the thought that within these walls people were being protected, cared for, loved so that they might heal or at least live the best possible life that they could.

I parked along the wall of one building, got out and breathed in the fresh country air. I had actually become lost while trying to find my way here. I had followed the map I had purchased but had gotten lost early on. I had ended up in some remote village and had to find someone to ask directions. I had wandered into a small machine shop of some kind, and a young man there had never heard of Burrswood, but thought that I had turned right when I should have turned left at a small intersection up the hill north of this village. He offered to make a phone call for me. I listened as he asked questions and drew a small map. When he hung up the phone he laughed and said that even he would get lost if he didn't know the area well. "It's like that here in the country," he said with a jovial smile. I thanked him and offered to pay for the phone call. He shook my hand and said in his British accent, "It's the least I can do for you, mate... it's just country friends here for you." And I smiled and shook his hand in turn, thanking him greatly.

When I tried to follow his drawing, I once again somehow got turned around. But after reversing myself I finally found the small road leading to this wonderful place. Burrswood is about an hours drive south of London, but you really do need a good map to find the place.

Now breathing in the fresh country air I really could not believe I was here. Someone walked by, and I didn't know if it was a staff person or perhaps even a patient. I smiled and said, "Do you know where I might register?" He replied, yes and pointed me to the second doorway down the carpark. I thanked him, left my bags in the trunk of the car and found myself standing in a lobby, similar to that which you would find in a hotel. There was a registration counter and several people in the wood paneled lobby. I stepped up to the counter and introduced myself. The woman behind the counter laughed a light cheerful laugh and said, "Oh yes! So I suppose it was a little difficult finding us? I am the one the young man called. It is so nice to have you visiting Burrswood. If you will sign in here, I will give you the key to your room. Here is your itinerary. Our director has written out a schedule for you to meet with each of our staff, and has invited you to sit in on the staffing meetings each morning you are here. You will also take your meals with the patients who are here in the dining room. You will meet our chaplain who will serve as your host. If you have any questions while you are here please do not hesitate to ask. We are very happy you have come to visit us here at Burrswood. Do you have any questions now?" I replied that I was very grateful for the invitation and after looking at the three day schedule said I was very impressed with the outline of activities. I also asked if perhaps they might have a bookstore on the premises. She smiled and replied, "Yes, we are very proud of our bookstore. I think you will find one of the most complete selection of books anywhere that fit your topic on prayer and healing. You will find the bookshop just down that hallway to your right," as she pointed the way.

Then she handed me my keys and had one of the staff escort me to my room. She said that the chaplain would meet me in a half hour to begin my visit at Burrswood.

While I waited for the chaplain to arrive, I went to the bookstore and found a very large collection of books on healing. One introduced me to the research done by the Church of England. I also saw a book by the Linns. I had read other things by them. Next to it was a book of daily prayer by Maddocks. I also found a book co-written by the former director of Burrswood. He had been featured in the video I'd seen on prayer at the Anglican House in Toronto.

The Burrswood chaplain, named Steve, met me a bit later, and after welcoming me, escorted me up to the Chaplain's Office. He offered me a seat and told me a little of the history of Burrswood.

At the turn of the century, a woman named Dorothy Kerin was extremely ill and slipped into a coma. Not expected to live but a day or two at most, her family gathered at her deathbed. Then, miraculously, Dorothy suddenly sat up in her bed... and demanded her nightgown! She said she was ready to get out of bed, and that she had had a vision in which Christ called her to do the work He had laid out for her. That work was to provide a healing place for people. Her miraculous healing caught the imagination of physicians in London who came to inspect her. Her story became well known throughout London and its countryside. From the day of her healing until the day she died many years later, she worked tirelessly for those who were ill and in need of healing.

Her legacy is Burrswood. Burrswood completed her vision from the Lord. She knew that she was to find a place where her dream of a full healing ministry could be carried out. Now on several hundred acres, the Burrswood community had become a reality. Staffed with medical and spiritual personnel, it offers a hospital, a whirlpool and health spa area, a wing to treat mental health issues, has outpatient housing, provides chaplaincy services, and includes a chapel in which healing services are held three times a week, open to the public, and plenty of walking trails for spiritual renewal and serenity.

It even has its own tearoom and gardens. Steve then escorted me outside to something he was quite proud of. It was a small tiny building, which when you entered, you discovered was a tiny little chapel for personal devotion. Just outside of this small place was one of the prayer walks which Steve had designed five years before when he had come to be the Burrswood full time chaplain. Along this pathway were stations for reflection, prayer, inner renewal and contemplation. It was apparent that Steve was deeply spiritual.

But Steve was also a very fine theologian and pastor as I discovered over the next few days. During staff meetings, he listened carefully to the discussions about each patient. When appropriate he would ask a pertinent spiritual question or seemed to grasp the underlying spiritual malaise of a person that may be contributing to the emotional/physical disease or malady. He led one of the morning devotionals which the staff never miss. They gather in a side room off the main Dorothy Kerin chapel, and one of the staff plays guitar while everyone joins in singing and praying for each other and for those who have come to Burrswood for healing.

Steve's use of the scriptures deepened my own personal healing journey, and his fresh use of texts and Scripture's wisdom was in and of itself a minor miracle to behold. From psychiatrist and nurse to groundskeeper and volunteer, all listened carefully to the words and music that strengthened their souls for the work of each day. They were clearly bonded together as a healing team. Each station was seen as integral to the smooth working of the whole.

Everyone was viewed as equals and each person prayed fervently for one another. It was clear that to work at Burrswood takes an extraordinary person who is ordinary. I was most impressed with the physician who lives in one of the nice homes near the central buildings. He and his wife invited me to their home. There I heard how the Holy Spirit was moving and working through the staff and patients to deepen their work and recovery. I loved his sense of humor. He told stories of how Burrswood had changed over the years and how it was continually adapting to new expectations from the community and from the staff itself.

While it clearly was meeting the high standards required to have its hospital status intact, it also sought to be the spiritual place envisioned originally by its founder, Dorothy Kerin. What was most profound, was the deeply personal faith of this physician, and of his humility in the face of the disease processes. He clearly saw spirituality as a treatment modality and a source of healing for each of his patients. He prayed "with" his patients and "for" his patients daily. He was himself transformed in the Spirit and in turn was transforming them physically, emotionally and spiritually.

During my three day stay at Burrswood, I was an observer of a unique holistic approach to integrating mind, body and spirit, with full services to the entire human being. Thinking back to what Canon Linda Nicholls had said when I had visited her in Canada, she was absolutely right. This is a very unique place and perhaps there is nothing else like it in the world.

As I sat in on staff meetings, the lead nurse would pull up a file on a patient and give a brief history of the patient's illness, either mental, physical or both, and she would describe the patient's family support system (or lack thereof), the circumstances surrounding this patient's intake, and what some of the psychosocial aspects that might be playing out in the patient's overall health picture. For confidentiality reasons, I cannot describe any one particular patient profile, disease, or psychosocial circumstances. What I can tell you is how all of the other staff, usually six or seven of them along with the primary nurse would ask questions, make comments, or speculate on a holistic approach to healing. Existential issues that may be underlying the etiology of the disease or disorder were openly discussed. The patient's spirituality or belief systems were taken into account. Strategies for asking pertinent questions were discussed, and a "team" approach from the chaplain to the psychologist to the hydro-therapist were formulated.

How did the patient perceive Christ in their lives since they had indicated they were Christian? What did the patient feel they needed, beyond medicine and hospital treatment, for their overall ultimate recovery? Did the patient wish to participate in the "laying on of hands" healing services held in the chapel? Observations of what family member was coming to visit, and which ones were not, was integrated into the treatment plan. Those patients in the "outpatient" mental health program were integrated into the meals with in-patient treatment. Even the patients seemed to be integrated together around meals where patients both hospitalized and ambulatory rubbed shoulders with those who were outpatients.

I observed excellent psychiatric, nursing and chaplain services throughout my stay. Funded by both public governmental support as well as private donations, this seemed to be a perfectly blended model of care unlike any I had ever seen before.

The Director of Burrswood, Michael, was a licensed psychiatrist. While in charge of the overall administration of Burrswood's operational functioning, he also involved himself in the staff meetings, patient care, and overall support for all his staff and ancillary employees. His winning smile and professional caring demeanor were, to use a British phrase, "spectacular."

Michael invited me to sit with him in the back of the church at one of their community healing worship services, led by Steve, the Burrswood chaplain. What I witnessed as well as participated in was a service very much like the one I had seen on the video described earlier and one which I would be part of later in 2004 in Canada.

During this service, dozens of people from the surrounding countryside, and some from urban London, came for healing. The outline for the service they experienced is reproduced in small pamphlets just outside the chapel doors. There are two versions of this worship service. Both include the laying on of hands for healing.

When the time came, Michael led the way for me to the line where people stood waiting their time for the laying on of hands. Each person would kneel, speak softly for what they wished to be prayed for, and then Steve would lay hands on the person's head or shoulders, and pray for healing of the person. I tried counting the number of persons attending the healing service I attended, and I think it was more than 150 persons in this service.

Michael knelt before I did, and while I could not hear for what he prayed, it was obvious that this executive director was like everyone else there, praying for his needs. It was a very reverent experience witnessing this service for healing. When it was my turn to kneel before the altar, I told the chaplain what I wished for healing, and he laid hands upon me and prayed exactly for what I had requested. A warmth spread over me as he prayed and laid on hands. I could understand why so many people would travel so far to be at Burrswood for their public services of healing.

The next day, the chaplain, Steve, invited me up to his office, and showed me the large group of materials he uses to understand the nature of disease and the eight categories of disorders for which he prayed with persons. Using color charts and protocols worked out over several years, he and the staff of Burrswood had a point of view from which to provide healing ministries for all who came for help.

The heart of the matter for Burrswood care is the insight that all diseases and disorders carry within them a spiritual component. From that center of spirituality, each patient was "diagnosed" not only for physical or mental "disease" but also were considered for spiritual "disease." The integration of mind, body, spiritual, and relational needs was very unique in the care of the patient. Even if on occasion the actual talking with patients about spiritual dimensions of their care did not always happen, i.e., a particular patient was resistant to talking about spirituality or had closed themselves off to this dimension, still the staff at the meetings thought about how this patient was doing from a spiritual perspective. I was impressed with the staff's gentle spirit in these matters, even as they approached each patient with professional care from their own medical perspective.

The degree to which the entire staff prayed for each other and each patient was prayed for spoke volumes of the deeply held spiritual convictions of each staff member. Prayer was at the core of their ministry of wholeness and healing. Their humbleness in their approach to each patient, and their profound listening skills as they listened and documented each patient's story was something to behold.

Here in the countryside of England were many "lighthouses of hope" in the forms of psychiatrist, nurse, chaplain, physiotherapist, hydro-therapist, nursing volunteers, and dietitian. The team itself was a "lighthouse of hope" as was Burrswood itself, and its founder, Dorothy Kerin, a Catholic woman at the turn of the 20th century, who was deeply religious and completely devoted to caring for the whole person.

Once again I was blessed to see another form of healing and another great example of a "lighthouse of hope."

Chapter 17
The Midlands: Healing in the Parish
Brian Leathers, Spreading the Healing Message

I was driving from London, England up to the Midlands towards the home of Brian and Joy Leathers. Brian is a minister in the Church of England and he and his lovely wife had invited me to visit them sometime. I had met both of them at the 7th annual pastor's conference held at the Toronto Airport Christian Fellowship (TACF) gathering.

During that first day at the pastors' conference I walked around the auditorium while the band played prior to the opening of the conference. I finally made my way down a row of chairs when suddenly a couple of British accented chaps called out to me, and made me feel welcome. They had me join them further down on the row. We each introduced ourselves over the music and that was the beginning of a wonderful week with all of them, especially Brian and Joy.

I wrote earlier that the Toronto Airport Christian Fellowship has been called the laughing church. I soon discovered why it had that reputation as one by one many of the several thousand pastors or spouses in attendance began to start laughing or calling out praises. The caricature of British as those "stiff upper lipped" people made me glance over to see if any of the Brits I was sitting with would also react the way many in the building were doing. I had the thought that these "brothers" from England certainly wouldn't succumb to emotions or whatever was happening, but many of them were also laughing and full of great joy. It was amazing to watch. One or two of them did not get carried away but many of the non-Brits around us were having the time of their lives, clapping and laughing as the music continued on.

I knew that this would be a unique experience for me, having never been in such a huge hall with so many charismatics being swept up in a grand cacophony of sound. It is impossible to describe on paper what it sounded like. Men and women moaning and groaning, and crying out, and shouts from every direction, hands raised, clapping, singing, some looking as if they were in deep trance, bodies swaying, some people falling down, and falling out and writhing on the floor. Thank goodness Francis MacNutt had prepared me for this experience. It became infectious.

Soon it seemed as if the sounds and movements of so many was a great outpouring of the Spirit. I knew that this was exactly what it was in the hearts and minds of those who were here. I smiled kindly and sang the songs as they were posted up on the screen and the band continued on with praise songs.

Later on, after the first major break in the service, I made my way through the bookstore, selecting some CDs of some of the music we had just sung. When I exited the bookstore in the rear of the building, I saw Brian standing alone. I went up to him and we chatted about the music and the service, and it was a most pleasant conversation. He told me that his wife, Joy, had gone to use the restroom outside the hall we were in.

Several minutes passed by when I saw Joy come back in from the outside wing. She had just stepped into the building again when she started giggling.

Then it got worse and she found herself laughing. She was not the only one. Brian told me that when it happens like this to her she can't stop it.

I asked naively what he thought was happening. He said that it was the power of the Holy Spirit in her, and that sometimes it just grabs people and makes them start laughing. I had never seen anything like this before, but it did appear to be something which strengthened many in their faith and brought them closer to God. Many people throughout the hall were giggling and laughing, reminding me of the passage in the New Testament where the disciples are accused of drinking wine, as the explanation for the tongues they were speaking in. Now right before my eyes I watched people become "slain in the spirit" as it is often called. People everywhere were really high on God. Then after awhile, as the service continued, things began to calm down a bit and the band finally stopped playing. There was now a time for prayer. Some people went up on stage to receive prayer. When prayed over they would fall backwards into the waiting arms of some "Catchers." In fact, everyone who went up for prayer fell backwards into a Catcher's arms. Brian and Joy explained this to me, and made me feel very comfortable at all times.

At the end of the entire week of the pastor's conference, Brian and Joy and I had become fast friends. They invited me to their home in the Midlands. It was now towards their home that I was driving.

This was my very first time to visit the Midlands in England. As I drove through various small towns, I noticed that this region was very much a working class area, and in some spots, even poor. There were some factory smokestacks in the distance, and signs of poverty and decline. I even saw a strange sign near the road. I had no idea what it meant. It was just one of those weird little signs here in the Midlands. Knowing that first impressions are not always true and lasting, I decided to ask Brian about this when I visited.

I finally found Brian's church, parked my car in the driveway, and saw Brian approaching me in the driveway as my engine died. He was so happy to see me, hugged me, and he invited me into his home nearby. His kids were terrific, fun and playful. Joy came over, gave me a warm hug of welcome and offered me a beer. We all sat in their living room while their kids played and battled for my attention. They were young children, and as children often do, they drew me into their games while their parents continued talking with me over that delicious beer.

Our conversation came around to the revival going on within Anglican churches all over England. After years of declining attendance and the reputation of the Church of England as being rather boring and unemotional, Brian began to talk about the revival catching fire across the country.

He explained how for he and his wife, Joy, the Toronto Airport Christian Fellowship provided the kind of energy and Spirit-filled Christianity that they had hungered for. He explained that this was true for a growing number of Anglican clergy, such as those I had met in Toronto. Brian and Joy explained how the week in Toronto is the highlight of the year for them. It is a time when they are "refilled" and "replenished" for the hard work in the Midlands.

Brian explained how the Midlands have been through various changes and that his ministry often was directed at blue collar workers. He spoke of some gang activity, mostly economically driven.

I asked him about the banner outside his church that advertised something called The Alpha Course. He explained that this form of Bible study grew up from a church in London, and has grown all across England. I asked him more about it. I learned that there is within it a special emphasis on the Holy Spirit and also on the topic, does God heal today? I was intrigued by this because I had never seen a Bible study that raised this question. Brian explained that this was what was so exciting about this Bible study. It is informal, often is found acceptable by new seekers and makes for a relaxed gathering of people in homes around good food and fellowship. The Alpha Course seems to make basic Biblical concepts easy for people to grasp. He felt that this Alpha Course and the things he was learning at the TACF were going to definitely grow his church and bring many more people to the Lord.

I am featuring Brian in my book because he represents another kind of "lighthouse of hope" for those who are in need of healing and prayer. Of course, since first learning about Alpha in England, I've since met others involved in The Alpha Course in the United States. Many clergy and lay people love it because if its renewed emphasis on the Holy Spirit and the healing power of prayer. It has now come to America and is used in many places in many different denominations. Of course, like all new Bible studies, it has drawn some criticism by some for not being doctrinal enough or is too experientially based, or has too many connections to charismatic renewal or to the teachings of John Wimber and others. I am not endorsing this Bible study, but what I am doing is reporting to you what I saw and learned during the course of my study on prayer. (For a positive look from a Lutheran perspective see this article, A Lutheran Critique of the Alpha Course at https://web.archive.org/web/20160119211727/http://postcessationisttheology.blogspot.com/2012/01/alpha-course-critique-of-steadfast.html)

For people like Brian and Joy, The Alpha Course and religious experiences such as those in Toronto undergird their new excitement for prayer and healing and spiritual renewal. They go to Toronto to fill up, and more than one person I met at what is known as the Toronto Blessing seemed to experience TACF as a kind of spiritual gasoline station where they fill up for the work back home over many nations and continents.

As Harvey Cox, a famous theologian of yesteryear, points out in his book Fire from Heaven, the charismatic renewal is the fastest growing Christian movement in the world. He reports that there are now over four-hundred million Charismatic Christians on the planet. However you wish to describe this phenomenon, whether Pentecostal, or Charismatic, or Revival, or Spirit-led Christianity, it is a fast growing "fire" of renewal that has swept Africa, Central and South America, and Southeast Asia as well. In this case, I met a wonderful clergy couple who were very welcoming when I was feeling a little uncomfortable in Toronto. Joy was also very open with me, describing her physical experiences in Toronto, and how they cannot be controlled and yet they are a powerful reassurance to her that God loves her deeply. Brian is an example of a very loving husband, very supportive in his relationship with his wife who experiences the direct power of the Holy Spirit (her words). They represent thousands of persons worldwide who have been touched and affected by what is known as the Toronto Blessing, which is an unusual manifestation of prayer and healing within Christianity, which is criticized as not being Biblical and is even considered a counterfeit Revival by some.

What is true is that this religious revival has enlivened more and more Anglican priests and has made them feel more emboldened in proclaiming the Gospel of Jesus Christ. While some may argue it does not go deep enough and is not rooted enough in traditional doctrine, the up-side of it, which Brian brought home to me, is that it has brought a new spirit of renewal and hope within what had been stodgy churches and a declining membership all over England.

Brian and Joy are another kind of "lighthouse of hope" in the Midlands. I wish them well in all they do.

(Update on Brian and Joy, Fall of 2013 - Joy is now serving as pastor of a local free church where she has started a new youth group. She will be ordained next year. Brian is the Rural Dean which means he coordinates the churches and ministers in the Church of England in his region. Their four children are grown and successful. Dan (24) is training to be a minister in the Church of England. Rachel (23) an aspiring writer, hopes to ghost-write Christian books and she also leads worship. Thomas (21) has been evangelism secretary for the Christian Union and recently graduated from York University. Timothy (19) finished school and wants to work in education or tourism. Recently Brian was introduced by the Archdeacon to a missionary from overseas saying, "This is Brian - all four of his children love the Lord." He was very proud of that moment.)

Chapter 18
Notre Dame Cathedral, Music and Prayer

Many consider it the jewel of Paris: Notre Dame Cathedral. Its impressive flying buttresses, its many gargoyles, and its beautiful entry way are awe inspiring. I had first seen this magnificent cathedral when I was 18 years old. Now I was seeing it again, but this time I appreciated it so much more. Unfortunately, the front facade was being cleaned so it was shrouded from view. But once inside, I nearly gasped at its beauty.

I was there in time to hear singing in some remote part of the cathedral. First came the sound of young boys' voices, which were accompanied by adult male voices. I found a guard, hoping that he spoke some English. I asked if the choir was practicing. He replied with a deep French accent that they were preparing for a brief Mass. I had forgotten that Mass was held often in this magnificent church. I made my way forward, so I could watch and listen better.

I sat and watched the priests and the assistants and the choir members lead the parishioners, visitors and tourists in the celebration. The music was beautiful. The organ music throughout the cathedral filled the air with sweet sounds. I was to purchase a couple of CDs later on in the gift shop to remember that unique sound.

Following the Catholic Mass, I moved forward and sat in the area of wooden seats that faced across to the other side. I do not recall what the name of this section is, but earlier it had held those singers and participants in the service. But the music lingered. Somewhere the singers continued or perhaps they were new singers. A number of people sat in the same section as I did and listened to the music echoing throughout the nave.

One's eyes are drawn upwards to the beautiful stained glass windows everywhere and back to the rose window in the back of the cathedral. I felt dwarfed in this place. Huge colonnades hold the high vaulted roof. The Gothic style of architecture was magnificent to behold. A woman sat nearby and bowed her head in prayer. Looking around there were many entranced as was I by the music and beauty of Notre Dame. Many bowed their heads in prayer. It was truly a holy moment as people of many nationalities were drawn together in prayer and worship.

I cannot describe how the light came in through the windows above or the feelings one would get from looking up at all of the magnificent stonework and artistry in the construction of such a magnificent cathedral. All I know is that I was transfixed, like the woman near me, and the tourists across from me. The thought came to me that you did not have to be religious to be moved by the spirit of this sacred place.

Through the centuries, through the numerous upheavals in Parisian life and culture, this church has stood the test of time. I felt I could spend hours here in prayer and meditation. The wonderful organ music, choirs, and worshipful atmosphere were infectious. Who would want to leave this house of God? Notre Dame de Paris with its rich history and great architecture is unique in all the world. When I had first entered it's hallowed halls I was thinking like a tourist, looking at everything, taking it all in and not feeling particularly spiritual. That had all changed with the music and the worship. Now I was no longer the tourist. Now I was part of the gathering of people who sought healing and connection with God. Around the cathedral votive candles burned brightly, carrying the petitions of many, hoping for positive outcomes from the whispered and silent prayers. How many people had come into this great cathedral over the years? How many had prayed and worshiped and called upon God for His healing hand?

In the moments I spent inside Notre Dame, my thoughts gave way to spiritual things. I prayed. I listened. I was still, motionless, in the presence of God. I thought of the ancient song, "O Magnum, Mysterium." The mystery and majesty of the Lord filled this place.

The time came when I reluctantly made my way back out into the busy city of Paris. I looked up at the gargoyles with ugly faces staring down. I made my way down the sidewalk still filled with the sensations I had experienced while inside. Several minutes later I came to the Jewish war memorial in which hundreds of tiny lights shine representing each of the Jews taken from Paris during the Nazi regime, never to return home. I was struck by the juxtaposition of the Notre Dame Cathedral and what it signified and this Jewish Holocaust Memorial so nearby. I thought of the glory of God and the horror of what men do to each other. The words of Jesus came to me, "Father forgive them..." I thought of my own light and darkness within me. I was glad I had prayed in Notre Dame as I continued on my way into the expanse of Paris. The sounds of city came on stronger: honking horns, motor scooters, a policeman's whistle. The luminous moment inside the Cathedral still burned inside me like an eternal light as I made my way back down the busy sidewalk filled with shoppers and those out for a lovely stroll. Life was good. My sabbatical was a blessing. I smiled and headed for the Metro towards the train station. I wondered what would come next.

Chapter 19
Chartres Cathedral and the Labyrinth

Not only can people be "lighthouses of hope" but so can cathedrals bring the light of hope into darkness. One of the best examples of this, and some say it is THE best example, is the Cathedral at Chartres, about a 45 minute drive or train ride south of Paris, France. Built hundreds of years ago, it has stood as a monumental "light" for those traveling on pilgrimage. Long ago this massive structure dwarfed the tiny village that surrounded it. Now the village has grown up around it, so that while it is still visible for miles before you reach it, its dominance over the plain on which it sits has been diminished over the centuries. Still, it is a magnificent cathedral that draws you in.

I drove out of Paris to see this heavenly place. I had first learned of it from colleagues and friends who urged me to make sure to put it on my itinerary. Reaching the town of Chartres, I found some public parking, and then began my climb up through walkways, stairs, and streets until I finally reached the entrance to the Cathedral. I had already read much about the incredible light that shines through the beautiful stain-glass windows at various times throughout the day. It is said that Napoleon was so moved by the light inside the Cathedral that he claimed if the Devil visited Chartres, the light itself would scare him away. Inside the Cathedral I was struck immediately by the holy silence which greeted me. My eyes were drawn upwards to the massive roof overhead, and then my eyes were drawn to the huge columns supporting the roof of this incredible cathedral. As I made my way around the sanctuary, I found myself in awe of some of the places which were very dark for lack of light while other places stood out in magnificence as the light from the windows far above shone in beams of colors and shapes onto the floor far below.

The feature of the Chartres Cathedral which is so famous worldwide, is the labyrinth carved into the floor. I had heard of this ancient labyrinth and had read about it before coming here. I was disappointed that there were chairs covering the labyrinth. I knelt between some of the chairs and looked closely at one of the lines in the floor which delineate the labyrinth. I had read that Napoleon had members of his army dig up the lead which filled these lines in order to melt it down for canon and musket ball for his legendary march to conquer the world.

People who saw the labyrinth long before Napoleon's desecration of the labyrinth described it as beautiful and exquisite. Even now in its rather plain state, it still appeared to me as something very special. I only regretted that I could not walk the labyrinth as I could at some of the places in America where this very labyrinth had been painstakingly copied. The unique pattern of this labyrinth is still in use for religious services and for spiritual renewal as part of the growing labyrinth movement world-wide.

I had read that there were historically six cathedrals for official pilgrimage for French Catholics during the middle ages. Chartres was one of those six cathedrals. As I stood on the massive floor of the Chartres Cathedral, I could imagine thousands of people making their way for days, perhaps weeks, until they came to this holy place. They would come into the cathedral, kneel before the altar for prayer, rise and break off into small groups that would wander into every nook and cranny of this magnificent building to once again kneel before smaller altars, praying for health, good crops, family members, freedom from evil spirits, and the like.

Standing in this giant space I thought that although I am separated from those pilgrims by many centuries, I too, would still pray for the same things, for good health, family members, a safe food supply, and freedom from harm from evil people and life's tragedies.

With these thoughts in mind, I noticed a woman standing alone, still as a statue, head bowed, hands at her side, deep in prayer. She stood next to one of those massive pillars holding up the building. I watched her for awhile. She didn't move. Her lips didn't move. She stood there for some time, lost in her own world of prayer and meditation. Chartres does that to you. It draws you into a relationship with God. Perhaps this woman was a person of strong religious convictions. Or perhaps she was on her own personal pilgrimage, just now beginning to explore her relationship with some Power greater than herself. As I looked around, I saw others in prayer as well. Some of those kneeling made signs of the cross as they knelt or stood up to leave. Those who were walking around walked quietly. The hush was audible. Chartres is a sacred place and you can feel the energy present from the millions of pilgrims and faithful who have come to pray here.

The woman nearby slowly raised her head, as if coming up from some deep place, and slowly looked around as if noticing where she was for the first time. Then she walked slowly into the shades of darkness and light, down a passageway of the great cathedral. Others who had just entered the cathedral were moving in that direction as well. So many thoughts and feelings moved in my soul as I made my way around this great place of God's presence.

I stayed for a long time inside the Chartre's Cathedral. It makes you want to stay. It somehow beckons you to stop your life for awhile, and pause, and go inward to have silent conversation with your Creator. Gothic structures are built to draw your eyes upward, to the heavens, to bring your thoughts upwards to sacred things, lifting your soul from the ground of everyday living and the mundane of life. The same thing happens to you at Chartres. It stirred even someone like Napoleon to be moved in his spirit.

I watched as the light in the Cathedral changed over time. I went once more to the labyrinth determined to learn more about how it was used, why it was built, who used it, and what became of other labyrinths over time. As strange as it may sound, the labyrinth was somehow becoming a lighthouse of hope to me. I wanted to participate in whatever it was that drew pilgrims here to walk this eleven circuit floor design. I wanted to know how it renewed one spiritually and how it brought you closer to God, or perhaps deepened your walk with Him.

I also wanted to know why you could no longer use it, why chairs were covering it, as if to prevent people from using it. Perhaps it was to keep it safe for future generations to look at, or perhaps over time its use had been forgotten or neglected. I wondered who might know the answers to my question. Later on in my sabbatical study I learned that indeed there was someone who knew a lot about labyrinths, and this one in particular.

But for now, I felt as if I had come into an altered state of awareness inside this wonderful place at Chartres. I decided that any time I came back to France, I would make this a special pilgrimage place for myself.

Finally, my time had come to an end, and as I walked back out into the sunlight, and looked back at the ancient outer walls of the Cathedral, I knew that I had found a very special place, and that even buildings could be "lighthouses of hope."

Chapter 20
Paris to Munich
Healer on a Train

The train car I decided upon for my train from Paris to Munich was a couchette. This is a car with rooms that have beds stacked three on each side, like bunk beds. My car was full of people as I boarded in Paris, and my room had six people assigned to it. Just before all of us settled into the room, the female conductor came by and picked up all of our passports. They do this for security reasons so that while you are sleeping someone does not steal your passport, or so I was told.

After she had gathered our passports, we began to introduce ourselves to each other. I think there is a natural curiosity to know who you are traveling with since you are among strangers. One of the passengers in my room was a very large black man who was from Nigeria. He had a winning smile and a deep voice. He asked me what had brought me on this train. He had selected the bottom bunk beneath mine, and he seemed very pleasant to me. I told him about my sabbatical studies in prayer and healing. He grinned bigger and told me he had just come from Nigeria where he participated in one of the largest healing services ever. I asked him how many attended. He replied, "Four million." I gasped! "Did you say four million?" "Oh, yes," he said, "Over a period of several months we had a continuous healing service and over four million attended. This is not unusual for Africa. We have an AIDS epidemic and the power of God's Spirit is strong in our country."

The only reason I actually believed him is that on a recent Benny Hinn television program on Christian TV, Benny had interviewed a German evangelist who had brought along videotape of his own recent healing services conducted in Africa. (Benny Hinn is a famous television evangelist and charismatic healer). One of the German evangelist's videotapes revealed that during a night time healing service, the camera panned the gathered crowd in a 360 degree sweep. It was an amazing sight. African people stood shoulder to shoulder in a massive wave of humanity. As far as the human eye could see, in every direction, you could see people together, pressing against each other. There was not one place unoccupied by a human being, as far as you could see to the horizon! Had I not seen this with my own eyes I would not have believed it. The German evangelist on the Benny Hinn show estimated over a quarter of a million were in attendance that night. Huge lights and gigantic speakers were everywhere so that all of these people could hear everything being said and done on the central dais in the middle of this sea of humanity.

It reminded me of something I had read in Harvey Cox's book I had been reading before I left for the European portion of my sabbatical. In his book, Cox reported on the growth of the phenomenal charismatic movement world wide. All over the world, and especially in Africa, millions of persons were coming into the Spirit. As I reported in another chapter, the estimated world-wide total of Pentecostals is over 400 million souls. Absolutely astonishing!

The train pulled out from the station, and swayed back and forth as we continued to talk about healing. I could not believe I had met this large black man from Africa who was a healer, involved in healing ministries! Coincidence? Serendipity? Perhaps. But I don't think so.

He gave me his business card and he told me about various famous healers now in Africa. In one case he spoke about a Christian healer who was doing dramatic healings of people with cancer, and AIDS and other terrible diseases. He said that people were flying in from all over the world to come to this healer.

As my sabbatical went on, I was to learn that there are several world famous healers in Africa, to whom thousands of Europeans, north Americans and others are coming to see for a miracle cure. These healers are drawing in droves of people. While I was in England visiting my friend Melanie Warren, she had a friend visiting from South Africa at the same time. Her friend spoke to me about these kinds of healers before I boarded this train in Paris. She said she would send me a videotape of one of these healers because she had seen him in action and told me I would not believe what I saw. When she returned to her country she got me a video of this healer and mailed it to me.

This particular healer heals in the name of Jesus Christ. His words and actions are incredible and it is easy to see why so many come to see him doing his miraculous work. It gives one goose bumps to see his results. I suspect that there are many healers such as this.

I really cannot express adequately how surprised I was to be on this train from Paris to Munich with someone directly involved in healing ministries in Africa, almost exactly as was described to me several days earlier by Melanie Warren's friend. Rather than coincidence or serendipity I believe God placed him there for me to anchor the reality of my study. It was also like a sign to me that God was revealing the pathway for my study, showing me that the world is full of healers for whom prayer is central to all that they do. In fact, over and over again throughout my sabbatical quest, it was as if God was leading me, and placing people like this man into my pathway. I felt "led" at all times. The train continued on into the night and I thanked this man for sharing his insights with me. I pocketed his business card, and made my way up to my bunk as the clickety-clack of the train began to lull me to sleep. I looked down at the other passengers now also falling asleep. A lady on the top bunk across from me said goodnight and I said the same. I looked out the small opening at the head of my bunk and watched the lights fly by, mesmerized by the sights and sounds of the French train hastening its way towards Munich. It was there that I was to meet my son who was himself traveling down from Amsterdam where he had been lecturing for the computer company he worked for in the Silicon Valley in northern California. He had purchased and had built for himself a BMW from the factory in Stuttgart, Germany, and I was to pick it up from him in Munich. He had offered me the car for my sabbatical journey.

I closed my eyes and went to sleep as the railcar still swayed back and forth. The African man below me was another 'lighthouse of hope' and his ministry to millions was a real surprise. I was to have more surprises along the way. And I would meet another healer on a train, coming back to Paris at the end of my journey. Simply amazing!

References:

The Elijah Challenge (www.theelijahchallenge.org/): Just one example of healing ministries in Africa similar to the ministry of the man I met on the train.

Chapter 21
Salzburg and a Night at the Castle

Is there a more beautiful city than Salzburg was my thought as I made my way up towards the castle high above the city. I was planning to have a delicious dinner overlooking the Austrian Alps as seen from the window of the restaurant atop the hill. Afterwards I was going to enjoy a concert in the small, famous hall in the castle. A string quartet from Czechoslovakia was playing. On the program was Eine Kline Nachtmusik by Mozart. I had a ticket in the front row. What I did not know at the time is that this hall is where the most talented performers throughout Europe come to play and sing their music. A list of all those who have performed here would literally be a Who's Who of the deep musical world of classical music.

Earlier in the day I had walked the cobblestone streets of Salzburg, taking in the vast array of shops, professional buildings, cafes and specialty stores of all kinds. I crossed the river, walked into magnificent squares, and visited churches. Images and places featured in the movie The Sound of Music came to me. I walked by the famous horse training area of Salzburg and even found offices of healers and practitioners of homeopathy. The day was magnificent and the beauty and sparkle of the city was unparalleled.

I thought back to the nice drive down from Munich, and the well wishes from my son as he handed me the keys to the white California model of the BMW he had built in Stuttgart. I had use of the car for two weeks, and was a little worried about putting any nicks or marks on the car. But he had reassured me not to worry because the factory guaranteed complete coverage bumper to bumper for the first thirty days. With that thought still lingering in my mind, I took a deep breath and relaxed as I walked through the city of Salzburg.

Towards evening the lights began to light up the city. I made my way to the castle, anticipating the magical evening to come. Indeed it was magical. I was able to get a table beside a window so that I could see the Austrian Alps in the distance. The setting was perfect. So was the meal. A glass or two of wine relaxed the

body and heightened the senses. High above the city I sat and enjoyed every second of the ambiance in the restaurant.
Following the meal, I made my way over into the castle. Once inside, one makes a series of twists and turns as you make your way to the concert hall. People were excited as they walked towards the much anticipated music of the night. Some were dressed in fine attire while others wore ordinary clothing. Regardless of dress, there was an air of high expectation that something good was going to happen.
Entering the hall, I looked around at how simple everything was. The hall is a large rectangular setting, with a raised platform in front. I made my way down to the front row, sitting left of a couple, and right of a single woman. I looked up and the music stands were not more than 10 feet away. The string quartet had not yet entered the room, but I could clearly see their music posted on the music stands.
Within fifteen minutes the quartet entered. Following a rousing ovation they sat, readied their bows, and began to play in unison: Eine Kleine Nachmusik, the music of Mozart. Earlier in the day I had passed the home where Mozart was born. It was clear that this quartet was highly skilled and played with vibrant exuberance. I sat back and let the music wash over me. The couple to my left held hands while the woman to my right was smiling. Every eye was on the players and every ear took in the rich and warm tones of this magnificent piece. The quartet played two additional pieces that night but I have forgotten what they were. At the end of their concert they were met with a standing ovation. They continued their bows, smiling and genuinely pleased by the audience's reaction. They exited the stage, leaving their sheet music behind. A number of people lingered afterwards and stepped near the stage to look at the quartet's music. One woman sat on the piano bench and fingered the music of Mozart. I heard a man nearby say he had never heard Mozart better played. Soon the hall emptied of appreciative fans, and I made my way back out to the wall of the castle that overlooks the city. What a magnificent sight!!! Like a fairy tale city, the sparkling lights reflecting off the water of the river and the windows lighted so brightly up and down the valley

brought a smile to my face. I soaked in the magnificence of Salzburg for as long as I could.

I retired to bed that night full of pleasure and contentment. What a day and night it had been. I had not done any study on my sabbatical that day but I had taken in the romance and sensuality that is Salzburg, Mozart's home. The meal, the wine, the view of the Alps, the concert, the lights of the city, so filled me with a glowing appreciation of this magical city.

The next day everything would change.

Chapter 22
September 11, 2001
The Day Everything Changed

It was a beautiful day as I drove my son's new BMW sport model automobile under the bright sun. I had left early from Salzburg, Austria where the night before I had spent the evening in the Castle overlooking Salzburg, listening to the chamber orchestra play Eine Kleine Nachtmusik. I had had a lovely dinner in the Castle restaurant. Far out into the distance you could see the wonderful Austrian Alps, snow covered, and shining in the late afternoon sun. The view was spectacular! Breathtaking! Then the concert following this lovely meal was exquisite. I sat in the front row, so I could see every detail as the strings were plucked and the bows were moving. The CD I purchased following the concert features some of the same artists I saw that night, and some of the same music.

So it was that as I drove from Salzburg, through Innsbrook, then south towards Verona, Italy, I was completely content with life. My sabbatical was going smoothly. I was happier than I had been in ages. My heart was full of joy; My mind unburdened from cares and concerns. The engine of the BMW purred like a kitten. The music was calm and soothing from the radio. As mile after mile swept by (actually kilometer after kilometer), and village after village moved by my window, I smiled inside. I was traveling towards Venice, home of gondolas and famous restaurants. The Italian countryside of northern Italy was colorful as I drove through it. The hillsides were full of vineyards and each tiny village in the distance had a church spire rising up to the skies. I was completely content and satisfied as the countryside passed by.

I had pledged to myself that during my travel I would not allow the gas gage to get below the halfway mark. Glancing down I saw that the needle rested on the halfway mark. So I began to look for a petrol station. Within twenty minutes I found one off in the distance. I was looking forward to having the service station attendant wash my windshield. They still do that in Italy, just as they used to do all across America.

I pulled into the petrol station, turned off the engine of the car, and sat waiting for the attendant to step outside the small building to my right. No one came. I waited a little longer, but still no one came. So I stepped out of the car, and checked out the price of fuel on the pumps outside, then made my way into the building. No one was there.

I walked through a small souvenir shop looking for someone, but there was no one there either. This was very puzzling to me since I had never been in an unattended souvenir shop.

This complex turned out to be much larger than it appeared outside. Inside there were many places to sit. There was also a pizzeria and some other places to get food and drink. But I saw no one anywhere. I made my way along the corridor, seeing not one single person anywhere despite the fact there were cars parked outside. Then I came to the end of the floor, and made a turn, and stopped dead.

I couldn't have been more surprised! Standing in front of me was a group of perhaps 15 to 20 people, all with their backs to me, all staring up at a television set mounted overhead. There, on the screen, was a news broadcaster speaking in Italian. Behind him was a still photograph filling the background of what looked like water hoses pouring water onto some kind of wreckage.

My first thought was that there had been a terrible accident on the autobahn, so I wanted to learn firsthand where it had occurred in case it was along my route to Venice. The news broadcaster never spoke a word of English so I did not have any idea what he was saying. Then, in the lower left hand side of the screen, a message began to flash in English. It said: "America Under Attack."

I froze. What could that mean? America Under Attack? My first thought was that this must be another type of Oklahoma City bombing, but then, why would the message say that America was under attack? Why was it saying America? The "talking head" just kept reading from notes as they were handed to him. I thought that perhaps a car bomb went off in America and the media was hyping this, whatever it was, I knew I had to find out. I asked several people standing there if they spoke any English. No one did. This was surprising to me after being in Germany

and Austria where nearly everyone spoke some English. But no one spoke English here.
Then, a young man came up next to me, also curious about what was on television. I turned to him and said, "Excuse me, you don't speak English do you?"
He replied, "A little bit, yes." I asked him, "Do you also speak Italian?" "Of course," he said. "I am Italian."
"Could you please translate what they are saying on the news? It says America is under attack so could you tell me what they mean?"
"Sure," he said. Then I watched him... his lips moved quietly as he listened. Then I saw tears forming in his eyes. His face became drawn and ashen, and he turned to me. "Are you English, Australian or American?" he asked.
"I'm an American from California," I replied.
"Oh my god," he said... "Your country has been attacked by terrorists... They are saying... you know, those two big towers in your country?"
"The World Trade Center?" I asked. "Yes," he said. "They are saying that awhile ago a... how do you say it... commercial aircraft?..." "Yes, commercial aircraft," I replied. "A commercial aircraft crashed into the World Trade Center tower... It exploded into a fireball... then... a little while later..." (he kept looking at the television screen, then would glance at me, then turn his eyes back to the monitor) "another commercial aircraft crashed into the other Tower... then... they say... another plane crashed into... a five-sided building, do you know this place?"
"The Pentagon?" I asked?
"Yes! The Pentagon. This is the picture we see now on the television... the water is being sprayed on the Pentagon. Wait... now he says another commercial plane crashed into the woods in a place... something about a pencil... a State... do you know this place?" he asked.
"Do you mean, Pennsylvania? It's a state in the United States," I answered.
"Yes... the plane crashed in a field in this Pennsylvania!"
I had to sit down. I wanted to sit down. But I stood there transfixed by what he was saying. I had read many spy novels and this was worse than any plot line I had ever read in any of

those novels. This was inconceivable to me. I just couldn't comprehend what was being said. My mind was racing and I was overwhelmed by emotion and I could barely hear what else he was saying to me. My eyes filled with tears. Then I thought I heard him say that the twin towers had collapsed. "What did you say?" I asked. "They are saying that the towers have completely collapsed, they have fallen to the ground."

I just stared at him. This was impossible! I couldn't remember at that moment exactly how tall those towers were... something like 110 stories I thought I remembered from when I had visited them myself. I had stood on the top of those towers and looked north at all of Manhattan, and south to the Statue of Liberty and Staten Island and the entire panorama surrounding the south of Manhattan. How could these towers be gone? Weren't they the tallest buildings in the world? How could a plane take them out? Oh God... and what about all of the people in those buildings and those on the ground? What about emergency workers, policeman, fire crews, red cross and the like?

The still picture behind the Italian announcer never moved. It was like a bad painting, the stuff that nightmares are made of. The words "America Under Attack" kept flashing. The blurred picture behind the announcer did not move. The announcer did not move except for his lips and the people standing in front of me did not move.

The world had stopped.

I had stopped.

I don't know how long I stood there. It was beyond comprehension. It reminded me of how my parents had described themselves the day the news came that America had been attacked at Pearl Harbor. It reminded me of the day in high school when the principal of my high school suddenly interrupted all of our classes over the Public Address system, announcing that he and some teachers were in the faculty lounge watching TV when the program was interrupted with a news bulletin that President John F. Kennedy had just been shot in Dallas. A few minutes later it was confirmed by Walter Cronkite that the President was dead. The world stopped. My teacher burst into tears and said, "I'm sorry" and left the classroom.

America Under Attack

Then I heard the young man continuing on... "They say that all airports in America have been shut down and that over 4,000 airliners have been grounded and taken from the skies... They say that the President of the United States has left Washington D.C. to a secret location, and that perhaps he is on Air Force One but no one is saying where he is... the White House has been evacuated... America is on Full Alert... jets can be heard flying over the Capitol... they say the chaos in Manhattan is great... much smoke everywhere..."

Suddenly my beautiful day was gone, in a flash! Thousands of miles away from where I stood, people were dead and dying. My home country was under attack. I grew cold inside. Numb. I was in shock. A sudden thought occurred to me, "What am I doing here when my family and loved ones are scared?" I thought of canceling my sabbatical and going home. But how could I get home? With airports closed and the country under attack, the borders would surely be closing or closed.

In that moment I thought only of getting an English speaking hotel for the night, one with a television that would broadcast CNN.

I asked the young man who had been translating if he would please help me find a hotel somewhere in Verona. He spoke with the pizza store manager in Italian and then translated back for me to take the "Verona Sud" exits and how to find a hotel where they spoke English.

I thanked them both, used the "WC" (water closet/restroom), went out and fueled my car, and headed towards Verona. Before the sun went down I had secured a room with CNN broadcasting from England, and sat up most of the night watching the horrible scenes unfolding in and around the World Trade Center location, the Pentagon disaster, and the flurry of reports from all of the news agencies. I think I finally fell asleep exhausted around 3:30 AM, a restless, fitful sleep from all of the hell of this day.

As I write these pages of my book I think now about the song later written by Alan Jackson entitled "Where were you when the world stopped spinning, that September day?"

It is one of those moments in time that burns into your brain forever. More than your brain, your entire body and psyche! Here I was, on a sabbatical on prayer and healing and psychoneuroimmunology, and almost like a cosmic joke, I found myself drawn ever deeper into the reality of the need for prayer and healing. I prayed deeply for those I did not even know... victims, survivors (surely there had to be some), rescue workers, first responders, my government leaders, anyone I could think of. Prayer now was not for an individual, but for an entire community, a city, a country, for the world. America, the symbol of security and freedom, had now had its soul rocked! No more invincibility. No longer safe. "Pray for us now and at the moment of our death," are words that came to me from the Rosary. I am not a Catholic but still those words came to me. I uttered silent prayer for our nation and my family and those whom I love dearly and for their loved ones.

I became focused on healing. How would first responders heal from the images of this day? How could America ever heal? In those first hours of this terrible inferno there was throughout the world, mass fear and shock. Who had done this bad deed? Who was responsible? Why didn't we know about it beforehand? What had been done to try to stop it, prevent it?

Did those passengers on board know what was about to happen to them? How had pilots been overtaken? What had air traffic control done?

A thousand swirling thoughts heated my mind, and in the midst of it all, there was great great need for prayer, and somewhere down the road, there must come the genuine need for healing. But for now my thoughts were not on healing at all. My prayers were for all those people at what would later be called "ground zero..." for all of those caught on video in horrific moments... for those who hung out of the Twin Towers with no one to rescue them... some falling to their deaths... for those who videotaped while facing death, like the physician who captured on videotape the wall of smoke that came when one of the towers fell.

The next day I was to be in Venice, Italy. But it was now nearly impossible to focus on my sabbatical study when the world had suddenly gone crazy! Several hours later the front page of the Italian newspapers would show horrible scenes of death and debris and people in all phases of injury. There would be first estimates of how many firefighters and police officers died in the collapse of the towers. First reports of the Pentagon fires, and the report about the plane that crashed in the Pennsylvania woods would be printed.

When I finally awoke, I noticed I'd fallen asleep leaving the television on. The coverage of the attack on America continued. The broadcast still transmitted relentlessly the horrible pictures of what had happened. Now there were new video clips of the planes crashing into the World Trade Center towers. One showed the plane on a long approach, then slamming into the first tower, a huge ball of jet fuel exploding everywhere! Then they showed another view of it captured by someone else. Then there was the view from ground level looking up as the plane went overhead into the building. I think it was later that day or perhaps the next day that other views came of the second plane hitting the second tower.

My visit to Venice was certainly not going to be the way I had originally imagined it would be. I wondered what the future held. I showered and dressed, turned in my keys at the front desk of the motel, and got into my son's car outside. I headed towards Venice, with a heavy heart and high anxiety.

Chapter 23
Venice - The Day After 9/11

I was so exhausted from staying up most of the night watching the videotape and live feeds from America of the horrible images of the planes crashing into the towers and the news of the terrible loss of so many police and fire rescue units in the collapse of the towers. All of the images gave me a fitful, troubled sleep as I finally managed to fall asleep towards morning.

By the time I awoke and began to make my way into Venice, I was feeling worn out, yet wanted so much to enjoy Venice. I drove to the outskirts of town and parked. Then I made my way on foot through the twists and turns of the outer part of Venice, until I managed to arrive at a small cafe for some late breakfast. Nearby two older couples sat, talking so that I could easily overhear their conversation. They spoke about the terrible news from America. They were having a discussion about how the United States should respond. One of them said it was time for America to get tough on terrorists and that they should find out whoever did this and bomb the hell out of them. But one of the others said that would be too dangerous. That might escalate everything into an even larger world-wide mess, and that the U.S. should make sure who they were going to attack before doing so. Back and forth went their discussion, each one spinning off from the previous comment. It was clear to me that it was going to be difficult to really enjoy Venice, with the events unfolding across the ocean in America.

I paid my bill and made my way to St. Marks' square. The square was crowded with people and the ever present pigeons. The pigeons flew around the square and some people ignored them while others stopped to watch. My destination was the church in the square.

I walked into the darkness of St. Mark's. This is a very old church which is often crowded and thick with tourists. I didn't have anything specific that I wanted to see. I just wanted to find some comfort here after the sights and sounds from the television set a few hours previous. I was having a difficult time concentrating on the beauty of St. Mark's, and I didn't stay long.

I went back out into the square and made my way down to where the boats were docked on the water. Looking across the water I could easily see other parts of the Venice area, the islands and places only accessible by boat, made famous in so many movies. I wanted to experience a part of Venice that would help take my mind off of the hell of yesterday. So I purchased a one hour gondola ride which was very expensive but very helpful in calming my worried mind. The gondolier pushed my gondola through narrow passageways, and once in awhile would sing something that was soothing and pleasant. This ancient city on the water and its long rich history helped me remember that this too had been a city known for so many battles and difficult times. That while the events in America were awful, that viewed through the long time of history that perhaps in time the current troubles of terrorism might someday be resolved. But in the short run, it didn't feel like that at all. But I listened to the singing and the soft sound of water lapping against the side of the gondola and tried to lose myself in the beauty that is Venice.

My day was nearly at an end. On the way out of the city, walking through it's narrow passageways of shops and markets, I stopped in a few places just to sight see. Venice is known for its masks so I considered taking a small one home with me. It is also known for its glass-blowing. I stopped in a special blown-glass shop, and looked at various figurines and glass works, some in blue, some in pink, some in various shades of colored glass. All of them were remarkable, especially the ones of intertwined figures. While Venice is known for its Mardi Gras and colorful masks, it is hard to find a better place where glass blowing is such a magnificent art. It is a collector's paradise.

I was thirsty and as I made my way out towards the outer part of Venice, I came upon an Irish pub. They say you can find an Irish pub in every major city of the world. I believe it. So I ducked inside, found a booth, and ordered a Guiness. Nearby a group of young men were playing some kind of game, and one spotted me and called out, "Are you an American?"

I replied "yes" and he looked over at the bar tender and called to him, "Come and change the channel of this TV for our American friend over there. He will want to know what is happening back home." A television was anchored above the table where the lads were playing. The bartender pointed a remote at the TV, and found the BBC and turned up the volume. More news in the aftermath of September 11 was being broadcast. I thanked the guy who had requested the channel be changed for me.

They motioned for me to come closer. One of the young men told me about his grandfather's time on Anzio Beach during World War II, and how Italy would be forever in America's debt and how Italy would stand shoulder to shoulder with America in its war on terrorism. Another young man talked about his friends in the military and also said that Italy was one of America's true allies, and if he ever got the chance to get back at those killers (the terrorists), he would do it without hesitation. They all toasted that comment, and I thanked them for all of their support. Nearby were a couple of young people who were backpacking in Europe, and they were not so enthusiastic about what the other young men were saying. One of the backpackers expressed fear that President Bush would be too trigger happy with his cowboy diplomacy and could lead the world into nuclear warfare. His companion, a girl, said all of this talk of war scared her, that America must show restraint in her response to yesterday. She said she was afraid that if cooler heads did not prevail that she and her generation would be doomed to live in a world of constant warfare.

I reflected on the older couples I had seen earlier in the day who were up for a fight, and the young men at the nearby table who also were in a fighting mood. Then of these two backpackers who clearly wanted an alternative to war, and were feeling quite scared.

It was a scary time, a sobering time. Here I was in Italy sharing the same thoughts and feelings as these European strangers who did not feel like strangers at all. Because of the power of television, the Internet, and instant communication of global news events, people of all races and nationalities were able to engage in conversation about survival and international policy in cafes and pubs and a thousand other places in a heartbeat. What were other parts of the world thinking about the terrorist attack on the World Trade Center and elsewhere in America? Were there those around the world who found this evil appalling? Were there those in ecstasy, hoping for further attacks on the

West? Would there be a way to find out who had done this and bring them to justice?

Then I heard the news broadcaster saying something I had not heard before. That yesterday, over 4,000 planes over American soil, were all made to land based on an order, not from military command, but by an FAA official who did not know what they were dealing with and so ordered all commercial flights to be grounded immediately. And they all managed to land wherever they were within an hour! I was amazed. But I wondered, where was our military? What were they doing? For that matter, where was our President and Vice President and what were they doing? In the absence of so much information, my anxieties remained high as I paid my bill, thanked everyone and said goodbye, and headed for the parking lot, to begin my travel back up into France.

My day in Venice had not gone as I had originally imagined it. The world had changed, and at least for the time being, nothing was going to be normal. Would it ever be again?

Up to now my travel and my sabbatical had been rather idyllic. Now it was very difficult to focus on the journey being completely compelled almost instinctively to focus on the attack on America.

People were trying to go on in shops and restaurants as if business was usual and life was good. But you could see it in strained faces and discussions everywhere. Everyone seemed to know that the world had changed. Terrorism had already come to Italy, Germany, France, and England. Now the United States was reeling under perhaps the greatest attack in it's history.

September 11, 2001. The day that changed the world. The day that changed my sabbatical and plunged it into utter seriousness around prayer and healing.

Chapter 24
Taize, France: Prayer as Music

I had departed Venice, Italy in the late afternoon, and traveled long into the night until I came to a small motel off of the Italian autobahn near the city of Milan. After a brief sleep, I continued on in the early morning, driving over the famous St. Bernard Pass of Switzerland. At the summit of this pass there is a shop that has the most enormous St. Bernard stuffed animals, complete with the small keg underneath their chins. If I were a child I would truly want to take one of those great dogs home with me!

My friend, Richard, had strongly urged me to visit Geneva, Switzerland. He had suggested that I visit St. Peter's, the church where John Calvin was preacher.

To get there I drove on the road south of Lake Geneva. I hummed a song by Chris de Burgh as I drove along. The song is called Say Goodbye To It All. One of the lines is "took a boat across Lake Geneva, it was raining all night long, we were lucky and we saw no enemy..." At one point I passed through the town of Evian, famous for its water. The water is high up in the mountains. But I stopped to have a photo taken at one of the signs.

Calvin was launching the Protestant Reformation in Geneva and became the translator of the Geneva Bible. At St. Peter's, I was in awe of the stark portrayal of the Geneva Protestant leaders in the paintings within the church. Their countenance looked no nonsense and quite severe.

Richard also had suggested I visit the Wall of Reformers in a nearby park.

I first walked along the long wall with all of the Protestant reformers represented, with the exception of Martin Luther. *(see Photography section)*

Luther had his own marker, which I interpreted to mean that Luther was seen as not quite welcome on the Wall with the Protestant reformers. On the other hand, a friend suggested to me that Luther was set apart, since he was recognized as the Father of the Reformation. Whatever the explanation, I had my picture taken in front of the Luther monument. *(see Photography section)*

Eventually I passed into France, and made my way towards the little village of Cluny, France near the Taize community. My good friend and colleague, Richard Binggeli, had been here previously, and had suggested that I drive through the winding country roads to stay in Cluny. I took his advice and am so happy that I did. I was afraid that I had timed my drive wrong because it was very late in the day when I finally came to a small petrol station on the outskirts of Cluny. The proprietor was so kind, and spoke nearly no English. He somehow managed to understand that I needed lodging for the night and that I was going to Taize that night for their prayer service. He made a phone call, speaking in rapid French, and pointed me to a tower in the distance. I drove there, and found a cute little hotel, the Hotel De L'abbaye on Avenue Charles-De-Gaulle. After a quick check in, I drove through the country again towards the even smaller village of Taize. It was now a race against the sun which had already begun to set.

I nearly missed the tiny sign marking the village of Taize. I drove onto a very small road, past small farm houses, and ancient looking village homes. After driving awhile, I knew I had gone too far. I turned around... drove back, and this time saw an old looking fortress complex on a hillside, and drove up the steep incline. Suddenly I was passing young people who were out walking in the evening, and I passed one young man who was seated on a wall reading what looked like a Bible. Within a few hundred yards I was there. Parking was off to the left in huge fields. The Taize compound was to the right, and there were now dozens of young people everywhere. Some were laughing, some singing, some talking. Everyone looked in high spirit.

I made my way to the reception office, and found where the evening service would be held. This left me some time to visit the small gift shop, and to look over the dozens of papers in many different languages describing Taize around the world. I bought a CD of Taize music (I already owned a couple of other Taize CDs), and then made my way up towards the building where the evening worship would be held.

When my colleague, Richard Binggeli, first told me about Taize, he described it as one of the most moving experiences of his life. He spoke about the music sung in the church by young people in many different languages at the same time. I sat in his condo and watched a videotape with him about Taize before leaving for my sabbatical. The video told the history of the Taize community and how it evolved into a gathering site for young Christian pilgrims from all over Europe and the rest of the world. During the summer time as many as 50,000 young people will come to Taize. They come for many different reasons, but nearly all of them are on a spiritual pilgrimage. The centerpiece of everything at Taize is the worship held three times per day.

Now I was about to enter this very place I had read about on their website and had seen on video. I was feeling very excited to hear the music sung by these young spiritual pilgrims. After all of the terrible news from the 9/11 attacks over the past two days, I was anxious to hear something uplifting.

At the entrance, you pick up a song book in your native language. Then you enter into a church room that is actually a building that is expandable. Depending on the size of the number of people gathering for worship and praise, the walls of this building expand or contract to surround the people.

At the top of the worship place are all of the many, many candles in various shaped holders. Draped behind these candles and around them are very large ribbons of red cloth, creating a most reverent yet exciting and stirring worship decor. Along one side of the building are various levels where guests and visitors may be seated. Older persons such as myself sit higher up, leaving the lower levels for the young people, almost all of them under the age of 30.

The central floor area extends from where the candles are at the top of the worship space, all the way to the rear of the worship space, and it is a very large open area, where hundreds and sometimes thousands of young people kneel in song and prayer. They are joined by the monks of Taize who come dressed in their traditional monk habits as they also kneel with the young people. Some of these monks are blessed with gorgeous voices. A single one of them will incant the first verse of a Taize song (or so they did when I was there) and then the entire community will sing the refrain in unison, each in one's own native tongue. There is no way in a print form to communicate adequately the incredible sound of prayer in song that wafts through the building when all of these monks and young people and guests are singing together. The Taize community has musicians who accompany the singing, and the music actually brought goosebumps to my skin. Each Taize song is simple. Each song is easy to sing. I attended worship there just a few days after the September 11, 2001 attack on the World Trade Center, so that the mood of the music was more somber than perhaps at other times. It was a mood of reflection and spiritual introspection. We sang songs of dependence upon God and requests for deliverance from evil. We intoned the great mercy and saving grace from God and prayed for protection and sustenance of others. Many of the songs we sang prayed for healing and health.

> For a sample of Taize music go to their Learning the Songs webpage at www.taize.fr, then click on the song title, "Jesus Remember Me" and then print out the song, then click on the tab "together" and listen to the music, and sing along with the words. You can also order Taize CDs from this website.

By the fourth song I broke down into tears. I was profoundly moved by the words and music and my own heart's prayer. I felt very powerfully connected to God. Perhaps a better way of saying it is that I felt as if I had been wrapped up in the very heart of God by His Holy Spirit. Teardrops dripped from my eyes. I made confession of my sins during the moving music. I prayed for persons I dearly love. I lifted up to God deep concerns of my soul and heart. Twice I simply could not sing... I was so overcome with emotion that my lips trembled and I could not sing. I could not see the pages of the songbook I held because of my tears. Even as I write these very words I long to return to Taize. It is a deeply spiritual experience of refreshment and renewal. I felt my burdens release. At Taize they say that song is prayer. I cannot ever remember feeling so at one with the Lord as I did through the prayers I said in song in that tiny village in eastern France.

"Oh Lord, hear my prayer... Oh Lord, hear my prayer... when I call... answer me... Oh Lord, hear my prayer... oh Lord, hear my prayer... come and listen to me..."

At one point I raised my head and looked around, and saw many nationalities represented in the faces of young people. North American, Europeans, Africans, South Americans, Asians... all with bowed heads, all being transformed by the musical sounds of everyone in one voice. I close my eyes right now and I am "there"... I can hear the music and the voices and feel within my body the Spirit of God dwelling within me.

For me, going to Taize was one of the highlights of my sabbatical, if not the very highlight of it. When we consider prayer and healing, it is my belief and experience that there is no more profound way of prayer than through music. Music has healing properties. Spiritual music opens us up in ways that no spoken word can. Music resonates within us. Music makes vibrations which can profoundly change the vibrational rhythms of our bodies. The work of Stephen Halpern, world famous musician and music scientist, brings conclusive evidence of how sound waves can soothe or excite. Halpern and others create music at different wave pulses in order to enable persons to reduce stress, become calm, have pleasant feelings, and release endorphins. I attended one of his workshops in Los Angeles when I returned and saw his photographs of music waves and the corresponding responses within human beings.

Here at Taize, it was not just the healing words of the songs of praise, or the ambiance of the worship setting, but it was also the healing music I was hearing and soaking into my being that began to open me up in new and different ways, allowing me to release thoughts and feelings held in from the stress and toxins of my work. I began to breathe deeper, and slower, and it felt as if my heart was slowing down in a deepening calm sea of love from God. Yes, I use the word transformational for this experience. My friend, Richard Binggeli, who had recommended I visit Taize, has spent many hours here. He reports like I do about how moving the experience is at Taize. In light of the 9/11 attack, I also was decompressing and feeling very dependent upon God for His love, protection and guidance.

One of the bishops of the Evangelical Lutheran Church in America, Bishop Murray D. Fink, from the Orange County/San Diego, California area, often leads early morning prayer times before conferences he attends. He invites anyone who wishes to join him at 6 a.m. for this special prayer time. He has created different prayer postures for people to move into as they make supplication to God. The first time I actually heard the music of Taize was at one of these conferences. I decided to join Murray as he led us into various prayer postures and played music not only from Taize, but also played Tibetan music, and music from Marty Haugen. Though I would later order and listen often to the music of that early morning prayer time with Murray, that first hearing was truly moving. It is music that not only draws us inward but it also connects us to God at a very deep level. When listened to in a prayer posture, the physical and the spiritual are connected in many ways. Our minds and hearts are changed, and we encounter the Spirit of God in a new and rich way. One feels truly in the presence of the Holy One. In this place, who would want to leave? That's why thousands visit Taize every year. It's why the music of Taize has made it into Christian hymnals of so many denominations. It truly is deeply spiritual. (Murray Fink later published a book of his prayer postures which is available to you entitled "Stretch and Pray: A Daily Discipline for Physical and Spiritual Wellness," Augsburg Fortress Publishers, 2005)

It is important that I say something about Brother Roger. Brother Roger was the founder of Taize. He was an extraordinary priest. He was one of the resisters against the Nazi invasion of France. He managed to move south into Taize and founded a community of monks. After the war, this monastic community continued and Brother Roger's teaching became well known. Then years later, music by an extraordinary musician was added. Students from all over Europe began to hear about this prayer as music. Soon thousands of young people flocked to Taize, to equip themselves for witnessing their faith throughout Europe and beyond.

There are several videos about Brother Roger's remarkable life available through various websites. This gentle spirit is seen walking with students and teaching simple messages about God's love and blessing.

Brother Roger was 90 years old when he died in August, 2005. He was stabbed to death by a Romanian woman, Luminita Socan, age 36, during an evening service in the church. Roman Catholic priest, the Rev. Alois Leser, a priest from Germany, who would become Brother Roger's successor, prayed for forgiveness for the woman who murdered Brother Roger. He said, "With Christ on the cross, we say to you, Father, forgive her, she does not know what she did."

Newspapers covering this international story wrote about how Brother Roger began his monastic work in 1940 during World War II, and that his vision was intentionally ecumenical. Today the Taize community consists of about 90 members from 20 countries or so, from virtually every Christian denomination. Consistent with Brother Roger's lifestyle, he was buried in a simple wooden coffin and was carried into the church by brothers from Taize. One newspaper reported that the coffin was followed by a group of Romanian children who had been visiting the community when Brother Roger was killed.

I stayed in the town of Cluny, just about a ten minute drive from Taize. The Cluny Abbey, destroyed during the French Revolution, was the best known abbey in all of Europe before its destruction. You can see the remains of much of that abbey while in Cluny. As I thought about Brother Roger's death, I was thinking about the destruction of the Cluny Abbey. People can tear down buildings or destroy people's lives, but the ideas and spirit of these special places and people cannot be destroyed. Taize developed in the 1970's as a pilgrimage site where people from different countries and faiths could gather, especially annually at Easter, to worship together in ecumenical harmony. At the mass held for Brother Roger, both a Roman Catholic priest and a Protestant minister led the worship, which also symbolized Brother Roger's tireless work of ecumenism.

My brother, Leroy, knew that I had visited Cluny, and upon hearing of the death of Brother Roger, he forwarded me several emails including various commentator's reflections on Brother Roger's life and work. One of those was from Jim Forest, secretary of the Orthodox Peace Fellowship and editor of the quarterly journal In Communion. I quote one paragraphs from his editorial:

"Few people in the past century have done so much to inspire a thirst for unity among Christians. Sixty-five years ago, when Roger Schutz founded the Taiz_ community, divisions among Christians were as formidable as the Iron Curtain. Catholics took pride in not being Protestant while Protestants rejoiced in not being Catholic. As for Orthodox Christians, they weren't even on most people's radar screens. Brother Roger, a young Swiss Protestant pastor, dared to imagine Christianity's healing. The ecumenical monastic community he founded became a center for intimate encounter between Christians from every confession and continent."

Jim Forest's insight into Brother Roger's daring to imagine Christianity's healing is profound. It was this exact thing I experienced at Taize. People, young and old, Protestant, Catholic, Orthodox, each singing in his or her own native tongue, singing the same piece of music at the same time, all one ecumenical Voice singing praises to the One Lord God of us all. May Brother Roger rest in peace. May his vision of peace and healing between Christians continue on in his absence. He truly was a great "lighthouse of hope." His beacon of hope during World War II and beyond shines as bright today as ever. Thank you God for Brother Roger and Taize.

Chapter 25
Rue Cler, Paris, France

It had only been four days since the world changed. The images of the planes crashing into the two towers, the collapse of those towers, the images of people hurling themselves out of those highrises, the terrible billows of smoke and fire, the loss of firefighters, police and rescue personnel, the hole in the Pentagon, the disintegration of the plane in a Pennsylvania field... all of these images still swirled in nightmarish fashion as I stood on Rue Cler, September 15, 2001.

It had only been four days since I had stopped for fuel on the Italian autobahn only to learn of the terrible events in New York City– only four days since I'd seen those flashing words on the television screen: "America Under Attack!"

On September 10th, I had been in the Salzburg castle high above that magical little Austrian town..without a care in the world bathed in sweet quartet music. On September 11th, the sounds from the television were sirens, screams, shouting, and urgent words from broadcasters trying to describe the terrible unfolding events.

Visiting at Taize had helped calm me and had given me some solace. I'd finally connected via phone to the United States. Indeed airports were closed, the U.S. borders were closed, and life was far from normal for anyone. Reassured that my family was alright lifted my spirits. Yet the pall over America was heavy and the dominant conversation in Europe was about how the United States would respond.

I'd made it back into Paris, and checked into the Grand Hotel Leveque at 29 Rue Cler. In Paris, like in the rest of the world, a great sense of uncertainty permeated everything. A high level of anxiety and the enormous psychological impact of it all was everywhere.

Many were still numb with disbelief. How could this have happened? Would anyone wake up from this nightmare? Sadness and depression was like a dark, wet, heavy fog over everything. So much destruction and loss, and the constant images of pain and suffering, brought a sense of oppression and despair... and hopelessness.

Yet... there was still hope. It came in the most unexpected way in a most unexpected place. It came in the form of a little boy on a street in Paris, called Rue Cler.

September 15, 2001 on Rue Cler, Paris, France

The little boy stood still, watching.... His eyes followed every movement. Before him stood a violinist on the street called Rue Cler, in the city of Paris. Rue Cler is a street of many wonderful shops.

You can smell the aroma of fresh fish and meats wafting out from one side of the street mingling with the fragrances of freshly baked bread and fresh coffee from the other side of the street. It is a busy avenue with local Parisians mingling with tourists making their way up and down the Rue Cler. There are the traditional outside French cafes where people can sip their favorite beverages while in conversation. If you wish you can also tuck yourself into a wine and cheese shop or find a favorite dessert in another shop nearby. Down the street are the best waffles to be eaten in the world and the aroma of cooking swirls in the air with all the other wonderfully delicious smells.

The little boy stood transfixed, his mouth parted slightly as he took in each clear note played by the street violinist. Nearby a woman watched this scene. Her breathing had slowed as if she were in a trance. Her eyes brightened as she looked at this little boy in whose face was great awe. He stepped a little closer. The violinist had not yet seen the boy. He had not seen him because his eyes were closed in rapture as he played sweet music on the strings beneath his nimble fingers. His bow drew down and back up, relentlessly, as that sweet music poured out of the belly of the violin. Then suddenly, the violinist's eyes opened and as if drawn by a magnet, his eyes slowly were drawn to where the little boy stood nearby. A slight smile crossed the violinist's lips and he sort of nodded towards the little boy as if to say, "Yes... yes... I see you... you like my music don't you?"

Nearby on the other side of the boy stood his Papa. The little boy's father bent over and said in French something about "come now, we must be going." The father placed his hand gently on the boy's shoulder to move him down the street, but the boy moved his shoulder forward, casting off his father's hand. He took another step towards the man playing the violin.

I watched the little boy's eyes. They were wide now as if staring into the deepest magic that ever was. My heart skipped a beat. The cloud that had hovered over the world was being lifted through the eyes of this little boy. He stared up intensely now, at the violinist and his violin, hearing the music pouring from its strings, first in slow moving passages, then in little spurts of flurry. Violinist and little boy were becoming one in the music, in the magic. On played the musician while the little boy now stood as if a statue of contentment, his eyes aglow with wonder and delight at this thing he had never seen nor heard before. I watched his tiny fingers twitch involuntarily by his side, almost as if he were playing too.

His father made another attempt to break his little boy away from this scene. The woman nearby had tears in her eyes, as she too was moved by this little boy's riveted fascination with the music and the magic. She felt this little boy's transformed countenance in the presence of such sweet music and the promise of hope in the air. The scene was picture perfect. The French violinist on the market street with the little boy staring up, never blinking his eyes, the father making feeble attempts to tear his little boy from the music, the woman nearby understanding in the depths of her heart what was transpiring here on this street. The sounds and smells and the near still life little boy standing with fixed gaze at the man playing his heart out, while passer-byes began to sense this event unfolding, they too now pausing to take it all in... almost as if time itself were beginning to slow down and come to a stop, while the violinist modulated his violin into soft rich passages of slow chords.

The images of September 11 were no longer present as I asked the woman nearby what she thought of this scene. She turned to me with a glow on her face and some tears in her eyes and said, "This is precious, so incredible." In her very being she was being transformed by this little boy's awe. Sometimes we have difficulty putting into words what a spiritual experience is, but at this very moment in time, this woman was experiencing spirit deep in her heart and soul, and this little boy and the music anchoring him, transforming him was also part of this spiritual moment.

I wish you, dear reader, could have stood there and seen this with your own eyes, and listened to the music from this violin with your own ears. There really are no words to express what this moment in time was like. On played the violinist, at times closing his eyes with passion and then opening them to see the little boy.

The little boy now stood absolutely motionless. In this very moment I felt as if I were in the presence of a miracle.

I stood motionless as well. In the presence of the Sacred we do not move. We barely breathe. In this luminous moment the glimmer of hope against the darkness of four days earlier burst forth in my heart as the music and the image of this little boy, the woman and the street violinist became like a masterpiece hanging in a Metropolitan Art Museum.

The inner healing I felt was like no other soothing I had ever experienced. It was as if the hand of God had descended upon this small street in Paris and through music in the most unexpected place a healing began for all who were there. In the Nativity we think upon one little boy who transformed darkness into light. The Old Testament declares, "By His stripes we were healed."

Here on Rue Cler another little boy, in his own disarming way, was also transforming darkness into light. The violinist and little boy were lighthouses of hope. That little boy reminded me of all the little boys and girls who would be growing up in a post September 11 world, a world that would need healing and prayer.

I knew that this scene would stick with me for a very long time. Boy, violinist, father, woman, Parisians, the street full of fragrances and sounds, all mixing together into something mysterious and magical, touching hearts, touching souls. God comes to us through these kinds of moments.

It had only been four days since 9/11 but like the first buds of spring after a harsh winter, there was once again a spark of hope. I stood there for several minutes. Soon my eyes filled with tears and I laughed deeply inside. I got it. I got what was happening to me, to the woman near me, to all who stopped and paused from wherever they were going or whatever they were doing, paused from whatever concerns they had that day. I got it. All of us were connected, bound together, through the eyes of a child, in the sweetness of music. I could feel a very deep calm wash over me. I could see in the eyes of the woman nearby that she too was taking it all in, feeling that deep soothing healing and calm.

It has now been many years since that moment on Rue Cler. I can close my eyes and see the violinist and the little boy and I can hear the sweet music anchoring all of us and threading our hearts together. The closest word I can think of is... Love.

God's love can heal us through music, through laughter, through touch, through relationships. God's love has the capacity to stop us dead in our tracks, and revive us, change us, transform us. Love can renew us, refresh us, and even turn us around. Love makes a new pathway in wilderness journey.

It was not until the violinist came to the end of his piece that the little boy blinked. The violinist held his bow in one hand and the instrument in the other... looking at the boy. The boy smiled. The violinist smiled. They looked at each other and in that look was the love of ages. The boy's father now whispered that it was time to go. He slowly placed his hand on his little boy's shoulder as he lifted his own eyes to the violinist, nodded, and the violinist looked up with loving eyes to this loving father. Even the father had been swept up in the moment. The boy slowly turned towards his father and took his hand. The violinist's eyes sparkled as he watched the boy and his father move back into the Rue Cler, among the pedestrians now beginning to also move back into the routines of their day. The woman... turned, ready to move on. I moved on too.

It was now, as if, the moment had never happened. Oh! But it had! It really had!!

In life, we carry these moments in our hearts and minds. They live in us. We "carry them like a fire in our hearts" as a songwriter has penned.

This book is about miracles and mystery. There are mysteries about prayer that are just beginning to be understood. There are miracles of healing that still remain a mystery. What began for me as a very simple study of prayer and healing and mind/body health became a study of complexities and deep realities for which often there is no language in which to express these experiences and learnings.

There is a scene in C. S. Lewis's book The Lion, The Witch, and the Wardrobe in which the great lion, Aslan, is slain, and the triumphant forces of evil are dancing in merriment for now they believe they have ended Goodness once and for all. But then, something unexpected happens. The lion Aslan who was slain comes back to life. In this scene Aslan stands before the Snow Queen who had killed him. She says incredulously that this can not be happening, that Aslan must surely be dead because she had used her deepest magic upon him. Aslan replies that there is a deeper magic still of which she knew nothing.

There is a Deeper Magic Still. I do not mean the magic of magicians or charlatans. Perhaps human language can not contain it nor express it very well. That Deeper Magic Still is God's healing presence, that holds the promise of transformation and change in our bodies, our minds, in our world and in everything we hold dear.

C.S. Lewis, expressing it in a child's language in his Chronicles of Narnia series, shows us the image of New Life. Things are not always as they seem to be. When facing cancer or heart disease or any other kind of life threatening experience it is possible for us to lose hope because of what we see or hear or fear. We can become quite frozen and become overwhelmed by hopelessness and doom.

But through the eyes of a child we remember that things really are not always as they seem to be. Through the eyes of a child we can see hope. We can see life. We can hear music. We catch a glimpse of resurrection. In the kingdom of Narnia, C. S. Lewis shows us how the bitter cold of winter's darkness now melts with sunshine springing forth as the clouds disappear. Yes, of course, order is turned into chaos in our real world. But there is Deeper Magic Still that can restore order.

Healing and restoration are at the center of God's heart. We can experience His everlasting healing Presence in the very midst of whatever is breaking down in our life or in our world.

There will always be a day when the world changes. There will always be One who changes not and who promises to be with us even to the close of the age. "Fear not, for I am with you," He said. Healing happens in this life and in the life to come.

Chapter 26
Amsterdam to Prague

I left Paris on a rainy night. I recalled a song by my favorite musician, Chris de Burgh called "A Rainy Night in Paris." Indeed it was. I had to depart in a pouring rain, leaving behind my warm hotel room. I turned for one final look up at the Grand Hotel Leveque, then I turned and moved on into the soggy night. My study sabbatical was almost at an end. I still had a trip to Prague ahead of me, and I was traveling up to Amsterdam to meet my son and the rest of my family who had managed to get out of the U.S. on a non-stop. Still nothing was going into America, but some planes were now departing the States.

My son was glad to see the return of his BMW. I had used it for several weeks, and it was broken in when he got behind the wheel and drove he and his girlfriend, my wife and daughter, and myself through the countryside to what used to be known as East Germany. We came to the town of Chemnitz. It looked like an industrial city, and there were many indications that, like many cities of the old East Germany, this town had also suffered neglect. A huge, gigantic bust of Karl Marx stood across the street from our hotel. It was my first time in the former communist controlled area of the country, and the stern face of Karl Marx was a reminder that things take a long time to change. Eventually we caught a train to Prague. The train seemed to run on rough track at times. For me it was another sign of troubled eastern Germany. Then shortly after we crossed over into Czech territory, during the slowing of the train to move onto another track, the unthinkable happened. The train somehow came off the rails.

The train came to a complete halt. Conductors and other train officials got out to look at the problem. We were now going to be stranded for several hours while officials figured out how to get the train back onto the tracks. It gave all of us a chance to get off the train and walk around a bit on the gravel siding.

I thought back to all of the exciting people and places I had seen. I was looking forward to seeing Prague, a city which my son said is one of the most beautiful in all of Europe. At the moment I was wondering if we would ever get there. The train voyage had been so slow, and now the train had several cars off the tracks. I could only be patient and enjoy the pause.

Eventually the cars were placed back on the tracks and we progressed slowly again towards the city of Prague.

Arriving in the train station in Prague, my son got us into a taxi cab and whisked us away to a beautiful old hotel. I was amazed at the beauty of the city lights as we passed through various streets and avenues. At the hotel, we got checked in, had supper at a very intriguing restaurant within walking distance of our lodging, and then returned for a much needed sleep.

My main goal here in Prague was to see the Holy Infant of Prague, known the world over, as a healing symbol of peace and hope.

But my son was right. Prague is a beautiful city. Its architecture, buildings, bridges, statues, historic landmarks, old world charm and outstanding food make it one of Europe's best travel destinations. Prague is often used by film makers of espionage films or romantic stories. Words can not adequately capture the sights and sounds of either daytime or night-time Prague. Its cobblestones, multiple stairs, beautiful spires and excellent hotels make this a brilliant city to visit. It is an old city with deep traditions and old-world culture. Yet it is a modern city as well with active night life and many young people gracing its streets. Someday I will return to Prague. There is so much to explore and do there, and my time was much too short.

Chapter 27
The Infant Jesus of Prague
Venerations and Miraculous Healings

When one thinks of healing, one thinks immediately of places like Lourdes, France, or Fatima, Spain. These are places with long histories of reported miracles and miraculous healing. While I have not yet visited Lourdes or Fatima, I have visited one site that has long been associated with healing. It sits high on one wall of a Catholic church in Prague, Czechoslovakia. It is a small figure of the child, Jesus, and it is known to the world as the Infant Jesus of Prague.

As I stood looking up at this strange figure, strange for a Protestant such as myself, I wondered how it came to be that this figure of the child Jesus, crown upon its head, wrapped in a robe, came to be so famous. After studying the figure for some time, I looked down to find a small plaque in front of the entrance to the figure. It read: "Heal me and I shall be Healed." It is from a place in the Bible that speaks of healing (Jeremiah 17:14). Perusing the Internet, I learned some facts about the Infant Jesus of Prague. The figure is made of wax and stands 47 cm high. Some kind of silver casing protects the figure from damage. This casing reaches down to the waist. The sculpture was made by an unknown artist. It likely has a wooden core covered with material that can be seen through the wax. The Infant Jesus wears a white undershirt. On top of the undershirt has been placed a white rochet (like a surplice worn by bishops and abbots) over which is a covering of a silk top with frills around the neck and hands. Looking at it, it reminds me of a pluvial worn by priests. The Infant wears a crown on its head.

It is believed that the history of this work begins in Spain. The so called cult of the Childhood Jesus is associated with the Baroque period of artist presentations of the Christ Child. Research reveals that this figure I was staring up at came from a convent somewhere between the Spanish towns of Cordoba and Seville and is a copy of a venerated wooden sculpture that was in that convent.

A Spanish woman named Dona Isabela Manrique de Lara a Mendoza obtained it and gave it to her daughter as a wedding gift. Her daughter married a prominent Czech Nobleman. The figure remained in the family after another marriage, and upon the death of this husband, it was donated to the monastery of the Teresian Carmelites near the church of Virgin Mary Victorious in Prague Mala Strana.

In the year 1631 the Saxons invaded Prague and the monastery was plundered. The sculpture of the Child Jesus was thrown out but was later recovered by a priest who had it restored. The broken arms were repaired and it became an object of worship once again, and miracles began to be associated with the figure. The figure was later moved to another church, and in 1655 the Bishop of Prague crowned the Infant Jesus with a crown.

Because of the great number of pilgrims coming to the Infant, it was moved once again to the side altar of St. Joachim and St. Anne in its current location.

According to some websites, it was in the 19th century that the fame of the miraculous Infant Jesus spread to Spanish speaking countries of South America and also Italy. Some monasteries developed special liturgical prayers to the Infant Jesus of Prague. There are many legends and miraculous stories attributed to the Infant Jesus of Prague. I'll just share one of these. A two year old little girl in Brazil was born with disconnected hips. She could only walk with difficulty with the help of special equipment. It was very difficult for her to walk, but the parents decided to pray a novena to the Infant Jesus of Prague. Six days later the little two year old took her first steps without the special equipment. The doctors were said to be astonished. Friends and relatives could not believe what they were witnessing. In 1995 the whole family came to the church of the Miraculous Infant of Prague to give thanks for the miracle.

Central to the belief systems of those who venerate the Infant Jesus of Prague are the words which the Infant Jesus of Prague says to his people: "The more you honor me, the more I will bless you." One website says that the devotion of the Infant Jesus of Prague is surrounded with so many miracles and wonders that it rapidly spread to the whole world. Quoting from this website, "The Little King has been enthroned as the Great King of the world to assist His subjects in their trials, difficulties, and crosses. He Who Himself has suffered so much, desires to assist those who come to Him. He wishes to attract all hearts to His own through the attractiveness and simplicity of His Divine Infancy."

Venerations such as these are not uncommon throughout the history of the Roman Catholic Church. The well-known veneration of Mary is worldwide and tens of millions of Catholics call upon her daily through rosaries and Mass and individual prayer and supplication. Mary is sought after for miraculous healing and for protection in difficult times. I think the Infant Jesus of Prague is worshiped, honored, prayed to, and called upon in a similar way. Whether it is Lourdes, Fatima, Prague, or as we will see in another chapter, Chumaya, (so-called Lourdes of the North America), people seek out healing and help from icons and saints throughout the world.

Of course, this is not the Protestant viewpoint that sees no need for intermediaries in coming directly to Christ for help and healing. But for millions and millions of Catholics, the Infant of Prague is but one avenue for healing.

It is important for us to remember that there are many "lighthouses of hope" even in the form of a wax statue. Somehow it calms the inner spirit of men and women, who believe that they can be and indeed are healed by the power of Christ through these saintly intermediaries. (In a future chapter we will learn of the 14 Helpers whose role is similar.)

Once again, I want the reader to know that I am not endorsing these beliefs or practices, but I want you to know that there are millions of believers who seek healing through this veneration process. Many claim healing and cures come from these prayers and petitions. One story I read reported that a woman with a terrible health condition dreamed about the Infant of Prague and was cured. In my travels I came upon many such stories associated with places of visions or appearances of the Virgin Mary or the visitations by Saints. In the human heart there are the deepest yearnings for healing and health.

These too are 'lighthouses of hope.' Faith, belief and prayer are all part of this phenomenon called healing. Whether one believes the thousands of healing stories reported by the faithful, one thing is certain: millions believe in miracles and scientific explanations are not always able to be given for each case. The man crossing the sidewalk heard a voice telling him to have no fear, that his wife would be alright. A woman with metastatic cancer sees the vision of Jesus standing at the foot of her bed comforting her with words that all will be OK. A woman, while dreaming, sees the vision of the Infant Jesus of Prague and finds her disease disappear. While there are plenty of skeptics (even at Lourdes there is a panel especially appointed to make sure of the veracity of healing miracles), there are also plenty of stories of healing within religious circles. Venerations of statues and icons are but one more way we see people's belief in the healing power of God.

Chapter 28
Prague to Paris
Another Healer on a Train

The train I rode from Prague passed through luscious pastures and fields of endless green. It traveled near ancient villages and passed alongside cliffs dotted with old castles perched on top or hidden behind trees. The passing view was breathtaking as the train swayed back and forth as it crossed over into Germany. The train now was running parallel to the Rhine river, the river I first visited when I was 18 years old. Nothing seemed to have changed in the past 35 years. Barges still chugged up and down the Rhine. Occasionally one would see a tourist boat loaded with sightseers. Flags fluttered colorfully off of the rear of many vessels moving on the waters. The color of the water was dark and foreboding in places. In other places on this large river the color would change to a lighter green as my train rounded various bends. The sunlight glistening off of the water made the river shimmer and sparkle with light and life! What a glorious trip this was. Across the Rhine one could see more castle ruins high up on the hills. What had life been like in the Middle Ages? What healing remedies did people use in that age?

I checked the train schedule in my hand, and knew I had about a half hour window of time to make my connection to my next train after we pulled into Cologne. There I would transfer to another train to Brussels where I would switch again to a train bound for Paris. I didn't want my sabbatical to be coming to an end, and I wondered how America would be changed after the September 11 attack. I even wondered if I would be able to fly home, and how safe it would be to fly.

As I looked at my train schedule again I heard the voice of the conductor announcing something over the intercom in German. I asked a man next to me what the announcement was and he told me that on this day there would be a change. Instead of continuing on the fast track, this train would cross the Rhine and go the slow way through several villages, making stops to take on passengers.

This was horrible news! I asked him if he was a regular passenger on this route and he said he was. I asked him how much additional time would this slower route take. He replied "a half hour, perhaps forty-five minutes." I groaned, "Oh no." He said, "What is the problem?" I told him about my train connection. He said he did not think I would make the next train in Cologne. Then he began to tell me that there would probably be other trains later in the day.

He then began to tell me that he had just returned from a vacation in the United States, and how much he loved America. We chatted about all of the places he had visited over the years in the States. He spoke of places he planned to visit on future trips. His laughter as he spoke about things he had seen and done calmed me. I think he sensed my anxiety and was helping in his own way to help comfort me. Somehow in our exchange I was no longer thinking about September 11 or about missing my train connection. His voice and the images that I had of his trips brought me deep pleasure and a very deep calm. He was helping restore and heal me. I was learning a lesson. "Be anxious in nothing" was a phrase from Holy Scripture. I took a deep breath and thought, "everything is going to be OK."

Before long the train began to slow to a crawl as it made its slow pace around the outer ring surrounding Cologne. By now I was taking it all in stride. If it was meant to be it was meant to be. Then the man said, "come" and stood up, inviting me to step out of our compartment into the hallway of the train. He led me to a door at the end of the train through which we could see the huge spires of the Cologne cathedral rising far in the distance. I recalled first climbing those towers when I was 18 when the choir I was singing in had stopped here in Cologne in the summer of '65. I remembered climbing those towers a second time just a few years before while visiting my friends Thomas and Astrid during a Chris de Burgh fan club gathering. Thomas, who was in very good shape, led me up the hundreds of steps inside of the Cologne Cathedral. At one point I asked him if we could rest as my legs ached and my heart pounded in my chest. He smiled and said, "Of course." He was so gracious. Eventually we did reach the top, and as we looked out across this great German city, he told me that as far as we could see, there had only been ruble after allied bombing during World War II. He said this was in retaliation for what German bombers had done to the England city of Coventry. He said that now there was a city exchange between these two cities and a very good friendship between the leaders of both cities. He seemed very pleased with this. He pointed to one place along the river off in the distance and told me about how the ancient Romans had come to this place.

All of this came to me and more as the train made the slow crawl now up the west side of the city. I could still see the spires in the distance although now they were blotted out at times by the buildings we were passing on the way to the train station. My German friend was describing various buildings and some of the history of this cathedral city. The Cologne Cathedral is such an impressive structure. If memory serves me right, the tradition is that the remains of the Three Magi from the Christmas story are buried inside the cathedral. For centuries, pilgrims have visited the cathedral to view these remains.

As I stood at the window of the train car, my German friend was explaining to me how the platforms worked, where to go when the train stopped, and other essential details. By the time my train finally came to a halt it was fifteen minutes past the time of my next train's departure. My friend said it would take at least eight minutes to reach my next platform. This would mean that my next train would have to still be there twenty-three minutes beyond the scheduled departure time. That made me chuckle since the number 23 is my favorite number. But knowing the reputation for on time train departures in Switzerland and Germany, (they say you can set your clock by the promptness of trains in Switzerland), I decided to calm myself even further by taking some nice deep breaths. I just told myself that my train would not be there, to be "calm and relaxed" and find out when the next train would depart towards Paris. I heard my friend saying to me "I have a feeling your train is still here." Then with a twinkle in his eye he said, "If it's not here, I know of a very nice hotel nearby. Perhaps you could change your schedule." He gave me the name and number of the hotel, and wrote down his own phone number. I thanked him for his gracious hospitality. I shook his hand and suddenly the door in front of me opened and he said "Go... go!" and I stepped down onto the platform and walked rapidly, following the directions my German friend had given me. Down two flights of stairs, then along a long corridor past masses of people, then left (sweating now), up a staircase, then another (heart pounding... automatic thought, "is my train still here?"), then up towards the next platform, turn left...

Two trains! As I reached the platform at the top of the stairs, I saw two trains, one on the right and one on the left. The last of passengers were boarding on either side. "Bitte!" "Please can you help me!" I called out. A conductor raised his head from looking at some manifest and looked at me. I walked rapidly towards him. "Brussels" I called out. He was young and smiled but did not say a word. Perhaps he spoke no English or maybe he didn't understand me. But his right arm came up from his side and he pointed to the train to his right. I continued walking towards him, then, I was standing right in front of him. I showed him my ticket and he motioned for me to hurry to the next car. I rushed to it and mounted the high step onto the train. I began to make my way down the aisle when I felt the train begin to move. I'd made it with less than a minute to spare! As I dragged my luggage down the center of the train car, a friendly couple seated to my right looked up at me and smiled, saying something in German. I replied in English, "Hello." They replied in English, "You just made it." "Yes" I said, "I can't believe the train is still here!" "Well there was some kind of problem up ahead on the track so we were delayed here for more than twenty-five minutes or so." I replied "God is with me," and smiled. The woman replied "God is with all of us."

What an interesting reply I thought. Somehow her words calmed me further. I had been anxious for no reason at all. Here I was, returning from the final leg of my sabbatical journey, and once again I was feeling led by God. I replied to her, "You are so right... God is with all of us." I passed them, found my seat, and felt the sweat on my back, and wiped my face. I had been walking fast and now my heart rate was up. God had one more surprise waiting for me.

I don't like riding backwards on trains but the seat I was assigned was facing the wrong way. It was so late in the afternoon and the shadows were lengthening as the train crossed into Belgium. I had never been here before and suddenly it was like being in a fairy land. Quaint villages flashed by as the train picked up speed in the open countryside. Over bridges, across rivers and streams, we moved as if on a magic carpet. The roadbed of the railroad tracks had been built in places above the villages so that you could look down into the streets and below. The scenery was wonderful! You could clearly see village shops and homes in great detail. Over and over the train would cross first to one side of a small river then switch back to the other side of the river. Back and forth the river would slip beneath the train only to emerge on the other side. Soon the sun was sinking into the west, beyond the furthest hill in the distance. Village lights began to flicker on. I began to doze. It had been a very long day and I was beginning to feel the fatigue. As I closed my eyes I could hear the clickety-clack of the rails beneath my feet. Miles stretched into endless miles as I slipped beneath the waves of dream-like brain fog. There is that sweet twilight place between the awake state and the dream state, and it is in that middle ground that I dozed. I had finally crashed.

My sleep was disturbed by the voice of a conductor announcing arrival into Brussels. There are actually two or three stops in this city, and once again local persons helped me by telling me not to get off at the first two stops, but to get off at the third stop. Soon the train came to my final stop. This time I had about twenty minutes to make it to the next platform. I still hurried just in case something else went wrong.

I was really looking forward to this final leg of my train ride because this time I would be on a bullet train to Paris. I had never been on one of those sleek, fast trains which have become world famous. Like before, I had to climb stairs to the right platform. As I took the final step up from the stairs, I was amazed at what I saw. Wow! Right before my eyes was the front of this modern marvel. The nose of the bullet train was just a few feet from me. I could see the engineer/pilot clearly through the windshield of his very special train. I could not believe how beautiful this train was.

I found a conductor. He looked down at my ticket and said in very good English that my seat assignment was on the very last car of the train. So once again I pulled my luggage behind me and walked past car after car. I finally came to the rear car, and stepped up into a beautifully decorated interior. But the most astonishing thing was... no one else was in the car with me! I was alone.

So I got out a book and started to read. I glanced at my watch. Just a few more minutes and the bullet train would pull out of the station.

With less than two minutes to go, someone came on board behind me, and sat across the aisle from me. I took a look over at whoever had just entered. There sat a woman who was dressed in such a way that I thought she might be a religious person, perhaps even a nun in contemporary dress. She was wearing a beautiful cross around her neck. So I thought I would start with that.

"Hello," I said. She smiled and in a quiet pleasant voice said a soft, "Hello." I said, "That's a beautiful cross you are wearing. Does it have meaning for you?" "Oh yes!" she said. "I am a follower of Jesus Christ. Would you like to see my cross?" I replied, "Yes, I'd love to look at it." "May I join you?" she asked. I moved over to make room for her and said, "Sure, come sit here." She crossed the aisle just as the train began to move. She sat down right next to me and held her cross out from her chest so I could see the cross clearly. "It's beautiful," I remarked. She smiled and said, "Thank you," and told me she was a devoted nun from Paris, and a member of a healing community. I couldn't believe it!! Once again I was being led in my sabbatical. I felt the presence of God strongly. "Are you an American?" she asked. "Yes," I said. "What brings you to Europe?" she asked. I smiled and told her that I was on a study sabbatical on prayer, healing and mind-body medicine. She looked very surprised and said, "Really? That is amazing." Then she paused, looked away, as if contemplating something, then she looked straight ahead, then turned her head and looked at me and said, "God has brought us together I am sure." I grinned, "I think you are right." Then I asked her to tell me more about her healing order. She described that their order is based on some visions a young girl had in Paris in the mid 1800's, very much like St. Bernadette at Lourdes. She asked me if I had gone to Lourdes. I explained that following the September 11 attack on

America, I had lost a day or two and did not make it to Lourdes. She explained, "Oh that is too bad... it is a wonderful place, and you must go there and spend several days sometime." I told her that the medical director of Lourdes had offered to spend some time with me, but that we could not match our dates together as he was going to be out of town while I was nearby. Then she made me a remarkable offer. She said that the next time I came to Paris perhaps she could accompany me to Lourdes. She went on to explain what happens there and various things for me not to miss.

Our conversations somehow turned to music. She was explaining how great a role music played in their order. She had with her a small French hymn book of some kind. She asked if I might like to hear some of their music. "Of course," I said. I could tell that our train was approaching a very rapid rate of speed as my new friend began to sing in a light, bright high voice. She of course sang in French. The melody was sweet, perfect. I smiled inside as the train sped through the night time towards Paris, France. I asked her to translate the song she had just sung, and she did the best she could. She said that the first song was about God's healing, and how God's love is for everyone. The second song was of praise to God. It also thanked God for all His blessings. She asked me if music was important to me. That question really made me grin since music is my soul, my favorite thing on earth. "Oh yes," I replied. "Music is very special to me in my worship of the Lord," I continued. She was delighted with my response and asked if she could share more music with me. I smiled and said, "Of course!" And we spent the rest of our time singing, chatting, and sharing with each other about spiritual things.

Then, she paused and offered to pray for me and for good things to arise out of my sabbatical. She took my hands in hers and proceeded to pray, first in simple English, then in French. Tears flooded my eyes. I didn't know why. Was it the gift she had become to me on this train? Was it the grace I felt coming through her from God? Was it that once again God had given me a sign of his love and support of me? I thought of "signs and wonders" and thought that this woman of God was a very special "sign and wonder" in my life. The thought "train lady" came to my mind. Perhaps she was an angel in disguise. I didn't understand anything she was saying in French but by the tone of her voice I knew instantly that she was communing with God. I could feel the energy of her spirit flowing into mine. More tears welled up. Her head was bowed in prayer so I felt relief that she wouldn't see my tears of great joy. When she was done praying, she looked up at me. The smile that came to her face was of such serene peace that I felt I was looking into the eyes of an angel. Perhaps she was one.

Before we arrived at the train station in Paris, she wrote her name down on a piece of paper, handed it to me, and asked me to keep she and her order in prayer. We felt the train come to a stop. We were in Paris. She slid off the seat, and wished me God's speed, and walked out of the train car and down the platform. I felt as if I had been touched by an angel. Instead of riding to Paris alone on the bullet train, I sang and prayed my way to Paris with a profoundly spiritual person. Then I laughed out loud and looked up to the heavens and said "Thank YOU, God!!! You are amazing!!" Then I left the train and walked down the platform towards the airport for my flight back to the United States.

What had begun so many years ago when Elleston Trevor and Betty Lareva had both shared their pain with me was now coming to completion with joy and sweet resolution. I had begun this sabbatical with just a notion... to explore the world of prayer and healing and to learn a little more about mind-body connections. What was just a simple thought, a seed, at the beginning, had grown to a fully grown tree under which I now rested within the knowledge that I had experienced a very full sabbatical, led by the Spirit, and that I had been profoundly impacted by so many people along the way. I had no idea how I would ever communicate what I had learned or experienced with other people. My heart was full and my journey had become a turning point in my life. My very being had been touched in such a way that my own personal spiritual walk was rejuvenated. Somehow I now knew that God would make me one of his healers. Perhaps the first step along the way would be to share my sabbatical experiences with others through some workshops. The thought of writing a book had not yet crossed my mind. That would come later as friends asked me to share with them what I had experienced.

Finally, I was at the airport, and now on the plane. I settled in, fastened my seat belt, and recalled the many things I had seen and done on this sabbatical journey. My plane lifted off the runway. I looked out at Paris below. The Eiffel Tower stood in the distance. I had spent some wonderful time there one night. I had walked past it in the day time, and had mounted its steps to the top on two occasions, once in late adolescence and now as part of my sabbatical. My thoughts turned to Rue Cler and the street violinist and that little boy in the aftermath of September 11. I was now that little boy, listening to the sweetness of the melody played by the street violinist. That music was now playing in my heart. The title of C.S. Lewis' book, Surprised by Joy, popped into my head. It truly was all about joy. It was all about love. I looked one last time at the Eiffel Tower and breathed a silent prayer of deep gratitude for everything from my entire sabbatical experience.

And I thought of the lady on Rue Cler, who had stared at that little boy... and heard the same sweet music from the street violinist, the music of hope and healing in the aftermath of 9/11. It had been a luminous moment.

I closed my eyes, tilted my seat backwards, and felt content. I had met many lighthouses of hope.

Section II – Beyond the Sabbatical Places, People and Issues: 2002-2013

Chapter 29
Walking a Prayer
Labyrinths and Healing

The moon was round and full and bright white like a huge beach ball hanging in the sky. It was about 9 p.m. under an Arizona night sky, and I stood near several rings of candles flickering in the light warm breeze blowing across the backyard of the home of Kent and Nina Matthews. Kent had been a Director of Christian Education (DCE) on the staff of a Lutheran church in Arizona. It was through their pastor that I learned of Kent and Nina's work in the area of healing. They had invited me over for supper to share with me their work in the healing arts, and to walk their homemade labyrinth.

As I stood in their backyard with Kent and Nina, I prepared myself for the experience ahead. Kent had laid out a labyrinth pattern on his grass, in the shape of an ancient Celtic cross known centuries ago to the peoples of Europe. This design was different than the labyrinth I had visited at the Chartres Cathedral outside of Paris, France. The labyrinth at Chartres is a huge eleven circuit pattern literally laid into the floor of the cathedral. The Matthews' pattern was small by comparison, and in a very different shape. Yet having walked other labyrinths before, I was preparing myself for another opportunity to be with God in this most wonderful way.

As I stood underneath this beautiful Arizona night sky, I took off my shoes and said a prayer... and then removed all thoughts from my mind as I stepped into the circular pathway of the labyrinth. I felt the grass beneath my feet as I followed the outline made by the candles, creating the labyrinth route. The previous time I had walked a labyrinth, I didn't sense or feel anything different or special. It just seemed like a nice walk inside of the pattern. But, this time I was struck by a powerful wave of emotion. Tears welled up in my eyes. I felt truly touched by the Spirit. While the space was smaller than other labyrinths I'd walked, somehow, under the light of the moon, and the glow of the candles, and the spiritual presence of Kent and Nina, I was feeling very close to God. I felt lighter, freer, happier, and content. All of my worries, concerns, and anxieties were put away. My life was in God's hands. This time I didn't pray for family or friends, not even for myself. I simply emptied my mind of everything, and breathed in the presence of God. I simply rested in the silence of my mind. I began to repeat a simple mantra: "Thank you God... Thank you God... Thank you God." I would later learn about the work of Herbert Benson and the relaxation response that comes with repeating a word or phrase. That night at Kent's I didn't know about the relaxation response. All I knew is that I felt very relaxed and calmed completely. Just this simple word of thank you to God made me feel overwhelmed with gratitude. More than once my eyes moistened with tears of gratitude.

Eventually my pathway ended as I left the labyrinth. I felt refreshed, renewed, different. I could tell that Kent noticed. I have always been a deeply feeling person and also very cognitive, but on this night I had an unusual experience. As I had entered this labyrinth I seemed to see something out of the corner of my eye. It was a white robed figure and my first thought was that it was an angel. I was reluctant to tell Kent of this experience but upon completion of my walk in the labyrinth I did share it with him. I couldn't explain it very well, so I described it as a sort of transparent, white personage. I asked him if he thought I was crazy. He smiled and said, "no not at all."

One of the people I most admired was Carl Sagan, the great American scientist who brought a keen critical eye to anything that might smack of charlatanism or fakery. Most Americans know him for his humorous "billions and billions" when he would describe stars in the sky. The comedian of the NBC Late Night Show, Johnny Carson, would chuckle to himself when he would do his monologue at the top of the show, and mimic Carl Sagan's "billions and billions."

Before he died, Sagan wrote a final book entitled *The Demon Haunted World* in which he set out to debunk just about every kind of "sighting" of UFOs, Ghosts, Demons, etc. So, because I was such a huge admirer of Carl Sagan's scientific approach, I was very skeptical of someone who would say they could see angels or any other disembodied spirit.

But now, on this night, I had "seen" something, or thought I had. Perhaps my mind was playing tricks on me. To my relief, Kent didn't laugh when I told him what I had glimpsed. In all my life I had never perceived anything like this. And it had not come from any suggestion from Kent because we had not talked about the labyrinth or anything else in this realm. But I had "seen" something as I entered the labyrinth. It was a figure, and it stood at the entrance to the labyrinth. And it seemed it was watching me, protecting me perhaps? Had I seen a glimpse of my guardian angel? I do not know. I didn't see it again, and haven't had that experience again.

After my labyrinth walk, Kent and Nina invited me back inside where we had a long and serious talk about many forms healing, including therapeutic or healing touch. It was a wonderful night and I enjoyed getting to know this couple very much.
* * *

The purpose of walking a labyrinth is to meditate on one's relationship with the Lord or for deepening one's sense of oneness with God's Spirit. *(see Photography section)*
Labyrinths have become very popular in recent years. Today labyrinths can be found in many places throughout the United States and, indeed, the world. It was my good friend Roxanne Whitelight and her partner Ruth who came down from their home in Spokane, Washington to Santa Barbara, California to lead a group of spiritual persons in the walking of their labyrinth patterned after the one at Chartres. It had been handmade to the exact measurements of the Chartres labyrinth. I believe Roxanne told me that their beautiful labyrinth cost in the neighborhood of $3,000 to make. In some places, communities of people have pooled their resources and skills to make labyrinths. Some labyrinths are portable while some are permanent. Labyrinths are made in many different materials.

Roxanne explained the history of labyrinths, and how to make the best use of them. She and Ruth spread their labyrinth out on the large lawn on the grounds of the former Jesuit school, and had participants remove their shoes. She and Ruth modeled how to walk along the pathway of their labyrinth, leading the rest of us one by one, with sacred steps and quiet hearts. When my turn came, I closed my eyes and thought of friends far off, and lifted them to God in prayer. Then I slowly opened my eyes and began slowly walking the cloth labyrinth laid out before me. When I finally reached the center of the labyrinth, I paused for perhaps five minutes, letting my spirit join with the Spirit of God. I prayed for members of my family, for all of the participants who had come to this gathering, and all those people who had been special in my life. Then I focused once again on my breathing, thanking God for the privilege of communing with Him. Then I rose and walked slowly back along the pathway that leads out of the labyrinth.

The design of the labyrinth helped me focus and go inward in thought and prayer. There is nothing magical about the labyrinth. I can come into the Lord's presence at an altar, in the woods, even sometimes while in my car along the rush of L.A. freeways. But the uniqueness for me of the labyrinth is that it gives me another different way of approaching God. I think of it as leaving behind the distractions of my everyday life, and as I walk slower towards the middle of this pattern, I feel as if I am being drawn into the heart of God. You may experience it in that way too, or in some different way. That's the beauty of the labyrinth. There is no "right" or "perfect" way to walk the labyrinth. *(see Photography section)*

Rev. Lauren Artress of Grace Cathedral in San Francisco wrote a wonderful book entitled Walking the Sacred Path. Her thoughts about the labyrinth might initiate new appreciations for this ancient design.

Christian writers have also written about the use of the labyrinth. Just as there are many different ways to pray, there are different ways to utilize the labyrinth. In her book Lauren says that at the height of the early middle ages, when huge Gothic cathedrals were being erected, there were 22 cathedrals (such as those at Chartres, Amiens, and elsewhere) that had labyrinths. Now after all these centuries, only the labyrinth at Chartres remains of the great eleven circuit forms from those other famous cathedrals. Historians point out that it was Napoleon and his army that dug up the Chartres labyrinth in order to use the lead in it to make lead balls for the coming Napoleon war campaigns. What a tragedy. It saddened me to think of those men digging up something so precious and beautiful. It is said that during Napoleon's campaign deep into Egypt, one of the cannon balls fired during the battle blew off the nose of the Sphinx. I shudder to think of what the lead from the Chartres cathedral did during Napoleon's campaigns.

You don't have to go to Chartres, however, to walk this form of labyrinth. All you need to do is go to Grace Cathedral in San Francisco, or find a labyrinth in one of your nearby communities. Inside of Grace Cathedral, an exact duplicate of the famous Chartres eleven circuit labyrinth has been expertly redesigned to the detailed specifications of the one in Chartres, France.

Outside the walls of Grace Cathedral is a second labyrinth which you can walk as well.

The Labyrinth Project of Grace Cathedral, under the outstanding leadership of Rev. Lauren Artress, has become internationally famous.

\Thanks to this project, there are now many places throughout the U.S., Canada, Europe and throughout the world where you can walk the ancient labyrinth. In a moment I will share with you about some of my earlier labyrinth walks and my recent pilgrimage to Grace Cathedral on a labyrinth weekend.

* * *

Later as I read the work of Larry Dossey and others, I learned that it is often those who approach God with gratitude and openness who often do better when they are ill or overcome with disease. That night in Arizona, I again was not aware of this research on prayer. I only knew that I was praying what was in my heart that night. "Thank you God... Thank you God... Thank you God." I spoke no words aloud. I was no longer aware of Kent or Nina, nor the light of the moon, nor the feel of the grass beneath my feet, nor the soft heated wind of the desert. All I became aware of was being in the presence of God. At one point along the labyrinth path an image of Jesus standing very near me came to my mind. I was open to whatever God wanted me to be aware of. I was simply filled with gratitude.

Some years later I heard Dr. Daniel Amen lecturing about the brain. Dr. Amen is a pioneer in brain research, and has become nationally famous because of his spectacular "before and after" pictures of the diseased brain. Special photos of the diseased brain are taken before treatment. Then after treatment the diseased brain is once again photographed. The outcomes are often very dramatic and easily seen in the colorful plates of photographic evidence.

Dr. Amen had spoken at a Healthy Congregations annual update, a program developed by my friend, Dr. Peter L. Steinke. During the question and answer period following Dr. Amen's talk, in response to a question, he commented that the temporal lobes of the brain are often associated with spiritual experiences as well as the paranormal. A follow up question asked about how the temporal lobe processes information, and whether or not Dr. Amen believed that the images of God and other spiritual experiences were just part of our imagination or just all "in our heads". Dr. Amen replied, "If God created us then why would he not create a way for Himself to communicate with us?"

The implication, of course, is that God does indeed communicate with us. As I think back on that night in the Arizona desert, I was being communicated with by God. He sent a millisecond brief "sight" of His guardian angel. The "image" of Jesus being with me was certainly not something physical outside myself. It was an inner image of the Son of God with me. It would later remind me of the vision that a woman had of Jesus at the foot of her bed speaking words of encouragement during her battle with cancer. My "seeing" was in my mind. These images were in my mind. For the earlier lady reported on, the vision was of the Lord standing at the foot of her bed. I have heard many other stories during my sabbatical of persons feeling the touch of God on them or of seeing a vision. Certainly through the use of guided imagery, when used spiritually, one can deepen one's relationship with God. I have learned that religious images and thoughts can be very uplifting and helpful when we open ourselves up to those images. It's like when a preacher is telling the story of how Jesus met the woman at the well, or Jesus stood up in the boat to calm the sea, or any other story of Jesus... you are able to picture it in your mind. That night in the labyrinth I felt God's presence and saw the image of Christ with me, and God's guardian angel present as well. I've not had any of these images or thoughts since that night. But if I close my eyes right now I can see them clearly and I can remember how they made me feel so safe and full of gratitude. "Thank you God."

My friend, Mary Myers at Timothy House, on Kelly's Island, north of Sandusky, Ohio, in Lake Eerie (where I am writing today) shared with me today that she has felt something else while using a lap version of the labyrinth: deep relaxation. She and her partner at a retreat, both began their finger tracing at the same time in the lap labyrinths they held. They moved their fingers through the labyrinth, relaxing and tuning out distractions. When Mary had completed her finger walk through the labyrinth, she looked up only to find that her partner had finished her finger walking at exactly the same time. She felt very calm. She went on to tell me that teachers have used these smaller labyrinths with children who calm down while using them. Other teachers have used pictures of the labyrinth for children to color. Again, the effect is the same, calming the children and relaxing them.

I love the labyrinth. For me it is another tool to deepen my walk with God and to let go of distractions in order to meet with God. Recently I decided to do one of the pilgrimages at Grace Cathedral. Once again it was a profound experience. But first let me share with you a little of the history of how the Labyrinth Project came into being as shared by its originator, Rev. Lauren Artress.

She says that it was in 1991 that she felt restless, wondering what would be her next step in her ministry at Grace Cathedral. She had already been innovative in several other things and, creative spirit that she is, she felt that something was nudging her forward to her next step. She had no idea what it was. One day she found herself walking around in a room at her home. She paced back and forth, but in a circle. At one point she remembers literally saying out loud, "What?!" Within a short period of time she would find out what the WHAT was.

Through a series of events she came to learn about the labyrinth. She was invited to walk one for her very first time. Her experience was personal and moving. She learned that she was walking the eleven circuit pattern of the labyrinth at Chartres Cathedral. Somehow she knew that she was being led to this place.

In 1991 she and six others from the Grace Cathedral staff and community traveled to Chartres, about 45 minutes outside of

Paris. When they arrived they met disappointment (much as I did my first time at Chartres) when she discovered that the labyrinth was covered with countless chairs. It was obvious that the labyrinth was not being used here at Chartres. They searched for the local priest and found none there. They asked the souvenir shop lady about it, and got no help there either. It was as if no one understood anything about the labyrinth's use. So the Grace Cathedral group took matters into their own hands, literally. They went over to the chairs, and lifted them off of the labyrinth. She reports that the chairs were linked together 8 across which made it easy to move them. Then the group began their labyrinth walk. Other visitors to the Chartres Cathedral began to join them so that perhaps 35 to 50 persons walked it for the first time. Upon their return to America, Lauren wrote to the Chartres cathedral each year until they finally heard from someone in 1995. A priest there was interested in what Lauren had been discovering about the ancient use of this tool for spiritual development. Lauren inquired about the records kept by the Chartres cathedral only to learn that they had been moved for safe keeping during the Allied bombing during World War II. Unfortunately, bombs fell on the museum storing these ancient records and all were lost.

Rev. Artress explains that there has always been a deep connection between the Grace Cathedral in San Francisco and the Chartres Cathedral. So beginning in 1995 they once again traveled to Chartres to walk the labyrinth under special permission from the priest there. In 1997 the priest traveled to Grace Cathedral to walk their labyrinth. The surprise came when the priest from Chartres was so impressed that he announced that they were going to open the labyrinth at Chartres on Friday evenings for walking.

* * *

Because Grace Cathedral is a welcoming church, it came to Lauren to plan labyrinth pilgrimages. These are offered once a quarter under different themes. So it was that I decided to attend one of these pilgrimages in November 2002. The theme of the weekend was "moments in time."

I arrived for the 3 p.m. registration, and there were already many persons registering. Labyrinth items were on various tables for sale during the entire event, and so I took time to look at T-shirts, scarves, mugs, music CDs, sweatshirts, umbrellas, earrings, necklaces, and other items all with the labyrinth design. When Lauren herself came among us she was warm, friendly, outgoing, and very welcoming. I began to really look forward to the weekend.

Lauren spent some time finding out where everyone had come from. Then she began to tell the history of how the Labyrinth Project evolved. Then she asked who had experience with the labyrinth, and began to tell interesting and fascinating stories about people's experience with the labyrinth over the years. Then she began to prime us for how we might best use our time on the labyrinth. She also spoke about the musicians who would be there to play music to deepen our experiences.

Following this wonderful discussion there was a cocktail and hors d'oeuvres time when we got better acquainted with one another. Then came our supper together.

After supper we entered into the cathedral itself to walk the labyrinth. In addition to the planned quarterly events, the second Friday night of the month the labyrinth is also open to the public. People from all over the Bay Area and visitors to San Francisco were already walking the labyrinth. A host at the opening pathway to the labyrinth allowed time and space before letting the next person to enter the labyrinth. This made for a very pleasant experience.

Before walking the labyrinth I decided to partake of the laying on of hands service being conducted in one of the small chapels in the Cathedral. Two ministers, a male and female, waited patiently behind the railing as one by one each person requesting prayer and the laying on of hands came forward. When my turn came, I knelt before the female minister. She asked me my name and for what I desired prayer. I had been in constant pain of an undiagnosed condition for nine weeks at the time. I prayed for spiritual strength and physical healing. She laid her hands on my head and prayed for my healing. Her warm and gentle words opened my heart to the fullness of God. She prayed for the healing of my body and called on the power of the Holy Spirit to restore me to health. After several moments of fervent prayer she anointed my head with oil, and made the sign of the cross in the name of the Father, and of the Son and of the Holy Spirit. I whispered a thank you and rose from the kneeler and walked towards the labyrinth.

Already many people were in the queue awaiting their turn to enter into the labyrinth. I got into the queue and began my prayer as I patiently waited.

When my turn came, I began to walk as I had before. But this time what came to me was sadness and grief that welled up from a deep place inside of me. I found myself with each step feeling my throat constrict and my heart heavy as I thought about the loss of my mother and father over the past several years. I remembered my father playing baseball with me and my mother's cooking. Here I was walking on a Friday night and the memory of my father bringing my mother candy on Friday nights as was his habit came to me. I thought about the loss of my friend Carol, a catholic girl from high school who taught at Alfred University in Medieval studies. I remembered her farewell letter to me and other of her friends just before she passed away a few years ago.

For the past several months I have been battling with two medical conditions, one life threatening and the other creating chronic pain for weeks. I grieved the loss of my health and gave it up to God while walking the labyrinth. I thought about close friends who had moved away and special friends carried in my heart. Tears flowed down my cheeks, and when I finally came to the center of the labyrinth I sat down... and wept. Others were seated nearby in the center as well. I noticed another woman crying. Others were in poses of reverence and awe. Some faced the altar a hundred yards away. One person was smiling. I placed my head down and just let my tears fall. I prayed to God as I have never prayed before. I thanked God for all of these persons in my life, for my parents, for my friends, for my family. My tears of grief became tears of gratitude for the life I had been given and for the opportunities to touch lives through my counseling and other events. I became aware that I was being cleansed, released from all of these griefs. The old hymn came to me... "What a friend we have in Jesus... all our sins and griefs to bear... what a privilege to carry... everything... to God in prayer."

The harpist, named Destiny, was playing music that seemed to heal my soul, and touch my heart. I don't know how long I stayed in the center of the labyrinth, but I felt as if I was in the heart of God, and that God was holding me in His hands... that the Spirit "knew" me and what I was and who I am and held me like a mother holds her infant. I thought of the Pieta that I had seen in Rome at St Peter's Church, that wonderful sculpture of the Mother of Jesus holding her son in her lap as he lay dying. I also heard the voice of Charlotte Church singing Pia Jesu. I felt the voice of God saying "I Am With You" and I felt a deep peace come over me. I felt safe, at home.

Just before I rose to leave the center of the labyrinth I noticed a young woman sitting near me. She was singing in a very soft voice a song that was so pleasant but she sang so softly that I could not hear the words. She was at one with the Spirit and seemed at peace.

I slowly rose and began to walk the path leading back out of the labyrinth. Finally I went and sat in the darkness of the cathedral and thanked God for being with me since my birth. I asked for wisdom for the future and a special prayer of thanks for love in my life.

I left the cathedral for the parking structure to get my car so that I could drive down to Mountain View, south of San Francisco, to spend the night with my son who lives there.

I arrived at the entrance to the garage only to see the same woman who had been singing in the center of the labyrinth with me approaching on the sidewalk going somewhere.

"Hi," I said. She looked up and there was a moment of recognition. I said, "I loved what you were singing in the center of the labyrinth. Do you mind telling me what it was?"

She smiled and introduced herself and told me it is a song that is often sung at her church on Sundays. She said, "It's called Use Me." "Wow," I said, "Use me. So why were you singing that?" She replied that that is what she wants. She wants God to use her in any way He decides. I replied, "Well, I needed to hear that song right at that moment." She replied with great sensitivity, "I saw the tears on your face and knew it was a meaningful moment for you. It was an important moment for me too and that song just came to me." I replied, "Well God used you in that very moment to bring me joy and a deepening presence with Him." We continued to talk a few more minutes and she invited me to her church in Los Angeles. It was amazing to me that I was meeting someone in L.A. too. We said we'd see each other in the morning, and I went to get my car.

The next morning I returned to Grace Cathedral. This day was full with a video about the labyrinth, small group discussions, and Lauren Artress's wonderful leadership in deepening spirituality. There was also private time to walk the labyrinths or spend some time in the excellent bookstore there, and also time to network. There were also mini-workshops led by various staff from Veriditas, the Labyrinth Project staff, and time for prayer and meditation.

The evening was once again full with a wine and cheese reception like the evening before. Then we were once again treated to outstanding food prepared by wonderful volunteers. Then we prepared for the second evening in the Cathedral. Following supper, Lauren introduced the musical group for this second night just as she had done the night before. The previous night Desire had told us of the ancient tradition of the harpists in Egypt and how they played special music. On this second night another outstanding group would accompany our walk.

This night the Cathedral was closed to the public. Only those on the pilgrimage weekend were present along with the wonderful musicians and their unusual instruments. We began our entrance into the Cathedral by being handed a small votive candle by Lauren. We processed quietly throughout the entire cathedral. All of the lights in the cathedral were out except the few lights near the nave of the Cathedral lighting the labyrinth.

As I passed by the chair in which Bishop James A. Pike sat, the famous priest of Grace Cathedral in the 1960's, I thought of how Pike had pushed against the walls of tradition within the Episcopal Church. I thought that as we walked this quiet reverent walk in the candlelight procession that once again Grace Cathedral was moving beyond the bounds of tradition again.

The candlelight procession came to a halt at the entrance to the labyrinth. Each of us placed our candle somewhere where it would not be stepped on or kicked. The nave of the cathedral was alight with flickering candles as soft sweet music filled our ears and opened up our senses to whatever God would bring to us this night.

I took off my shoes and again waited in the queue. This time when I entered the labyrinth I was filled with a lightness so unlike the night before. This night I felt like dancing. The previous night had cleansed me. Now I felt lighthearted and close to God in a perkier way. Others on the labyrinth must have sensed this as well as some of them began to pick up their feet in a sacred dance. Soon many on the labyrinth were dancing to the unusual rhythms and wonderful beat of the musical ensemble nearby. Perhaps five minutes into my labyrinth walk I felt something touch my cheek. Then something else touched my eyelid. I looked up only to see dozens of rose petals falling out of the sky. Grace Cathedral is a huge Gothic-like structure with high vaulted ceiling. Somewhere high up where we could not see, rose petals of red, white and pink were spiraling down upon us on the labyrinth. I stood and placed my arms out straight, palms turned upward, watching to see if any of the hundreds of petals now falling might just land in my open hand. Suddenly one landed right in the center of my palm! Others around me were doing the same thing. We were becoming like little children, surprised by joy and smiling at one another. The rose petals just kept on falling. Those in the center of the labyrinth stood, knelt or sat motionless... everything was as if it turned to awe!

It was as if God's grace was being showered down upon us. I thought of the flower petals strewn in front of the bride in the wedding as she makes her way to the altar. This reminded me of Jesus the bridegroom claiming His bride the Church. I thought of Love, often portrayed by the rose, and how often lovers give to one another the gift of roses. I thought of gentle rain, in this case the "rain" of flowers and the sweet scent that was beginning to rise all around me from these gracefully falling, twirling petals. It was like magic! I could not help but smile wide as I began to think of these falling petals like the many blessings God had bestowed upon me in my lifetime... each falling rose petal was like another blessing, and soon there were too many to count. They just kept falling out of the sky. That reminded me of the ancient Hebrew people who during their wilderness journey were fed with manna from the heavens. It reminded me of the ancient prophet Elijah who received the gift of ravens while he fled out into his own personal desert. And I thought of the old Bert Bacarah song, "Raindrops Keep Falling on My Head," when I scraped ice and snow off of my car in St. Louis one time when snow kept falling on my head.

Thank you God came into my head again. Thank you for sustaining me and leading me. While the night before on the labyrinth had been a time for tears, this night was a time for laughter and gladness!

When I arrived in the center of the labyrinth I stood for a few minutes, looking down the center of the cathedral to the altar area so far away. I remembered sitting in this cathedral when Pike preached. I remembered sitting in this cathedral for a huge Reformation rally. I remembered walking this labyrinth with friends and loved ones. This "Moment in Time" was refreshing and renewing my own spirit. Suddenly I laughed right out loud! "Thank You God!!" Someone near me echoed my words. It was a wonderful moment.

That evening I again traveled south to visit with my son and his girlfriend. The next morning I arrived a little later than I wanted to having overslept. The parking lot beneath the cathedral was already full. I had to find another parking structure nearby. By the time I reached the cathedral's first floor rooms, I had missed part of Lauren Artress's live interview with Matthew Fox, the outspoken former Dominican priest who had been silenced by Rome and then later had been removed from the priesthood. In the past few years Matthew Fox has brought his Creation Spirituality to Oakland, California in the Bay Area. His new book had just been published and he was speaking to a live audience as well as the Internet audience on Grace Cathedral's website.

After his talk many people queued up to purchase his book. I got in line without purchasing a book, and when I got to where he sat behind the signing table, I simply introduced myself and thanked him for his many writings. He asked about my work and we chatted for a minute or so.

As the last of the people came to Fox's table for the book signing I made a decision to buy a book too. I stood as the last person in the line. When I reached the table Fox looked up and said, "So you got a book after all," and I chuckled, "Yes." He signed my book, and I told him about my sabbatical in prayer, healing and mind body medicine. He in turn told me about the Mass he leads in Oakland and then said they had a healing at their most recent gathering. He said that a lady had been suffering from some kind of abdominal pain (as I was at the time) and that she had been to several doctors who could not determine the cause of her constant pain (at this point I got a chill down my spine for he was describing my condition perfectly). He said that during the Mass she suddenly felt her body healing. Afterwards she came up to him and thanked him for the Mass and described how all of her pain had left and she felt healed. Then he said, "You should come and join us some Sunday evening in Oakland."

I had gone to school in Oakland during my first two years of college and so it was as if I was being invited back "home." And I could NOT believe that a woman with a condition sounding very much like my own had been healed at their service. I told Matthew Fox that I would come up again soon for his Mass. He shook my hand and wished me well on my book. It was a wonderful moment for me.

Then it was time for worship in the Cathedral. I decided not to join in the worship but to remain an observer. I noticed that the pews and chairs were quite full when I entered in the rear of the Cathedral. A processional cross service began with great music and a wonderful sounding organ. People sang loud and with enthusiasm. As they made their way through the liturgy I thought about how welcoming Grace Cathedral had become.

Intentionally welcoming Muslim, Hindu, Jew and any other seeker of spiritual life, Grace used words and symbols to welcome visitors to this wonderful vacation city of San Francisco. The spoken message from the leader was excellent, and a Eucharist meal was reverentially presented as one by one persons knelt around the huge square to receive the body and blood of Christ. I sat in a pew behind one of these kneeling groups and observed the reverence with which people knelt together.

At the conclusion of the service, the Cross was led out of the cathedral followed by all of the clerics. The thought crossed my mind that this was something unusual: the Cross of Christ moving near the upper area of the ancient labyrinth. Modern Christian and ancient Christian, and all other seekers, together being led by the Spirit of God. It was a wonderful moment. I whispered again under my breath, "Thank You God."

After the worship service the pilgrims gathered together for our final time with Lauren. She invited us to attend the forthcoming summer's events and pilgrimage to the Chartres Cathedral outside of Paris. We also met all of the staff of Veriditas, and we said our farewells to new friends and fellow pilgrims. It was a great Moment in Time.

I made a few purchases of labyrinth products before departing. I bought a finger labyrinth made out of beautiful wood in the shape of the Chartres Cathedral labyrinth. I also bought a pendant for myself with the same symbol. I bought postcards for friends and spent a little time listening to some of the CD music that I had not listened to previously. I bought a few of these CDs for my own spiritual nourishment.

I thanked Lauren for a wonderful inspiring time. I also ran into the new friend who had sung "Use Me" that first night on the labyrinth. We exchanged emails and promised each other to meet sometime to learn more about our experiences of the labyrinth.

One of the things I purchased before leaving Grace Cathedral is a video about the labyrinth narrated by Lauren. I plan to show it to friends, colleagues, ministers and churches to show how the labyrinth can be used from a Christian perspective. Christians have used this meditative form throughout Christianity even though it has been promoted within the context of the New Age movement. It is another form which Christians can easily use to deepen their walk with the Lord.

The New Age movement likes the labyrinth because it allows one to get in touch with their higher power, inner light or spiritual energy, whatever that may be. For Christians, however, in the tradition of pilgrimage done for centuries throughout Europe, people walked to pilgrimage sites like Chartres and then walk with God in the labyrinth. In many ways the labyrinth itself symbolized the Christians walk of faith. You begin on the outside with your cares and concerns, then praying, you move towards the center where you rest with God as you enter His heart. Then when you have finished your time with God, you walk back out from the center back out into the "world" where one lives out one's faith. The labyrinth then becomes a powerful tool to strengthen one's unity with the Lord and prayer life. It is an experiential way to be with the Lord. It is another way to become equipped for the mission before us.

If you get an opportunity to walk a labyrinth somewhere, by all means do so. And if you are ever in San Francisco, make sure to visit Grace Cathedral and walk their inside and outside labyrinths. Labyrinths can now be found throughout the world, especially at Christian retreat centers and special places of prayer.

I hope this has given you a glimpse into the world and use of the ancient labyrinth. There is an old Christian hymn entitled, "It is Well With My Soul." When I think of the times I've been in the presence of God in the labyrinths outside of Paris, in San Francisco, in Santa Barbara, or in Arizona, I always feel that all is well with my soul. I invite you to experience walking the labyrinth sometime. If you feel as if you stand outside a door and God is on the other side waiting to welcome you, the labyrinth is another way to open that door of your heart and invite God inside. I pray it for you.

Chapter 30
In Memorium: David Larson
The National Spirituality and Health Conference

Earlier in my book I told the story of meeting David Larson and what an enormous influence he had in the field of spirituality, religion and health. I told how he spent several hours with me and his assistant Dr. Tom Smith at their offices at the International Center for the Integration of Health and Spirituality (ICIHS) founded by Dr. Larson. It was now 2003, two years after the close of my formal sabbatical travel, that I received an invitation from Dr. Tom Smith, David's assistant, to the conference in honor of Dr. David Larson. It was to be a research report conference, and was to be a virtual Who's Who of experts in the field.

The title of the conference was Integrating Research on Spirituality and Health and Well-Being into service delivery: a research conference to be held on April 1-3, 2003 at the Natcher Conference Center in Bethesda, Maryland. The keynote speaker was to be Dr. Harold Koenig whom I had also previously met. As I looked down the list of guest speakers I saw the name of Dr. Robert Ader, the father of psychoneuroimmunology I had met in Rochester. I also saw the name of Andrew Weaver who had been so instrumental in setting up my interviews with Doctors Larson and Koenig. Also on the program was another name I recognized: Michael McCullough who had co-authored Religion and Health with Larson and Koenig. Other names were also familiar to me, and I knew this would be an important and historical conference. The purpose of the conference was to present strategies for integrating the growing knowledge base that exists on the impact of spiritual factors on physical, mental and social "health and well-being" into clinical practice and the delivery of health and human services.

As I looked over the three day conference, I saw that the research papers would be presented on three areas of spirituality. Day one would be on spirituality and physical health. Day two would be on spirituality and mental health. Day three would be on spirituality and community health.

The International Center for the Integration of Health and Spirituality (ICIHS) was one of the many sponsoring agencies, and was the overarching sponsor. Its mission statement was included in the program announcements (remember this was the organization established by Dr. David Larson). It read:

ICIHS is dedicated to the integration of health and spirituality. We provide strategic direction to define and advance this emerging field through multi-disciplinary collaboration with organizations, researchers, educators, clinicians, and patients. These alliances, along with our comprehensive research-based resources, assist our members in achieving excellence.

Unfortunately this would be the last major conference sponsored by ICIHS because with the loss of its leader through death (David Larson) ICIHS would be closed within a year or so. Dr. Smith did an outstanding job trying to keep ICIHS afloat but the effort could not be sustained. To his credit, Dr. Smith and ICIHS did a fantastic job in bringing together many of the top names in spirituality, religion and research.

I think about 500 persons were in attendance at the conference. I met pastoral counselors, psychiatrists, scientists, social workers, researchers and many others interested in this growing field of knowledge. The conference began with a welcome by Dr. Smith, and a slide of David Larson was shown on the large screen in front of us. His surviving spouse, also a researcher, was introduced and she received a wonderful ovation. The structure of the conference was for each speaker, about 15 per day, to be given 15 minutes to present the major research findings in his or her area. Each also generated a prospectus on the research in hard copy which was in our manuals.

What struck me right from the beginning is how many speakers came to the podium and took two or three minutes of their 15 minute allotted time to talk about the personal influence Dr. Larson had on their careers and on their lives. It was amazing to hear each anecdote and story about Dr. Larson. I learned very quickly that just as he had been magnanimous with his time with me, he did the same for all who knew him within the scientific community.

The first speaker on day one, "Spirituality and Physical Health," was Robert Ader. As I have described him earlier, he is a scientist par excellence, and is a detailed and spirited researcher. He spent most of his time speaking of the descriptions of Placebo Effect. In laymen's terms, this refers to the belief a patient has in the helpfulness of the treatment. For example, if a physician gives a patient a sugar pill and the patient believes it is a pill with a real medication, the patient's belief in the health benefits of the pill, may in fact have similar effects on the patient, as if he were taking the real medication. Dr. Ader reported that variables which influence placebo response include the size, shape and color of the pill, clinical versus experimental situations, the intensity of the symptoms, qualities of physician and patient-physician relationships, beliefs and expectations, and the meaning of the illness and the treatment. He then went on to say that spirituality mediates placebo effects. He said that this is a philosophical point of view, and that it can be poetic and personal. It relates to one's feelings and there are anecdotal stories about these effects. Then he said something important; he said that placebo effects are confused with spontaneous remissions, prayers and miracles. That this is an unknowable effect of the art of medicine. He called this the non-medical self-healing caused placebo effect. Spirituality effects, he went on to say, are placebo effects. He said "spirituality is associated with placebo effects." He felt that people who identify themselves as more church going are more likely to have these spiritual placebo effects. He also concluded his remarks by saying there is a general lack of agreement on how placebo effects come about. What I understood from his brief presentation is that (and I apologize to Dr. Ader if I misunderstood) spirituality is like a sugar pill. You "believe" in the spirituality and it has this possible salutary effect on you, and can be quite beneficial. In other words, it is more important what the patient believes than on the reality of the pill. This makes research, in Ader's opinion, very difficult to do in relationship to spirituality and physical health.

These opening comments from the day's first speaker set into motion a growing debate as to what is indeed spirituality and how does it actually effect physical health and treatment of illness.

Another speaker on this first day was the famous researcher from Harvard University, Dr. Herbert Benson, author of the Relaxation Response and Timeless Healing. He reported his research into what he considers ingredients to healing. One of the illustrations he used in his talk was one I had seen him make on the video reported earlier when I was in Canada: The Power Within. In this illustration, Dr. Benson said that the treatment of the body is much like a three legged stool. The first leg is pharmaceuticals. The second leg is surgery and other procedures. The third leg is self-care and in it is the relaxation response including good nutrition, exercise, cognitive restructuring and spirituality. The challenge he said, at the mind-body institute, is to combine good self-care with pharmaceuticals and surgery for ultimate outcomes.

Then he went on to describe how the physiology will be the same in the relaxation response no matter what phrase you repeat. For example, if a patient uses the phrase "One Lord Jesus Christ Have Mercy On Me, " it will be the same physiological response as if you use the single word "Peace." Benson continued by saying they are seeing the same physiological responses to repeated phrases no matter what the phrase is. Quoting Larry Dossy, Dossy said that prayer brings about healing. For Benson there are two kinds of prayer. One kind is the prayers that interrupt your everyday thoughts. These might be random or intentional but they are not repeated phrases. The second kind of prayer is that taught by St. John of the Cross. This type of mysticism is the result of a repetitive focused phrase. It is this type of prayer, according to Benson, that brings about the relaxation response, the reduction of stress, and leads to healing. He said that intercessory prayer requires more study to see if it has the results that good scientific papers require. However, the research on repetitive phrases, to self-induce a relaxation response, that can last 24 hours or more, is conclusive. According to Benson any disorder that causes stress can be treated by a relaxation response. Words repeated such as "peace," "one," "our father," "shamel Israel," "the lord is my shepherd," any sacred word repeated will lead to the same relaxation response. This is similar to the mantra concept used in meditation. He added, "You should exercise if you cannot sit well."

Another speaker the first day was Richard Contrada, on the topic of Spirituality and Cardiovascular Disease from the Department of Psychology, Rutgers State University in New Jersey. Among his findings are that surgery patients pray and find it helpful. Prayer lowers depression in "one year survivors" of cardiac surgery. Prayer also creates optimism prior to surgery. He reported on the Rutgers project on religion and spirituality. The results of this study finds that religious beliefs predicts few surgical complications and lower lengths of stay in the hospital. The strength of religious beliefs increase superior results.

A woman speaker also took the podium, Dr. Ellen L. Idler, Ph.D, head of sociology at Rutgers University. Her topic was Religion and Physical Health: Historical Perspectives and Current NIH Research. She began her presentation with these words: "If it hadn't been for David Larson, we wouldn't be here this morning." She went on to say that because of Larson's pioneering work and motivation, now more than ever before there were emerging models of religion, personality and health becoming integrated as never before. She brought many insights and research from 1980 to 2002. Among them was a question she asked about attending religious services and health, a much researched concept. She asked, "What does it mean to attend religious services and be part of religious groups?" Her answer: "They are exposure experiences. They are exposed to social experiences," which she concluded may be helpful for health through interrelatedness as opposed to being alone. She referenced the novelist Mary Gordon who was asked "Why do you go to church?" Her reply was something like, "Church is the one place you don't have to be rich or attractive or wealthy or even sane to attend."

This gives you a flavor of some of what was shared on day one. Research projects on spirituality and irritable bowel syndrome, obesity, smoking, drinking, hypertension, social support, pain, moods, joint pain, etc. were covered. A good overview of the famous Alameda Study was reported on, and laughter broke out in the audience when Dr. David Spiegel produced a Los Angeles area series of freeway signs which, instead of listing names of street off ramps, listed the names of drugs: Prozac, Valium, Pain killers, etc. as if you were driving in L.A. and saw the drugs signs to take you along other pathways.

Day two was on spirituality and mental health. Among the speakers was Roger Fallot on Chronic Mental Illness. He stated that people with serious mental illnesses are a neglected population. One patient he knew said, "My own recovery happened with a spiritual dimension." Fallot continued, "We don't talk about spirituality because we frankly don't know what to say. Now a few years later we know something to say." He said that there are about 15 million seriously mentally ill patients in the United States. Serious mental illness categories are major depression, schizotypal personality disorder, the schizophrenics, other personality disorders and chronic mental illness categories. He spoke of high rates of substance use and abuse, high disability incomes, homelessness and the history of violence. He then asked, "How does religion support or interfere with recovering processes?"

Many surveys and studies point to spirituality and religion as one of the most important sources of support. Over 80% of those surveyed report that spiritual support/or religion is important to them. The most single arena reported is personal devotions, prayer books, etc. Religion or spirituality are positive coping resources, sources of social support, help with enhanced sense of self esteem, and give a sense of hope. Prayer, attendance at religious services and studying the Bible brings comfort. Religious involvement may be a way of reconnecting with a group. One study showed that parents with schizophrenic family members who insist that they go to church find that these schizophrenics have less problems. Many experience the power of loving relationships through religion and often experience serenity. Making reference to theologian Reinhold Neibuhr, the creator of the Serenity Prayer, he pointed out that letting go where change is possible often leads to serenity and health. He also touched on some of the potential negative effects of spirituality and some religion, but mostly he felt that there were possible positive outcomes from this kind of activity. He felt that the next set of research steps to be taken are key questions for research such as: What aspect of spirituality or religion has what impact on which dimension of recovery for which people in which situations. A longitudinal emphasis is needed, and intervention outcome studies are important.

This brought us to the keynote speaker whom everyone had come to hear: Dr. Harold Koenig. His talk was entitled Overview of the Relationship between Spirituality and Mental Health. (With Dr. Koenig's permission, this keynote address is produced at the end of this chapter. This paragraph is a summary of that address). Dr. Koenig reported that religion and mental health care has a long historical connection. He cited treatment of the mentally ill in first century Western Europe, then spoke about the first mental hospital in Jerusalem run by monks in the 5th century. In the 6th century monasteries cared for the mentally ill. In the 12th century in Belgium the mentally ill were brought into people's homes to become part of family life and to expose them to religious teachings. By the 15th century the church began witch hunts to try to persecute demon possession. In the 15th century there was also St. John of God in Spain where he stressed care and compassion. His story is that he had experienced a dramatic conversion but then became destabilized in a mental hospital in Spain. He was later put out on the streets, then later was allowed in front of a house where other mentally ill people were allowed to sleep in a small little area. That little area grew into a hospital, and then the entire order came up around it, the Order of St. John of God, and hospitals around the world today exist to care for mentally ill. By the 18th century moral treatment for the mentally ill was in full swing. In the United States, the first psychiatric care was established founded in moral treatment. The Quakers brought this idea with the Friends Asylum. Members of the Harvard retreat center and other retreat centers founded the American Psychiatric society made up of ministers who lived on the grounds to work with the mentally ill, and gave care. The history of this work was reported in the 1998 American Psychiatric Journal. In the 20th century Freud influenced modern psychiatry with ministers learning his theories and applying them to pastoral care and counseling. In the 21st century with changing times, training and research mushrooms into the impact of religion on mental health. Following this portion of his presentation he covered many research reports on various aspects of religion on mental health. Among these studies on religion and depression, religion and positive psychology, Newburg's research on looking at the brain to see what happens during spiritual experiences (are our brains just creating God or are our brains receptors of that which goes on around us? Or is the brain actually acting on a neurological response to spiritual experiences?)

Much of what he reported can be read in his book by the title Religion and Mental Health. It is a fascinating study into how religion helps or hinders mental health.

Throughout the rest of the day there were reports on PET scans and SPECT images during meditative states, as well as aspects of brain function during prayer states. Different types of activities in the brain occur with different kinds of prayer. One example was a study done on nuns in prayer. Centering prayer and more vocal types of prayers were studied as to how they relate to mental health. There are reports on the function of forgiveness and mental health from a religious context.

Another report focused on religious coping. One interesting aspect reported on was three types of religious coping. Collaborative coping which is defined as, "God and I work together." A second style was described as Self Directing coping characterized by, "without relying on God." A third type, called Deferring, was reported as "giving yourselves over to God." Another outstanding report was the relationship between religion and Post Traumatic Stress Disorder.

On day three the focus was on spirituality and community health. The keynote was given by Byron R. Johnson, on the topic, "Overview of the Relationship between Spirituality and Social Issues." He began his talk this way: "My kids are Dave Larson fans. If there was an email they would cry out, 'There's a Larson message!' He would leave funny messages and tell how much he loved me and cared about me. Larson would send two or three faxes a day updating me on some research finding or question he had. Then there were those apples... he ate these green apples constantly, and carried big bags, trunks of granny smith apples.

One of the things so compelling about Dave was to mentor people to do research the way he learned and I was one of the ones David invested some time in." He then went on to talk about social science research and the study of the role of religions on social phenomena, including religion and health outcomes. He reported that in the religion and health outcomes research, there are over 400 studies dealing with hypertension, mortality, depression, suicide, sexual behavior, alcohol use, drug use and delinquency, all having major impacts on social functioning. His overview on the benefits to community health because of spirituality and religion was excellent.

There were many other reports on day three on the impact of the social good because of religion and spirituality. These far outnumbered the research indicating negative aspects of these dimensions. One speaker pointed out that spirituality has long been neglected as a research phenomena. One reason is it has too many definitions. There is no universal agreement as to a definition everyone agrees to, which makes research extremely difficult. However he went on to say that many studies show prayer is therapeutic. Prayer is a good resource for coping. Spirituality studies show this improves the ability to cope with problems and stress. A most interesting report was also given by Andrew Weaver on the role of religion in the treatment of Alzheimer's disease. One of the things discovered in research is that family members who use religious belief to cope with the task of providing care have been shown to have better quality relationships with the persons receiving care. Clergy and members of congregations can help caregivers by providing emotional support and participating in difficult decision making. Admission into a nursing home can be very traumatic and religious persons and communities can offer tremendous support. Weaver also reported on another critical aspect of religion; man's search for meaning. Referring to Victor Frankl, in his 1959 book, "Man's Search for Meaning," Weaver said, "It has been argued that religious faith gives caregivers an added sense of purpose and meaning in their work." Frankl wrote with powerful conviction after surviving the Nazi death camps that the search for meaning is the primary motivation of life. Then on caregiving, Weaver said in conclusion, "Finding meaning and purpose in one's work helps to counter the negative aspects of care-giving because they provide a reason for giving good care. Meaning and purpose can provide psychological rewards." At the time of Weaver's comments, he was at the Healthcare Chaplaincy of New York City, in the Research Department. Following this third day of the conference, participants were pretty exhausted, and we welcomed the bus ride back to our hotel.

Summarizing the three-day conference, it was clear that a great deal of groundwork and research had already been done by very competent researchers. It was also clear that much more needed to be done from a research point of view. As I wrote this, I received an email from Harold Koenig who was once again seeking researchers in a wide variety of research related to religion, health and related matters.

All of these presenters are among the cream of the crop as "lighthouses of hope" for better insights into how spirituality can be used to better life and foster hope. An excellent place to begin learning more about health as it is related to religion is The Handbook of Religion and Health by Harold G. Koenig, Michael E. McCullough, and David B. Larson. Be sure to read the strong endorsements for this book, many which read "Recommended Without Reservation." It is an easy to read book and covers areas such as depression, anxiety, heart disease, hypertension, stroke, cancer and risky and destructive behaviors such as substance abuse, smoking, and certain sexual activities. A little pricey but it is affectionately known as "the bible" in this ongoing field of research study.

Dr. David Larson's legacy will live on in the hundreds of colleagues and students he trained and touched by his excellence in research and passion for truth. I was truly blessed to have met him before his untimely demise, and I was enriched deeply by Tom Smith's invitation to attend the conference in Maryland. Harold Koenig and others continue research into religion and health, so that the story goes on. I look forward to what new findings are discovered as to the role of religion on all aspects of health.

Following the death of Dr. David Larson, the Library of Congress named a section of its vast collection in memory of Dr. Larson.

It is a tribute to what he stood for and what he did. May his beacon continue to shine bright as other "keepers of the light" tend to their lamps.

* * *

With permission of Dr. Harold Koenig, the following transcription of his keynote address (summarized above) entitled "Overview of the Relationship Between Spirituality and Health" is reproduced here in its entirety. It is especially helpful to clergy, ministers, and others looking into the history of care of the mentally ill.

Keynote Address: "Overview of the Relationship Between Spirituality and Mental Health"

Harold G. Koenig, M.D.

DR. KOENIG: It is a pleasure to be here and to see so many faces that are familiar and to be talking about this exciting area. I have a lot to talk about, so let's start with the first slide.

DR. KOENIG: I think introducing this area by giving you a little bit of a historical perspective on the topic is important to understand that religion and mental health, although separated for so many years, them coming together now is not something entirely new. In fact, their being apart over the last 100 years is really what is new.

In the first century in western Europe, there was no treatment, basically, for the mentally ill. They were kept away from the population because the people didn't want the mentally ill to be scaring the people in the general population, so they were kept in dungeons and in dark cells. So that was the form of treatment: there was no treatment.

Then, in the fifth century, one of the first hospitals for the treatment of the mentally ill, specifically mentally ill, was established in Jerusalem and, of course, was run by monks. In the sixth century, monasteries throughout western Europe brought in the mentally ill to provide care for them. This is particularly true in Spain.

In the twelfth century in Belgium, the mentally ill were brought into the houses of many of the devoutly religious people. So they were actually included in family life. Of course, there were religious reasons that they brought in these mentally ill who otherwise would have been oftentimes living on the streets.

In the fifteenth century, however, the Church began to persecute the mentally ill probably with the intention of trying to maintain a faith that was pure and that was not heretical but also the issue of this demon possession. The idea that people were possessed by demons and that the demons had to be exorcised. If they weren't successful, then the person would be burned or beheaded, whatever. So this was the witch hunts.

Also in the fifteenth century, there was a fellow by the name of St. John of God. Interesting story. He was in Spain. I believe he was a book salesman. What he did was, he was in his 40s and he had a spiritual experience that changed his life. He had a dramatic conversion experience. Then he went into the mental hospital.

Apparently, it destabilized whatever it was that was going on in his mind and he became psychotic, and he ended up in a mental hospital. He stayed there for several weeks and then came out and was living on the streets.

Then someone allowed him to live in, actually, the little area in front of his house that was covered by a roof. He lived there and he brought in other people to sleep with him on the streets, other mentally ill people. He brought them into his little area there that he had to sleep.

Eventually, that grew into an actual hospital. Then, this kind of a hospital that brought in the mentally ill into their midst, this entire order came up, the order of St. John of God. This, even today, still has literally hundreds of different hospitals around the world that bring in and care for the mentally ill.

The eighteenth century moral treatment is the whole beginning of American psychiatry. You don't hear much of this in the literature, particularly with regard to psychiatry, that American psychiatry had its origins in what is called a moral treatment. The first psychiatric hospitals in the United States were built by the Quakers bringing moral treatment over from Europe. The first one was Friends Asylum in Philadelphia, the Friends Asylum. Then the Hartford Retreat and the Worcester Retreat were all modeled after Friends Asylum.

What we don't realize, though, is that the founders of the American Psychiatric Association and the "American Journal of Psychiatry" were the superintendents of these institutions. They included chaplains and ministers very much as part of the treatment team of the mentally ill. In fact, these ministers lived on the grounds of the mental institutions and provided not only services for the patients but also provided some spiritual care. A lot of this was documented, in fact, in the "American Journal of Psychiatry" in, I think it was 1998, in an article that was published there.

Now, of course, over the next 100 years, that was all to change with Freud's influences on modern psychiatry. Since the late 1800s, psychiatry, psychology, and religion have been very separate.

However, in the twenty-first century, things are changing. This includes the training in psychiatry and psychology as well as research and the volume of research.

Now, I would like to get this part of it out of the way. We do know that religion does have negative effects in individual cases on people's mental health. It is unclear whether or not it is the mentally ill person or emotionally ill person that then globs onto religion or whether it is the religion that actually makes a person neurotic or mentally ill. That is up to question.

I think for a long time mental health professionals assumed that it was the religion that was making people unstable, neurotic, mentally ill, rather than vice versa, the mentally ill person seeking comfort and health, globbing onto religion.

However, religion can be used to justify hatred, aggression, and prejudice. That we see at some level all over the place and in every religion. It can be used to gain power and control over others. It can be used to foster rigid thinking, obsessive practices. It can foster anxiety, fear, excessive guilt. It may be used to deny the facts in a kind of magical, unrealistic way. It can be used defensively to avoid addressing issues common in the thought content of psychotic persons. It can interfere with mental health care. People may feel that they have been healed of their bipolar disorder, is probably the best example, and they will stop their lithium.

It can foster negative attitudes towards mental health professionals. Given the negative attitudes of mental health professionals towards religion, many religious groups have also discouraged people in their congregations from seeking psychological or psychiatric care.

It can delay diagnosis and effective treatment. People may be treated locally, say, within a church setting by counselors or by a minister and they may have a severe depression that may worsen. They may commit suicide. That happens.

Now, let's take a look at some of the definitions here.

Spirituality versus religion. Now, not everybody agrees with me on this. So if you all think differently on this, you have plenty of other company nationally, but since I'm giving this talk, I'm going to give you my view of the situation.

Spirituality is popular, religion is not. However, for researchers, spirituality tends to be very diffuse. It can be almost unique to every different person. So, how do you actually measure a construct and then correlate it with different mental health outcomes, that is diffuse, that includes mental health as part of its definition? How do you do that?

I usually speak in terms of religion, not spirituality because I can measure religion: religious beliefs, religious practices, religious activities. However, I use a broad definition of "religion" when I talk about it. I don't mean just going to church with "religion" or institutionalized religion.

Religion, as I talk about it, includes personal religious beliefs, personal commitment, practices, prayer, devotional reading, faith, community involvement, attending services, practicing the rituals, group religious activities, volunteering for religious reasons.

This is very important here. Religion may impact but does not necessarily include forgiveness, meaning and purpose, sense of connectedness, or sense of peace, wonder, beauty, and awe that oftentimes is folded into the term "spirituality." When you include all of these other things in your spiritual predictor variable, you create a circular type of reasoning here. If you define spirituality as being able to forgive, as meaning and purpose in life, all of those things are naturally connected with mental health.

There have long been very strong correlations between those factors and mental health. They are almost kind of pseudonyms for mental health variables. Therefore, if you include that as part of your definition of spirituality, what are you really measuring then when you are looking at the correlation between spirituality and mental health?

So, I encourage you not to include these things as part of your predictor variable, part of your spiritual variable, but rather look at the correlation between religion or spirituality and forgiveness, meaning and purpose, et cetera.

Again, this is my view on it. Many of you may have good reasons not to do this, but this is what I would suggest, to keep things more pure and to avoid the circular type of reasoning.

Now, let's look a little bit at the research prior to the year 2000. This is summarized here. It is in the "Handbook of Religion and Health." If you look at purpose and meaning in life, you can see that of the 16 total studies in the literature, 15 find that the religious person has greater purpose and meaning in life.

Now, this is important to establish this connection, to look at it scientifically, to measure one and then correlate it with the other because many atheists and agnostics would say, hey, I have purpose and meaning in life, why should purpose and meaning be part of the definition of religion and spirituality? So, it is important to establish then the connections between purpose and meaning in life and religious practices or beliefs.

Well-being, hope, and optimism. Of the 114 studies that have looked at this in the last 100 years, we find that 91 find a connection. Greater hope, greater optimism, greater well-being. Social support in virtually all of the studies. Marital satisfaction and stability in 80 or 90 percent of studies. Depression and its recovery, two-thirds of studies. Suicide, again, 80 to 90 percent. Anxiety and fear, about 50 percent.

Now, why is that? Why are there fewer studies showing this correlation for anxiety and fear? Part of it has to do with the fact that fear and anxiety are powerful motivators for people to become religious. Think of September 11th. Think of since the war began. How has the U.S. population reacted?

After September 11th, given the fear and uncertainty, nine out of 10 Americans turned to religion as a way of coping. This was reported in the "New England Journal of Medicine" the week after September 11th, that there were really no other coping behaviors more common than Americans turning to religion, 90 percent of the population. This was a national sample.

About two or three weeks ago, the Gallup organization released findings from early March of 2003. Weekly church attendance had risen about 10 percent, with 49 percent weekly church attendance, 49 percent based on a national Gallup poll.

So the idea here is that anxiety and fear motivate people towards religion, but don't always reduce the anxiety and fear immediately. Therefore, when you look at cross-sectional studies, which most of those studies are, you find sometimes religion and anxiety are positively correlated because it is the anxiety that caused people to turn.

Substance abuse, a lot of research on that. Delinquency, quite a bit.

In summary, of the 724 quantitative studies that we could identify in the previous 100 years, 478 find a statistically significant positive correlation with the religious variable.

Now, what about since the year 2000? Since 2000. We have been talking about prior to the year 2000. Now let's look at since 2000.

Now, there is a growing interest in this field. Entire issues of many journals have been devoted just to religion and mental health. The entire issue. Now, prior to about 1990, I don't think this ever occurred before, that you had an entire issue of a secular journal devoted to papers on religion, spirituality, and mental health.

This only includes about 70 percent of the journals. There have been several journals since I developed this slide that have actually come out with entire issues on the topic. These are secular journals.

Now, growing amount of research. If you remember nothing else, nothing else of what I say, I want you to look at this. Look at this right here. I want you to start down here.

You can do this yourself, and I encourage you to do this. Go into "Psychlit," which is the largest on-line database for research studies in psychology and psychiatry. Go into the "Psychlit" database and simply put in the word "religion." Search for it, focus it down, and then see how many studies you get, but restrict the year to 1980 to 1982, down here. Then take the word "spirituality," put it in "Psychlit," run it, focus it on the articles, and see what you get out, again focusing on just 1980 to 1982. What you find is you will find 101 articles on religion and zero on spirituality because spirituality, there was no such term in 1980 to 1982 in the scientific world. It didn't really come about until 1990.

Now, at that time, 1980 to 1982, there were 406 articles on social support. So therefore, the ratio of articles on religion or spirituality to social support was 25 percent.

Now, simply move up in time and let's look at 2000 to 2002. This time do exactly the same thing, but restrict your time period between 2000 and 2002. What do you find? You find 410 on religion and 821 on spirituality. You now have 1108 articles instead of 101 articles for the same period of time. Now, what does this suggest?

Now, more important, look at the number of articles published on social support during that time, 1590. Now look at the ratio. It's no longer 25 percent, it's now 70 percent.

I encourage you to do this. I think there is no better evidence that this area is growing rapidly within the mainline academic community than if you just look at the literature out there.

Now, there are also a growing number of posters and presentations and dissertation abstracts. If you just go to APA or you go to the American Psychiatric Association meetings, American Psychological Association. Look at the abstracts that are being presented. There are a lot more on religion and spirituality than there were 10 to 20 years ago.

Qualitative research, in addition to quantitative studies, have been coming out in this area, particularly in women, AIDS, African Americans, caregivers, and those who are stressed. These are very important populations to be looking at religion and spirituality because it appears to be in stressed populations that you see these effects emerging.

Now, I am just going to give you kind of a very brief overview on some of the recent studies that have been out. This is very quick. I don't want to take much time on this, but I think it is interesting.

I have divided them up. They are all since 2000. I have divided them up by different conditions, one being adaptation, a section on depression, substance abuse, et cetera. Let's just look at some of these.

Matthews – not Dale Matthews, another Matthews – clinical trial with intercessory prayer. Patients who expected to receive intercessory prayer felt significantly better than those who expected to receive positive visualization. So the expectation that one is going to receive prayer seemed to help the well-being of these patients.

Dale Matthews, by the way, also found in his study of rheumatoid arthritis patients that patients who thought they were being prayed for in the double-blind part of the intercessory prayer experiment did better than those who didn't think they were being prayed for, whether or not they were actually being prayed for. So thinking that you are being prayed for seems to make a difference.

Here is a study of caregivers of patients with schizophrenia. Strength of religious beliefs predict greater well-being. Now, this kind of confirms what Peter Rabins at Hopkins found in his longitudinal study of caregivers of Alzheimers and cancer patients, that the more religious the caregiver was, the faster the emotional adaptation.

Now, although many of these studies find a positive correlation here that I am going over, my intention when I did this literature review, which was fairly rapidly, was not to just find the positive studies.

I tried to put up here the most recent studies that were quantitative that were published in the literature. So this should be fairly representative, although there is probably some bias in selecting out some of these articles. It is, I think, fairly representative of the research that is out there, perhaps a little bit biased on the positive side, but not a great deal.

Here is one in the "Journal of Adult Development," 195 adults with recent vision loss. Spirituality buffered the effects of negative life events experiencing impact in control ratings. So again, in a stressed population you see this effect.

Three-hundred nineteen psychology undergraduates getting the NEO Personality Inventory and these other scales. These spirituality scales correlated with extroversion, agreeableness, and conscientiousness.

Here is one in England: 179 adults. Again, spirituality related to extroversion. Extroversion on, this time, a different personality scale.

This is one of 230 low-income women with HIV and AIDS. Spirituality significantly correlated with adjustment. Once again, you have these stressed, oftentimes medically ill populations where you see these effects coming out.

Let's look at depression. A study in Canada by Dr. Baetz. She is in the audience here. I hope you all get to meet her. She is doing a series of studies in Canada. This one is one of, I think, four or five studies she has recently done, 88 psychiatric inpatients. The more frequent worship attendance, the less severe depression, the shorter length of stay, the higher satisfaction with life.

Here is 156 spouses of lung cancer patients. Again, the caregivers. Curvilinear relationship between religious coping and depression. Those who had moderate religious coping had higher depression. Moderates had higher depression than those who had either high religious coping or did not use it at all.

So if you were atheistic and you were absolutely positive that God didn't exist, you coped relatively well. If you were absolutely positive that God did exist, you coped pretty well, too, but if you were kind of in the middle and weren't sure whether or not he existed, or she existed, then that's when you had more depression, at least among the spouses of these lung cancer patients. It is the uncertainty, the uncertainty.

Here is an interesting study of 227 Iranian and 220 U.S. college students. Intrinsic religiosity in both samples correlated with greater adjustment, less depression, less anxiety, less perceived stress, and greater self-esteem. The opposite was found for extrinsic religiosity.

Again, in the "British Medical Journal," 135 relatives and friends of terminally ill patients, spiritual belief predicting faster resolution of grief symptoms, helping with the bereavement process.

Here is a study: 303 psychology students providing a significant moderating effect for both depression and anxiety, but more for depression than with anxiety. Again, because of that mixture with anxiety of turning to religion with depression, giving hope, giving meaning, giving purpose, et cetera.

Substance abuse. Let's look at a few here. Longitudinal analyses of 1,526 alcoholics. Alcoholics Anonymous significantly associated with abstinence and reductions in drinking intensity whether the person who attended AA was religious or atheistic. Clients unsure of god beliefs – see, again this uncertainty, unsure of their god beliefs – reported significantly higher drinking frequency. Atheists and agnostics were less likely to attend AA, but if they did, they did just as well as believers.

Four-hundred seventy-five youths, those involved in religious activities predicting probability of never using alcohol. Spirituality predicting never using marijuana or hard drugs. Forty-three HIV-positive injection drug users, independent of other predictors. Strength of perceived religious and spiritual support was a significant predictor of abstinence.

Another one: 252 in a treatment setting. Spiritual well-being predicting length of recovery and recovery barriers.

Now remember, the spiritual well-being scale has in it an existential well-being scale and a religious well-being scale. We're not too sure, if you're just looking at the total score, whether it's the existential well-being score that is actually predicting things. The existential well-being score is really a proxy for a mental health variable, like well-being.

Here are 236 recovering substance abusers. Religious faith and spirituality associated with increased coping, resilience to stress, greater optimism, more perceived social support, and lower anxiety.

So now, yes, there is probably a file-drawer phenomena, that many of these studies all seem to be positive. Those are the ones that tend to get published. The ones that you don't find any relationship probably end up not getting published.

Certainly, you would expect, if you found a negative relationship between religion and mental health, that that would get into the mental health literature, given the secular departments of psychology and sociology, but you don't find those relationships very often. You don't find the negative relationships between religion and mental health or substance abuse, et cetera.

Treatment application. This is 228 participants. Inclusion of spiritual process in counseling. Spiritual intervention perceived similarly to a cognitive behavioral intervention, regardless of the spirituality of the patient. So in this particular study, including the spiritual process in counseling, was fairly acceptable to patients, regardless of their spirituality.

Here is one from the "Journal of General Internal Medicine," a focus group with 22 seriously ill patients. The willingness to address religious and spiritual discussions, this time, was correlated with the physician-patient relationship, which means that patients didn't particularly want to discuss their intimate religious and spiritual beliefs with a physician they didn't know, but would rather do that with a physician that they had a relationship with, that they trusted.

These are very sensitive issues that people experience with regard to their religion and spirituality, and they wanted to have a connection with their doctor in particular that would be helpful if these issues were brought up.

Here are 95 parish nurses and 91 mental health nurses who were compared on spiritual issues. Both groups reported high spiritual perspective scores and similar interventions.

So apparently, at least in this study, parish nurses and mental health nurses were fairly similar in what they did with patients. Here is a study in Canada, a study of 200 Canadian and 210 occupational therapists. Do we have any occupational therapists in the audience? Yes, one at least. Good. There is a lot of interest in occupational therapy. I'm excited about that.

Now, here is a study that patients have a preference for discussing spiritual and religious issues in counseling. So this summary is here to suggest that patients would be open to this.

Miscellaneous studies. These are interesting ones here. This is one looking at 340 community-residing and institutionalized elders. Personal meeting, religiosity, spirituality contributed more to well-being than did social resources, physical health, or negative life events. Isn't that interesting? These factors contributing more to well-being than these standard predictors of well-being and mental health.

Here is one looking at 254 students and psychotherapy outpatients' religious straying, feeling alienation from God, religious fear, religious guilt. This is the other side of the picture, when people feel like God is punishing them, has deserted them, doesn't love them.

This is work that Ken and I did at Duke – not this – but we did a study looking at survival after hospital discharge from Duke and found that those people with negative religious coping, like what these guys are describing here, was correlated significantly with death after discharge, independent of their physical health and their mental health. So this doesn't only have mental health applications, this has physical health applications as well.

Here are 76 African American and white primary care patients. Intrinsic spirituality, extremely important for depression care; three times more likely in African Americans than in whites. So in African Americans, in particular, religious and spiritual issues in treating depression should be very important.

Now, here is religious coping. The practices of 400 psychologists were assessed and correlated with their distress levels. No differences observed between religious and non-religious therapists. That's interesting.

So we have the question now: Is it the religious therapist that has more or less distress versus the non-religious therapist? At least, this study showed there was no difference.

In any case, more research needs to be done. There haven't been a lot of studies, and I think there needs to be, on, actually, the effects of the caregiver's spirituality, the mental health provider's spirituality, on their ability to relate to patients and on patient outcomes in therapy. Very little research on that.

Here is a good one. Two-hundred subjects underwent genetic subtyping and answered questions on a spiritual scale. The DRD4 gene and spiritual acceptance were significantly related. The gene may play a role in personality trait of spiritual acceptance. So therefore, someday we may be able to develop a pill to activate this gene in people to make them more spiritual. Let's look a little bit, quickly, at the kinds of studies needed. Further qualitative studies, we need more studies that are qualitative in nature, that actually look at some of the mechanisms, try to explore how religion and how spirituality impact mental health and various aspects of mental health and mental disorder.

Second of all, we need more longitudinal studies on the outcome and the course of major mental disorders: schizophrenia, bipolar disorder, major depression. Very few longitudinal studies looking at those outcomes.

We need clinical trials using religious interventions. There have been a few studies, maybe five to 10 out there. They're not really well designed, but there are some studies out there that are clinical trials looking at religious interventions, mostly in religious patients. They should serve as models for more studies that need to be done looking at better samples.

The idea of clinical trials, where you look at a religious intervention in a patient with a mental disorder, I think it's important that we have more studies done like that because there are very few out there. That, of course, helps to determine the causality.

A lot of those earlier studies were cross-sectional or longitudinal. Cross-sectional studies don't provide any evidence for causality. Longitudinal ones provide some circumstantial evidence for causality, but no direct evidence because you need a clinical trial to establish that.

Program effectiveness. Evaluations need to be done. For example, faith-based delivery of mental health services. What difference does that make, if mental health services are delivered in a faith-based setting versus a secular setting? There are no clinical trials looking at that, and so we need to have program effectiveness studies done.

This is particularly important if the faith-based initiative might, in the future, grow from just the substance abuse area into the mental health area, as well, the faith-based and community initiative of our government.

Theologically-informed instrument development needs to be done, instruments designed specifically for different religions, instruments designed that are valid across religions. We need a combination of these specific for different religions, and also some valid across religions.

We need instruments that include an individual's historical exposure. A lot of times, these instruments only capture right now, as far as immediately, how spiritual or religious a person is. We need some evidence for the history because we know that

that changes over the lifetime of an individual. People spiritually mature over a lifetime, and we need to get that exposure.

We don't really have any studies looking at the level of exposure to religion, spirituality, and mental or physical health outcomes. Instruments that tap activities and behaviors through monitoring, in other words, people wearing a device that they might be beeped every 10 minutes and say, what were you thinking about, what were you doing. See to what extent, how much of the time do people spend thinking about religion or spirituality in their lives rather than making them just do a retrospective report. It would be nice to be able to monitor that.

Studies addressing application and clinical practice, including impact of the health professional's spirituality on outcomes, as I said earlier.

This is the last slide before we have some time for questions. This is kind of a summary of the talk. Lots of research showing connections with mental health, lots of research, but we are still only at the very edge of a field that is growing, that is emerging. We're at the very edge of it. There is a tremendous amount of research that needs to be done to define better what is going on and what these relationships are all about.

What I showed you here is, there is a lot of research being done now. There has been a lot of research that has been done, but a lot of it, like I said, is cross-sectional. A lot more research needs to be done in terms of these more sophisticated study designs, to give it some sense of what this means, and then how to apply it. Amount of interest and research is rapidly growing in this area. More sophisticated measures of religion and spirituality and methods of studying religion and spirituality are needed, more longitudinal studies. Clinical trials are needed, especially of the impact and acceptability of religious and spiritual approaches to treatment.

Religion and spirituality are starting to become mainstream. This is now starting to become popular, believe it or not. Before, you couldn't get a study through the IRB or get NIH to fund a study on religion, but now, if you include religion or measuring spirituality, it's almost like, okay. This is kind of the trend now. You really haven't done a complete grant unless you have included a couple of variables on this and kind of look at it. It's almost like social support was five years ago, where you almost had to look at social support if you were looking at some kind of mental health outcome. Now we are starting to get almost to the point where you need to be measuring a few religious variables, as well.

NIH is more receptive to this area. I think that the evidence is that there is growing receptivity within NIH. I think there is some concern about the review groups. Many of the review groups don't have people on them with experience in this area, or knowledge in this area, and therefore, people reviewing the grants may not be real familiar with the area.

So that is a concern that I think needs to be addressed within the study sections at NIH, that some experience gets included on those study sections.

Funding issues remain a challenge. There is no doubt about that. Getting any studies funded on religion and spirituality, although, like I said, growing interest in this area at NIH. NIH funds are not expanding this year, so that's an issue on getting more money. Therefore, a lot of times we will have to be piggybacking these religious variables on studies that we have funded through other means, through more conventional means, adding, say, a few questions on this and then looking at it along with what else you are looking at.

Question-and-Answer Session

DR. KOENIG: Let's open it up now for about six minutes worth of questions. Yes?

QUESTION: Thank you. In substance abuse treatment, spirituality has played a mainstream role for 50 years. I even note the mainstream is like an aquifer. We don't talk about it outside the treatment facility. A clear distinction has long been made between religion and spirituality. What is your reaction to that, both to the fact that it has developed subrosa over the years and without any review in the literature, any testing, and to the question that a clear distinction between spirituality and religion has long been made in that field?

DR. KOENIG: Yes. AA was the first, really, that made in-roads into psychiatry, the first in-roads that religion/spirituality had in the field. There is no doubt about that.

Now, the way I talk, I would say it was religion within AA that was being utilized, the evidence of a higher power and the idea of turning over one's life, that one is unable to deal with this situation and having to turn over one's life to a higher power and then acting this out by providing support to one's neighbor, the other alcoholic, supporting that person in their recovery. These are very elemental religious principles.

That is the way I would call it. Some people would call it spiritual principles. So, to me, I think, whatever you call it, whether you call it spirituality or religion, it was the first inroads.

In 1953, the "American Journal of Psychiatry" published a paper that talked about alcoholics and what were aspects among alcoholics who survived, who didn't die of their illness. This was even before AA, I think. I don't know when AA was developed. Was that before AA? 1936?

Before AA became real popular, 28 percent of recovery was due to religious conversion. Religious conversion – it said this in this "American Journal of Psychiatry" article – among the alcoholics. They said this before AA became more prominent, but there is no doubt that AA and the principles there in AA and all the substance abuse, whether it is alcohol, whether it is drugs, whether it is eating disorders, are all the same. The idea that these are powerful disorders that completely take over the person. The idea that this person literally becomes helpless in the face of this powerful addiction, and having them to counteract that by saying, I can't deal with this, admitting that, giving it up, and then living that out by caring for one's neighbor, so to speak, the "love God, love my neighbor" kind of idea, is instrumental, I think, in recovery.

Yes, sir?

QUESTION: I have a comment about the gene, the DRD4 gene. It is known in the nutritional literature, for example, that certain modifications like caloric restriction can activate a longevity gene. Maybe it is possible that religious practices or spiritual practices, meditation, prayer, can activate that gene.

DR. KOENIG: That is interesting. Studies need to be done. Very interesting. An activation of a spirituality gene.

QUESTION: Maybe there are other drugs that can do that.

DR. KOENIG: Maybe not. Maybe there are other practices that can be used. Excellent. Yes?

QUESTION: I really appreciate your historical perspective on the renewal of shifting around between negative and the positive view of religious effect. The ones we see the field moving on, we may see a more complex picture, I think, especially when we move from the mainstream religion to different perspectives when the people have different experiences with different religious beliefs under different conditions and in conjunction with different disciplines.

Do you think we will see a more complex picture, for instance, both ways, negative and positive impact of religion and spirituality? Mutual influence, I am talking about there is a likelihood that in some aspects religion will contribute a manifestation of mental illness. Also, at the same time, mentally ill patients will turn to religion and spirituality to seek comfort.

DR. KOENIG: Yes. I think that there is no doubt that the picture ahead will be complex as we look at many different religions and as we study them. However, I think that you would be surprised at what we will find, that some religions that might seem to us very destructive or very neurotic or very obsessive or very constrictive may turn out to be, for the people who choose those religions, very beneficial for them, depending on who chooses, who selects themselves into the religion.

So, as we also deal with cultural issues, things may be very different than we expected. So, I agree with you. It will be a complex picture ahead. There is no telling what we may find as we start to look very specifically into different religions and different cultures in their natural habitats as well.

Next?

DR. SMITH: I'm sorry. Those of you who would like to ask more questions, please join Dr. Koenig this afternoon at the "Meet the Presenters" so that we can be faithful to the time. We could spend the entire day with Dr. Koenig; I understand that. But at the same time, we need to be faithful to the other presenters who have prepared so well and made themselves available to us.

Thank you very much, Dr. Koenig.

References:

Faith, Medicine, and Science: A Festschrift in Honor of Dr. David B. Larson

Chapter 31
The Blumhardts at Bad Boll, Germany
Battling Darkness and a Birthplace of Healing

I had met with my psychotherapist support group before my sabbatical had begun. We were meeting at the home of my colleague, Pieter Noomen, a pastor originally from Holland, who had been serving many years as the Associate Pastor at First Congregational Church in Los Angeles. He is also a licensed Marriage, Family, Child Counselor and published author. Over drinks before dinner, Pieter asked me if I had ever heard of Bad Boll. I said I hadn't and he said, "It is a very famous center for healing, well known in theological circles in Europe. If you go to Germany you should go there. I was there once, many years ago when I was a pastor in Holland. I attended a conference there with clergy from all over Europe. It is a very important place with a long association with healing."

So I made a mental note of Pieter's suggestion. I was planning a European portion for my study on prayer and healing, and if I got to Germany, I would definitely look into Bad Boll. A few months later, when I was meeting with Francis MacNutt in his Christian Healing Center in Jacksonville, Florida, he asked me if I knew about the Blumhardts of Bad Boll, Germany. His question took me by surprise because here was a reference again to Bad Boll. I said, "No, but I have a friend named Pieter, in my therapist support group, who suggested that I go to Bad Boll. So, no, I don't know about the Blumhardts. Who are they?" He replied, "I'm surprised you do not know of them, because they were Lutherans, and are very famous in Germany." Francis then told me that it was Johann Christoph Blumhardt who founded Bad Boll and battled the demonic for two years before saving a young woman's life. Francis smiled and said, "Have you read the book, The Awakening: One Man's Battle With Darkness?" I said I had never heard of it. He got up from his desk and went over to the library in his office, reached up, and drew down a small paperback book, and handed it to me. Then he said, "This is my personal copy. Keep it. Read it. From your Lutheran background you should know this story. And if you decide to go to Bad Boll, you'll know what you are looking at." I took the book, thanked him, and later read it. After reading the book, I decided to visit Bad Boll.

My opportunity to visit the Bad Boll region of Germany was not to happen until after my study sabbatical had officially ended. A few years ago I traveled to Germany and met with a German friend, Hillu, who at the time was living in the general vicinity of Stuttgart. During my visit, she offered to drive me to Bad Boll and to help in any translation or communication of things we might discover there. She had never been to this area herself. So together we set out on our adventure to Bad Boll, not knowing what we might find.

Hillu proved to be an excellent guide and translator. We drove into the region of Bad Boll, and found a parking place. Leaving our car, we set out for the very large, bright yellow, grand hotel-type building that dominated the area. There were trees lining the pathway, and off in the distance there was another set of buildings. We were to discover later that those distant buildings are a Lutheran seminary at Bad Boll. *(see Photography section)* The sign beside the pathway listed various treatment modalities offered inside the Bad Boll spa. This is not the type of spa one visits in America where you simply get a massage and perhaps a mud bath. No, this Spa at Bad Boll is more like a holistic treatment center for physical, emotional, and even spiritual ailments. The sign beside the pathway had arrows painted on it indicating which direction to go to receive services such as Aromatherapy, Psychotherapy, Hydrotherapy, and Physiotherapy. It was obvious that this large hotel-like building was not a hotel at all, but a holistic healing center. After reading the sign, Hillu, in her upbeat cheerful way, looked at me and said, "OK, let's go inside. Let's see about these Blumhardts."

We walked up the walkway and entered through large glass doors. We entered into a large entrance way and to the left, was the reception desk. Hillu led the way, and exchanged greetings in German with the pleasant woman behind the counter. Soon she was smiling and nodding and Hillu was gesturing, and, because I do not speak nor read German, the only thing I could surmise was the body language, and it said that something exciting and good was happening. Both women kept speaking and gesturing upwards and then back behind me. Hillu said, "Thank you" and turned and said, "This is the place!"

A staircase leading upwards was behind me, and I followed Hillu to the right of the staircase. There in the corner of the entrance was a glass case with artifacts in it. Looking closely I discovered that these were books written by Johann Christoph Blumhardt. There was a translation of the Psalms, and also what looked like a form of the Catechism he had penned. The glass case was locked, but there were other documents under the glass. I took some pictures of what I was seeing. Then we headed upstairs. Hillu was talking, "You are going to be amazed. The lady said that upstairs is the Blumhardt room. It is dedicated to the memory and history of the Blumhardts." I was getting excited. We came to the door and Hillu opened it. We entered an enormously large room. On the long wall to our right were two huge portraits. One was a portrait of the elder Blumhardt, Johann Christoph (1805-1880). The other grand portrait was of Christoph Friedrich Blumhardt (1842-1919). *(see Photography section)*

In the center of the room was a very long table with chairs around it. In one corner of the room was a book case with old books in it. We looked at them and discovered that they were a collection of many books written by the Blumhardts and written about them. We laid them out on the table one by one and I photographed them. Then I had Hillu take my picture next to the Blumhardt portraits. There were other documents in the room praising the Blumhardt's work. There was also a copy of The Awakening.

The Awakening tells the story of a very young Pastor Johann Christoph Blumhardt who was initially an unknown parish pastor in Mottlingen, which at the time was an obscure village of Wurttemberg, southern Germany. There was a young woman in his parish by the name of Gottlieben Dittus. She came to Pastor Blumhardt's attention because of the strange situation surrounding this young lady. She acted unusual, made odd sounds, probably suffered from some kind of severe nervous disorder, and in the words of one commentator, "her household was visited with strange psychic phenomena."

Blumhardt had never seen anything like this. His seminary education provided inadequate training for facing these strange phenomena. Blumhardt began to believe that he was in the presence of something dark, indeed, perhaps even demon possession. He read the New Testament again and studied how Jesus had dealt with demons and spiritual warfare.

He came to the conclusion that indeed this young lady was somehow possessed by some kind of demon, and he set upon a pathway to rid her of her torment. This would become a two year battle for the young woman's soul. For Blumhardt this was a season which would change his life and bring him into greater reputation as well as closer scrutiny.

According to the record, Blumhardt approached this situation at first with good counsel. He was not at all sure what was going on, but knew enough about pastoral care to befriend the young lady, to listen carefully, and to work with her. Over about a two month initial period, it became clear to Pastor Blumhardt that he certainly did not have any means available to overcome the woman's malady, and in fact, Blumhardt was not sure what the malady may be. As is reported in The Awakening, Blumhardt invited the girl to join him in prayer. "Lord Jesus, help us. We have watched long enough what the devil does; now we want to see what the Lord Jesus can do." This became the initial salvo in what would drag out for two long years into a spiritual battle with the demonic. Whatever these demonic attacks were, Blumhardt did not hesitate now to bring all of his pastoral training and experience to the encounters with whatever held possession over Gottlieben Dittus. The Awakening is a powerful drama of this conflict between the forces of light and those of darkness, of Christ's power and the resistance of the demon. After two long years the spiritual warfare ended abruptly! Gottlieben's sister, who had also been under some kind of demonic attack, cried out suddenly, "Jesus Is Victor!"

Her voice was strange but suddenly everything was over. The battle ended. Blumhardt had persisted in bringing the Lord Jesus and His power against the devil, and saw the healing victory come to pass. Word of this miraculous healing spread throughout the countryside. The girl's possession was over and she was never again to have these difficulties. In fact, she became part of the Blumhardt's household and served there all the rest of her life. Blumhardt would later report that he believed fully that the demon or demons that had possessed young Gottlieben had been conquered by Jesus Christ and that the outcry of "Jesus Is Victor!" was the final act in this tumultuous encounter. Whatever this dark force had been, it had now been expelled by God's power.

What I find so compelling in this straightforward account is that Blumhardt himself was not a man of sensationalism or emotionalism. He was even-mannered, calm, thoughtful and measured in all of his pastoral duties, and brought this same kind of presence to this spiritual warfare. So he found himself involved in something that "grew him up" as they say. He grew from knowing little or nothing about dealing with forces such as those possessing the girl, into a famous pastor of healing through his humble yet steadfast battle against the powers of darkness during those two years.

Suddenly news of what had taken place began to transform the village of Mottlingen. "Signs and wonders," as the New Testament describes them, began to happen. As the story of the miracle continued to be passed on throughout the countryside, people began to come from all over. The Awakening says that not only was the congregation renewed, but that there were many healings, some of these of a physical nature, and some of a psychological nature, as some who were in opposition to this outpouring of the Holy Spirit were themselves transformed. People with bad marriages discovered that their relationships began to heal. Some with physical ailments witnessed the cure of these disorders. In my own assessment of the story, I think this became a kind of Pentecostal event which we call a revival. The church revived, enemies were reconciled, new volunteers came forward to evangelize the neighboring villages and countryside. As one writer described it, it was a place of missionary zeal and fervor.

Of course as people began to drop out of their own churches and gravitate to this exciting, renewing, signs and wonders place of God, other pastors of the region began to complain, and Blumhardt began to receive criticisms. These lasted over a few years, and finally Blumhardt tired of the criticisms, left the church in Mottlingen, and moved to the area known as Bad Boll, where he purchased a run-down spa-resort hotel and turned it into a spiritual retreat center. It was here that Blumhardt had the freedom of expression of his understanding of God's direction. The retreat center was created for prayer, meditation, rest, study, communion with God, and a place where you could receive the wisdom of a pastor who cared deeply about you and your life. While I do not remember seeing the phrase in The Awakening, Lutheran clergy would understand this place as a place for sealsorge: soul-care.

Here, now, at Bad Boll, I was standing at the very place where the caring of the soul had expanded in modern times to include care of the whole person: body, mind, and spirit. The small beginnings in a humble country parish where spiritual warfare burst open into victory over the devil had now led to a tradition of healing in Bad Boll. Pastor Blumhardt continued his ministry until his death in 1880. His son, Christoph, also helped his father operate the retreat center. Both were Lutheran pastors who found themselves in the midst of a revival that began to look like the Pentecostal outpouring in the book of Acts. One can imagine how these activities would fly in the face of traditional worship and practices, and in time, the relationship between the two Blumhardts resulted in severed relationships with the Reformed Church.

Seeing the books on the first floor of the Bad Boll spa and retreat center, I could well imagine the two Blumhardts, father and son, teaching and counseling people from all around. They both wrote well and were very bright. For those reading this book who may know some of the great names in theological circles from the last century, it was the great Karl Barth who believed the Blumhardt account of what happened, and defended the Blumhardt name against any voices who were critical. Barth is just one of the great theologians of modern Germany who did not see any of this as simply "faith-healing" or Pentecostalism, but believed that what had happened to the Blumhardts and continued at Bad Boll was something indeed extraordinary but was played down and considered calmly as another form of God's love for His people. For the Blumhardts, what happened to the young girl and what came after at Bad Boll, was evidence of God's kingdom breaking into the real world just as it had been in the book of Acts at Pentecost. But their response was to downplay the "signs" and to reemphasize that it is Christ's victory over the devil and his darkness and was not something to bring about the praise of the Blumhardts. Indeed, both the father and his son believed that the purpose of ministry and the life lived in Christ was to strive for Christ's justice and his kingdom on earth. For the elder Blumhardt, this meant fighting to bring Christ's kingdom on earth through the ousting of the demonic in a real life situation. For the younger Blumhardt, it became a kind of thelogia-politico, a kind of political theology, which led him away from the spiritual healing ministry of his father and into German politics. The son became part of the workers' movement of the Social Democratic party of his day. He was elected to a six year term in the legislature of Wurttemberg. He became well known in his advocacy of making a difference in the lives of workers through the Social Democratic party.

It is said that the father was the worker pastor of healing while the son was the thinking pastor for social movement. While the son did not follow in his father's footsteps at Bad Boll for any length of time, he did manage to continue his father's firm belief that the Kingdom of God has come and is still coming. For the elder Blumhardt the proof was in the healings and "signs and wonders" that were miraculously taking place. For the younger Blumhardt the Kingdom of God has come and is still coming in what Luther called the Left-Hand Kingdom of God, in the social, political order of creation.

There are those who clearly see the Blumhardts as predecessors of Dietrich Bonhoeffer's theology of suffering in the real world to give evidence of God's kingdom breaking in. As Bonheoffer once wrote, if God calls a man, He calls him to die (The Cost of Discipleship). The Kingdom has to break in, in a very tangible way, even if it means participating in the suffering of God. In this sense, there are some who see this as a very real existential involvement in the Kingdom of God, and are reminded of the writings of the theologian Soren Kierkegaard. In fact, Karl Barth wrote that he thought both Kierkegaard and Blumhardt were the progenitors of the Neo-Orthodoxy Movement in theology, a mighty statement indeed.

On a side-note, in my research, I discovered that there were connections among various German theologians at the turn of the 20th century. In fact, I had read a number of works by these writers. I discovered that Emil Brunner's father was converted by Christoph Blumhardt (the son), and that Brunner in his writings gives credit to Blumhardt for many of his influences on his thinking. Also, Pastor Eduard Thurneysen, who was part of the team with Karl Barth, had himself studied under Blumhardt at Bad Boll in 1904. Because of this connection, it was Thurneysen who introduced Barth to the literature I had been looking at myself in Bad Boll. Thurneysen wrote a brief introduction to the Blumhardts in 1962 in German which had not been translated into English. He also wrote a book entitled in English, A Theology of Pastoral Care in which Thurneysen writes extensively on the contribution the Blumhardts had on pastoral counselors.

Hillu and I left the upstairs of the healing center at Bad Boll and thanked the receptionist for her hospitality and guidance. She responded cheerfully and said that before we left we must visit the cemetery to see the large headstones over the graves of both Blumhardts, their family members, and that of the young girl who had been cured of demon possession.

We went back outside and found the graveyard some distance away. Respectfully we walked around trying to make out the names on the many tombstones in the cordoned off grave site. We found them all: Johann, Christoph, Gottlieben, and others. I pondered why I had never before heard of these wonderful warriors for healing, healing of souls and the struggle for justice (for the workers) which has its own kind of healing. Partly it may have been that World War I came, so that when the senior Blumhardt died, it was in the shadow of the war to end all wars, which eclipsed any information from crossing the Atlantic about the younger Blumhardt. The elder Blumhardt was, after all, pastoring at a kind of spiritual retreat center in a small place called Bad Boll, hardly the kind of earth-shattering place of famous persons.

Yet today in Germany, you can still go into a book shop and find the writings of the Blumhardts. I know, because I did it easily. Also, in America there is one small publishing house, the Plough company, and a small group of people who work to preserve the writings, history and name of the Blumhardts, for what they believed, what they stood for, and how they made a difference. That's what "lighthouses of hope" do. They make a difference. They show the way for people, even in small places like Bad Boll or in legislatures such as in Wurttemberg. I remember an old saying, perhaps from the '60's that went something like this: bloom where you are planted. The Blumhardts bloomed where they were planted, and sowed seeds spiritually and politically which still bloom even to this day.

As "lighthouses of hope" their legacy is that they have continued to be part of the awakening for healing as they believed that God's kingdom has already broken into this world and keeps on breaking in.

References:
Pneumatology and Theology of the Cross in the Preaching of Christoph Friedrich Blumhardt: The Holy Spirit Between Wittenberg and Azusa Street
https://www.amazon.com/gp/product/056747240X
Pastor Johann Christoph Blumhardt: An Account of His Life (Blumhardt Series)
https://www.amazon.com/gp/product/B0095JQ3YO
Thy Will Be Done: Sickness, Faith, and the God Who Heals by Johann Christoph Blumhardt, Christoph Friedrich Blumhardt
https://www.amazon.com/gp/product/087486867X

Chapter 32
The 14 Helpers and Healing

In Franconia, Germany, there is a beautiful cathedral dedicated to healing. The Vierzehnheiligen, which is the Cathedral of the 14 Helpers, sits in a section of Bavaria, about one hour from Bamburg. I traveled to this magnificent church to see for myself who these fourteen helpers were, their involvement with healing, and to see the place of veneration of these saints.

Arriving outside the church, one is first struck by the many small shops on the street outside to the right of the cathedral. Here many booths line the avenue where candles, rosaries, postcards, and other souvenirs can be purchased. When I arrived, there were people in tuxedos exiting the cathedral. A wedding had just occurred and the ushers were filing out down the long staircase which spreads out in front of the cathedral.

Upon entering the church, one is struck by the wonderful baroque and rococo architecture of the 1774 structure. In the center of the huge church is a very large artistic altar with large sculptures depicting the 14 helpers. Each of the helpers are holding in their hands symbols of the diseases/conditions for which they help the petitioner. Inside the cathedral and in the shops outside, you can purchase lists of these 14 helpers and the diseases which they cure. There are also several websites which give the same information. Below I have listed the disease, condition or situation followed by the name of the Holy Helper:

For headache: pray to St. Achatius
For fever and sudden death: pray to St. Barbara
For throat conditions: pray to St. Blaise
For sudden death (again): pray to St. Catherine of Alexandria
For bubonic plague: pray to St. Christopher
For temptation: pray to St. Cyriacus
For headache (again): pray to St. Denis
For intestinal problems: pray to St. Erasmus
For family discord or problems: pray to St. Eustachius
For domestic animals: pray to St. George
For plague or for a good confession: pray to St. Giles
For childbirth: pray to St. Margaret of Antioch

For physicians: pray to St. Pantaleon

For epilepsy: pray to St. Vitus

After making a complete tour of the Basilica Vierzehrheiligen (Church of the 14 Helpers), I was drawn to the rear of the church, to the small room which would be to your right as you enter the basilica. Here I was met with an incredible room full of testimonials to the healing powers of the Helpers.

The room of testimonials is perfectly square and very large. Everywhere you look there is some kind of symbol or written report of a miracle that has happened in someone's family. On one wall, chiseled into the stone itself, are stories of miraculous healings from the 14th and 15th century. These include recoveries from falls, from being crushed by a horse, or cured of some blood disease. The other walls of this healing room also have written testimonials of other kinds of healings. One testimonial really touched me, a letter from a young woman, who wrote to say that her healing would be in heaven. There are crutches on the walls, left at the church after a miraculous healing. These crutches reminded me of those at Chumaya, the Lourdes of North America in New Mexico (more on that later). There were also shelves of other gifts given to the cathedral as thank offerings to God for being spared or healed or cured. One particular one was a very, very tiny lighthouse. It made me smile instantly because of the title of my book. I looked closely at it and next to it was a tiny note in small handwriting which said simply in German, "Thank you God for your healing light." It brought a tear to my eye. High above I could also see dolls given by children who also were giving thanks for being healed. Everywhere you turned this room was filled with literally hundreds of appreciations of the healings and cures people had experienced. It was almost overwhelming.

For Roman Catholics especially, this kind of healing place draws thousands of pilgrims each year. They are drawn to the altar to pray to one of the Holy Helpers. They are drawn to this room I was standing in, to be encouraged and motivated by hope for whatever condition they are experiencing. It is a profoundly moving experience to stand in this place and think of the hundreds of thousands of people who have come here for centuries, professing their hope and praise to God, seeking help and relief.

So how did it happen? How was it that this particular place was created for healing? What was the story and how were the 14 Holy Helpers discovered?

The story is this:

On September 24, 1445, in the small village of Bad Staffelstein not far from Bamburg, Germany, a young shepherd named Hermann Leicht (Leicht is "light" in German!), from the Franciscan monastery, was out walking one morning along the narrow dirt road when he saw a small child crying in a nearby field. Curious about what he was seeing, he walked into the field toward the child. He finally reached the child but when he bent down to pick up the child, it suddenly disappeared. This was a huge shock to the shepherd. He couldn't believe his eyes. Was he hallucinating? Was he ill? What had he just witnessed and what did it mean? He looked around to see if anyone else saw what had happened. There was no one around to share what he had seen.

Not long afterwards, Hermann Leicht once again saw the child reappear in the same spot out in the field. Once again the child was crying. The appearance was exactly as before except this time there were two candles burning near the crying child. Once again as the shepherd approached, the child disappeared. Hermann Leicht then shared what he had seen with other brothers in the Franciscan monastery nearby. No one knew what to make of it.

Then about 11 months later, in June of 1446, as he walked along the same pathway, the shepherd saw the same child for a third time. He slowly and cautiously approached the child, afraid it would suddenly disappear again. To his surprise, this time the child didn't disappear, and the shepherd noticed a red cross on its chest. As he arrived to face the child, he became aware that they were not alone. Now, an additional 13 children were also present. The shepherd was astonished! The child then spoke its first words to the shepherd. It said that they were the 14 Helpers and that they wished for him to build a chapel there in the field. They explained that they wanted to rest. The shepherd listened intently to the child as he looked into the faces of all the other children. Then the child spoke again saying, "If you will be our servant, we will be yours!" Once again, the shepherd looked around to see if anyone could confirm what he was seeing and hearing. Not far away, a woman standing on the same road was seeing the same thing as the shepherd. Later she would tell him what she had seen and heard, verifying this amazing experience. Shortly thereafter, the shepherd saw two burning candles descending to the very spot where he had seen the 14 Holy Helpers.

The shepherd hastened to tell others what had happened, and a party was organized to carry out the 14 Holy Helpers' wish for a chapel to be built where they might rest. The small wooden structure was finally completed, and then something unexpected happened. Someone praying for healing received a healing. Then there were other healings. The miraculous healings grew as people sought out the fourteen Holy Helpers. To this day pilgrims come from all over Germany and beyond to seek out healings. If you wish to read more about this you can find several websites that will tell you more.

The cathedral or basilica is on a high hill overlooking fields and hillsides. It is a beautiful setting conducive to holy thoughts and deep reflective prayers. The basilica itself is a beautiful, grand tribute to the belief in miracles and extraordinary undertakings by the power of the Light which comes from the Creator God. Venerations and prayers to saints are part of the heart and fabric of traditional Catholicism. As I have said elsewhere in this book, there are many "lighthouses of hope" that I do not necessarily endorse nor suggest anyone follow. What I find important, however, is for you the reader to know that there are many lighthouses of hope which people find comforting and indeed healing. This is but one more example, and a dramatic one it is, of the search for close encounters with God which translate into healing works and drawing closer to God. Looking at the many testimonials and thank yous from people healed from their belief and prayers to the 14 Helpers, one must at least acknowledge that there is strong belief in saints and their supplications before the throne of God. Hundreds of millions of Roman Catholics worldwide find sustenance in the prayers to Saints. The 14 Holy Helpers are centered in healing. They are venerated and sought out in times of crisis. They must be considered "lighthouses of hope" even though they date back to the 1400's. Even if they were a vision or story to give peasants of that day great hope in dismal times, they are still there, as intermediaries in the minds of the followers of the Roman Catholic faith. From this standpoint, they are examples of ongoing lighthouses which beam hope to thousands.

I close this chapter with an old children's rhyme which actually comes from the veneration of these 14 Holy Helpers. Members of my own family recall this rhyme from their own childhood. It goes:

When at night I go to asleep,
Fourteen angels watch do keep,
Two upon my right hand,
Two upon my left hand.
Two who warmly cover
Two who o'er me hover,
Two to whom 'tis given
To guide my steps to heaven.

Chapter 33
"Little Switzerland" Germany

There is a part of Germany, to the east of the towns of Bamberg, Forchheim, and Erlangen, towards what used to be called "East Germany." This part of Franconia is called "Little Switzerland." It is called that because it is an area filled with small mountains and hills, and villages tucked away in and between those smaller mountains. It is a wonderful holiday area for many Germans. Today people travel down from Berlin, others travel west from parts of former eastern Germany, and many from west of Little Switzerland travel east along its pretty scenery, lush forests, and quaint villages to breathe in the fresh air and to find a relaxing vacation spot. It is also an area with a number of caves. The one called "The Devil's Cave" is one of the best I've ever hiked through. It is ideal for children because it is filled with many narrow passages that are spooky and fun.

It is into this region that I have traveled a couple of times. One of those times brought me to a small village that had an old Catholic church in its midst. On the day I was there, the final mass was just finishing and there were many people coming out of the front doors of the basilica.

I had been told that there was a place of healing in the rear of this church. I wanted to see it but first I wanted to poke my head inside the church. I did not have much time as other events were beginning, but I enjoyed seeing the structure of the church, pews and statuary including the stations of the cross.

I came out of the church, and made my way to the rear of the basilica. There in the distance was a grotto for St. Mary. Here pilgrims prayed for healing and for help. This particular grotto was not very attractive and did not seem to me to be very conducive to a mood of tranquility and peace. But perhaps it need not be attractive. The statue and painting of Mary was simple and straightforward. My overall impression was that perhaps this grotto was quite old and had been there for many years. Either way, it was clear that it served the purpose of drawing people into God's presence.

Then I heard singing. It was coming from my left. I turned just in time to be treated to a rare sight. I saw a few young people at the tail end of a line, carrying flags and banners which rippled in the breeze. They were singing Easter music as I watched the end of the line disappear from sight as the line went around the far outside wall of the church. I didn't know what was happening. The singing rose on the wind, and I turned and ran back from the direction from which I had come, hoping to learn more of what was happening. The young people holding and waving those flags above their heads and singing were also wearing white robes. At least most of then were. A few wore red stoles or sashes.

As I emerged out onto the sidewalk, I looked to my right and saw a rather long processional led by priests with a few young adults in the front of the parade. They were moving away from me, and their singing grew louder and there was a happy spirit in the air. Whatever this was, wherever these young people were going, they were walking in the streets of the village singing and shouting and laughing and waving banners and flags with great joy.

I did not speak German, so I had to turn to someone to tell me what was going on. I learned that they were singing Easter songs and shouting "the Lord is Risen!" I stood and watched them head through the village, and even when they disappeared I could still hear them singing and shouting. Eventually I could not hear them anymore. Then many minutes went by as I made my way down one of the streets. I heard them again, across the village somewhere and imagined their processional winding through the streets, up into the surrounding hillside, singing and laughing and enjoying the warm summer sun.

When they were done taking their singing and message throughout the town, then they would return to the church. I thought about how rare this was, to see something like this. In America, people did not go through the streets of their town, holding up banners and singing Easter songs and shouting "the Lord is Risen!" But somehow, in this country village in Germany it seemed quite appropriate. It was clear that these young people were enjoying what they were doing. I thought of an old Doobie

Brother's song about "Taking it to the Streets." That's what they were doing. Taking their message of hope to the streets.

I connected that to healing. I thought that perhaps somewhere in an upstairs bedroom, someone might be laying ill or discouraged. Then I imagined them hearing singing coming from a distance, getting closer. I imagined the struggling person's heart being lifted for a moment, perhaps a smile breaking out in their heart or on their face as they heard these young voices. Then perhaps as the procession moved beneath that window, the music and verse would ease the burden a little for the one in the midst of some ailment, some setback, some difficulty. Even if you didn't have the same belief system as the people in the procession, just their voices alone might bring relief and hope.

That was not the only grotto I was to see on my post-sabbatical travels. While driving a very narrow country road in another part of Franconia, I came to a lush picnic area. Across the way was another grotto, away from the road, deep in the woods. It was an ideal location to build one, because it was so peaceful and quiet and green in those woods. It was in a secluded area and very conducive to quiet prayer and meditation. Here people could sit or kneel and raise their thoughts to heaven. Here in nature one could imagine a sense of deeper closeness to God and His creation. I could easily imagine a person's stress being lowered and a peaceful tranquility settle within the troubled breast. The only sounds were those of an occasional bird or the rustling of leaves in the small breeze.

Throughout Europe I was to see numerous places along the sides of roads specifically showing a Madonna figure, a symbol for prayer. Along the winding road which leads to Colmegna, a little north of Luino, along Lago Maggiore (Lake Maggiore), there is a shrine with Mother Mary deeply recessed back into the structure. Surrounding Mary on three sides of the inside walls are written the names of those soldiers, both Italian and German, who were from the village of Colmegna and the surrounding area, who died in World War I and World War II. It reminded me of the line from the song by Chris de Burgh, a song called Say Goodbye to It All. The song in part is about the boys who gave the ultimate sacrifice on the beaches of Omaha, Juno and Gold (the D-Day invasion, June 6, 1944). One of the lines speaks about "whisper a prayer for the boys who said goodbye to it all." That line came to me as I stood in front of that Madonna shrine on the winding road of the village of Colmegna.

Then I thought about Lourdes, France, one of the most famous grottos in all the world, where St. Bernadette is said to have had a vision of God. It has become a world famous healing place, like Fatima in Spain (there are others). These are special gathering places for people to come to pray for healing and miracles. Miracles of healing have been verified by Catholic authorities at Lourdes. Many shrines like that of Lourdes have crutches hanging on walls, and wheel chairs abandoned, by those who have been healed. Like the site of the Fourteen Helpers in another part of Germany, or Chimayo in New Mexico, of the United States, people gather with hope and prayers that healing will take place.

Relics were believed in the Middle Ages to also have healing properties. In the medieval town of Bamberg, it was believed that if you saw the relics from the time of Christ, you would receive a healing. In fact, monasteries and churches throughout the Middle Ages were said to have relics from the stories about Jesus and His times. Scholars believe these were ways for monasteries to receive financial support. Whereas today monks make bread or work a farm or produce hand made oven fired ornaments for financial support, the relics "business" of the middle ages provided similar ongoing support. The people believed what they were told and made pilgrimages to view these holy relics. As I've mentioned elsewhere in this book. the remains of the Three Magi are said to lie in state at the Cologne Cathedral in Germany. Other places claimed to have pieces of the cross that Jesus died on, while others had the shroud that covered Jesus' face and body, and still another claimed to have other pieces from the Biblical accounts.

Little Switzerland is just one of thousands of places throughout the world where there is a grotto or a place of prayer which features a Marion connection (St. Mary) or some other blessed saint to whom petitions are made. While the Reformation and subsequent protestant groups growing out of the Reformation reclaimed the direct prayer connection with Jesus, within Catholicism the system of saints was to remain a bedrock of belief. Prayers and petitions would continue to be offered up to an intercessory saint... carrying the request from the petitioner to the saint who would then approach Christ or the throne of God on the petitioner's behalf. Mary, of course, became the premiere saint for the vast majority of Catholics and that still continues today. Particularly in Latin American countries, a parade of the faithful will fill the streets, holding high a statue or icon of Mary, the Mother of Jesus.

A great example of this is what is known as Our Lady of Guadalupe. In a story reminiscent of the 14 Helpers (see the previous chapter), a 57 year old widower whose baptized name was Juan Diego, was walking on a hillside in a village just outside Mexico City. While walking he heard beautiful music, then saw a cloud and within the cloud was a young Native American Indian dressed like an Aztec princess. She spoke to Juan Diego, who was to go to the bishop of Mexico and the bishop was to build a chapel where this young Native American maiden appeared. The story goes that the bishop required a sign from this princess, and that Juan Diego was to bring him that sign. Around that same time, Juan Diego's uncle became ill. This made Diego decide to avoid the princess. But the lady came to Diego, and gave him roses to take to the bishop as a sign. She also told Diego not to worry because she told him, reassuring him, that his uncle would be healed. Diego then took the roses to the bishop. He was to carry them in his cape (or poncho). When he arrived before the bishop, he opened his poncho, the roses fell, and on the inside of the cape was the exact image of Mary as she appeared on the hillside to Juan Diego. This amazing event took place on December 12, 1531. Today, Our Lady of Guadalupe is the most popular icon of the faith throughout Mexico, and the veneration of the Virgin of Guadalupe (another name for her) is widely proclaimed. She became extremely popular among the indigenous Indians of that time and over the centuries her shrine in Mexico has become one of the world's most visited places for healing.

Chapter 34
Augsburg and a Healing Priest

I had always wanted to visit the city of Augsburg, Germany, where the Augsburg Confession was hammered out in 1530, to become the uniting document of Lutherans the world over. Little did I know that I would get the opportunity to go there, and that the reason, would be healing.

In the Catholic church of Augsburg there is an assistant to the Bishop, a priest who is in charge of healing ministries. Several of the archdiocese in Germany have such a person, and the one in Augsburg was willing to meet with me.

I had met Evelyn Walz through a search for a room to rent in Franconia. As it developed, she was willing to go with me to meet this priest, and to translate for me.

We drove into a very nice neighborhood in Augsburg, and parked in front of the address the priest had given. I walked up to the front door of his home, knocked, waited for a few moments, then heard the sound of someone on the other side of the door. The door swung open and before me stood a slightly built man with bright eyes, and a winning smile, but didn't speak any English. My translator introduced me to him, and he invited us inside. Once inside he took us to a pleasant room, with a small couch and two chairs. He sat in the middle of the couch, motioned for me to sit in the chair to his left and for Evelyn, my translator to sit in the chair opposite where he sat.

He spoke to Evelyn and she translated for me, that he was apologizing for not being able to speak English, but was very excited about my visit, and was eager to explain his ministry to me. I nodded, and replied that I very much appreciated his taking time for me, and I explained the nature of my sabbatical study, and that I was now following up in a post-sabbatical journey to learn more. He smiled as he heard my words translated into German.

He explained that he had about an hour and then he had to go visit someone ill in the hospital. He explained that he had been doing a ministry of healing for many years, and that he had been invited by his Bishop to continue to do this as a special ministry.

He said that he had always felt called to a healing ministry. When he was a younger priest, he always felt compassion for those who were ill or struggling with illness. Sometimes, it was not only physical illness, but also illness of the mind or spirit. Sometimes it was illness in relationships. But as time passed he knew he would dedicate his life to a healing ministry. He asked me if I understood and I said that I did, that I had a mental health background and had done years of pastoral counseling, and that very often I saw people manifest physical illness because of some emotional issue that was unresolved. His eyes again brightened and he nodded his head to demonstrate that we shared a similar understanding.

He asked if he could give me some examples of his ministry, and I replied, "Yes, of course." He then reached for a very thick file folder which lay in front of him on the coffee table. He picked up the folder in one hand, and pointed to it with the other. "These are all letters from people who have been healed," he said. He looked me straight in the eyes, and the smile was gone, and in its place was a look of serenity and awe. When the translation was finished I replied, "There are so many letters in there." I truly was astonished.

He nodded. "Yes, it is true. The power of the Holy Spirit is very strong, and I keep this file to remind myself that I am a mere instrument of the God who loves people, and wants them to be healed." I nodded my head yes. "Please go on," I said. "Please share with me some of your letters."

He opened the file folder and it looked like there were more than a hundred letters in the file. As if reading my mind he said that he had more than 250 letters of healing, and this one file was just part of those letters. Then looking down, he picked up the first one, written on thin blue paper, and he began to read. It was a letter from a woman in the congregation thanking him for coming to her home, laying hands on her, anointing her with oil, and praying for her. She had a back ailment and after the priest prayed for her, the pain and discomfort began to go away. The letter continued that from that day, she no longer had any painful symptoms. She said her doctor was glad to report that her back was now strong again.

He paused after reading that letter. He said that it was a typical letter. Many of the letters were like this, in that they were about ordinary aches and pains or physical difficulties, and that healing prayer had a profound positive effect on these conditions.

Then he took another letter from the file, written on lined white paper, this one from a man who had suffered severe headaches. The pain medication that his doctor gave to him sometimes worked and sometimes didn't work. A friend in the parish had told him about the work of the healing priest, and suggested that he should give him a call. The letter was a thank you letter for the priest's visit. It described how the man felt a warm, calm presence when the priest anointed him with oil, laid hands on him, and prayed for healing of his headaches. He said that he had a few headaches over the next couple of days, but they were less strong, and that after a few more days, they disappeared altogether, and he was no longer plagued by them. He gave praise to Jesus Christ for healing him, and thanked the priest for caring about him.

I asked the priest at this point if he thought he was a healer. He smiled and shook his head no. He replied, "I am not a healer. Only God can heal. I am but a conduit, an instrument in human form, for God to use as He wishes." I asked him if there is healing every time he anoints with oil and lays hands on someone and prays for them. His smile returned, "Oh, no" he said, "not always." He paused as if thinking about what to say next, and then added, "I never know what God is going to do. I only know I must be faithful in doing what I can to be the best instrument for God to use." I said that I understood. I told him that some believe that if a priest or pastor is not right with God, that as a human vessel, he can block the flow of the Holy Spirit's healing power. I asked if that is what he believed. He replied that he did not know. He explained that all men sin, including priests. He said he thought that the healing power of God can use even humble or sinful priests to do His will. He smiled and his look asked me if I agreed. I said that I agreed. I explained that Martin Luther said that God uses sinful pastors to administer communion, and that the communion was valid in spite of the shortcomings of the pastor. He nodded enthusiastically that that was right, that the sacraments of God are His sacraments, and that earthly men were forgiven of their sins, and that whenever he approached someone who was ill and needed the sacrament of healing, that he spent time preparing himself, making his own personal confession of sin, so that God would cleanse him and make him his holy instrument of healing.

I was in awe of this priest's seriousness with which he approached his ministry of healing. It was obvious that he loved his people, and cared deeply about what was happening in their lives. He seemed to work tirelessly and freely for the sake of his people, and seemed to be greatly beloved by the tone of the letters he shared.

As if to show me that the same appreciation for God's work among his people was the same in each letter, he would pull a letter at random from the stack and read portions where people shared their individual circumstances, and what had happened as a result of prayer. One letter shared that there didn't seem to be much change yet from the prayers, but the writer was not discouraged because she was receiving a blessing just from the fact that a man of God was paying attention to her. This reassured her that God had not forgotten her.

Our time had come to an end. I thanked him once again for taking the time to share all of this with me. He said that it was his pleasure and he loved it that an American would be asking about his healing ministry in Augsburg. I wished him well, and said that I would pray for his continued strength to carry out his important work among his people. He replied that his strength always came from God and that this would always be his ministry.

He saw us to the door, shook hands, and said a final thank you. As I turned to go I had the impression that he deeply appreciated my visit with him as much as I appreciated his sharing with me. Later on during the day, I saw several tapestries of the historical meeting of the protestant city states and the Catholic city states meeting before King Charles V, which was to help prevent war between protestants and Catholics during the Reformation. I was to learn that Martin Luther was several hundred miles north in Coberg castle writing instructions to Philip Melanchton who was arguing the protestant case before the Emperor. Luther would send a courier by horseback from Coberg castle down to Augsburg and Philip would reply via courier.

Later I had the opportunity to visit Coberg Castle, and see the Lutherzimmer (Luther's room) as it has been preserved as an historical place of importance in German history. If you visit there, you will see the original paintings of Luther painted by Cranock which are the very images of Luther which have come down to us from the 16th century.

I was also told that at Luther's time there were dozens of dialects throughout Germany. When Luther translated the Bible into German, and this German Bible was used for educational purposes throughout Germany, that it was Luther's dialect that became the main form of the German language which we hear today. Of course, there remain various dialects throughout Germany just as there is in nearly every country. But if true, it is an interesting historical fact of how the Bible (Luther's translation into German) effected language and perhaps even culture.

I also had a thought as I drove away from the priest that afternoon that he did not need relics or saints as mediators or petitioners of the deity for healing. No, he simply made the straight connection between God's healing power and the one needing the healing. He was just the conduit he said. Another lighthouse of hope.

Chapter 35
Chimayo, the Lourdes of North America

My therapist friend, Richard said, "You know, another place you should consider visiting is Chimayo." Leila asked, "Where is Chimayo?" Richard replied, "In New Mexico, not far from Ghost Ranch." I had learned about Ghost Ranch years ago from Presbyterian therapist colleagues Cecil Hoffman and Teresa Bremer. It is a Presbyterian ranch in New Mexico, near Santa Fe, where many go to study together, work together, and explore. It is also one of the places in America where ancient dinosaur bones have been discovered.

Then Peter asked, "Is it near Santa Fe?" Richard replied again, "Yes, it is near Santa Fe and is a place of healing. They call it the "Lourdes of North America." It's a small Catholic church on Indian ground. Inside the church is holy dirt. People come from all over the world to touch the dirt and bring it back home for healing purposes. It's been said for years that the whole area has healing powers. It was a place where Native Americans came because of the healing energy in the canyons and on the plains there."

I asked, "Is it a vortex center, the kind you hear about where healing energy is a special power or force emanating from the earth?" Richard said, "Yes, I think so, at least the Indians believed it. When the priests came they said they were aware of it too. So a church was built there. Over time it became a very special place of healing. You can go into the small room where the dirt is in this hole. The entrance way is pretty small so you have to duck your head to get inside. Then when you come out you can go into this larger room and see crutches on the walls and wheelchairs of people who have had miraculous healings there. There are testimonials you can read, and there are photographs and other things left there by people who have been cured. The chapel there is quite lovely as well. When you enter into it, there is this rather grotesque sculpture of Christ in torment. He is rather distorted, and bound in pain. It is a symbol I think of what people feel when they come to Chimayo. They are bound up with pain and disease and sometimes a sense of hopelessness. But the chapel and altar are quite beautiful. There is an old priest there who came there in the 1950's, I think, and he must be in his 80's now. If you are lucky you will get to see him and maybe interview him. He is a very short man but always has this kind of twinkle in his eye. He is quite delightful really." So I added Chimayo to my list of places to visit. I would get that chance in a most unusual way.

I love reading mystery novels, and one of my favorite mystery shops where I can purchase first editions, often signed by the authors, is the Mystery Bookstore, in Westwood, California, near the UCLA (University of California, Los Angeles) campus. I received an e-mail from this shop one day, announcing upcoming authors who would sign their new books. One of the book descriptions intrigued me. It was a mystery novel (Thicker Than Blood), about a woman who owns a parking structure in Los Angeles. She finds a body in the parking lot. What she doesn't know is that the discovery of this body will lead her into a maze of intrigue, which will ultimately involve her with the powerful forces of the Department of Water and Power. Since I had seen the film Chinatown, starring Jack Nicholson years ago which was also about the water and power company of Los Angeles, I thought this sounded like a good plot. So I went down to the Mystery Bookstore to meet this author by the name of Penny Rudolph.

I got there late and was afraid I had missed her. When I entered the shop, nearly everyone had left, but the author was still there. I went up and introduced myself. She was a very pleasant lady, and we got to talking about my work, her work, about Los Angeles politics, about California, and many things. I learned that she lived in New Mexico, in Albuquerque with her husband and dog. As we spoke I asked her if she had ever heard of Chimayo.

She knew it well and we discussed it for a few minutes and then I told her that someday I wanted to visit it and told her about the book I was writing. Then she said that perhaps she could help me out a bit, and then she invited me to come to her home to meet her husband. I said, "Really? That would be wonderful!" She said that when I visited, she and her husband would show me around New Mexico. She told me of a motel I could stay at not far from the airport. We made some arrangements to meet again in Albuquerque. As I walked out of the Mystery Bookstore I was just smiling, feeling once again, that I was being led.

A few weeks later my plane touched down on the tarmac in Albuquerque. The day was bright and sunny, and the mountains that I could see as I flew in were as beautiful as I had remembered them in past years. I got my rental car and drove out to where Penny and her husband lived. Their directions were great, and I pulled up in their driveway. They greeted me at the door, and I found myself standing in a beautiful home. I met Penny's husband, and their doggie, and they offered me something to drink. They orientated me on what to see and visit and told me how to get to Chimayo. They also drove me around to see some of the canyons and rock formations around the area. We also took a hike up a great canyon and forested area. They were incredible in their hospitality and I owe them a great deal of gratitude.

I was finally on my way to Chimayo. It is located in the Santa Fe area. After traveling through the artistic part of Santa Fe. I passed by the Georgia O'Keefe art gallery. I saw many interesting sculptures along the way. Soon I found myself on a country road with what looked like Indian dwellings and partly run-down houses. Then I finally saw the signs for Chimayo. As I turned off onto the next road, I felt myself being pulled back into time, back to a simpler way of life. I was reminded of long ago when there were no paved roads, only dirt ones. I was reminded of a time when native Americans traveled to streams for the water, and later, water wells were dug in the desert. I could imagine why someone might build a church out here where the winds blew and the foothills sang of spring flowers, and trees smiled at their winter snow coverings. I parked, got out of my car, and began to make my way over to the church in the clearing. There were very few people around. I saw an older man and woman exit their car and start to walk over towards the small church. A few others sat on stumps or the ground, talking or reading. I decided to follow the older couple into the church building.

If you look up Chimayo on Wikipedia or other websites, you will learn, as I did in my personal visit, that this church site is known as the "Lourdes of North America." It has this title because of the miraculous healings which have occurred here. If you do some more research, you find that the church with its two bell towers was created on a "holy dirt" site. The Native Americans in the region believed in the healing powers of the dirt in this place. In fact, the entire region is known for its healing properties. Because of the church and holy dirt inside its walls, pilgrims from around the world come to Chimayo for healing. About 300,000 are estimated to come each year.

The main attraction is, of course, the small room to the left of the main altar, where the dirt lays inside the hole. When I reached the main sanctuary of the church, I stepped inside, saw the large sculptured figure of the Christ in pain which Richard had described to me. Then I went deeper into the church and discovered a wonderfully small beautiful sanctuary with places for pilgrims to sit, kneel, and pray before the altar which contains a statue of Jesus Christ. There were a few people here and there, deep in silent prayer. No one spoke at any time I was in this chapel. It is a holy place and the atmosphere and surroundings draw your attention to silent prayer, not speech. I took my place along the left wall and also prayed. After several minutes of prayer I opened my eyes and now only one or two persons were with me. I got up quietly, walked to the front of the alter, looked at its detail and then made my way through the entry way to the left of the chapel.

I stepped into a long rectangular room. There were objects everywhere, on walls, on the floor, just everywhere. Along the west wall were crutches hanging from the walls and standing next to cabinets. Also there were some wheel chairs, canes and other objects left behind by those who had come here to receive healing. It is a moving sight to stand and see these objects, knowing that this is not fakery. This is the visible evidence of a healing power that changed people's lives.

There are also candles and things you can purchase. It is a very busy room in that there are so many objects to take into view. I turned back to my right to see the small entrance leading to the holy dirt. I took a few steps, bent in order to enter the sacred room, and once inside, stood and looked around the room. It is a very simple box size room. Only a few paintings and art work hang on its walls.

But my eyes were drawn immediately to the center of the room. On the day I was there, perhaps because of the coloring of the weather outside, there was a kind of luminous light on the floor. There, in the center of the room, is what I and hundreds of thousands before me, had come to see: the holy dirt. I bent down, reached into the hole, and drew up dirt into my hand. It was cool to my touch. I held some in the fist of my hand, then slowly let it fall out of my hand like sands through an hour glass. It looked like plain old ordinary dirt to me.

Was this dirt imbibed with some healing powers? Was it the people's expectations of what this dirt could do that brought about healing? I had heard that some persons came here with bags, and would fill them with this dirt, and take it home with them to place on a beloved's body for healing. I had also heard that while in this room, people were known to open their clothing and rub the dirt on whatever part of their bodies were diseased or suffering. I had some history of lipoma pain (also known as Dercum's Disease also known as Adiposis Dolorosa) in my abdomen so I took some of the dirt, opened my shirt, and rubbed the dirt on my abdominal skin. I was alone in the room so I knelt in prayer, asking God to use this dirt to heal me. I felt calm in this room. There is a peace about it that is wonderful. After several minutes, I retraced my steps through the low opening, back into the large room which holds the crutches. I looked at other objects in the room, and then made my way outside.

I had not yet seen the priest who oversees Chimayo. I hung around outside under the warm New Mexico sky. I did see one man who, for some reason, looked like a local to me. He was seated by himself inside what I took for a kind of courtyard in front of the sanctuary. I walked over to him, making sure I was not disturbing him in case he was in prayer. He raised his head, aware of my presence, and I said, "Hello, are you from around here?" He smiled brightly and said, "Yes, I've lived here for many years." I asked, "Do you mind if I ask you a few questions? I am writing a book and wonder if you would allow me to interview you for a little bit?" He replied that he would be honored. He suggested we move out from underneath the sun, and he led us over to a bench west of the courtyard. We took a seat underneath a very nice shade tree where the temperature was definitely cooler. I took out my notepad and asked him if I could get his name, and if I could include things he might say in my book. He said, "Of course you may do so. This is my home. This is a healing place. I, myself, have been healed here. I would gladly tell you anything you wish." I felt thrilled to meet someone like this man.

He told me his name and said that he had come here for healing. He said that he had in fact been healed of two things. He described these to me, and told me that he has neighbors who have also been healed.

I asked him about the priest. He said that the priest was a wonderful man, who had come here sometime during the 1950's and stayed. He said that the priest was now in his '80's, was very short in stature, but has a great heart. I smiled and asked him if he was around today. He said, "Oh, of course. I just saw him fifteen minutes ago. I think he went into his office with some pilgrims. Do you wish to speak with him? Come, I will introduce him to you. He knows me."

With that he got up and led me back into the courtyard, and went into an archway, then stood outside the priest's office. His door was open and we could see he was behind his desk speaking with several people.

We waited.

The three people concluded their conversation, and it was then that I noticed there was another man in the room with the priest. As it turned out this is a companion of the priest's who assists the old man.

We stepped into the priest's office, and he said, "God bless you," and started to walk back out the door. My new friend said, "Padre, will you have five minutes for my friend, here?" pointing at me. The small priest looked up and his old eyes twinkled. He looked into my eyes and said in a soft voice, "How may I help you my son? Have you come for the Holy Dirt?" I replied, "No, Father, I have actually come to ask you a few questions for a book I am writing on prayer and healing." His eyebrows rose and then he stepped forward and said, "You are writing a book on prayer and healing?" "Yes," I replied, "And I wonder if you could tell me what you think is happening here with these healings? Is there some powerful source of healing inside of the dirt?" His voice shifted, and almost as if in a conspiratorial tone he said, "Do you want to know a secret?" I was drawn in by his presence. "Yes," I spoke softly. Without hesitation he said, "I do not believe in the dirt. I believe in the healing power of Jesus Christ. Many people come here from all over the world for the dirt. I do not think it is holy. I think it is dirt. But people believe in it. I think that the only power that heals here is the power of Jesus Christ."

I was absolutely surprised by his response. In the back of my mind I had recalled that the Catholic church in the middle ages had established a relic system whereby pilgrims would travel great distances to see a piece of the wood of the cross of Jesus, or visit the place where the Three Magi were buried, or would visit a shrine with the tears of the Holy Mother, and that pilgrims would place money into the coffers of the churches and shrines which they visited. This was perhaps, as some historians have said, the only way some of the monks were able to sustain themselves and their monasteries and convents. I do not know if this is true, but this thought occurred to me as the old priest said this to me. Did the old priest really not believe in the holy dirt yet allowed pilgrims to come from all over the world to get this dirt? It was absolutely clear by his tone and his eyes that the power of healing available from Jesus Christ was what he completely believed in.

As all these thoughts jetted through my mind, the priest continued speaking to me. "I will tell you a story. I do not think I have told this story before. But long ago, when I was a young priest here, a man brought his young son. He could not walk. His leg was paralyzed. No doctor could cure him. He brought his son for the healing dirt. They got the dirt. They used it. Nothing happened. The father was so broken hearted. His young son was disappointed. They came to see me. They asked me where the healing power is. I said to them, 'The healing power is in Jesus Christ.' The father said, 'Father, show us the way.' So I told them to come with me. They followed me right in there... to that very altar. We knelt. All three of us. I prayed for the power of Jesus Christ to heal this boy and to take away the sadness of this father. I prayed with them for many minutes. I turned to the boy's father and told him that we would see what the Lord would do. The father turned to his son and said that they should have hope. It was then I saw my first miracle. The boy got up and walked. He walked. He walked up and down the aisle. I was astonished. I shouldn't have been. I am a priest. I am supposed to believe in Jesus Christ. The father praised God. I praised God. The power is not in the dirt. It is in Jesus."

He turned to his assistant and said, "I haven't told that story before have I?" A question mark on his face. His assistant glanced at the priest, to me, then back to the priest and said, "Father, I have never heard that story before. In all the years you have held interviews, I do not remember you telling this story. It is an amazing story!"

"Yes!" said the old priest. "It was time that I tell it, and it is to you (pointing his finger at me) that I tell it to." I asked him, "May I include it in my book?" He smiled and said, "Yes, of course. If it tells people about the healing power of Jesus, put it in your book."

With that he turned away and as if dismissing us, he walked with his companion towards the door that leads back outside. As he took a step, a man appeared in his doorway. "Father," he said, "I have come from Germany. I have a man, a friend of mine, who is dying. Can I please have some of the holy dirt I have read about?" This man was holding a couple of plastic bags in his hands. The plea in his eyes was genuine. Whatever the condition was of his friend, he was desperate to try to do something about it.

The priest replied, "Bless you my son. I shall pray for your friend. Go into the sanctuary, then to the left of the altar through a small opening you will find the dirt. Take as much as you wish."

Turning back to me the priest said. "They come from all over for the dirt. They scoop lots of it out. I have the dirt replaced in the morning. There is always dirt for healing."

With that, he walked with his companion close behind, out into the hot New Mexico sun. I turned to my friend and said, "Thank you for introducing me to the priest. He is quite a man." My friend replied, "He loves the people. And I am surprised to hear the story he told you. No one has ever heard that story. When he said the power is in Jesus, not in the dirt, I was surprised." I could tell by his bewildered look that he was trying to comprehend what had been said. Then, looking at me he nodded, "I think I understand. Maybe it wasn't the dirt that healed me but Jesus Christ. Or maybe it is both. It is an amazing story."

We both walked from the priest's simple office and saw him with more pilgrims. He was pausing to have pictures taken, blessing people, and listening to their griefs and pains, sorrows and hope. He was there clearly that day standing as a lighthouse of hope.

Chimayo itself is a lighthouse of hope for hundreds of thousands of pilgrims seeking healing, coming with hope.

I spent the rest of my afternoon with my friend. He told me more stories of healing. Then he said, "Would you like to buy something to take back with you?" I said that I would love to do that. He explained how the buildings surrounding the church are co-ops and places where local people, and local Indians, make pottery and beads and objects for pilgrims. He led me into one shop being operated that day by two women.

They also told me of healings, and one of the rooms in this shop was created in memory of a young girl. Her picture and her story are on the entrance to her room. I stepped in. There are dolls and other girl's things on sale. All of them very pretty and kept very well.

When I came back to the main room, my friend said, "Come, let me show you something." He led me over to a wall that had homemade crosses hanging on this wall. He pointed to several. "I made these," he said. The shopkeeper said, 'We are very proud of his work and the work of all the native artists in our community." I asked if they were for purchase. He grinned and said, "Yes, of course!" I pointed to the two that I wanted, and the clerk took them down, brought them back to the counter, wrapped them up, and I paid for them.

We spent more time, the four of us, two shopkeepers, my friend, and myself, talking about other healings in the community. We talked about the power for faith, about the holy dirt, about God.

Here in this ancient Indian area, where native Americans believed in the power of the holy dirt long before any European set foot in this country, there was an ease talking about God, faith, and healing as naturally as if you were talking about the weather. This was not conversation for the Gringo tourist. No, this was holy talk, reverential, grounded in real people's pain and suffering, with an awe that God in His Grace, healed people and transformed their lives.

When the time came for me to leave, so that I had some daylight left to drive out of the area, I thanked them all, and told my friend to keep in touch. Later he would mail me some articles he had from his home about the history of Chimayo. I will be forever indebted to him for his kind friendship and wonderful story-telling. He too, as unknown as he is, is one of those special lighthouses, who on that day, was my beacon.

Chapter 36
Rev. Bill Dasch and Prayer for Healing

I walked into the baggage claim at Hobby Airport and immediately saw the sign with my name on it. Holding the sign was a tall, handsome man wearing a big smile. When he said, "Are you Ron?" I noticed his deep voiced Southern accent. "Welcome to Houston!" he grinned. "Let me give you a hand with that luggage," he continued. That famous Southern hospitality was in strong evidence. You could see a sparkle in his eyes when he looked at you or anyone else. I liked him instantly. We were to "bond" quickly and well.

His name is Bill Dasch, Rev. William Dasch to be precise, and he was (at the time of this first meeting) the senior pastor of St. Mark Lutheran Church, Houston, Texas. Bill had heard about my interest in prayer and healing through a colleague of mine named Rich Brumfeld. When Rich found out that St. Mark Lutheran Church had a dynamic "prayer for healing" ministry, he suggested that Bill contact me. Bill phoned me and we spoke about our mutual interests and he invited me to visit him at St. Mark's. It would be the start of a wonderful time together.

St. Mark Lutheran Church, west of downtown Houston, was a 55 year old congregation, first begun by working people and farmers from Lee County, Texas. Traditional in Lutheran ritual and values, they grew this church at a time when it was a kind of mission area west of Houston. Over time it became a church that has had several senior pastors, and has gone through a number of transitions. During my stay I would learn about the most important transition the congregation had seen to date: the transition into prayer as the central core value of its identity.

I had come into the William P. Hobby airport on Wednesday afternoon. That evening I attended the Wednesday night service. It was a low key, warm, inviting informal service of easy music, scripture readings, and prayerful comments by Pastor Dave Schultz. A young, talented musician sat at the keyboard and led the small gathering of people through old and new music. When Pastor Dave invited the people gathered to sing I Am Jesus'

Little Lamb, he turned to the young musician and asked him to start. The young man, perhaps a little embarrassed said, "I don't know it."
Pastor Dave chuckled and said something about how one could tell that there were different generations here. I think in the Lutheran Church you would find that nearly everyone over the age of 40 knows I Am Jesus' Little Lamb. I don't know how old the young musician was but it was clear that he was perhaps a middle to late 20's person, and that clearly, this small little event in this worship service pre-signalled another possible sign of transition as St. Mark's attempted to relate to an entirely new generation of young Christians.
At the conclusion of this evening service of praise and prayer, the prayer teams of St. Mark's Lutheran Church moved down front in preparation for any who wished to receive prayer for any situation they were facing in life. A number of persons came down to the prayer teams after the conclusion of the service. Since I had been experiencing some discomfort from the rare disease I have, called Dercum's Disease, I decided to walk down to the foot of the altar steps to receive prayer as well. *(see Photography section)*
The prayer teams at St. Mark's are highly trained and very welcoming. They greet you with smiles and surround you with the presence of God. They listen carefully to the prayer request, and they are very respectful of the need placed before them. They ask you a single question, "What would you like Jesus to do for you tonight?" The question focuses you immediately on a relationship between Jesus and the one being prayed for. It signals that members of the prayer team do not have their egos involved in this process at all. They are very clear that it is Jesus who does the "work of healing". They see themselves as people of God who believe that God can do anything. They offer fervent prayer that the power of Jesus will meet the need of the person needing prayer. They do not pretend to know what will happen nor do they predict outcomes or raise unrealistic expectations. After receiving the specific prayer request, they ask if they can touch the person being prayed for, and if given permission, they place a hand on a shoulder or back or above the place on the body where there is a physical malady or disease.

Each member of the prayer team, if so moved, offers a three part simple prayer. The first part gives adoration to God, the second part is a prayer for the concerns specifically requested by the petitioner, which is followed by the third part of the prayer which is thanksgiving to God. In following these three part prayers, prayer team members are asking for God's healing presence and that Jesus would meet the need of the request.

In my own case my prayer team asked me, "What would you like Jesus to do for you tonight?" and I told them of my disease, my discomfort, and asked that the pain be removed so that I would not be distracted from the purpose of my trip. One of the team members asked if they might place a hand on my abdomen where I had the discomfort. I said, "Yes, of course." She placed a hand on my shoulder and on my abdomen. Another person stood behind me and placed her hands on my back. Another team member placed a hand on my other shoulder and my arm. I could feel heat emanating from the prayer team member on my left... heat that warmed the area of my abdomen that had been hurting me for the past 8 months. This was not the first time that I had asked for prayer for healing, but it was the first time that I felt the heat on the direct spot affected. (I would later learn that often the person who is praying with what feels like hands of heat, actually has cold hands, and that prayers are still effective even if the petitioner feels no heat from any hands laid upon him or her). Each person prayed for me in their own way. It felt good to be surrounded by people of prayer. I felt calmer and more relaxed as they prayed for me. I could actually feel the discomfort being alleviated during their prayer. It felt good to have the stinging sensation so common with my disease just fade away. I felt just a little tearful from gratitude that the symptom was fading. Following the prayer time, I was taken back to a new hotel in town that they had arranged for me to stay at, and I slept deeply that night without awakening in the middle of the night from disease symptoms.

The next day I met Rev. Dave Schultz, associate pastor on the staff of St. Mark's. Pastor Dave shared with me that he is a strong believer in the power of prayer. I asked him how he first got into prayer for healing, and he chuckled and said that it happened sort of by accident. Early in his ministry he went to make a hospital visit on a young girl who was extremely ill. The girl's mother asked Dave to lay hands on her and anoint her with oil. No one had ever asked Pastor Dave to do this, and it had not been part of his seminary training. He sort of gulped and let her know that he didn't carry oil with him (he now does everywhere he goes). The mother challenged him by saying she had read in the New Testament that the laying on of hands and the anointing with oil was part of the healing ministry of the church as recorded in the book of James (in the New Testament). Dave said that was true, so he went to a grocery store and bought some simple cooking oil, returned to the hospital, anointed the girl with oil on her forehead, laid hands on the girl, and prayed for her healing. A week or so later he learned that the girl was much better. Not long afterwards another family who knew about this healing also called for Dave to come over and lay on hands and anoint with oil. This time he had the oil and he went over and laid on hands and prayed for healing. Again, a few days later he learned that this patient also was improving.

I asked Pastor Dave (who at the time had been in pastoral ministry nearly 40 years) what his thinking was about healing. He said, "I believe that healing takes place through Medicine, Miracle or Mercy. We don't know what God will do. Sometimes He heals through the physicians and nurses and medicines and medical procedures. Sometimes we see a miracle, something that the doctors cannot explain... that's happened many times in my ministry. Sometimes it is God's mercy in that he takes the loved one home to Heaven. That can be a healing too."

Pastor Dave strongly believes that where two or three gather together for prayer and are in absolute agreement that something definitely happens from that prayer.

Pastor Bill Dasch and Pastor Dave Schultz are both powerful men of prayer. It is through their dynamic leadership that St. Mark's has sustained a powerful prayer team. They are joined by Katie Toon, a layperson, who also began to pray for healing out of necessity. She found that God answered her prayers, and she became more interested in learning more about prayer. Over the years she has gone on to become a very fine student of prayer. She has received prayer training from a variety of persons. She has completed the first, second and third training sessions offered by Francis and Judith MacNutt of Christian Healing Ministries of Jacksonville, Florida. She has also been trained in Theophostic prayer through which she has seen powerful evidence of God's transforming lives.

During the congregational meeting held on Sunday while I was there, Katie spoke gently and encouragingly to the members about prayer and healing at St. Mark's. One of the stories she told was powerful. She said that she had heard a story about people's relationship with Jesus being sort of like having a car and wondering where Jesus fits into that car. She said that for some people a relationship with Jesus is like driving down a road and passing Jesus who is standing on the side of the road. You wave at Jesus and He waves back. But some people have Jesus in the trunk of the car. If you need him like during an emergency then you take him out of the trunk and use him like a jack or a spare tire or flares. Some people have Jesus in the back seat of the car. He isn't a back seat driver, He just sits there and looks out the window and watches the countryside pass by. He doesn't say much but he's sort of nice to have along for company. Some people have Jesus sort of hanging over the seat of the car... just sort of watching what's going on. Then there are some people who have Jesus on the passenger side. He isn't driving the car. He is just a companion who may not say much but he's up there in the second seat. We are in charge, he isn't. But he wants to drive the car. That's what he wants to do. One person that Katie worked with was shocked to learn that Jesus wanted to drive the car, to be in charge of her life. It had never occurred to this person that Jesus might want to drive her car. Katie talks about what it is like when Jesus is driving the car of one's life. Sometimes He takes us to new places and into new experiences. But life becomes exciting and interesting when you know that Jesus is in charge. We have to surrender to him, and often we don't want to do that. We don't want to give up control.

There are several powerful stories on a video of testimonies that Pastor Bill Dasch sent to me before I visited. Members of St. Mark's report their healing stories on camera. There are many. One of the most dramatic stories is of a young man who lay in a deep coma for weeks. Three out of four doctors finally agreed it was time to harvest this young man's organs. Needless to say the family was extremely reluctant to do this. They were filled with sadness, fear, uncertainty. One doctor said, "OK, let's give it one more day." At this point, a family member called Pastor Bill to come over and pray for healing.

Pastor Bill arrived and stood by the young man's bedside. He laid his hands on the man and within a few seconds the boy sat up in bed and opened his eyes. Pastor Bill says he jumped back four feet! The boy wanted to speak but the tubes in his mouth prevented this. Everyone in the room was astounded! The doctors couldn't believe their eyes. Pastor Bill told me that on that day, he didn't want to give the family false hope by praying for the boy. But he also believes that anything can happen when you pray for healing. He also wanted to honor the family's wishes. So he anointed the young man with oil, laid hands on him and prayed for healing. What happened was the most dramatic moment to date in Pastor Bill's ministry of prayer.

On that video were other testimonials of healing. Each person healed spoke simply about what had led them to ask for healing prayer and what happened afterwards. They were not as dramatic, perhaps, as the story above, but each person was truly grateful for the prayers on their behalf.

I came away from that first visit to St. Mark's with a new awe for the power of prayer in Jesus' name. I liked the three part prayer for its adoration and thanksgiving to God, and that the prayer team members prayed exactly for what was requested, not adding or subtracting from the petitioner's response to the question, "What would you like Jesus to do for you?"

I also liked the honesty, when prior to prayer time, the pastors and prayer team leaders say that they did not know what will happen as a result of prayer. They simply say that they believed God wants His people to pray for others, and that for them, Jesus is the healer, not them. They are only the hands of God carrying out His command to pray for healing.

I recalled the teachings of Jesus from the New Testament. There he taught His disciples to preach, teach, and heal. In the Gospels there are many examples of Jesus' healing ministry. (See the Appendix). In the book of Acts one reads of the healing acts of the Apostles. Beyond the first century, there are further testimonies of early church fathers reporting healings. Down through the centuries, other Christians have anointed with oil, laid on hands, and prayed for healing.

And there in Texas, I heard of another group of Christians learning how to pray for healing, and some of the results of those healing prayers.

It would not be the last time I would learn from Pastor Bill Dasch. Later he and I would host 16 prayer seminars over nine days in the Pacific Southwest District of the Lutheran Church - Missouri Synod. Later still he and I would host our first national training at the Reclaim Conference held at St. John's Lutheran Church, Mansfield, Texas, the next congregation Pastor Dasch would be called to serve. There we would bring together many speakers and gather together many who were eager to hear how to reclaim the healing power of Jesus. That experience is documented elsewhere in this book.

Chapter 37
My Personal Story of Healing Prayer

My study sabbatical officially ended in 2001 but I decided to continue to read about prayer, healing and psychoneuroimmunology. Little did I know that I personally would be in need of healing prayer in the not too distant future. My ordeal began when I noticed pain in my abdominal area, just beneath the skin. At first I thought it might be a bout of shingles since I had known of this painful condition from friends who had experienced it. I looked it up on the Internet but the descriptions didn't quite match my symptoms. So I decided to make an appointment with a doctor at Kaiser hospital, under my health insurance.

The physician I met with was young and very personable. While I waited in one of the treatment rooms for his arrival, I read some of his Certificates on the wall, describing where he had gone to school, and his degrees. I was impressed. I would later discover he was in the top of his medical school class at UCLA, the University of California, Los Angeles, Medical School, one of the best in the country.

He finally arrived, greeted me, and asked me what was the problem. I told him that sometimes I could feel little rice-like nodules just beneath the surface of my skin and that they were beginning to cause significant pain. He had me take off my shirt, examined my skin, and could not feel the tiny rice-like objects I had described. I could no longer feel them either but I could still feel the pain. He ran some tests, took some blood, and we rescheduled.

I soon discovered that the pain increased, and that it was becoming increasingly difficult to work or concentrate. Chronic pain can become so debilitating. I called to return to see the physician as soon as possible. A week or so later I went in again. Once again the doctor was unable to find the cause of this pain. Nothing had shown up in the lab work. It didn't match any condition with which he was familiar. I went home that day with some pain killer pills, but I was no closer to understanding what I was dealing with. The doctor did say, however, that the next time I was in pain and could feel the tiny objects beneath the skin of my abdomen, to come directly to his office, and by-pass the regular waiting room procedures.

A week or so later, I was in great pain. I was in so much pain I was on the verge of tears. So I decided to go in on Monday morning. When Monday came, I could feel the tiny objects shaped like rice that had resurfaced just beneath my skin. I could barely drive to the medical center. I went directly to my physician's office and he came into the medical room immediately. He had me take my shirt off promptly and placed his fingers on my abdomen. "I can feel them," he said. His fingers moved across my belly, then up higher and then lower. "I can feel nine of them," he said, his eyes peering at where his fingers were moving. "I don't know what this is," he said. I told him that I had looked up "the abdomen" on the Internet and had discovered that there were seven layers of skin before reaching the abdominal cavity and that this felt as if the rice size nodules were in between the 4th and 5th layers of skin. He nodded and smiled slightly, "Yes that is where they seem to be. Its as if these things are along the nerve endings in the skin." Then he paused and said, "I will be right back," and left the room. A few minutes later he returned. "I have just spoken with a colleague of mine, and I told him my hunch and he agreed. I think these are lipomas. But they don't usually become inflamed or diseased." I asked him, "How do you spell it?" He replied, "L - I - P - O - M - A. They are all over the body in many people. I can give you some stronger pain medication. I will have to do some research on this condition."

I thanked him, had his prescription filled, and left his office grateful that he had given me a clue as to what this might be. That night I went again to the Internet and typed in two words together: "lipoma" and "nerve." When I hit the search button, nine websites came up. One of them was a description of the physician who discovered Dercum's Disease. A French doctor had discovered this condition over a hundred years ago, where small lipomas became painful and grew, sometimes to the size of oranges, grapefruits, and in untreated patients, to the size of watermelons!! My God I thought. Is this what I have? The website said it was almost always a condition in women and rarely in men. The more I read about the symptoms, the more convinced I became that this was the disease I had. I looked it up on the Center for Disease Control website and discovered it was on the rare disease list. Oh great, I thought to myself, leave it to me to somehow get a rare disease!

I looked at the other websites, and none gave me much more information. One of the sites was an oncology site, so I clicked on it. It was the website of a physician in Orange County, California, who was a specialist in cancer. I scrolled down through the various cancers described on his website, and then suddenly, on the list, was the condition of Dercum's Disease. Was this a form of cancer, I wondered? I could barely move from the pain level increase. This was a Friday night and I spent most of the weekend in bed fighting the pain. But on Saturday morning I called the doctor's office, and made an appointment for Monday morning. He did not take insurance and the cost would be $400 for a half hour consultation. At this point, the money was no longer of concern. I was in pain, not sure I could ever work again. I had to find out if there was a treatment for this condition. I would pay any price to get this taken care of.

With great difficulty, I drove down to his office in Laguna Beach. When I finally arrived at his receptionist's window, I was nearly doubled over in pain. She said the doctor would see me immediately. I was ushered into a room. Within a minute the doctor came in. He was tall, thin, an older man with wise and kind eyes. "So I hear you think you have Dercum's Disease. That's rare for a man. Let's have a look." He helped me take off my shirt, had me lay back on the bed, and began to run his fingers across my belly and said, "Oh yes, I can feel them. I think you are right." Then he said, "You don't mind if I explore your skin elsewhere do you?" I replied, "Please, anywhere you want to look." He could tell I was in pain. He checked my back, chest, legs, and whenever he would discover more lipomas he would show me where they were. Those on my legs and elsewhere were not in pain. He explained that many people, probably all people, have lipomas but they never become inflamed. He explained that mine were, and then he had me put my clothes back on and said, "Come next door to my office and we'll discuss this."

I got dressed, made my way to his office, took at seat next to his desk and he took a chair and placed it in front of his desk so he could talk directly to me. He handed me a sheet with all the known treatments for this condition. He also told me that there were probably not more than seven physicians in the country who really knew this condition well. He told me that lipomas are mainly found in red fat, not white fat. I had never heard of red fat. He then told me the Latin title for this disease and it literally means "red fat." He also told me that it tends to run in Germanic people. He also stated that it probably went back to Neolithic man and described how he thinks of the disease as coming down through hundreds of centuries. He said that my lipomas were too small for surgery. He also thought that the best treatment for me was a antidepressant drug which had pain killer properties. He told me to take the next few days off, because the drug he was recommending would probably kill the pain but also knock me out.

I looked down the list of perhaps 17 different treatments for the disease. Then I said, "You know, there is one treatment that you don't have on the list." He raised an eyebrow, and said, "What is it?" I said with a pained smile, "prayer." "Ahh," he said, "I believe in the power of prayer. If you know of some people who can lay hands on you and pray for you, I would recommend that in addition to the medication I am going to give to you. I have seen remarkable things happen through the power of prayer. Go and do that."

I thanked him greatly for his help. When I went to pay for my visit, I noticed that the doctor had spent and hour and a half with me, not the half hour consultation first stated. I knew I was going to have to pay more for the time but it was worth it. I had brought cash with me. I placed four, one-hundred dollar bills on the counter. The receptionist only took three of the bills. I said, "But I've been here an hour and a half and I was told it would be $400 for a half hour consult." She smiled and replied, "He likes you. He only wants $300." I could not believe it!! I paid my bill and left.

When I got home I took the first of the pills prescribed. I was very sensitive to it and slept all night and through the next day as if I were dead. I could not tolerate the full dosage, and I called the doctor's office and they advised me to take half a pill. That would still make me drowsy and help me to sleep. While sleeping I had no pain. But upon waking the pain would come back although sometimes at a lesser degree.

About a week later, I ran into a friend of mine, David Kruger, at a conference. He and I sat down for a drink and he invited Rev. Tom Rogers over to join us. Tom listened with great interest to my story about the pain. Then he invited me to his church. He explained that they would write a healing service for me. I could not believe it! He said that they had a healing tradition, and that the men of his church would be very willing to come out and pray for me. That is exactly what happened.

I drove down one evening soon after that meeting, and Tom had written a beautiful prayer and healing service in my honor. Several men of his congregation came and assisted him. When the time came, after worship and praise, Tom and the other members of his church surrounded me and laid hands on me, and prayed for my healing. Each man in turn prayed for me. I was profoundly moved and grateful for what they did for me that night. During the prayers the pain subsided. It was amazing. I drove home that night without pain. Gratefully, I would remain pain free for several more days. Then the pain began to return as did the lipomas beneath the skin.

I continued to battle the pain for another two weeks. I was able to work most days while tolerating the pain. Then one afternoon I made an announcement following a circuit counselor's clergy gathering in which I also made reference to an upcoming district meeting where I was going to speak on prayer and healing. My announcement was the last one for the day, and I noticed a pastor hung around for a few minutes afterwards. He introduced himself to me. He said his name was Jess Knauft and that he had done some study of healing.

I told him briefly about my study sabbatical on prayer, healing and psychoneuroimmunology, and then I told him about my battle with the pain from my lipomas, telling him that what the doctors had been able to do so far was limited, and that I needed to find a place where I could go for some healing prayer.

He smiled and said, "I think I know just the place. Do you have the rest of the afternoon free?" "Sure," I said, "Why?" He replied, "I have a friend, an Episcopal priest who does healing prayer down in Oceanside. Let me make a phone call and see if he is in." I was astonished that this "coincidence" was happening. Or was it a coincidence at all?

Jess made his phone call, then turned back to me. "It's all set," he said. "Come on, I'll drive," he continued. We left my car there and we walked to his car. Once inside Jess began to fill me in on the history of his own research on healing and prayer. He asked me if I had ever read Morton Kelsey. I told him that Kelsey's book on Healing and Christianity was the first book I read during my sabbatical. "Great book, isn't it?" he asked as we pulled out onto the highway. "Kelsey had this secretary who helped edit all of his books," Jess said. I replied, "I know, I saw he always thanked her in his books for her tireless dedication to his manuscripts." "Yes," said Jess. Switching lanes he said, "Her son is in my praise band at my church. He plays bass guitar and is at all of our healing services." (Later I would learn that his name is Fred Roach, and that his mother was not just Kelsey's secretary, but she was the major researcher for Kelsy's books.) "Morton Kelsey's secretary's son plays in your praise band at your healing services?" I asked incredulously. "Yeah, that's something isn't it," he replied. Again I was a bit overwhelmed. "I didn't know you have healing services at your church," I responded. "Yes, I think it's a really important ministry that we let get away from us over the years," Jess said. Later I would discover at least nine churches in my own denomination in Southern California that held healing services regularly or upon occasion.

We continued to discuss the history of healing, why it was not taught at the seminary where both he and I had graduated. Finally we arrived at the healing center in Oceanside. I followed Jess inside and he introduced me to his Episcopal priest friend. I liked him right away. He invited us to see the facility where he worked. The center of his ministry there was a healing ministry.. Then he took us into his office where we became better acquainted. He shared his story of how he became involved in healing ministry, and the breadth of the work done in this place. Eventually, he invited Jess and me to a place where there was an altar. The plan was that each of us would kneel before the altar, while the other two would lay hands on the one kneeling and pray for him. He said it was important to pray exactly for what the petitioner requested. We agreed. Jess said he would go first. He knelt and I joined the priest in front of the altar while Jess got to his knees in prayer. The priest asked Jess what he needed prayer for. Jess said what was on his heart. Then the priest laid hands upon Jess's head and prayed for the issue Jess had identified as his wish for prayer. When the priest was done praying, it was my turn to pray for Jess. I laid my hands upon Jess's head and prayed for his concern.

Next came my turn. I knelt before the priest and Jess. I asked for prayer for complete pain relief, and complete healing of the lipoma disease. Jess began by laying his hands on my head and offering one of the best prayers I have ever heard, and it was for me personally. As he prayed, the pain in my abdomen began to lessen. Soon the pain was half what it was. When Jess finished his prayer, the priest laid hands on my head and prayed for me. The pain in my abdomen decreased more. I kept thanking God for what he was doing to heal me, even as the priest continued praying over me. Again, the priest's words were soothing, encouraging, uplifting as he asked God for healing and wholeness in my body and in my life. When he had completed his prayer, I rose and took my place next to Jess. It was the priest's turn to kneel in prayer and to state what he wished prayer for today. Jess led by laying on of hands and praying for healing. When he was done I did the same thing for the priest.

Afterwards we thanked each other and spent some more time talking about the ministry there in Oceanside and its future. While we talked I noticed that I had no more pain. I wondered if it would come back again later as it had done previously.

When our visit was over, we thanked the priest and went north out of Oceanside back to where my car was parked up at the other facility. I thanked Jess for introducing me to his friend, and for the opportunity to receive healing prayer. He invited me to come to his church some Sunday and to participate in his congregation's healing prayer service, and to meet Morton Kelsey's secretary's son. I agreed I would do that, and later on I did attend worship there and meet the secretary's son.

I drove home that night without any abdominal pain. When I got home I checked to see if I could feel any of the lipomas. I couldn't feel any of them. I slept very well that night.

The next day, and the day after that, I still had no pain and no symptoms whatsoever associated with the disease.

That was several years ago. Since that prayer time with the Episcopal priest, I have never had the lipomas return nor have I had any pain in my abdomen. I praise God for it.

One of the lessons I take away from this experience is that healing is sometimes gradual. We sometimes think that healing should be instant. It doesn't always work that way. Sometimes it takes multiple times of healing prayer before a particular symptom decreases or disappears altogether. Sometimes the symptoms or the disease do not go away in spite of our best efforts at healing prayer. There is no set pattern to these things. Much of it still is a mystery.

I was recently at a workshop put on by the California Association of Marriage and Family Therapists, a professional organization to which I belong, and the speaker was making a presentation on the effectiveness of our work as Marriage and Family therapists. He asked a question, "Do you know how effective medicine is?" Then he posted a slide which showed that medicine is about 43% effective overall. Less than half of the time, medicine works the way it should. Then he asked, "Do you know how effective counseling therapy is?" He posted another slide showing the research that talking therapy was about 43% effective. You could begin to hear some of the soft laughter through the room. "Yes," said the speaker, "Your work and mine is just as effective as medicine." Then he asked a third question, "Do you know how effective prayer is?" He added that you don't have to be of a particular religious persuasion and that he was not here to try to convert anyone to anything. He just wanted us to see things in perspective. Medicine is 43% effective and psychotherapy is 43% effective, he said. "How effective is prayer?" he asked. He posted a slide. "Prayer is 44% effective." Then he went on to say something similar which I had heard Larry Dossey say and it is this: Nothing works 100% of the time. Medicine, psychotherapy or prayer in the opinions of significant researchers is not always effective. Just as some medicines do not work for some patients, some psychotherapy doesn't work for some clients. Some researchers believe that prayer is a similar situation. Prayer does work, but like medicine or psychotherapy, it doesn't work all of the time for all of the people praying. Sometimes prayer works instantaneously, sometimes it works gradually, and perhaps sometimes it is not effective at all.

What should we do then? My answer: keep praying. One of Larry Dossey's books is entitled, Prayer is Good Medicine. Dr. Dale Matthew's book called The Faith Factor has a chapter entitled "Prayer and Prozac." The emphasis is on the "both and", both prayer and Prozac. If prayer is good medicine then why can it not be combined with other medicine? Why not as Dale Matthews, a Christian physician, is suggesting that we not take prayer and Prozac together? For that matter if a patient can take one pill for a headache, and another tablet for his ulcer, and another medication for his arthritis, why can we not combine medications, prayer and psychotherapy. Each of these separately works some of the time for some of the people. Why not do them in combination? I was taking pain pills for my lipoma, receiving healing prayer, and was talking with a few psychotherapy colleagues about my thoughts and feelings during my painful condition. Their unconditional love and support in combination with the medication and the healing prayer felt like the right thing for me to do.

The point here is not to limit yourself just to healing prayer. See your physician. Talk to a good psychotherapist or trusted counselor. And go where you can have people of prayer lay hands on you and pray for your healing as well.

One other thing: To hear that prayer is sometimes "ineffective" as some researchers say, is certainly a challenging issue for those who are religious, particularly those who are Christian. We are not used to thinking that prayer is ineffective. In fact there are some who believe that even trying to do research on prayer is not a good idea.

Be that as it may, Christians believe that God hears prayer and answers prayer. The answer is either "yes" or "no" or "not yet." Still we pray our petitions. Luther, when he prayed for his friend and colleague, Melancthon, said he would hold God to his promises to answer prayer in the affirmative. Christians may not think of prayer as medicine, and wonder what is wrong with those guys who try to do research on prayer and healing. On the other hand, I find it somewhat reassuring that research shows that medicine and psychotherapy are not always effective, and my own experience of people in prayer is that they do not always receive an answer or an answer that they want (is that the same as saying prayer is as effective as medicine or psychotherapy, that is, it works but not all the time?). For Christians the point of reference is God. God answers either yes, no or not yet. For researchers the point of reference does not seem to be God but rather it is on the effectiveness of prayer. Is taking a pill the same as saying a prayer? No not at all. But we do want to believe in the effectiveness of the medicine we receive. And we do want to believe that there is a God who listens to our prayers, who loves us, and does answer our petitions.

For me, the lesson in all of this was patience. In the midst of the relentless pain there were times I wanted to give up, to resign my work, to just lay in bed all day, suffering. I pushed myself through the pain and did what I could to continue working while seeking good solid medical advice, which we should always do. My doctors were compassionate and helpful. The medications that they prescribed worked reasonably well but in a limited way. My first attempts with healing prayer seemed to work temporarily. But I was not going to give up. I had read in one of my books on healing prayer that sometimes the healing comes gradually. I held onto that belief.

I thank Jess and his priest friend for taking the time to pray with me, for me, and to offer relentless hope for a positive outcome. Over time I believe I was healed by prayer. It was not my faith or lack thereof that healed me. It was a gracious and loving God who wasn't done with me yet, had more work for me to do, and removed my disease and my symptoms. I thank and praise God for the relief and the opportunity to give witness to His tender mercies.

* * *

I graduated from Concordia Seminary, in St. Louis, in the spring of 1973. I had taken no courses on prayer or healing because there were none offered. The term "psychoneuroimmunology" had not yet been coined. There was a sort of shunning of anything that smacked of the "charismatic" so there really was no one looking into the gifts of the Spirit or what those might have to do with healing in the world today. And of course, the seminary, in fact the very church body that I was in was in the midst of a huge firestorm over the methods used in Biblical interpretation (the historical-critical method was under attack at the seminary where I was trained). While we seminary students were taught how to preach well under the rubric of "Goal, Malady and Means" or "Problem, Point, Power" methods, I had not done any deep study whatsoever of the healing stories in the New Testament, nor had I done any research of the miracles done or seen by the early Church Fathers (after the first century). Like most people, I had experienced some physical trauma in the form of accidents which were painful and scary. During my study sabbatical I was drawn back to consider these once again. The first event was when I slid a broken test tube into my right wrist, by accident, when I tried to avoid the plastic bullets my little brother was shooting at me at the time. I was in the 7th grade, and my parents had gotten me a chemistry set. During an experiment I dropped one of the glass test tubes. When the test tube struck the cement slab where I was working, the top of the test tube shattered, leaving a sharp jagged edge around the top of the glass tube. Even though I should have thrown it away, I kept using it for new bubbling experiments, being very careful with it so as to not cut myself.

Then one afternoon I was walking along the side of my house towards the rear kitchen door to show my mother one of my experiments that was bubbling in the broken tube. Suddenly my brother, Leroy, came out from behind a bush, shooting at me with his new six-shooter gun which shot plastic bullets. As he blazed away at me, I dodged the bullets, but slipped on the sidewalk and fell, and somehow managed to run the test tube into my right wrist. Blood began to spurt everywhere. I dropped the test tube and ran to the side door holding my torn wrist as best as I could. I yanked open the side door and yelled, "Mom! Mom! come quickly!" I could hear the vacuum cleaner in the other room and my mother's voice calling out, "Just a minute, honey." I yelled back, "Mom, I'm bleeding, come, hurry!" I heard her drop the vacuum hose and run into the kitchen into which the side door opened from the outside sidewalk. She saw the blood erupting from my wrist, and immediately turned me around and grabbed a dish rag and her keys and we ran to the car. Quickly we got inside, and she ordered me to press the dish rag very hard at the base of the deep cut. She then shakily put her car keys into the ignition, started the car, jerked it into first gear and off we went, driving faster than I had ever seen her drive. I pressed the dish rag as hard as I could, trying to stop the bleeding, trying desperately to hold my skin together. Suddenly we were at the single car underpass which led to the other side of town where the doctor's office was located. Without hesitation, even though other cars were about to enter the single car tunnel from the opposite direction, she pounded her car horn loudly and blasted on through the tunnel. I was amazed that the cars on the other side of the tunnel stopped quickly! They must have thought her a mad woman.

We got to the doctor's office within a few minutes. Rushing out of the car ahead of me she went through the doctor's office door. The doctor came out immediately, did a quick look at my wrist, and ushered me into a room. I watched as he looked down into the parted skin. I had never seen skin apart like this so it made me a bit queasy. He sighed a sigh of relief. "The cut came close to the artery, but it didn't penetrate it. You are going to be fine." So he gave me a shot to relieve some pain, and went about stitching my wrist. I still have that scar today.

I went home, and after a matter of days, I returned to the doctor's office to have the stitches removed.

It completely healed.

I had not done any praying about this situation. Somehow my body knew how to heal itself. I took that for granted then. I was a good baseball player, throwing right handed and batting right handed. This scar on my wrist didn't interfere with baseball or anything else. I just never stopped to think about how my body knew how to heal itself.

The next event was during one of my high school football games. I had kicked off the second half of the game, and the receiver of the kick managed to run up the sidelines, eluding all of our tacklers. I was the last guy left between he and the goal.

As I lunged to make the saving tackle, I felt someone suddenly crash into the backside of my right knee. My body was moving upwards to make the tackle while my lower leg was being pushed towards the ground as I was clipped from behind. My knee gave way. I crashed to the ground, and tried to get up, but I couldn't put any weight on my right knee. I was in great pain and couldn't get up. Teammates came over, and I told them that I couldn't walk. My coach ran over. After examining me, he called an ambulance. I was carried off the field on a stretcher.

A day or so later I was having surgery done on my right knee. I think it was called a meniominiscectomy. The meniscus had torn and had to be removed. I was devastated. My football, baseball, and basketball interests were being dashed to the ground.

My leg was placed in a cast. I still remember clearly the physical weight lifting I had to do to re-strengthen this leg.

But once again, I didn't do any praying over it. I just followed the physician's directions, and the knee recovered, and although I missed out on the basketball and baseball seasons, the knee was good enough for the next season of high school football.

Somehow the body knew how to recover.

Unfortunately, during a church league basketball game, I was slammed hard into the pole holding the basketball net, came down hard onto the floor, and tore my knee again. That was the end of my sports career.

I completed high school, college, seminary, got married, and adopted a new born baby, and named him Matthew. Two years later we discovered that my wife was pregnant, and God gave us a little girl. We named her Kimberly.

One night my wife and I and our two little children went to a store. After getting out of the car, I placed my son on my shoulders. He loved this. My wife did likewise, placing our daughter (who was about two at the time) on her shoulders. I was ahead of them by a few feet when I heard a thud. I turned and saw my wife laying on her side, trying to keep our daughter's head from hitting the cement. She had slipped in an oil slick. Kimberly was crying. My wife was terrified, got up with our daughter, and together we walked over to stand underneath the outside lights of the store to examine Kim. There didn't seem to be any swelling or any unusual marks. We were relieved.

But our relief was short-lived. Unknown to us, our daughter's head had in fact hit the cement. Within a few days my wife woke up to find our daughter laying in a fetal position on the couch. My wife asked her what was wrong and cradled her in her arms. That's when she felt the lump on Kim's skull.

I had already gone into Los Angeles to teach a class for California Lutheran College when the phone call came that my wife had found this lump and was extremely worried. I told her to take our daughter to our pediatrician right away and call me when she knew something.

A little more than an hour later, my wife called again. The pediatrician was sure it was a hematoma, and that a blood clot had formed. He told her to get to the specialist he recommended and to do it right away. I was scared when I heard this bad news. I turned my class over to Agnes McClain, my assistant, and drove out to the San Gabriel Valley to the specialist's office. He had done a preliminary exam and wanted to do a CAT scan. We went with him into his lab, and we watched our little girl being placed into the machine for the CAT scan.

We watched as they injected the dyes, and watched the monitors as dozens of pictures of our daughter's scull began to appear. My wife grew faint and we had to step out for a while.

After the procedure was done, we returned to the specialist's office. He went around his room placing the pictures of our daughter's head condition on screens that illuminated the pictures from behind. Then he moved us closer to some of these pictures and showed us that there was in fact a double hematoma. He told us that an operation was necessary immediately. He said we had two choices: we could have him do the surgery now although he had just done some and was not feeling at his best, or we could have him get a good night sleep and do the surgery first thing in the morning. He told us that already one side of her body was non-responsive so that tomorrow would be the latest he could do the surgery. He also told us the odds of a safe surgery, and some of the possible things that could happen as she grew older as a result of this surgery. He was very honest and we could feel his genuine compassion and empathy for what we were facing. We had complete confidence in him.

My wife and I decided it would be best for him to do the surgery in the morning. We left our daughter in his good hands, and traveled home.

We called our good friend Wahli Vanstrom. She had had several terrible tragedies in her own life, including the death of a first husband, as well as the death of her son when he was young (I think he was 7). We called her for prayer. Somehow we intuitively knew that we needed someone who had been through the valley of the shadow of death. She agreed immediately to meet us early the next morning at the hospital at our daughter's hospital room.

I didn't sleep much that night. I prayed as I had never prayed before. I prayed for a good outcome but I also prayed for our doctor and nurses who would do their best. I prayed for my wife to help her see this through. I prayed for myself, that no matter what happened in the morning, that He would be with me. I prayed then for my daughter, and I placed her in His hands. Whatever happened, I was giving my daughter's life to Him. It has always been His anyway.

We went to the hospital early the next morning. Wahli Vanstram was already there, standing outside Kim's hospital door. When she saw us coming down the hallway she had tears in her eyes. She hugged my wife, then hugged me, and said that she had already been praying for Kim and for us. Then she paused and spoke much quieter, "I don't know if you remember that my little boy died years ago." We said we remembered. Then she said, "What makes this so important to me is that my little boy died in this very hospital, and the last time I saw him alive he was in this room, in the bed Kim is in." I felt a shiver go through me. Here we had asked her for prayer, and now she stood at the very place where she last saw her son alive.

Then Wahli looked at us and said, "In a few moments Kim is going to go through those double doors into the operating room. I remember watching my boy wheeled through those doors, and I remember praying for him. God decided to take him home, and I didn't get to see him alive again. Now the three of us are going to pray together when Kim is wheeled through those doors. God will be with her no matter what. He will be with us too, no matter what." Tears rolled down our eyes, all three of us arm in arm stood in a tiny circle with prayers on our lips and in our hearts.

A little while longer, the orderlies came and took our two-year old child through those double doors. It was a moment in which I was aware as I have never been, that life is fragile and that I had to handle it with prayer. "Thy will be done, Lord," I whispered.

We went into the waiting area and the hours slowly ticked away. After two and a half hours the doctor came down the hallway in his scrubs. He was wearing no expression on his face.

He got to us and we rose and he said, "The surgery went well, and we were able to relieve the pressure. Your little girl now has a hole in her skull about the size of a quarter. She will be in intensive care for a few days. Why don't you go home and get some sleep."

We thanked him which seems such a trite thing to do, knowing what a great service he provided. He reassured us, "I think she is going to be fine."

And so we turned down the hallway and made our way back home.

I knew that there was a possibility for infection or for any number of other things to happen. But I continued to pray.

The time finally came when we could see our little girl. It was difficult to see her head all bandaged and in an oxygen tent with a tube coming out of her skull. She slept with her eyes closed each time we visited.

When she was awake she became known as the "No Way" girl. When nurses would come to bring her food or medicine she would say, "No Way! No Way!" She clearly did not like being in the hospital.

One of the times when we returned to the hospital, Jim, my father-in-law, was coming out of Kim's room. We hugged him and thanked him for coming such a long way to see her. He smiled and said, "She's going to be alright, and I'm going to tell you why." We looked at him expectantly. "Why? What did she do?" my wife asked.

Jim chuckled. "Well, I was talking with her and she was looking past me and she suddenly said, "Throw the ball! Throw the ball!" At first I thought she was delirious but then I looked in the direction she was looking, and down across the room someone

else had a baseball game on TV. Someone had hit a ground ball to an infielder who was holding the ball, and Kim was telling him to throw the ball! That's when I knew she would be OK."
Jim was a man of faith. He had directed choirs in the Baptist church. He believed that God answers prayers.
Kim grew up without any side effects from this skull surgery. Today she is a beautiful young woman who works at Loyola Marymount University. She has acted and danced throughout high school and college, served as a waitress and later as bookkeeper at an upscale restaurant on the west side of Los Angeles. Since that day of her surgery she has not had one problem resulting from that dreadful fall.
I suppose one could say that the surgeon was the reason our daughter got well. We certainly could point to the hospital staff, their machines and medicines as helpful as well. But I believe that prayer also played a part in the positive outcome for our daughter. Wahli Vanstrom was right when she said that no matter the outcome we are in God's good hands.
Looking back, I started out with a very simplistic view of healing. I knew that the body could heal itself, and if I thought about it very much more than that, being a Christian I would have said, God made us that way.
I also have prayed my entire life. Mostly it was prayers during worship services, and sometimes I would pray at home or elsewhere. But my prayer life had never been frequent or with much depth I think. As a child I prayed the "Now I Lay Me Down To Sleep" prayer, and the "Come Lord Jesus Be Our Guest" prayer that my parents taught to me as a child to say before meals. But as an adult I found myself being drawn to prayers by Michael Quoist (French Catholic) and Father Malcolm Boyd (Anglican/Episcopal priest of Are You Running With Me, Jesus fame). Most of the prayer books I bought seemed flat and devoid of anything that really deepened me. I suppose that is one of the reasons I wanted to include prayer as part of my study sabbatical. I am truly glad that I did for I am now praying regularly and with purpose and intent. My prayer life has been deeply enriched, and I also see how much more profoundly prayer is connected to health and healing. I hope that

if you don't already know this connection, that you too may experience it.

In the past few years I have faced some additional health challenges. In 2008, I suffered two strokes, one in May and another in August. The first stroke left me with relatively no impairment, but the second one impacted my speech, my walking, and my fine motor skills. I had to have speech therapy, occupational therapy and physical therapy to assist me back to normalcy. In between the two strokes I also had a carotid surgery to clean out the carotid artery in my neck on the left side. This surgery was done at Scripps in San Diego. The preparation nurse came in shortly before the surgery and chatted with me. I asked her if she believed in the power of prayer. She said that she was a strong believer in the power of prayer and she offered to pray with me immediately before I was wheeled into the OR. At one time, she said, she had been a member of the Order of St. Luke and believed that prayer along with good medical treatment offered the best possible outcome. I did not see her again after the successful surgery but I remember her words clearly.

In 2010 I was diagnosed with prostate cancer. The prognosis was good as it was caught early, and as I underwent 45 straight weekdays of radiation treatment, I added prayer each and every day. In January 2011, I encountered another frightening episode of loss of power in my body, and was hospitalized for a a possible new stroke. After five days of hospitalization, the physicians could find no evidence for a stroke, nor could they find anything wrong with me. They decided to keep me for two more days.

Thank God they did! In the afternoon of that fifth day I went into a severe vertigo, and suddenly my heart rate dropped down to one beat every 13 seconds. A nurse monitoring my vital signs called a code on me, and a crash cart and team rushed into my room, moved me quickly from my bed to a gurney, and rushed me down to cardiology. There they stabilized me and the next morning I had a pace maker inserted into my chest. Once again I kept up my prayers for myself, my family and all of the medical personnel involved in my care. Today I am back at my full time job and am doing very well.

Someone once gave me a wall plaque which reads: Life is Fragile. Handle With Prayer. I couldn't agree more.

Photographs

Ron Rehrer with the MacNutts (Chapter 6)

Dr Koenig and Ron Rehrer (Chapter 9)

Dr. Larson, Ron Rehrer and Dr. Smith (Chapter 10)

Robert Ader (Chapter 11)

Abbey of the Genesee (Chapter 12)

The Abbey Psalter (Chapter 12)
The Book of Psalms Used by the Trappist Monks of Genesse Abbey

From The Abbey Psalter (Chapter 12)

Glastonbury Tor (Chapter 13)

Glastonbury Tor (Chapter 13)

Chalice Well (Chapter 14)

Chalice Well (Chapter 14)

The Outer Circle (Chapter 15)

Wall of Reformers, Geneva, Switzerland (Chapter 24)

Luther monument, Geneva, Switzerland (Chapter 24)

Taize (Chapter 24)

Candles in Prague (Chapter 26)

Common labyrinth layout (Chapter 29)

Walking a labyrinth (Chapter 29)

Bad Boll, Germany (Chapter 31)

Blumhardt portraits, Bad Boll, Germany (Chapter 31)

Prayer team at St. Mark's Lutheran Church, Houston TX (Chapter 36)

Bad Boll, Germany (Chapter 31)

Section III
Authors, Ideas and Research

Chapter 38
Morton Kelsey – On Healing and Christianity

For Christians, healing begins with Jesus of Nazareth. So claims Morton Kelsey in his monumental work called *Healing and Christianity: The First Comprehensive History of Sacramental Healing in the Christian Church*. Still the standard text on the history of Christian healing, Kelsey's book is an in-depth look at healing from a Christian perspective throughout the centuries from the time of Jesus to the 20th century.

While the medical community and many people often think of Hippocrates as the person we most have to thank for medicine, it is probably more true that the healing ministry of Jesus is a more holistic form of medicine. Through Jesus' healing touch, words, and very presence, people felt the love of God through Jesus' compassion for them. Whether you read through the writings of Christian healers or those of the so-called secular healers, all healers have come to the same conclusion. Rarely is there true healing if it is not connected with love. Oh sure, someone can receive stitches for a cut or have a medical surgery without the love from a physician. This is like taking my car to an auto mechanic and the mechanic need not feel love for me or for my car. He merely reaches in and changes the spark plugs or the oil. I suppose there are some physicians who operate in such a fashion. But healing is so much more than mechanical "cures", (e.g., removing a gallbladder or doing a coronary bypass.) Healing has to do with the whole person, not just the physical symptoms or disease, but one's emotional, relational, and spiritual well-being. True healing engages the entire whole person. In this sense, Jesus' ministry was to the whole person, and people felt the love of God enfolding them no matter what infirmity (emotional, physical, spiritual) that they brought to Jesus.

For those of you who may be unfamiliar with what Christians call the Holy Scripture (the Bible), there are two parts to the

Scriptures: the Old Testament and the New Testament. The Old Testament includes the story of Creation, the Garden of Eden story about Adam and Eve, and the history of Israel. The New Testament is the testimony about the life, death and resurrection of Jesus, and the history of His ministry through the life of His apostles and converts, especially Paul of Tarsus, who made three journeys, spreading the "Good News" about Jesus Christ.

Bible scholars agree the earliest of the four "Gospels" is the Gospel of Mark. Already in the first chapter of Mark, we see Jesus involved in the healing ministry that would characterize His entire life. In Mark 1:23, Jesus encounters a man in the synagogue who was possessed by an evil spirit. This spirit challenges Jesus. In Verse 24 this spirit recognizes Jesus as the Holy One of God and asks Jesus if He has come to destroy "us." In verse 25, Jesus responds sternly, ordering the evil spirit to "Be Quiet!" and then to the man who is possessed, "Come out of him!" In Verse 26, we read that the evil spirit shakes the man violently and comes out of the man with a shriek. The eyewitnesses to this event are amazed and marvel at Jesus' authority to cast out evil spirits. St. Mark in his Gospel reports that news about Jesus spread quickly throughout the region. Then Jesus continues healing many. Simon's mother-in-law is healed of a fever. Many who are sick and demon possessed are brought to Jesus. In Verse 34, we read that Jesus healed many who had various diseases and drove out many demons. Then at Verse 41, we read of Jesus healing a man of his leprosy.

At the beginning of the Gospel of Mark, Chapter Two, we read of the healing of the paralytic man. This man's friends have brought him to the place where Jesus was, and opening a place in the roof where they can lower the man down, they ease him down and Jesus sees their faith in bringing this man to Him. Chapter 2, Verse 10, we see Jesus telling why He is doing this healing. He is doing it so that the people may know He has authority on earth to forgive sins. He heals the paralytic man, and tells him to take up his mat and go home. The man arises, healed.

It becomes clear, I think, as you read through the first chapters of this earliest Gospel, that there are really three parts to Jesus' ministry. The first part, of course, is a ministry of preaching or proclamation. The early church continued this preaching ministry of Jesus wherever early Christians went. Lutherans, for example, during the Reformation and in modern times have made this a central act of worship.

The second part of Jesus' ministry was clearly teaching. Over and over again one can easily see Jesus teaching about the kingdom of God by the use of parables. Everywhere he goes he is preaching and teaching.

The third part of his ministry is healing. Morton Kelsey points out in his book Healing and Christianity, that nearly one-fifth of the Gospels is of the healing ministry of Jesus and the ongoing discussions that arose out of these healing signs of the Kingdom of God.

These three: preaching, teaching and healing comprise the work of Jesus. For Christians, of course, the ultimate work of Jesus was his death and resurrection, through which persons who believe in Him receive eternal life. This is the ultimate healing for all of us who follow Christ.

But during his lifetime, Jesus proclaimed, taught, and then demonstrated through healing, that the kingdom of God was "at hand" and that this Good News was breaking in on people's lives.

If you were to count up the physical ailments and mental/emotional problems presented to Jesus in the Gospels, you would find forty-one separate and distinct examples. There are seventy-two accounts in all, which include the duplications of some stories. Some of these passages, of course, describe Jesus healing many people, so that we know that there were many more healings than the specific ones separately recorded in the Gospels. It is clear that Jesus made healing a central aspect of His ministry.

We also know from a close reading of the New Testament record that Jesus passed his ministry onto his disciples and the apostles who followed Him. After His death and resurrection many early Church leaders continued His ministry of healing.

In Mark 6:7 Jesus calls the twelve disciples to himself and sends them out two by two, giving them authority over evil spirits. This was a continuation of His healing ministry.

In the Gospel of Matthew, Chapter 10, Verses 5-10, Jesus sends out his twelve disciples to continue His ministry, and here Matthew gives us more detail about what Jesus wants his disciples to do. He says (vs. 7), "As you go, preach this message: 'The kingdom of heaven is near.' (vs. 8) Heal the sick, raise the dead, cleanse those who have leprosy, drive out demons." Preaching about the kingdom of heaven coming "now" into their presence is combined with the healing ministry.

In the Gospel of Luke, Chapter 9, Verses 1-6, we have another version of Jesus calling his disciples to himself, giving them power and authority to drive out all demons and to cure diseases (vs. 1) as he sends them out to preach the Kingdom of God and to heal the sick (vs. 2).

So Mark, Matthew and Luke make it abundantly clear that Jesus' ministry of preaching, teaching and healing was passed onto his disciples, and when you look at the book of Acts you clearly see how these disciples and later apostles continued faithfully to fulfill his directions to proclaim, teach, and heal. For those of you new to the New Testament, the Book of Acts is actually part two of the Gospel of Luke. (In other words, the Gospel of Luke is part one, and the Book of Acts is part two. There are many healings in the Book of Acts as Jesus' disciples continue His ministry of healing).

Here are a few examples of healing recorded in the Book of Acts.

Acts 2:43. We read that many wonders and miraculous signs were done by the apostles.

Acts 3:1-11. We read that Peter and John heal a lame man, crippled from birth, by these words, "In the name of Jesus Christ of Nazareth, walk." The man's feet and ankles became strong and he jumped to his feet and walked.

Acts 4:23-30. We read of the prayer of the believers, who call upon the Lord to heal many with these words (vs. 30), "stretch out your hand to heal and perform miraculous signs and wonders through the name of your holy servant Jesus."

Acts 9:40-41. We read where Peter raises Dorcas from the dead. (Her Greek name is Dorcas, but if called by her Aramaic name, she is known as Tabitha.)

Acts 14:8. We read where Paul heals the crippled man at Lystra.

So here in Acts we see the early disciples and apostles healing in the name of Jesus. I've pointed out a few of the healings by Peter, John, and Paul, but there were many more.

Other books of the New Testament also speak of the ongoing healing ministry of Jesus through signs, wonders, faith, miracles, power, and other references. The books of Romans, First Corinthians, Second Corinthians, Galatians, Ephesians, First Thessalonians, Second Thessalonians, Hebrews, James, First Peter, Third John, and the book of Revelation all have references to healings through the faith as well as healings through the power of God in Jesus Christ.

(For a complete listing of the healing passages in the New Testament, turn to the appendix.)

So it is very clear that in the first century, the healing ministry of Jesus was a strong part of his overall ministry as the Incarnate Word of God (see the first chapter of the book of John, the fourth Gospel where it is written that in the beginning was the Word, and the Word was with God and was God. This is a reference to Jesus). It is also clear that this ministry of Jesus was handed on to his disciples and apostles and we have references throughout the New Testament canon as to how this healing ministry was thought of and how it was carried out. (Canon means the approved list of books agreed upon by the early Church).

The next question then is, did the healing ministry of Jesus end with the first century? I am told that at many seminaries within Christianity it is taught that the healing ministry of Jesus ended at the end of the first century. In prior years to when I attended seminary, professors there also taught the "signs and wonders" of Jesus' ministry were only for a "season", and that season ended at the close of the first century after Christ. These professors, as well as others in many other seminaries and Bible colleges, believe and teach that the gifts of the Holy Spirit and the miraculous healings during the time of Jesus and his disciples came to an end at the close of the so called Apostolic Age. The term often used for this belief is "dispensational" or as it is more often known today as "cessational." This is the belief that God withdrew from our world those dramatic and miraculous healings and interventions because these "signs and wonders" were only used by God in that first century to aid in the establishment of the Gospel. Once the Gospel was firmly in place, so these professors argue, God withdrew these gifts. In short, they believe God ceased to work miracles!

Are these believers in the "dispensational" or "cessational" viewpoint right? Did God withdraw dramatic healing miracles from our world? There are certainly those who believe this. But there are many more who do not hold this view at all.

Thanks to the outstanding research and writing of Morton T. Kelsey in his book Healing and Christianity, which was the first book I read during my sabbatical, there is evidence that the Early Church Fathers, as they are referred to, that is, the most influential bishops and others during the next three centuries following Christ's resurrection, believed and proclaimed that healings in the name of Jesus continued on.

Here are just a few examples cited in Kelsey's work:

a. Justin Martyr writing about exorcisms of demoniacs throughout the world in the name of Jesus.

b. Origin writing about how Christians are expelling evil spirits and performing many cures in the name of Jesus.

c. Cyprian referring to the healing of serious illness through baptism into the name of Jesus.

d. Tertullian giving very specific examples of healing, including the specific names of those cured and healed.

e. Quadratus, writing in Rome, that the works of the Savior are still continuing in his time.

f. Theophilus of Antioch giving his eyewitness accounts of casting out spirits by exorcisms as evidence that the resurrection power was beginning to work.

g. Minucius Felix (writing near the end of the second century) describing more exorcisms by the only and true God.

h. Irenaeus (writing in Gaul) references all kinds of healings like those in the Gospels and Acts, including the cure of different diseases and the raising of the dead.

i. Cyprian, writing fifty years later than Irenaeus, documenting about how healing continues to take place in the church.

j. Arnobius and Lactantius, writing at the beginning of the fourth century, are recording healings and exorcisms.

Kelsey spent over 25 years collecting his data on the history of healing in the Christian Church. I highly recommend that you read his book. I am indebted to him for the following Christian history of healing as the Early Church evolved and moved towards new structures, developing creeds and doctrines, electing bishops and leaders to preach and teach the fundamentals of the Christian faith, and to identify heresies and false teachings as this young religion expanded and spread far and wide. Nearly all of this framework occurred in the third century, and Kelsey points to eleven men who were the giants of the age. These eleven men also wrote about and were aware of the ongoing healings in the Name of Jesus.

These eleven men were:

1. Athanasius (for whom the Athanasius Creed is named as a staunch defender of the Trinitarian faith, lived from 296 until 393)
2. Basil the Great (329-379)
3. Gregory of Nyssa (331?-396)
4. Gregory of Nazianzus (329?-389)
5. John Chrysostom (345-407)
6. Ambrose (340?-397)
7. Augustine (354-430)
8. Jerome (340-420)
9. Gregory the Great (540-early part of the seventh century)
10. Sulpitius Severus, the biographer of St. Martin of Tours
11. John Cassian

After looking into the writings of the above giants of the early Church, Kelsey analyzes their worldview and describes them as men who believed that "demons attacked men's psyches directly, bringing physical and mental illness." He also describes them as men who "accepted the crucifixion and resurrection as events indissolubly linked, through which the demonic host was defeated, and believed that those who were filled with the Spirit of Christ had power to turn back demonic attack and to bring healing."

Kelsey is wise in stating that persons today who are "immersed in the almost wholly materialistic worldview of the 19th century," will have great difficulty in believing or accepting what many of these early Church fathers wrote about healings, and the casting out of demons. But Kelsey will not rest here. He argues that those who have verified some of the healings of an

Agnes Sanford or a Kathryn Kuhlman are seeing the same kinds of things "as was observed and recorded by these sophisticated and brilliant men who laid the intellectual foundations of all mainline Christianity."

Kelsey adds weight to his argument by pointing out that there are four historians of the first six centuries of Christianity: Eusebius, Sozomen, Socrates Scholasticus, and Theoderet, each of whom built upon the works of the previous historian. Each of them know of the ongoing healings within the Church, and Sozomen tells clearly of a man who was brought into the church and cured after receiving a divine revelation to dip his foot into honey, wine and pepper. He did so and his condition disappeared.

I don't have space enough to go into the details of how the liturgy of the church developed and how the sacraments were seen associated with healing. Please read Kelsey's section on Liturgy and Healing in his Healing and Christianity book. What I do wish to point out is that very early on, certainly by the third century if not before, that the ritual of Baptism as well as the ritual of the Eucharist (Holy Communion, bread and wine given in the name of Jesus Christ) were associated with healing. As one writer has put it, the sacrament itself was offered as "the specific medicine of life unto the healing of every illness."

Along with the Baptism and Eucharist, the early Church began to create services and procedures for visiting the sick as well as prayers for blessing or sanctifying of oil, or bread, or water to be brought to those sick persons to heal them. By the fifth century the Pope (Innocent I) wrote a letter in response to an inquiry from a bishop that not only did the clergy have the right to take holy oil to the sick, but that all Christians had the right to use it themselves "for anointing in their own need, or in the need of members of their households."

The use of consecrated oil, was instituted many centuries ago when on Easter Sunday, the day of Baptism, two different oils were used. The "oil of exorcism" was used first, followed by the "oil of thanksgiving" or chrism.

In addition, there is found in the oldest books from this period a form of healing that consisted of visiting, anointing, and laying hands on the sick. Until the 11th century this service was used for the healing of sick persons. In the Western Church, the purpose for healing was eventually discarded and the Roman Church began to use this service for preparation for dying. This is the so-called "Extreme Unction." It wasn't until Vatican II (in the middle 1960's) that extreme unction began to be set aside and the original intention of this service of healing was reintroduced into the Catholic Church. Over in the Eastern Church, however, the healing services were not used for preparation for facing death, but from the earliest of centuries had been used for the original purpose of healing.

This brings a memory to mind that I wish to share. I was five years old, living in the Inland Empire, in the small town of Colton, California, between San Bernardino to the north, and Riverside to the south, about 55 miles due east of Los Angeles. I slept in a single bed which had casters on the bottom of the bed legs. These casters (wheels) sat in small dish-like circles to prevent the bed from rolling.

One night I suddenly woke up because my bed was vibrating and moving, rolling along the hardwood floor. I looked out over my bed (we had a night light in those days) and I could see that the bed legs had slipped out of those tiny dish-like holders and the wheels on the ends of those bed legs were rolling fast across the hard wood floor! The floor itself was moving too, undulating like waves on a sea. I had no idea what was happening. I called out frantically for my mother and father, and they came in to reassure me everything was OK, that we were in the middle of a strong earthquake. I did not know what an earthquake was but I sure didn't like it! This is my first memory of an earthquake, but it made me very afraid.

My father had, some months earlier, purchased our very first television set, a very small black and white TV, The year was 1952 and television was in its infancy. When the earthquake finished, my father called all of us (me, my brother Leroy, and my mother who held my baby sister, Debbie) into the family room. He turned on the television. Channel 5 news was on and a very young news reporter by the name of Stan Chambers was reporting. (This would be the first mobile report by a television station in the United States). Chambers and his crew took the station wagon of the TV station and mounted a camera and a light on top and drove out to the town of Tehachapi, near

Bakersfield. It took several hours to get there in those days, but when they got there, they took the camera off from the top of the car and began to go mobile, taking in all of the terrible destruction from the Tehachapi quake.

The memory that remains from those pictures being broadcast to our tiny television screen is of a priest kneeling down beside a man trapped beneath the huge black steam locomotive engine at the front of a train that had derailed during the huge quake. The priest was holding a Bible in his left hand and a small vial of something that looked like water in his right. He was making the sign of the cross on this man's head, and was saying words over him, praying for him. Later on as an adult, I would come to know this as "last rites" or the act of Extreme Unction, used for preparation for death. I heard from my father later on that the man trapped beneath the locomotive died.

I wasn't sure that my memory of being 5 years old was accurate. A few years ago I met a pastor who was serving the Tahachapai community. He told me that it was indeed 1952 when that quake hit (so I was indeed 5 years old!), and that there is still a coffee shop/cafe locally known as the "earthquake cafe" which has the newspaper clippings, articles and photographs of that terrible day posted on its walls.

So I have a very early image of the anointing with oil for those preparing to die. But today the use of oil for healing purposes is once again within the Church and is being used widely. Within my own denomination there are many clergy using oil when visiting the sick and the infirm. While healing may not always occur in a physical way, the anointing with oil can bring about a profound sense of comfort in knowing that Christ is with us, which in turn can calm our fears, renew our hope, comfort us and sustain us when we are ill. This blessed oil along with the sign of the cross, and the reception of private communion, leads many back to the cross of Christ, and His resurrection, which gives us confidence for all the days of our life here on earth, and that time beyond this life where God has prepared a place for us.

Before we look at the Middle Ages and specifically the ministry of healing in the Reformation era, let's take a brief look at the thoughts of St. Augustine. It would not be too far to say that Augustine was THE theologian of the Western Church for over a thousand years. He was profoundly influential on Luther at the time of the Reformation, and he had a major impact on healing ministries: a negative one.

In Augustine's early writings he made it clear that his belief was that the healing gift so prevalent in the life of Christ and Apostolic era were no longer something that Christians should look for. The early Augustine felt that healing really wasn't that important and that it had disappeared. But in 424 during the writing of his tremendous work, City of God, he made the admission that he had been wrong. Here is what he wrote:

"...once I realized how many miracles were occurring in our own day and which were so like the miracles of old and also how wrong it would be to allow the memory of these marvels of divine power to perish from among our people. It is only two years ago that the keeping of records was begun here in Hippo, and already, at this writing, we have nearly seventy attested miracles."

Just three years before he died, Augustine wrote in the Retractions (also known as the "Revisions"):

"I also said, these miracles are not allowed to continue into our time, lest the soul should always require things that can be seen, and by becoming accustomed to them mankind should grow cold towards the very thing whose novelty had made men glow with fire. (De Vera Religione, cap. 25, nn. 46, 47) It is indeed true: that not everyone today who has hands laid on them in baptism thus receives the Holy Spirit so as to speak in tongues; nor are the sick always healed by having the shadow of the promise of Christ pass across them; and if such things were once done, it is clear that they afterwards ceased.

But what I said should not be taken as understanding that no miracles are believed to happen today in the name of Christ. For at the very time I wrote this book I already knew that, by approaching the bodies of the two martyrs of Milan, a blind man in that same city was given back his sight; and so many other things of this kind have happened, even in this present time, that it is not possible for us either to know of all of them or to count up all of those that we do have knowledge of."

Kelsey, in his work, gives details of what Augustine saw with his own eyes and personally knew about. Even during Augustine's

own personal illness before he died, a man came with a sick relative to have Augustine lay hands upon him. Augustine did not believe that he had this gift of healing, but the man told him he had had a vision in his sleep to go to see Bishop Augustine, to have a hand laid upon him. Augustine, hearing this, did not hesitate to place his hands upon this man, and the Lord made this sick man well and he departed from Augustine healed.
This brings us to the Middle Ages, Luther, Calvin and the Reformation. I will continue Kelsey's discussion in the next chapter.
References:
Interview of Morton Kelsey, Part One and Part Two (YouTube)

Chapter 39
Luther's Role in the Healing Tradition

To continue in my discussion of Morton Kelsey's great work, Healing and Christianity: A Comprehensive History of Christianity (see the previous chapter), Kelsey focuses next on healing in the Middle Ages, particularly on Martin Luther's viewpoint on healing.

Being from a Lutheran background, imagine my surprise to find out that it was Luther himself who not only downplays the role of healing, but suggests that the real miracles are not visible ones. Kelsey first quotes Luther from Luther's Sermons on the Gospel of St. John, Chapters 14-16, Luther's Works, 24:367 in which Luther says, "...now that the apostles have preached the Word and have given their writings, and nothing more than what they have written remains to be revealed, no new and special revelation or miracle is necessary." Apparently in his early writings Luther, as he was well known to do about other subjects, wrote colorfully against that with which he disagreed. Kelsey's footnote remarks: "In these early sermons the 16th century attitude toward healing and miracles is expressed with a vehemence and color which few other writers displayed."

In another place, Kelsey cites Luther's Works, Volume 46, edited by Robert C. Schultz (1967) where you will find this quotation from one of Luther's sermons, called "A Sermon on Keeping Children In School." The passage reads:

"Thus Paul says in Romans 8 that God will raise up our mortal bodies because of his Spirit which dwells in us. Now how are men helped to this faith and to this beginning of the resurrection of the body except through the office of preaching and the word of God, the office your son performs? Is this not an immeasurably greater and more glorious work and miracle than if he were in a bodily or temporal way to raise the dead again to life, or help the blind, deaf, dumb, and leprous here in the world, in this transitory life?"

Kelsey goes on to argue that Luther had two different viewpoints about healing that he never reconciled. One was that Luther agreed that no one raised the dead anymore and that the miracles of healing were really nothing but the work of the Devil. Realizing that Luther was so strong about "Sola Scriptura" (Scriptures alone) and the centrality of the Word of God (both in Bible reading and in the proclamation in preaching), the healing ministry of the church really was not very important to Luther. The other view Luther also expressed came later on in his life. This view was that healings were in fact occurring and that the Lutheran church should be involved in healing ministries. He gives the Church instructions on how to do healing, and talks about his own healing experiences (see below).

This division within Luther comes down to our very present day. There are those who argue for classic Lutheran theology and tradition which proclaims there is no healing within the Lutheran tradition. The most important thing is the proclamation of the word, and the celebration of the sacraments. They teach that healing ended at the close of the first century, and that feelings and experiences cannot possibly be any basis for faith or life since these feelings and experiences are subjective and only the objective Word of God is dependable. On the other side, however, are those who point to Luther's own experiences and teaching in his latter years in which he not only discusses his own personal healings but also instructs others on how to do healing ministries. Today this debate continues, particularly in the Lutheran Church – Missouri Synod, where classical Lutheran theology (of Word alone) is often pitted against those Lutherans more experientially oriented, particularly in healing ministries. Those who emphasize the work of the Holy Spirit within Lutheran preaching and teaching are often viewed as "suspect" by those of the classical tradition.

However, there is a new study out that seeks to find a bridge between this long standing conflict. The author, Simeon Zahl, has written a book entitled Pneumatology and Theology of the Cross in the Preaching of Christoph Friederich Blumhardt: The Holy Spirit between Wittenberg and Azusa Street. Zahl believes he has found in Christoph Blumhardt's preaching a way to reconcile the classical Lutheran tradition and that of the experience of the Holy Spirit. The reference to Wittenberg is where Luther nailed his original 95 Theses in the early 1500's and Azusa Street refers to where the Pentecostal movement began on Azusa Street, Los Angeles, in the first few years of the 1900's.

It is important to remember that Martin Luther was a Catholic priest whose desire was to reform the Church's teachings. Previous reformers had failed and had paid for that failure with their lives. When Luther nailed his 95 theses on the door of the Wittenberg church, he could not have imagined what would transpire throughout Europe and the whole of Christendom. It is outside the scope of this book to retell the story of Martin Luther and the Lutheran reformation in Germany and the great Reformation that took place within the Church and all of society. There are many books and films which tell this great story. What we are focusing on in this chapter is Kelsey's recounting of Luther's view of healing at the time of the Reformation. Kelsey is critical of Luther for saying very little about healing. He views Luther as emphasizing the teaching and preaching of the Gospel but one almost senses that Kelsey believes Luther either directly or indirectly was responsible for the suppression of healing and its practice in the emerging Reformation.

My personal view is that Luther, after posting those discussion points on the Wittenberg door, found himself in a firestorm of controversy in which he was focused solely on his defending his theological position (and writings) in the face of Rome. Luther was called to recant what he had written and what he believed. In his famous statement to Rome's representatives, Luther refused to recant by saying, "Here I stand." The result of that was that not only was Luther excommunicated from the Church but there was a great fear he would be captured and executed as had been done to others who had questioned the Church. Fortunately for Luther, he was whisked away and kept safe in a castle so that he could continue to write and develop his ongoing challenge to the Church's reformation. As this crisis deepened, Germany divided into Catholics and Protestants (Lutherans) and city states chose sides. Eventually in the city of Augsburg, Emporer Charles V gathered together all of the stake holders in an attempt, in part, to avoid total all out warfare. It is within this historical context that Luther had written prolifically and had been preaching to defend the "Sola Scriptura, Sola Fides, Sola Gratia" theological view point, and in this huge German upheaval that would soon transform all of Europe, that Luther was just not focused on healing. Further more, his early writings and preaching, quoted by Kelsey, is the early Luther arguing ferociously to protect the Gospel as he understood it. This meant peeling off and away anything that did not focus purely on the big theological issues of the day.

But Luther was very human. He loved Phillip Melanchton, his partner in his attack on Catholic doctrine and practices. So when Melanchton became very ill, Luther rushed to the bedside of his dying friend, and did what priests had always done in prior times (remember Luther was a priest there in Germany). He prayed for Melanchton's recovery, and stayed with his friend, hoping that his friend would not die.

In his book, Thelogy of the Heart: The Role of Mysticism in the Theology of Martin Luther, Lutheran writer Bengt Hoffman reports what Luther himself did and said while Melanchton lay dying. Hoffman writes that Luther rushed to Melanchton's bedside where he lay gravely ill. Luther turned to the window of the sickroom and poured out his soul to God. Luther passionately prayed for the healing and recovery of his friend. Hoffman reports Luther's words:

"This time I sought the Almighty with great vigor. I attacked him with his own weapons, quoting from the Scriptures all the promises I could remember, that prayers should be granted, and said that he must grant my prayer, if I was henceforth to put faith in his promises." (page 47)

Then Luther took the hand of the sick man saying:

"Be of good courage, Philipp, you will not die; although the Lord might see cause to kill, yet he does not will the death of the sinner, but rather that he should turn to him and live. God has called the greatest sinners unto mercy, how much less, then will he cast you off, my Philipp, or destroy you in sin and sadness. Therefore do not give way to grief, do not become your own murderer, but trust in the Lord, who can kill and bring to life, who can strike and heal again." (page 47-48)

It is clear from Hoffman's report that Luther knew Melanchton's inner struggle at the time, namely, (according to Hoffman) that Melanchton was blaming himself for too little stoutness in the defense of the evangelical cause. Melanchton would rather have passed away in peace than have to return to earthly strife. But God's power channeled by Luther's prayer recalled the sick man. We know from history that Melanchton recovered from what appears to be the brink of death. He wrote later, "I was recalled from death to life by divine power." (page 48)

Perhaps this was a turning point for Luther towards healing ministry.

I wondered if there was any way to collaborate Kelsey's writing about Luther's role in the demise and near recovery of the healing tradition within Lutheranism. Thanks to Rev. Bob Meyers, then Director of Ministerial Health of the Ohio District of the Lutheran Church - Missouri Synod, I found my answer. While visiting in his home, I noticed a book on his bookshelf behind him as we spoke together. I said to Bob, "What is that book behind you by Martin Marty?" Bob turned around and said, "I've had this book for a long time but never got around to reading it completely. Would you like to borrow it?" I said I would and he gave me the book. It's title was *Health and Medicine in the Lutheran Tradition.*

Martin E. Marty is one of America's greatest historians of religion, and also comes from the Lutheran tradition. He has written many books and many prefaces to other books. He is a much sought after commentator on church and religion, and often is quoted in Time, Newsweek, the Christian Century, and other leading magazines and periodicals.

As I began to read Marty's book, I was curious if I might find the Luther story about Melanchton. Sure enough, Marty had the story too. Essentially the same as told by Kelsey, Marty tells how Luther was very worried when his friend Melanchton became extremely ill. The impending death of Melanchton brought Luther immediately back to his early training as a priest, who had been taught how to anoint with oil, lay on hands, and pray for healing. Luther prayed without ceasing for his very close friend. When Melanchton began to recover, Luther praised God mightily and later began to reinstitute healing practices which had been neglected during the Reformation battles with the Catholic Church. But with the death of Luther, says Marty,

the healing practices within the Reformation churches faded and died.
I shared the above information with my friend, Rev. Paul Terhune, a clergyman and good New Testament scholar, at a conference of the Pacific Southwest District over a coffee break. He broke into a smile and said that this story about Luther is still alive in German culture today. He shared how his grandmother had told him this story about Luther. She told Paul to always pray for the sick just as, "sainted Martin Luther did." She went on to tell Paul that Luther had a friend, although she couldn't remember what his friend's name was, who was gravely ill. She shared that Luther went to his knees praying for his friend night and day until his friend got well again. She went on to say that she thought this friend later on may have caused some trouble for Luther because they didn't always agree on some things, but Luther was still a good role model for what a pastor should do. She said, "Pastors have to pray for people to heal them."
Kelsey documents Luther's changing viewpoint in his later years. Just five years after his friend Melanchton recovered, and the year before Luther himself died, Luther was asked what to do about a man who was mentally ill. The year was 1545. Quoting Kelsey again: "Luther wrote instructions for a healing service based on the New Testament letter of James, adding, 'This is what we do, and that we have been accustomed to do, for a cabinet maker here was similarly afflicted with madness and we cured him by prayer in Christ's name.'" (Reference for this story is taken from W. J. Kooiman, By Faith Alone: The Life of Martin Luther (1954), p. 192; letter to Pastor Severin Schulze, June 1, 1545, Luther: Letters of Spiritual Counsel (1955), pp. 51 f.) (see the full quotation later below).
Returning to the book, Theology of the Heart, quoted above, Lutheran author Bengt Hoffman documents a great deal more about Luther's thought and experiences with prayer and healing than that which is reported in Kelsey and Marty.
According to Hoffman, Luther wrote about his own suffering and illness. Discouraged and frustrated in his own battle with illness, Luther wrote to Gerhard Wilskamp saying, "Christ has so far triumphed, I commend myself to the prayers of yourself and the brethren. I have healed others. I cannot heal myself." (page

47) This passage makes it clear that Luther is requesting others to pray for him and for his illness. He says he has healed others. Healing was practiced by Catholic priests during Luther's time, and presumably he is referring to what was fairly common practice of praying for healing of those who were ill. Luther says he has healed others, but he cannot heal himself. He needs help. He needs the prayers of others. This means he is relying upon these petitions to God to make a difference. There is a tinge of despair in the words he wrote to Wilskamp. Even people of great faith, under the right conditions of illness, can slip into despair when they continue to suffer.

Bengt goes on to argue that Luther was aware that he himself was the object of intercessory prayer during his times of illness. The following paragraph comes from a letter Luther wrote to his wife in 1537:

"I was all but dead, I had already recommended you and our children to God and our Savior, in the full conviction that I should never see you again. I was greatly affected when I thought of you, thus on the brink of the tomb, as I thought myself. However, the prayers and tears of pious men who love me have found favor before God. This last night has killed my malady; I feel quite as though new born." (page 48)

After his recovery from the illness of "the stone", about a month later a good friend asked Luther what remedy he had used. Luther replied: "Prayer, for in all Christian congregations they fervently prayed for me according to the direction of the Apostle James 5:14-15." (page 49). It appears that Luther felt that, even though he had undergone some kind of operation, that intercessory prayer lay at the root of his recovery.

A pastor in Gotha, named Myconius, testified that Martin Luther healed him by prayer. It happened in 1541. In a letter to Myconius, Luther had written: "I will pray with you that God may keep you here long." (page 49). Myconius had been seriously ill with a lung ailment. The pastor wrote about Luther's prayer that it "showed a power" so that he recovered. Six years later, Luther died. That's when Myconius so moved by Luther, wrote the tract giving us this information about this healing matter.

Myconius believed that God brought him back to life through Martin Luther's healing prayer. Myconius wrote to his readers: "Now I crawl into my sick-bed to await the moment when the Lord bids me to put down my physical burden- I am now only skin and bone- and permits me to follow Luther to the Lord Christ. I would long ago have followed my dear Father Luther, had not the prayers of my brethren in several churches kept me here." (page 49)

So it certainly appears to be the case that pastors saw Luther as firmly anchored in Christ and that he did believe in the healing that can come from God through prayer. We certainly see it in Luther's praying for his fellow-reformer Philip Melanchthon. But if there is any doubt, the following writing by Luther (as reported by Hoffman) seems to clench it. While Luther believed that people who are ill should consult medically trained persons, he also counseled people to remain constantly in intercessory prayer. Read what Luther wrote to Pastor Severin Schulze on June 1st, 1545:

To Pastor Severin Schultze, Venerable Sir and Pastor:

The tax collector in Torgau and the councilor in Belgren have written me to ask that I offer some good advice and help for the afflicted husband of Mrs. John Korner. I know of no worldly help to give. If the physicians are at a loss to find a remedy, you may be sure that it is not a case of ordinary melancholy... This must be counteracted by the power of Christ and with the prayer of faith. This is what we do and we have been accustomed to do this for a cabinet-maker here was similarly afflicted with madness and we cured him by prayer in Christ's name.

You should consequently proceed as follows. Go to him with the deacon and two or three good men. Confident that you, as pastor of the place, are invested with the authority of the ministerial office, lay your hands upon him and say: "Peace be with you, dear brother, from God our Father, and from our Lord Jesus Christ." Thereupon read the Creed and the Lord's Prayer over him in a clear voice, and close with these words: "O God, Almighty Father, who has told us through your son, Verily, verily, I say unto you, whatsoever you shall ask the Father in my name, he will give it to you"; who has commanded and encouraged us to pray in his name "Ask and you shall receive," and who in like manner has said, "Call upon me in the day of trouble, I will deliver you and you shall glorify me:" we unworthy sinners, relying on these your words and commands, pray for your mercy with such faith as we can muster.

Graciously deign to free this man from all evil, put to nought the work that Satan has done in him, to honor of your name and the strengthening of the faith of believers. Through the same Jesus Christ, your son our Lord, who lives and reigns with you, world without end. Amen. (pages 50-51)

Luther continues:

Then, when you depart, lay your hands on the man again and say: "These signs shall follow them that believe: they shall lay hands on the sick and they shall recover."

Do this three times, once on each of three successive days. Meanwhile let prayers be said from the chancel of the church, publicly, until God hears them.

To the extent to which we are able, we shall at the same time unite our faithful prayers and petitions to the Lord with yours. (page 51)

(Original text also appears in Luther: Letters of Spiritual Counsel, Martin Luther, Theodore G. Tappert)

It is clear, I think, that in the last three to five years of his life, Luther received prayer for healing as well as prayed for healing for others, and even gave advice about the way to do prayer for healing. While I do not know if Luther thought in terms of a "healing ministry" since this seems to me to be a more contemporary phrase, it is clear from Luther's own testimony that he believed in offering prayers for healing and had a compassion for those who were suffering.

So if the great Reformer, Luther, was moving back towards a more accepting attitude towards healing, the Calvinist Reformation sweeping out of Geneva, Switzerland, buried the Reformation's tentative comfort with healing ministries. Writing in his Institutes of the Christian Religion, IV, 18, John Calvin said, "The gift of healing disappeared with the other miraculous powers which the Lord was pleased to give for a time, that it might render the new preaching of the gospel forever wonderful. Therefore, even were we to grant that anointing was a sacrament of those powers which were then administered by the hands of the apostles, it pertains not to us, to whom no such powers have been committed."

Marty goes on to say that those of the scholastic orthodoxy of Lutheranism were very militant against any claims of special gifts of the spirit, but those Lutherans more associated with the Pietist movements were Lutherans who practiced intercessory prayer as well as visitation of the sick. Marty accurately, I think, says that throughout the exceptions. One of those is the story of Pastor John Christoph Blumhardt, a German Lutheran who is called the founder of modern Lutheran healing movements. (See my chapter on the Blumhardts).

So having looked at Luther's letters about his own illness and others and the need for intercessory prayer and the laying on of hands, how did it come about that today most Lutheran clergy in the Lutheran Church - Missouri Synod and most in the Evangelical Lutheran Church (made up formerly of the American Lutheran Church, the Lutheran Church in America and the Association of Evangelical Lutheran Church) have never heard much about healing until just a few years ago? I do not know fully the answer to this question. I do know that in the early formative years of the Lutheran Church - Missouri Synod when certain theological conflicts were being battled over, that one side lost and another side won. What I have been told is that the side that won, lost as well the healing ministry theology which was not subscribed to by the winning side. The debates were not over prayer and healing but of other theological matters. But when one side was defeated and was no longer the endorsed opinion, that with their defeat on other matters also came with it the defeat of the healing tradition.

It was Wilhelm Loehe, in Germany, who sent over many German Lutheran pastors to America in the 1800's. Loehe was known in Germany in part for his support and practice of healing prayer. Much of his theology was a part of the losing side in the doctrinal controversies among German Lutherans arriving in America. With the fading of Loehe's popularity came also the loss of the ministry of healing which was part of his teaching and practice. One quotation from Wilhelm Loehe makes the point. "...in order that the church might carry on its task, even with the gifts of the Spirit even as in the same way Elijah gave Elisha this mantle, the gifts of grace were given to the church at Pentecost. Have these gifts ceased to exist? No, it is only unbelievers who hold this view. The Spirit is still present. Where the Spirit is there HIS GIFTS are also. It is possible to strive for these gifts especially through prayer."

Lutherans are a Word Alone group of believers. By that I mean Lutherans take seriously that God's Word is what sustains people and takes care of them. Central to Lutheran theology is proclamation of the Word and calling people to repentance. Luther's famous phrase about "Sola Scripture, Sola Fides, Sola Gracia" did not include words about healing or prayer. The Latin translated says that we are saved by Scripture alone, by Faith alone and by Grace alone. The emphasis is on preaching and teaching. That is what Jesus told his disciples to do: to go out and preach and teach. However the third thing Jesus told the church to do was to heal. The third part of what Jesus called them to do eventually got lost over the centuries. Eventually the viewpoint at most Lutheran seminaries was that the healing "signs and wonders" of Jesus ministry were only for "a season," meaning the First Century. The viewpoint held was that miracles ended at the conclusion of the First Century. However, as Kelsey clearly documents this is not true. Healing in Jesus' Name has continued in all centuries and has come down to us even into the 21st century.

But in our modern worldview and post Enlightenment philosophies there is reluctance to believe in a God let alone a God who heals. Reading Kelsey's book it becomes very clear that there has always been a healing ministry throughout history. Rediscovering Luther's viewpoint on healing is evidence that the Great Reformer did not believe healing ended at the close of the New Testament era, in that first century. Seminaries have a lot of catching up to do on this subject.

In his book, The Healing Reawakening, Francis MacNutt also explores how the Church nearly lost its healing ministries throughout the centuries. This work, previously entitled The Nearly Perfect Crime, looks at how influential the Christian practice of healing the sick and casting out evil spirits was in the conversion of the Roman Empire into embracing Christianity. However, over time and for various reasons, argues MacNutt, supernatural healing nearly disappeared from the mainline churches.

Today Christian healing is on the upswing. Nearly every Christian denomination now embraces some form of healing ministries. Many congregations are hosting healing services, and with the world expansion of the Pentecostal movement, healings are now reported from every continent. The Spirit of God does seem to be moving strong and swift throughout Christendom. It is good to know that Luther, towards the end of his life, placed a greater emphasis on healing, and that although sometimes neglected or perhaps even suppressed, the laying on of hands, anointment with oil, and the faithful prayers of believers once again is becoming a high priority in the life of the Church.

For Kelsey, Luther and Calvin, the two great reformers, were like a death knell on healing ministries. Kelsey makes an insightful point when he writes:

"The influence of these two men can hardly be stressed too much. Practically all Protestant theology begins from one or the other of them. Whatever reason they had for rejecting miracles- whether they were reacting to an emphasis in the medieval church, or perhaps responding to the first whispers of sophisticated humanism, or to the developing implications of Aristotelian thought- makes little difference. Calvin and Luther alike left the precedent that healing was a dispensation for a former time, and the matter was settled for later "orthodox" Protestants. The fact that the church fathers up to Aquinas, as well as the Orthodox churches, had a different point of view does not seem to have been much considered. (Note to readers: Aquinas was the great theologian of Catholicism writing in the later half of the 13th century. He pretty much rejected healing ministry in his writings. He did recognize that penance and healing had something in common, but the most he said was that perhaps a 'sanctified man's hand' might heal the physical, but his view of penance was that its validity did not operate through anything corporeal: there was no water, or bread and wine, or even oil. The priest would say 'I absolve thee', without anything in his hands.)"

My own view is that Kelsey is overly harsh in his critique of Luther's view of healing. Certainly the later Luther speaks strongly about healing. He doesn't seem to speak from a theological or doctrinal point of view as much as from a personal and pastoral care viewpoint. Certainly his healing writings which promote healing come during the last three to five years of his life. Perhaps it is an aging Luther who embraces healing in the last years of his life, or perhaps it is a man who has pretty much fought the good wars of the theological Reformation, who now turns more pragmatically to the issues of illness and life. Whatever the case, Luther in his sundown years gives pastoral advice to other pastors on how to pray for healing and shared how he has done healing prayer himself.

I'm so glad that Kelsey's work was the first book I read to launch my study sabbatical. It not only gave me an in-depth historical understanding of healing and Christianity, but it also gave me a framework into which I could understand other experiences during my sabbatical.

Martin Marty, a well known Lutheran historian and prolific writer said of Healing and Christianity, "This intelligent defense of the healing potential of Christianity merits careful attention." (Martin Marty, The Critic) The Union Seminary Quarterly Review said of it, "Of inestimable value to those who wish to understand the historical roots of the church's present attitudes toward healing. Prophetic and timely." The front cover of the work reads, "The first comprehensive history of healing in the Christian Church from Biblical times to the present."

From the beginning of his book, Kelsey informs the reader that he began the collecting of the historical material nearly 15 years before this book was written. (The hardcover version of this book came out in 1973, which means he must have begun collecting material around the later 1950's).

He says in the preface that there are a number of books that document the occurrences of sacramental healing in the present day. He also relates that his own first encounters with healing ministries had taken place 25 years before this book was written through Agnes Sanford's first book, The Healing Light. Kelsey's wife was just getting over the flu and to pass the time away she had read this book. When he came home one evening his wife handed him Agnes Sanford's book and commented that he better read this book because either Mrs. Sanford was "completely off base or she's saying something pretty important."

With this introduction, Kelsey sat down and read the book. This lead him to finding out for himself that healing still was occurring sacramentally. Later on Agnes Sanford moved to Monrovia, California where Kelsey was rector of St. Luke's Church in Monrovia. After Kelsey came to St. Luke's, a healing service was instituted which became an important part of this parish's life. Mrs. Sanford remained a close friend to Kelsey and wise consultant to him on sacramental healing. He also thanks his dear friend, John A. Sanford, (whose writings I am familiar with and like a great deal), for spending hundreds of hours with him as they discussed healing and other spiritual matters as they looked at the relationship of Jungian thought (Carl Jung) to various aspects of what he calls "modern Christian living."

From the beginning Kelsey asks whether the question is settled as to whether or not there is a place for the idea of Christian healing. If, as Kelsey believed when writing this book back in the early 1970's, that Christian healing was still a vital reality for people now, then he felt the need to "offer a rationale for practicing healing in the church today." In my opinion, he does a great job offering that rationale.

Chapter 40
Dr Garth Ludwig - Order Restored
A Biblical Interpretation Of Health, Medicine and Healing

Dr. Garth D. Ludwig wrote a tremendous book laying out a Biblical interpretation of health, medicine and healing. The title of this work, Order Restored, was written to provide a Scriptural lens through which to understand God's intention to restore the broken relationship with mankind, This relationship between mankind and God was perfectly ordered at creation but Adam's rebellion set into motion consequences which brought about complete disorder.

For Dr. Ludwig, the Fall, as it is known in classic Christianity, changed everything, allowing for disease to bring about disorder in human life, including physical diseases, mental illnesses, and corrupted relationships between human beings. As Ludwig describes these devastating consequences of the Fall, disease processes and disorder have permeated the bodies of many people. But this disorder is not confined to physical illness. It has also negatively impacted the minds and emotions of many, as well as led to broken relationships within society (divorce, business scams, greed, etc.).

In fact, Dr. Ludwig argues that this disorder is a cosmic disorder which can only be "re-ordered" again by the Creator Himself. To restore His creation, God sent Jesus Christ, whom Ludwig calls The Healer, to usher in the Kingdom of God, which can be seen through the healing ministry of Jesus.

I was not aware of Dr. Ludwig's book until his widow, Marlene, contacted me about it in 2002. I had gotten to know Marlene when I had a counseling office in the church where she served as a secretary. At that same time I was serving with Garth, her husband, on a ministerial health committee of the Lutheran church. Garth always brought wisdom and depth of knowledge to situations involving ministerial health issues. But what I didn't know was that he was writing a work on health, medicine and healing.

Ludwig died of cancer in 1998 and his book was published the following year. Marlene heard about my study sabbatical and contacted me about three years later, and sent me a copy of Garth's book. I am deeply indebted to her for sending me a copy of her husband's insightful and masterful book. It is clear from reading it that Ludwig had done a great deal of research and was thoroughly familiar with all of the major thinkers and writers in the field, and had developed his thesis over a great number of years.

What first struck me about his book upon reading it, was that many of the same people I was to read and visit during my sabbatical, and post-sabbatical time, were some of the very same people whom Ludwig writes about towards the end of his book. Of course, most of them were much younger when he was first learning about them. In one section of the book he points out a number of promising researchers and writers that the reader should keep an eye on. Amazingly, some of these have now become major health experts and leaders in the fields of body-mind medicine and the healing arts. By the time I had come along with my study sabbatical, many of them were already five to ten years or more down the road in their thinking and writing. I felt privileged to be following in Dr. Ludwig's trail-blazing path.

Another thing about Ludwig's book that struck me was how knowledgeable he was about the cultural aspects of understanding health and healing. He had worked abroad as an anthropologist researching among a number of different tribes in various locations. From his observations and studies, he learned a great deal about cultural differences in the way health and healing are perceived. This greatly broadened his world-view, for example, of the differences and similarities between folk healing in these cultures. He also gained respect for Eastern medicine in contrast to the Western medical system which he greatly respected.

He also brings his theological training to bear as he presents the Hebrew view of wholeness as presented in the Old Testament, in contrast to the new view of the human being as seen from the Greek perspective in the New Testament. For example, in the Old Testament, Hebrew worldview, there is no need for physicians because health was seen as a result of your right relationship with God (Yahweh). If something was wrong, then what one needed was to restore one's relationship with God. However, by the time of the New Testament era, the healing systems of Greek culture were already well-established and schools of physicians were well known. Thus you have the scene at the Pool of Bethesda, a healing place, where diseased and ill persons went for healing (see the Gospel of John, Chapter 5, Verses 1-15 in the New Testament of the Bible). Some had already seen physicians. Jesus is aware of physicians and their first century treatment methods. Even the writer of the Gospel of Luke is a physician. While restoring a right relationship with God was the key to health and healing within Hebrew culture (Old Testament), that is not the medical system for the Greeks. The body is now becoming viewed as separate from the soul (Greek dualism) and the body becomes the target for treatment. The move was away from a holistic worldview to a more secular, fragmented worldview.

This compartmentalization over the centuries would come down to our modern times. In the 20th century, specialization became the norm among physicians. One studied to become a heart doctor or a foot doctor, or a doctor of some other organ or appendage. As Robert Ader made clear in his comment reported in an earlier chapter, "no one was talking to each other." Before the rise of psychosomatic medicine's deeper research and the coming of psychoneuroimmunology, endocrinologists rarely spoke to cardiologist, and oncologists were unlikely to speak to podiatrists.

This is reminiscent of St. Paul's writing in the New Testament about unity in Christ. Using the body as his analogy, he writes in 1 Corinthians, Chapter 12, beginning at Verse 15:

15 "If the foot should say, "Because I am not a hand, I do not belong to the body," it would not for that reason cease to be part of the body.

16 And if the ear should say, "Because I am not an eye, I do not belong to the body," it would not for that reason cease to be part of the body.

17 If the whole body were an eye, where would the sense of hearing be? If the whole body were an ear, where would the

sense of smell be?
18 But in fact God has arranged the parts in the body, every one of them, just as he wanted them to be.
19 If they were all one part, where would the body be?
20 As it is, there are many parts, but one body.
21 The eye cannot say to the hand, "I don't need you!" And the head cannot say to the feet, "I don't need you!"
22 On the contrary, those parts of the body that seem to be weaker are indispensable,
23 and the parts that we think are less honorable we treat with special honor. And the parts that are unpresentable are treated with special modesty,
24 while our presentable parts need no special treatment. But God has combined the members of the body and has given greater honor to the parts that lacked it,
25 so that there should be no division in the body, but that its parts should have equal concern for each other.
26 If one part suffers, every part suffers with it; if one part is honored, every part rejoices with it."
(New International Version of the Bible)
St. Paul is making it very clear that there is one body with many parts. Each of those parts are important to the whole body. No part can stand alone. Twenty centuries later psychoneuroimmunology would be pointing to one body as well with each specialist needing to talk to other specialists for the sake of health and healing. This movement towards holistic thinking is now firmly established as a guiding principle in today's medical practice.
Towards the close of the 20th Century and this early part of the 21st Century, we are aware as never before that the body, mind, emotions and spirit of man are all one entity. Inside the body itself, for example, cells have intelligence, and they "know" what is happening everywhere else in the body. From the 1980's onward, "wholeness" begins to capture the imagination of scientists and medical doctors, and once again humans are starting to be viewed as a whole entity, not a collection of various parts. The concept of integrative medicine becomes more accepted and treatment modalities become multi-disciplined.

Dr. Ludwig's definitions of disease, illness and sickness also provide a helpful perspective in understanding health and healing. He describes "disease" as an observable, external process which can be diagnosed by the medical community. Illness is different. "Illness" is the internal interpretation of how a person feels as a result of disease. "Sickness" refers to the social implications of disease (process) and illness (personal interpretation, experience and meaning).

For example, a person has a disease or condition. It is properly diagnosed and a second opinion renders the same diagnosis. But one patient may respond to their illness (personal interpretation and meaning of the diagnosis and disease) a little differently than another. One person may see the diagnosis as a catastrophic death knell and simply give up while another patient with the same diagnosis may interpret it as a challenge which can be conquered.

Others would say of the person, "he is sick" and place that patient in the role of being sick. Depending on the disease, they may stay away from the sick person or they may come to help, assist, support the patient. Ludwig's understanding of these three different interrelated definitions helps clarify the viewpoint from which to understand health and healing.

Ludwig's detailed analysis of the healing ministry of Jesus is wonderful. Like Morton Kelsey, in his book Healing and Christianity, who writes that for Christians, healing begins and ends with Jesus, Dr. Ludwig similarly shows that Jesus is the Healer, and that it is He who ushers in God's plan for recovering mankind to Himself. Healings are a sign of the Kingdom of God which is restoring order in creation. This includes the people's restoration to health as well as healing disease and disorders of the mind, body, spirit and society.

In detailed analysis of the miracles of Jesus, Dr. Ludwig shows God's love for mankind. Pain and suffering are seen as enemies, symptoms of the result of sin in the world. He makes it clear that disease is not because of one's individual sin (he rejects the cause and effect retribution model that claims one is being punished for a particular sin). Still, you do hear a lot of people with this punishment viewpoint say, "I am being punished for my particular sin." Instead, Ludwig argues that all people are under the consequences of the broken cosmos, and that pain and suffering rain on both the just and unjust.

While Jesus does not heal everyone, He shows by signs what God intends to do and will do in restoring order. The final restoration is postponed until God decides to bring about a final and full reordering of the cosmos (as described in the book of Revelation in the New Testament of the Holy Bible where the writer sees a new earth and a new heaven). In the meantime, the church's mission is to establish its healing ministry, to pray for physical, mental, and emotional healing, and to work towards the restoration of society, and the many broken relationships within society. For many this broadens the work to healing the earth itself.

Ludwig urges us to think holistically. Instead of thinking (as in Greek terms) that "I have a soul," he urges us to think "I am soul." Instead of thinking "I have a body," he urges us to think "I am body." Instead of thinking that "I have a mind," he urges us to think "I am mind."

This certainly fits the recent paradigm shift in what Candace Pert in her book Molecules of Emotion calls the "body-mind" matrix. By this hyphen she means to say that it is not "mind" and "body" but rather it is one unity... "body-mind" or "mind-body." She claims "Mind" is everywhere in the body not just in the brain. Every cell of the body "knows" what is happening in the body. Cells automatically know what to do when you cut your finger or sever an artery or get cancer or are fighting a virus. Chemical and cellular processes "know" their roles. Killer T cells can identify what is "of the body" and what is "not of the body." While these cells do what is necessary to keep the immune system healthy, other cells go about their business of keeping the body functioning well.

Ludwig points out that if physical health is to be restored, it will depend on the efficient functioning of the immune system. But physical health can be impacted by one's thinking (mind) or emotional state. The immune system can be influenced by the power of positive suggestion but it can also be negatively influenced as well. Taking this one step farther, the recent writings and research of Dr. Daniel Amen, whom Ludwig did not live long enough to come to know, clearly indicate that

Ludwig was writing in the right direction. Amen's works such as Change Your Brain, Change Your Life, and Change Your Brain, Change Your Body, speak to the holistic nature of the human being. Amen's work, Healing the Hardware of Your Soul: Enhance Your Brain to Improve Your Work, Love, and Spiritual Life, reflects the new understandings of the unity of the body with the quality of social relationships. Interestingly, Dr. Amen is also a Christian who is challenging colleagues to rethink holistically, with the brain as the target of research. He is becoming well known throughout America through his PBS television programs.

To appreciate the importance of Ludwig's research, note his chapter titles of Order Restored are as follows:

Ch. 1 - Culture, Disease and Health
Ch. 2 - Health and Illness in the Old Testament
Ch. 3 - Health and Healing in the New Testament
Ch. 4 - The Biblical Model of Health
Ch. 5 - The Healing of Persons
Ch. 6 - Faith and Healing
Ch. 7 - Sickness and Suffering
Ch. 8 - The Ministry of Healing
Appendix 1 - A Service of Spiritual Healing
Appendix 2 - My Personal Journal

Unfortunately this book is still relatively unknown within the Lutheran church and may be completely unknown beyond that denomination. This is a shame because it is a rich and rewarding book, well researched and solid, and forms the basis of a way of thinking about healing and health that harkens back to Genesis, Chapter 1, where the creation is still in chaos, so to speak, and God is about to "order" it all.

Order Restored is a great title for this wonderful book. As a member of the Lutheran Church - Missouri Synod, Garth published his book through Concordia Publishing House's Academic Press. In my opinion it gives an outstanding presentation of Lutheran theology and healing that every pastor and congregation should study. Recently a pastor friend of mine, Rev. Keith Jones, pastor at Good Shepherd Lutheran Church in Goleta, California (near Santa Barbara), told me that he and his board of elders just completed a multiple week study of this book. He said it was trans-formative for them. One elder who had been skeptical because of his medical background came to find this writing very compatible with the scientific view of healing. It's like the phrase "prayer and Prozac" coined by Dr. Dale A. Matthews in his work, The Faith Factor: Proof of the Healing Power of Prayer. Theology, medicine, and healing can indeed be compatible within the holistic context of order restored.

At the Reclaim Conference (described elsewhere in this book), it was one of the books available on the book table. Many copies were bought, and the feedback has been tremendous from those who have discovered this wonderful tome. Order a copy for your pastor or church leaders. Walk through it and see if it doesn't profoundly alter your perspective on God's work of healing in His creation.

Dr. Garth Ludwig was a professor of anthropology on the faculty of Concordia University, Irvine, California. He was a scholar, educator, supervisor, theologian, and student advisor. He was also my friend. We often talked about the field of mental health, as he helped direct students either into Masters in Social Work or Masters in Marriage and Family Therapy. He also had an inquisitive mind, asking difficult questions about complex matters. He was a pursuer of truth, and was highly valued on the faculty at Concordia.

I recently met a man who told me of a younger Garth Ludwig when he was a parish pastor. The story I heard was of a Pastor Ludwig who cared deeply about the illness which struck the family in his congregation. The man told me how Garth was always there, praying for healing and normal health of the ill. I was told that the prayers were indeed helpful, and that it was Pastor Ludwig's tireless efforts towards healing that was so appreciated by this man and his family. He said that everyone felt that way about Pastor Ludwig. He was a man with heart and compassion. Hearing this made me appreciate even more the thoughts and structure's in Ludwig's writing.

What also is wonderfully surprising is his courage to describe the new talent of young secular writers (physicians, healers, others) who were just then at the cutting edge. One of those in his book is Deepak Chopra, who had just written his first book, Quantum

Healing. This was the very book that writer Elleston Trevor (aka: Adam Hall) had told me about when I visited him at his home, which later became one of the reasons I became interested in the area of healing and prayer. Ludwig was not afraid to look at any viewpoint on healing, whether secular or sacred, if he felt it provided another piece of the puzzle on healing. When I read some of his paragraphs about those first glimpses into many who now in robust, maturity, have led the field for a couple of decades now, I am proud that Concordia Academic Press published Ludwig's book.

Finally, just to underscore once again the point of Ludwig's writing, God wants order restored and will bring it about. God is not a God of chaos. God is a God of order. That is what God seeks: the restoration of the body, mind, spirit and all of creation. Certainly this is rooted in the ministry of Jesus' healing Time after time, Jesus confronts illness and destruction, and turns it around for healing and wholeness.

Even when the cross seemed to kill Jesus once and for all, there came a restored order in the resurrection of Jesus. Chaos would not have the final say. Order would win the day, and in fact, in the book of Revelation there is a description of "a new order" that is coming. The writer frames it as a new creation, a new earth, and that those who have died will indeed share in the resurrection with God when He comes once and for all to restore the order.

I believe that Dr. Ludwig's book is of great value to the church. It gives a theological framework in which to understand that the true nature of God is to heal. It is no accident that one-fifth of the Gospels in the New Testament are about healing. I agree with Morton Kelsey, that the healing works are not solely for the purpose of showing that God's kingdom has broken into the world or just as demonstrations of the power of the Gospel. In addition to these, the healing ministry of Jesus shows us that the center of God's being is for healing, for restoring, for ordering, and reconciling. In other words, Love is the center. Certainly God's love is translated into the forgiveness of sin, through the cross of Christ. As the Scriptures record, anyone who believes on Him will not perish but have everlasting life. (John 3:16) That's God's love, and it was shown in the sending of His Son.

Yet we also see the human Jesus weeping when His friend Lazarus is dead. Jesus has compassion for a man whose daughter has died. Jesus heals these two, but He heals others, and continues to heal, because love and healing and restoring order is what He has come to do. It is His essense. God so loved the world that He gave His only begotten Son.

I believe that Ludwig's book is a gift to the church, much like Healing and Christianity by Kelsey, in that it gives a solid basis for understanding the nature of illness, disease and even death. But it heralds "good tidings" that illness, disease and death are not the final act. Instead, Christ comes in resurrection power to trump these chaos producing processes. This is shown in the children's book by C.S. Lewis called The Lion, the Witch and the Wardobe. There is a scene when the Witch has killed the Lion, Aslan. (Aslan is the Christ figure.) He has been "crucified" on a stone tablet. When she comes next to look at the body of the slain Aslan, the lion's body is gone. The Witch is mystified because she used her Deep Magic to kill the lion once and for all. But then, Aslan appears before her. She cannot believe it. She is stunned. She tells Aslan that he cannot be alive for she used Deep Magic on him. He replies that there is a Deeper Magic still. It is this Deeper Magic (but not really magic at all) by which the Witch's intended chaos is reversed. All of the land of Narnia, that had been plunged into deepening hard freezing cold by the Witch, was about to thaw out. Order was about to be restored because of the "resurrected" Aslan. As He is brought back to life, so is the creation brought back to life. Green sprouts appear. Trees grow. Grass grows. Brooks and springs flow. Life beats Death. Warmth triumphs over cold. Love defeats hatred. Chaos is ordered. We see it in Lewis' children's story. We see it in the healings of people given up for dead or believed by their doctors to be beyond hope.

My parents taught me the game of Pinochle. More than once, when I thought I had the final hand, they would slap their final card on the pile of cards. "Trump!" they would shout. I had the winning card. I was sure of it. "Trump!" they would say as the trump card was played.

God slams down His final card... "Trump!" to the Evil one, to the Devil, and spirits of destruction, to the powers of darkness and disarray... "Trump!" to the minions of chaos and disorder. Theologically, that trump card, is Jesus Christ. In His very being, He was beaten, scourged, spit upon, wore a crown of thorns, was nailed to a cross (the Romans had perfected capital punishment), and left to die. The End. Finis.

But God is for ordering chaos. The trump card is played. Jesus is Victor! He rises to life, is raised from the dead. The Scriptures say "the first fruit of those who die in Christ." (First Corinthians 15: 20)

In so many ways, that is the theological basis for Ludwig's thought. That healing presence and healing power of God is part of God's very created order. Though it is now a "Fallen" order, it is an order restored. Sick people can and do get better. Dr. Bernie Siegel and others can write about "exceptional" patients. Some like Dr. Andrew Weil see these "miracles" as "spontaneous healings"; which lay within nature. Ludwig's view is that this very nature is part of God's good order. Embedded in it are the energies and seeds for healing. In my own words, it is the Creator God from the First Article of the historic Apostle's and Nicene Creeds which speak of the One who made all things, in heaven and earth. Then in the Second Article of those creeds, the focus is on the living Christ whose work continues even to today. The third article of both creeds describes the work of the Holy Spirit.

When Pastor Bill Dasch asks the petitioner, "what would you like Jesus to do for you," he is believing and proclaiming that Jesus is alive and that His healing presence continues. The Third Article of the Apostle's and Nicene Creed point to the power, the dynamic "power" of the Holy Spirit that breathes new life into people, that as the Scriptures say, when we are weak and do not even know what to pray for, that Holy Spirit intercedes for us in groans too deep for words. (Romans 8:26). That root word is the ancient word for heal... "sozo." God is the healing God as seen in the work of His son and the healing through His Holy Spirit.

I think that Ludwig's book is also a blessing on those in Seminaries and Bible colleges. His book grounds those students in a theology of healing. This empowers them in their first assignments (or Calls) to carry with them a viewpoint that reminds them how important hospital visits are, and how important sick and shut-in calls are to those needing the loving care of their minister. Instead of begrudging the sights and smells of hospitals, or aged bodies, or thinking that there are more important things to do, this book shows them Jesus and his healing ministry to which they are also called into.

When Jesus proclaimed His mission, He said it was primarily three things: preaching, teaching and healing. Pastors are not to shrink on the third one or believe that somehow the healing work of God ended at the close of the first century when the original 12 apostles, or the original 72 were sent out, or when the first eye-witnesses had passed. No, not at all. There is plenty of testimony in the next few centuries of the ongoing healing ministry Jesus Himself did and passed on to others. In the 20th and 21st centuries that healing presence has become more honored and recognized throughout all continents. Re-awakenings in the charismatic Christian communities, and the resurgence of healing ministries in mainline denominations are seen as powerful images of God's work of healing.

For Lutherans, Ludwig's theological presentation, of what he himself called the beginning thoughts, is well worth studying. Yes, there is a God that heals... heals in our everyday world in many different ways.

Chapter 41
Reclaim! The Healing Ministry of Jesus Christ

He said, "I want to stand."
Bill replied with a great laugh, "You're killing me here... You want to do what?" He said, with a twinkle in his eye.
The man replied, "I want to try to stand." He sat in his wheel chair and looked up at Bill.
Bill said, "Alright, gentlemen. Let's see what we can do. Ron, will you stand behind his wheelchair and hold it steady," and then he motioned for the four or five other men standing around to draw in closer together. Bill moved toward the man. It was clear that these two men knew each other very well... Pastor Bill who joshed with the man in the wheelchair, and the man in the wheelchair who trusted Pastor Bill implicitly. As I took my place behind the wheelchair, I was not exactly sure what was happening here, but I did my part in this moment along with some Elders and leaders of the congregation.
Then Pastor Bill said with his great Texas drawl, "You know I always get nervous whenever anyone is in a wheelchair and asks for healing prayer. I wonder if they think I'm one of these television evangelists who will strike their forehead and they will miraculously throw their wheelchair away." He was smiling and standing in front of the man seated in the wheelchair. He was still looking at him and was explaining to the men and to me, "We don't know what God is going to do for Ralph today but let's see what God has in store." (Author's Note: I've changed the man's name to Ralph to protect his anonymity). Pastor Bill continued, "Ralph has been in his wheelchair for about two years, and has had healing prayer before. He asked me as part of our Reclaim conference if we could pray for him before we go to lunch, and I told him we'd certainly pray for him." (The conference attendees had already gone to lunch and we were delayed for this special request for healing prayer.)
Again Pastor Bill continued, "So Ralph is it okay if we anoint you with oil and if we place hands on you?" Ralph said, "Yes, I would appreciate that very much." Then Pastor Bill asked him,

"What would you like Jesus to do for you today?" Ralph replied, "I'd like Him to help me stand up." Pastor Bill said, "That's what we'll do," and to us Pastor Bill said, "Ralph has not been able to stand on his own for a couple of years now, so we're going to see what God's going to do today."

Then Pastor Bill put a dab of oil onto his finger and made the sign of the cross on Ralph's forehead, "I anoint you in the Name of the Father, and the Son and the Holy Spirit." And then as others placed hands on Ralph's back and shoulders and forearms, Pastor Bill placed his own hands on Ralph's head as he sat in his wheelchair. Pastor Bill began by giving adoration to God. Then he prayed Ralph's request that today he might stand up, and rise up from his wheelchair. Then Pastor Bill ended with thanksgiving to God. When the prayer ended, Pastor Bill said to Ralph, "What was that like to have us pray for you?" Ralph said that it felt good.

Then he told Pastor Bill that he'd like to try to stand. Pastor Bill grinned and said, "Let's see it." And gripping the sides of his wheelchair, Ralph struggled to lift himself up. He was shaking and putting good effort to try to rise. We watched as he half-rose. I wondered if he could go all the way. Then with more effort, Ralph stood. He was wobbly but he was standing. Pastor Bill said, "Look at you!! Wow.. Look at that." Ralph didn't say anything. He just stood there. Then Ralph said, "I want to take a step." Pastor Bill said, "Now take it easy. Let's see what you can do." Ralph slowly put one foot in front of the other... and shifted his weight slowly... and took his first step. I pushed the chair a few inches forward to make sure the seat of the chair was positioned correctly in case he had to sit back down quickly. His fingers touched the arms of the wheelchair as he wobbled a little but kept standing. Them I was amazed as he took one more baby step forward. Pastor Bill said, "You're doing good, Ralph. Look at you." Then he added in a supportive voice, "Praise God." Then Ralph said "I've got to sit down now." And he lowered himself down into the chair. It was an amazing sight to witness. Then Pastor Bill and Ralph chatted a bit about how he was feeling. Then we all went to lunch.

This was in the summer of 2009. Rev. Dr. Bill Dasch and I had put together a three day training entitled "Reclaim! Recovering the Healing Ministry of Jesus." It was held at St. John's Lutheran Church, in Mansfield, Texas, about a half hour south of the DFW International Airport in Dallas, Texas. An invitation had gone out to many congregations of the Lutheran Church - Missouri Synod in those states surrounding Texas as well as many congregations and Districts nationwide. The response was terrific. People and presenters came from all over the United States.

As previously reported in this book, I had met Pastor Dasch when he was pastor in Houston, Texas. A colleague of mine had met him and recommended him to me. I was impressed with his work in healing prayer, and enjoyed meeting his prayer team members. Out of that came a series of 16 "Prayer for Healing" workshops held in the Pacific Southwest District of the Lutheran Church - Missouri Synod a couple of years later. Those were so successful that Bill and I decided to design and host a national conference for Lutheran clergy and congregations at the new church he was serving now in Mansfield, Texas.

St. John's Lutheran Church of Mansfield, Texas was stepping forward to host this very important conference, and was financially supporting it. Many of its members were providing transportation for speakers to and from the airport. Other volunteers were manning the registration desk, serving in hospitality roles, and coordinating the dozens of details necessary to make this a successful conference.

In planning this conference, Pastor Bill and I wanted to invite a couple of current District Presidents as keynote presenters. Each of the invited DP's gracefully agreed to assist us in this conference. In addition, President Ken Hennings, the DP of the Texas District brought greetings from his district and spoke about the importance of healing in the church.

President Larry Stoterau, DP of the Pacific Southwest District presented a moving keynote under the title of, "Why I Pray For Healing," which included his own personal experience of healing. Another keynote address was presented by former Kansas District President, Howard Patten. His presentation was entitled, "There's Power in the Blood: Healing and the

Sacraments," in which he spoke of the importance of the sacraments as a means of God's healing us. The Rev. Dr. Bill Dasch and I also gave a keynote address under the title, "Reclaiming the Healing Ministry of Jesus."

We also thought it would be good for participants to have choices of topics in "break-out rooms" in the afternoons of the conference. There were eight of these "sectional presentations". One of these was entitled: "Teach Us To Pray" presented by Rev. Dr. Bill and Sheila Dasch.

The other sessions were titled:
"Forgiveness and Healing" - Rev. Dr. David Kruger
"Soaking Prayer" - Rev. Steve Stutz
"How To Run a Prayer Train" - Chuck and Susan Heather
"The Healing Power of God in Lutheran Worship" - Dr. Wallace Horton
"When God Doesn't Heal" - Rev. Ron Rehrer
"How To Teach Children To Pray" - Bobette Stegall, MEd
"Healing the Healer" - Dr. John M. Hirsch

In addition to the presentations and workshops, there were also two planned evening worship services. One of the guest preachers was a friend from my old seminary days whom I'd not seen in over 30 years: Rev. Robert Preece, the First Vice President of the Texas District of the Lutheran Church - Missouri Synod. Also at each worship service, prayer teams stood at the foot of the stage praying for the dozens of persons who came for prayer. Some came with requests for physical healing, some with concerns about family members and beloved ones, while others asked for more of a quality, like patience or courage in the face of some life experience. Prayer teams asked if they could anoint the person with oil, followed by asking, "What would you like Jesus to do tonight?" Then with permission, members of the prayer teams would lay hands on the person who had come for prayer, and pray exactly for what was requested using that person's own words. There were many tears shed while the prayers were said and music continued in the sanctuary.

Back to Ralph: On the second day of the conference, Ralph once again asked if he could have special prayer. Again the same men and Pastor Bill prayed for Ralph as in a similar manner as the previous day. This time, not only did Ralph stand and take another step, he took many steps. All of them were slow and deliberate but I counted them as I pushed the wheelchair behind him. This time he took 37 steps. Then he had to sit down again. We were all witnessing the results of healing prayer.

The third day of the conference during the lunch break, we prayed for Ralph again. This time he rose... and walked slowly across the front of the sanctuary and into the older part of the building. This time, he walked about 180 plus steps! It was amazing to watch. I continued my role in keeping the wheelchair aligned behind him just in case.

The next day I left back for California. But Pastor Bill sent an email letting me know of Ralph's progress. On the fourth day he walked outside and a few days later he went to his physician to show him his progress. His doctor must have been amazed!

Pastor Bill, like previous ministers described earlier in my book, takes no credit for what happened to Ralph. Pastor Dasch is clear that it is we who pray and it is God who heals. This was not the first time that Ralph had been prayed for in the two previous years. Why was he able to stand and then be able to walk this time? I do not know the answer. What I believe is that God can do anything He wishes whenever He wishes. I've said elsewhere in my book that some healings are gradual in that they take place over time. Perhaps prayer has a cumulative effect. Sometimes things happen more rapidly, indeed, sometimes immediately. Sometimes things seem to never happen. As more than one writer in healing ministries has said, sometimes the healing is the "going Home to heaven," in other words, it is not an earthly healing, but rather, it is a healing in heaven.

The Reclaim conference was a great first step in teaching healing prayer from the perspective taught by Pastor Bill Dasch. There was to have been a Reclaim II the following year. However, Pastor Dasch's young son, Tristen, who had battled leukemia for years, turned for the worse. From May until August, 2010 Pastor Bill Dasch and his wife, Sheila, and Tristen's brother, Taylor, turned their fervent prayers towards the healing of Tristen. He had been transferred down to St. Jude's Hospital and Pastor Bill left his congregation in Mansfield to be by the side of his boy, Tristen, until the very end.

In spite of the best efforts of other prayer partners and prayer ministers who prayed without ceasing for Tristen, in the end, Tristen died. It was a terribly sad day and broke our hearts when Tristen died. Today at St. John's Lutheran Church in Mansfield, Texas, there is a memorial to Tristen with a shade tree and waterfall in memory of Tristen. I can easily remember playing pool with him, shooting basketballs and playing the game of HORSE with him, and watching him dribble the basketball down the court at school. He lost his battle to cancer but his life is a testimony of courage and great faith. He is one of those who received his healing in heaven.

So there was no Reclaim II. But Pastor Bill did finish writing and publishing a training manual for the Reclaim workbook that all participants received at the healing conference. Also, the entire Reclaim conference was recorded on DVD and is available as a boxed set from St. John's in Mansfield.

It was my honor and privilege to work with Bill in the development and presentation of the Reclaim conference in 2009. It touched the lives of many, and clergy and congregations who sent representatives took back with them practical ways to start healing prayer ministries in their own churches. I hope that in the future there will be a Reclaim II, and that the work we began in the past decade will continue on in the future.

(author's note in 2016, Pastor Bill Dasch retired from his church in Mansfield, Texas, and he went into full-time healing prayer ministry. He and his Team have done numerous training events in congregations and other venues. To learn more about his healing work, ask for a prayer for healing, or to schedule an event, go to Bill Dasch Ministries, www.billdasch.com)

Chapter 42
Arthur Umbach and The Many Forms of Prayer

My good friend and colleague, Arthur Umbach, has taught me many good things about prayer. One of the most interesting aspects of Art's teachings on prayer is that one learns there is a vast variety of prayer forms developed over centuries of time. I have heard Art present several times on the topic of Prayer and Spiritual Formation. With his permission, I am sharing some of the things he teaches in his course. Art is a deeply spiritual man and a great man of prayer. Art doesn't see himself that way at all. He will humbly tell you that he is just a beginner or that he is just learning. But he is an excellent teacher. I am indebted to him for much of what is in this chapter. During my sabbatical on prayer and healing, I came across nearly all of these forms of prayer, and did some primary reading (and praying) these types of prayer. But Art has done such a nice job of summarizing each of their salient points that I have asked him if I could share with you, my readers, from his presentation. If you ever have the opportunity to hear Art be sure you do so.

The center of prayer for Art is Jesus. His key question in his presentations always is, "How do we develop a closer walk with Jesus?" While it is true that you will find prayers in nearly all religions and most spiritual walks, for Art, the only pathway is with Jesus. He says right at the beginning that "our purpose is to introduce spiritual disciplines and prayer forms, to enrich and nurture your spiritual journey toward a greater awareness of God's presence and love in your life (Inner journey), to nurture a passion for Jesus and a life of service (Outer journey), and to build up the community of believers (Together journey)."

He begins by sharing from the New Testament of the Bible, words from St. Paul, in Romans 8:26-27, where Paul writes that we do not know how to pray as we ought. Then follows those wonderful words where Paul writes that God's Spirit intercedes for us, and this is described with groans that words cannot express. I've always found this to be comforting to know that the

Spirit of God is already there praying on our behalf, even when we do not pray as we ought.

Then Art focuses in on the person of Jesus. He quotes Luke 5:15-16 which describes Jesus as withdrawing from the crowds in order to pray. Next, he quotes Luke 6:12-13 where Jesus is described as going out to a mountainside and praying all night long. Next is Luke 9:28-31 where Jesus takes his friends, his disciples, Peter, John and James with him to pray. Then in two more quoted Bible passages, Luke 11:11 and Mark 1:25, we see Jesus praying in a certain place and also in a lonely place. Art makes the point that we see Jesus opening Himself up to God, and that during His entire ministry, Jesus is in constant communion with God through prayer. Jesus even said, "I can do nothing on my own."

At this point in his talk, Art reads from two well known 20th Century spiritual masters, Henri J. M. Nouwen and Thomas Merton, both well known Catholic priests familiar with the contemplative life as well as the way of the world. Out of Solitude by Nouwen speaks of how Jesus from a place of solitude, and the place of the lonely, finds courage to follow God's will and not his own. Thoughts From Solitude by Merton reflects upon the profound sense of not knowing where the road will lead that God leads us on. Yet, "I will trust you always." Both writings speak to the trusting of God to lead and to protect.

Art walks his audience through a variety of prayer types. Here are those from the first workshop I attended under Art's skillful leadership:

1. Breathing Prayer
2. Lectio Divina
3. The Examen
4. Jesus Prayer
5. Centering Prayer

Art describes each of these types of prayer, and gives examples of how he uses them in his own personal prayer life, and how they have been used historically by the church. He leads participants in experiences of these prayers, and describes when they may be particularly useful.

Then Art turns to other practices which may enhance one's spiritual growth and depth in prayer. These are:

1. Spiritual Direction
2. Praying Without Words (such as Praying Bible Stories and Praying Images)
3. Journaling
4. Christ Centered Fasting
5. Healing Prayer

Next Art describes a process for "Discerning God's Will." He describes the preparation for communal discernment and the "Discernment Process."

The next section speaks about "Dreams - A Way to Listen to God." He discusses "remembering dreams," and "ways of working with your dreams." There is a prescribed way of working with "symbols and images" from our dreams.

The final section of his workshop is about the use of the labyrinth. Referencing the ancient labyrinth at Chartres Cathedral near Paris, France as well as more contemporary examples of the labyrinth at Grace Cathedral in San Francisco and Christ the King Lutheran Church in Torrance, California, Art describes appropriate uses of this symbolic presentation of the pilgrimage to the Holy Land.

The labyrinth can open us up to God.

In the wrap-up of his workshop, Art lists additional aids to prayer. I found this to be a profound and challenging arena of prayer life. Among these aids are:

1. Prayer lists
2. Readings (Martin Luther, Early Church "desert fathers", Nouwen, Thomas Merton)
3. Prayer, Confession, Forgiveness (e.g. Matthew 6:14-15)

Here are additional recommendations Art makes:

1. Accept God's forgiveness
2. Acknowledge the anger and hurt caused by the offense of another
3. "Decide" to forgive - let go
4. Pray for the person who hurt you
5. Rule out revenge
6. Walk in the offender's shoes
7. Extend good will to the offender
8. Give yourself time to heal and take care of yourself

Art concludes by offering many practical suggestions for prayer and answers questions from the audience. Very often questions from the audience ask about various techniques in the implementation of these various types of prayer. Art graciously goes over these to help the person who asked the question deepen their knowledge. He also offers a very comprehensive bibliography for further reference.

But what is always the central motif at the ending of his presentation is "prayer is not a technique or way of getting God to do our bidding, but a relationship with a loving God, who 'longs' for our presence." He points back to Augustine's famous phrase that "our hearts are restless until they find their rest in You."

Art says, "Our desire for a deeper relationship with God is an invitation from God, who intimately cares about us and who invites us to participate in the divine activities of healing and transformation."

While there are many different prayer forms, the ones listed here are among the core. Of course, intercessory prayer is probably the most well known, in which the praying person asks God to intercede on their or another's behalf. This is often where the petitioner requests something from God or asks God to do something. In a recent study reported on CNN News, (April 2010), about a third of people do not ask God for anything. These persons pray prayers of gratitude. But about another third of people do ask for something specific they want God to do for them. Still another third prays a combination of these two forms... prayers of gratitude and thanksgiving and asking God to do something for them (intercessory prayer).

Whatever form one chooses to use for prayer, or combination of such, the wisdom of Art Umbach is that deep and prayerful listening in prayer draws us into a loving connection with God, neighbor, and self. It is listening that may be the greatest work of our prayer.

References:

Personal Prayer Forms, various forms of prayer, presented by Art Umbach and the Spiritual Life Team of the Southeastern District of the Lutheran Church - Missouri Synod

Prayer Resources, prayer services for congregations and personal prayer helps presented by Art Umbach and the Spiritual Life Team of the Southeastern District of the Lutheran Church - Missouri Synod
Abundant Living, Art's Blog
SED Prayer Ministry, Art Umbach on prayer life
A Minute With Art Umbach, Art speaks about his ministry as Director of Spiritual Life (Vimeo)

Chapter 43
Dale Matthews - The Role of Faith in Healing

We have probably all heard sayings like "Prayer Changes Things," or "Life is Fragile, Handle With Prayer." While millions of Christians pray and millions of other religious people of other beliefs including many non-religious people also pray, one wonders if faith makes a difference in the outcomes of prayer.

Two wonderful books address this very issue. The first is Dr. Dale Matthew's book, The Faith Factor: Proof of the Healing Power of Prayer, and Dr. Harold G. Koenig's book, The Healing Power of Faith: How Belief and Prayer Can Help You Triumph Over Disease. These are not the only two books available on this terribly crucial question, but they are excellent places to begin your own research.

On the cover of Matthew's The Faith Factor, there is an endorsement from Joan Borysenko, author of Minding The Body, Mending the Mind. She writes, "The Faith Factor will surely become the classic reference on religion and healing... A brilliant, masterful work."

On the front cover of Koenig's book The Healing Power of Faith, there is an endorsement from Herbert Benson of Harvard Medical School, author of The Relaxation Response. He writes, "This book is marvelous. Dr. Koenig has given us a compelling and accurate, highly readable synthesis of the healing power of faith."

A few years ago, I had the opportunity to hear Dr. Daniel Amen, a brilliant neuropsychiatrist, speak on the brain and it's marvelous capacities. During his talk he made reference to Dale Matthew's book and research. I was in a room with a hundred other clergy persons, and Dr. Amen was highly recommending that everyone read Matthew's work. I would agree with his endorsement as well as the other endorsement of Koenig's book. The hardback of Matthew's book came out in 1998 and the paperback version was out in 1999. At the time Dale Matthews, M.D., was associate professor of medicine at Georgetown

University School of Medicine. He had already authored a four-volume annotated bibliography of clinical research on many spiritual subjects, and numerous peer-reviewed scientific articles. While I was not able to meet Dr. Matthews during my sabbatical, he was third on my list of persons to meet with. This brilliant Christian writer has made a very serious attempt to explain the research on the faith factor. In his acknowledgements page I was not surprised to find that some of the very writers and researchers who have so influenced my sabbatical were persons he was thanking. He thanks many people including Judith and Francis MacNutt for introducing him to the ministry of healing. He thanks other pioneers who explored the boundaries of faith and medicine such as Herbert Benson, Larry Dossey, Morton Kelsey, Randolph Byrd. He also thanks Harold Koenig and many others who do research yet are grounded in faith. Reading along further you read of his blessing upon Dave Larson who had been his research colleague. (Dave Larson was a giant in the field as I wrote in a distinct chapter on his legacy earlier in this book). It is amazing to read how many persons Matthews acknowledges as influencing his work. Reading his acknowledgment page is sort of like reading a "who's who" in the field of faith research. All of them I read or met with during my sabbatical.

What Matthews does brilliantly in his book is to share with the reader the frontier of medicine and spirituality. He credits Herbert Benson and Larry Dossey and others for opening up the medical and scientific community to the possibilities of spirituality and faith. He details how physicians have been taught not to pray with their patients because of the great divide between medicine and religion, but goes on to share how he personally has come to see how important it may be for a physician to pray for his patients, if not with them.

It is wonderful to read of Dr. Matthew's strong grounding in the Bible. He had read it regularly throughout his life as a physician, and has probed its depths. He has learned that God does not always say yes to "our desperate prayers for healing," but he believes that God comforts us when we suffer through the loss of a beloved. Having read through the Old Testament and New Testament frequently, he has come to believe that God does heal.

He has seen this in the very lives of his patients, and he encourages his patients to seek God's grace and presence in their suffering.

Dale Matthews believes strongly that the faith factor can and does help people in a variety of ways and on a variety of issues. Some of the studies he reports on show that faith is involved in the prevention of disease, recovery from illness, in the treatment of emotional and mental suffering, especially with depression and grief, as well as conditions such as addictions, handling life's hurts, and overall happiness with life.

A number of studies have shown that the frequency of attendance at religious services is the strongest predictor of marital happiness for both men and women. Attendance at religious services is a stronger factor than age, income, education, occupation, number of children or other factors with regard to the prediction of marital happiness. This same factor of attendance at religious services is also found in studies done by Dr. Harold Koenig and others.

In other studies, Matthews found that 80 percent of students attending church three times a week were virgins as compared with 37 percent of those who attended less than once a week. This is seen as a very healthy thing for students since it helps prevent sexually transmitted disease such as AIDS, gonorrhea, syphilis, and herpes.

Other studies have shown that faith helps people cope with terminal illness, such as cancer and other life threatening diseases. It also plays a significant role with people on chronic hemodialysis and in coping with the stresses of life.

These reports about the positive role of faith in people's lives is but the tip of an iceberg. Space prevents me from sharing so many wonderful study outcomes reported in Dr. Matthew's book. However a friend of mine sent me an article written by Carolyn Conroy, who was the news editor of CompuServe at the time:

Do Religious People Really Live Longer?

The answer seems to be a resounding YES, if you believe 42 scientific studies that examined the link between religious involvement and mortality that were reviewed by the National Institute for Healthcare Research in Rockville, Maryland. The statistic: The people who were most involved in their religions were 29 percent more likely to be alive when the various studies were completed than were their nonreligious counterparts, reports WebMD.

Why? The short answer is that religious people tend to drink and smoke less and are less obese than nonbelievers. They also tend to have healthier lifestyles and exercise more. (The Seventh Day Adventists are well known for their healthier lifestyles). They have a positive support network that helps them better handle life's stress, and their beliefs help them make sense of their personal suffering.

The long answer is more complicated mostly because the researchers can't really figure out how religious involvement boosts health. But they do know that prayer, church attendance, abiding faith, and even singing in the church choir all seem to positively affect blood pressure, heart, and coping skills, according to Dale Matthews, a medical doctor and author of God for the 21st Century, an excerpt of which has been published on BeliefNet. He says, "The medical effects of faith are a matter not just of faith but also of science." He insists scientific studies demonstrate there is medical value in religious commitment. Prayer, worship attendance, and being part of a community of faith can help prevent and treat mental disorders, heart disease, cancer, and addictions. They can also prolong survival and enhance recovery. Matthews is quick to point out that physicians and clergy each have their own unique role in caring for the sick. One should not supplant the other. "We need prayer and Prozac, clergy and clinicians, faith and medicine."

–Cathryn Conroy, 12/16/02

Matthews says that the bond between religion and medicine is actually an ancient one. "Since the dawn of recorded history, these twin traditions of healing have been partners in the care of the sick, plowing together the holy ground of healing," he says. "In my office, I encourage everyone to exercise regularly, eat properly, stop smoking and excessive alcohol use, take medicines correctly, and even wear seat belts. Should I tell them to pray, read Scripture, attend worship, or work at a soup kitchen? My answer is yes!"

Of course, being religious does not guarantee good health. Most of us will get sick during our lifetimes. And it's a sure thing that we will all die no matter what our religious beliefs or practices. I urge you to get the Faith Factor and read it, and be amazed at how much his research is impacting how we think and live.

While I have a separate chapter on Harold Koenig, the focus of this chapter is faith and healing. In this context I want to discuss briefly Koenig's work on faith and healing.

Koenig's book The Healing Power of Faith was also published in 1999. His chapter titles invite the reader to delve deeper into the research literature. Some of his chapter titles are:

Religious People Have Healthy Lifestyles
Religious People Cope Well with Stress
Religion Offers Protection from Depression and Helps Those Afflicted to Recover Quickly
Religious People Live Longer, Healthier Lives
Religious People May Have Stronger Immune Systems
Religion May Protect People From Serious Cardiovascular Disease
Religious People Use Fewer Expensive Hospital Services
Helping Yourself and Your Loved Ones Benefit from the Power of Faith

All of Koenig's books are excellent reading and this one in particular gives a strong argument for the role of faith in healing. As Andrew Weaver pointed out to me, when you read about outcomes from studies on religion and medicine, or spirituality and health, or religious faith on outcomes of illness, most of the time you are reading from something Dr. Koenig has researched. Here is an example of what I mean.

Someone mailed to me a newspaper clipping from August 8, 2001, written by Nigel Hawkes, Health Editor of the Times (London). The title of the article is Loss of faith "increases risk of dying."

Nigel writes, "Christians whose faith is shaken when they fall ill are at greater risk of dying, according to a study in two American hospitals." He goes on to write that earlier research has shown that regular church attendance can lengthen life. This is the first study to show that there are consequences from a loss of faith.

The study was of 595 people who were 55 years old or older. They had various illnesses and were hospitalized in two hospitals in the Durham, North Carolina area. The study found that those people who died were people who felt abandoned or punished by God, as compared with those persons who survived their illness condition.

The study says that those Christians who reported feeling alienated from God, or attributed their illness to the Devil, or felt abandoned by their church community, were up to 28 percent more likely to die within the next two years than those who had no religious doubts.

This study was done by Dr. Harold Koenig and his colleague Dr. Kenneth Pargemant, a psychologist at Bowling Green State University in Ohio. According to Koenig, "Whenever anyone becomes suddenly ill with a disease that threatens life, or a way of life, they ask 'why?' or 'why me?'" He goes on to say "Some people experience anger at God for not protecting them or not answering their prayers for healing. Some feel as though God is punishing them and they question God's love for them, and sometimes they feel like others have deserted them as well."

I know of many pastors who have heard these kinds of words from their parishioners, or family members of parishioners. These words and feelings reflect the deep-seated thoughts and fears that come to many people when diagnosed with a serious disease.

Koenig addresses this by saying that these feelings are normal and expected during the stage of grief people go through. He says that most people come through this stage and do get reconnected to God and their spiritual communities, using their belief as a source of strength. But there are others that somehow get stuck, remaining in this state of feeling alienated or abandoned by God or others. Somehow they block anything spiritual from getting in.

What is clear from a report like this is that both pastors and physicians need to tune into people who have been shaken in their faith and are in big trouble. More and more medical schools are training physicians on how to take a patient's "spiritual history" but I wonder if any physician has the time to do such a history, especially if they are in an HMO or other such system.

Yet this is a serious issue that now is being surfaced from studies such as those done by Koenig, or Larson, or Pargemant and others.

What Koenig brings out so crucially in his writing is that in his four years of medical school nor in the first two years of his residency was there ever a hint that religious faith could "break the grip of addiction, shield people from depression, or calm them at times of emotional trauma." He says that in the mid-1980's the connection between health and spirituality or other "mind-body" research was embryonic and had not achieved widespread acceptance.

I remember when Joan Borysenko's book, Minding the Body, Mending the Mind first came out in 1987 that it was one of those ground-breaking books that told the story about the kinds of treatments that were used at the Mind-Body Clinic first established by herself and Dr. Klan Kutz in 1981. On page ten of her book, she introduces the concept of the power of faith and hope, and how science was just beginning to unlock the mystery of healing by beginning to understand the mechanisms of faith, belief and imagination.

When one stops to think about it, this entire field of inquiry is a little more than 30 years old with its serious research on the role of faith in healing and the mind-body connection. In some ways, perhaps, this field is just now beginning to leave its youthful adolescence, and is as a young adult, beginning to grow up more. On the Christian faith side of the equation, people such as Dr. Harold Koenig, the late Dr. David Larson, Dr. Dale Matthews, and other Christian researchers are trying to present good, solid research that demonstrates the importance of the "faith factor," regular church attendance, a deepening spirituality, the powerful role of prayer, and the importance of religious faith.

There are so many health benefits to religious faith that I strongly encourage you to read Koenig or Matthews or other such researchers. Koenig, for example, points out that religion is a significant factor in preventing suicide, and that frequent attendance at church when accompanied by a faith that is important to one's life consistently lowers blood pressure. People who have a deepening of faith and frequently attend religious services are shown to have a lower risk of heart attack.

While visiting Dr. David Larson in his office in Rockville, Maryland, he handed me a two page research summary of the Top 10 Research Studies on Religious Participation and Health Concerns, as published in peer reviewed journals documenting spirituality and health. He gave me permission to share these findings with ministers of our District. Because of copyright concerns, I am not permitted to give the details of these studies, but I can share with you in broad outline that all of the following health conditions are positively impacted with greater outcomes where faith is a factor: heart surgery survival, heart transplant recovery, high blood pressure prevention, immune functioning improvement, cancer and coping skills, depression recovery, a reduction of hospital stays, early death prevention, living longer lives and extending one's life by at least 7 years.

I am sure that there may be some person reading this book who might say, "Well, for heaven's sake, I already knew that there is a healing power of faith, or a healing power of prayer. Why in the world do I need some scientist or researcher to tell me this?" I think that from within the faith-based, religious community, it is easy to believe in the power of prayer or the power of faith. But research is enormously helpful in expanding our awareness of what we might consider in order to strengthen our faith, our worship attendance, our connection with God, etc., knowing of the greater health benefit from these practices born out by solid research at Duke University, or the National Institute of Religion and Health, and many other research universities and research centers.

I absolutely love Chapter 12 of Koenig's book in which he gives prescriptive suggestions of how you can help yourself or a loved one benefit from the power of prayer. He makes suggestions on attending religious services, of when and where to pray, how to take time to read religious scriptures, and about how to speak to your clergy person about your thoughts about God. If you are not a religious person already, he recommends that you keep an open mind to the existence of God, noting that 96% of Americans believe in the existence of God or a higher power. He gives a sample list of famous people who were "inspired people of great faith" who are worth reading, such as Mother Teresa, Dr. Albert Schweitzer, Harold Kushner, Martin Luther King, C.S. Lewis, and others. And for those not ready to consider religion, he even has some suggestions for them, including trying nonreligious meditation which may help you relax and help you receive other health benefits. He is aware that there are persons who have had negative religious experiences or have been exposed to negative or frightening religious ideas. He suggests talking this over with a loved one or trusted friend who will take the time to seriously listen to you. He suggests that spiritually healthy people accentuate the positive and not the negative. These healthy religious people "focus on God's love, kindness, generosity, and forgiveness– seeing all of us as imperfect, and dependent on God's mercy."

In May, 2001, Reader's Digest had a lead article entitled Why Doctors Now Believe Faith Heals. The writer, Lydia Strohl, writes that doctors now believe faith heals because they're finding medical evidence for it. She is right. In laboratories, in published studies, in peer reviewed journals, and in new books reporting these studies, we are learning a great deal about the healing power of faith. Now through articles like this one in Reader's Digest, researchers such as Harold Koenig, David Larson, and Dale Matthews are becoming household names. What the general public does NOT know about these three men is that they are Christians. They are men of faith who believe that there is a faith factor in healing, and that it is being evidenced by research.

These men are lighthouses of hope in that they encourage people to keep strong in their faith and to experience the healing and healthy benefits of that faith.

Chapter 44
The Byrd Study - Does Prayer Make A Difference?
Challenging Traditional Understandings of Prayer for Healing

The first and most remarkable study of healing I discovered in my readings during my sabbatical was reported in Dr. Larry Dossey's excellent book entitled Healing Words. In this brilliant work, Dossey reports on the extraordinary experiment done by Dr. Randolph Byrd in San Francisco in 1985. Dr Byrd is a physician (and a Christian) who wanted to test out the validity of healing through prayer. He had a number of cardiac patients and divided them into two groups, one which would receive prayer and the other which would not. He found Christian people in the community, both Catholics and Protestants, and gave them the first names of these cardiac patients with very little details about their condition. Each of the "prayed-for group of patients" were prayed for daily by people in the community while the "other group of patients" were not prayed for. Dr. Dossey records the results of this early experiment in his book.

The group that was prayed-for had a better outcome. They healed from surgery more quickly, had fewer complications and shorter hospital stays. The non-prayed-for group had more complications during the post-operative period, had longer hospital stays and in some cases did not heal well.

Dr. Dossey describes the remarkableness of the Bryd study. However, in recent years, the Byrd study has been criticized for design flaws and other difficulties, including the fact that it has rarely been duplicated. On the other hand there are studies (double-blind) that seem to indicate that remote prayer does heal. An excellent example of this kind of healing prayer (remote prayer) is reported in the film The Power Within in which Dr. Elizabeth Targ shares the results of her study of remote prayer. Again the design is similar to the Byrd study in that praying persons are given only the name of the patient and a brief description of the illness. The praying people are often at great distances (across state lines) and yet the results are promising. Those in the prayed-for group did much better overall than those in the not prayed-for group. What is also interesting to note is that Dr. Targ is not a Christian, and yet she strongly suspects that there is a process here that may be universal. This gave me pause to consider other "universal" powers which are unseen such as gravity, electricity, other forces in nature, and phenomena in the universe which I believe are created by God even if they still are mysterious. Scientists "discover" these realities and then create theories as an attempt to describe them, for example, "string theory," one of the recent attempts to create a theory of everything (also sometimes called the Unified Field Theory). Melissa Solomon, who served on the Board of Directors of the Pacific Southwest District of the Lutheran Church - Missouri Synod, sent me an article from a women's magazine that reports similar findings in hospital studies. Once again, where prayer takes place in double-blind studies, those in the "prayed-for" group have done significantly better than those in the group "not prayed-for." Later I was to discover other studies which did not come to the same conclusion. In some studies there seem to be no differences whether one is prayed for or not.

What does this mean? It means that we do not exactly understand why some studies such as the Byrd study and others show a clear benefit from prayer, while other studies do not seem to support the benefit of prayer. However, studies continue to be done to try to duplicate the Byrd study, or something similar.

It means that we should be praying for those in need of prayer. Prayer works. People do improve when we pray for them. Perhaps not all the time. But we should as the Scripture says, "pray without ceasing."

People ask the question: Do people always improve physically when we pray for them? No, it doesn't always happen this way. So why are some showing improvement when prayed for by strangers at remote distances while others prayed for show little or no improvement. The answer is: we don't know. We simply do not know why some reap a benefit from remote prayer while others do not improve, and in some cases, in spite of the prayers of others, they die.

What is significant in the Byrd study is that a Christian physician attempted a study on the effects of praying for patients with heart disease. Dr. Randolph Byrd did not gather together a well-known group of healers to pray for cardiac patients at San Francisco General Hospital. No, he took ordinary people who were known to be regular praying people within their faith communities in and around San Francisco.

Those who were prayed-for numbered 192. Another 210 patients were not prayed-for. The patients were randomly selected, and neither the patients, or doctors and nurses knew which group which patient was in. The group of 210 formed the control group in this carefully crafted experiment.

Those in the community who did the praying were only given the patients name and a little about the nature of the heart disease. No other information was made available to them. Since the name of each of the prayed-for patients was given to more than one person praying, the prayed-for group had between five and seven petitioners per patient.

The outcome results were considered numerically significant. The prayed-for patients only needed one-fifth as much antibiotic as the control group (not prayed-for patients). They also had less lung edema than the control group (three times less). Not one of them had to be placed on a respirator while twelve in the control group had to be placed on one. There were also fewer deaths in the prayed-for group although this was not considered statistically significant.

Furthermore, the group which was prayed for had less congestive heart failure and had fewer cardiac arrests. As indicated above, with fewer episodes of pneumonia, and requiring less diuretic and antibiotic therapy, this indeed became a landmark study.

The question then was: Could the study be duplicated? Duplication is the gold standard for scientific studies such as these. If a study can be replicated then it stands as a possible predictor of future outcomes, and can become a law of science. In this case, if future studies demonstrated that praying for cardiac patients always improved those patients' outcomes, then prayer would become a standard of treatment.

Unfortunately, while some studies have had similar outcomes to the Byrd study, other studies at other hospitals and clinics failed to replicate the Byrd study. As has happened many times in the world of science, when there is not a consistent series of outcomes, new studies are designed to try to find out cause and effect relationships. In the future I expect new studies will come forth which will show a direct positive effect between prayer and outcomes.

In 1997, twelve years after the Byrd study, Larry Dossey presented a paper at the meeting of Spirituality and Healing in a Medicine-II conference held in Los Angeles, California. The title of his paper was, "Prayer as distant intentionality: an idea whose time as come."

In this paper, Dossey argued strongly that "distant intentionality" as he calls it will have and does have a positive outcome on patient recovery and health. In this process one "intends positive outcomes for a friend or loved one who lives at a distance." For example, if you are in New York City and I am in Los Angeles, I can "intend" for you to get better, and because of those good intentions, you do get better. This is not like intercessory prayer in which one prays to a saint or Mary the mother of Jesus, or to Jesus Himself, to intercede for us to the God who heals. As Dossey has said in other places, it is not like an orbiting satellite which then beams our prayers to our beloved. No, for Dossey, this intentionality is more horizontal, directly from me to you, or from you to me. There is no "third party" involvement (no need for a saint or an intercessory). As Dossey has said before, the church does not have a monopoly on prayer. One's intentionality is like prayer in that the thoughts here impact there.

However, most traditional Christians think more of "praying to" Jesus (Protestant) or to Mary or a saint (Catholic) and that those prayers go "up" vertically to God who is above us. That is why it is called "intercessory prayer" because we pray to an intercessor on our behalf. At times, of course, we may pray directly to God (bypassing an intercessor). Even then we are often asking God to intercede or intervene on our or a beloveds behalf to remove a disease process, give us strength to persevere, or some other petition.

Dossey's paper: "Prayer as distant intentionality: an idea whose time has come" was presented at the meeting of Spirituality and Healing in Medicine-II, Los Angeles, CA. Another presenter at that same conference, M. J. Schlitz, delivered a paper entitled "Healing effects of intercessory prayer and distance intentionality." These two pioneers have argued strongly that distant intentionality will have and does have a positive outcome on patient recovery and health.

Millions of Christians believe that prayers are effective. Even when there is not an immediate positive outcome to our praying, we continue to pray. As the Holy Scriptures urge us, we are to pray without ceasing. Some pray, "if it be Thy will" by which they mean they acknowledge that God may have a different outcome in mind from what our hope is. Some leave this phrase off the end of their petition. Either way, the praying person asks God for something, and places his or her trust in Him. It seems clear to me that this is quite different than Dossey's "distance intentionality."

However, this does not mean that studies of Dossey's idea should not be conducted. Perhaps, similar to gravity, or electricity, there is a process (or force) for good that our intentionality can help facilitate or trigger. Just as some persons report feeling a warmth flowing through them when certain persons lay hands on them during prayer (or hold their hands above or near the body as they pray). So perhaps, although the distance may be greater between the praying person and the prayed for person, the efficacy may be similar. In the future, studies may indeed demonstrate that this is the case in spite of current skeptics and Nay-Sayers.

Before we leave the Byrd study and Dossey's thoughts about prayer, I should say a word about a book Dossey wrote in 1999, 14 years after the Byrd study. This work was called Reinventing Medicine: Beyond Mind-Body to a New Era of Healing. In this work, Dossey looked into the future of healing and medicine. He describes three eras historically of medicine. Era I medicine is that of mechanical medicine. That's traditional medicine practiced by most Western doctors. Era II medicine is what we understand as psychosomatic medicine. Era III medicine is what Dossey calls non-local medicine. This is the era of understanding the effects of prayer and intention. In this era, Dossey says we are beginning to comprehend the boundlessness of the non-local mind. In this concept we are all interconnected as we are all part of this non-local mind. That means our intentions and prayers are immediately received by others even at great distances. For most readers this will come as a rather novel and Avant-Garde form of thinking, some would even say it is radical. It certainly is not a Judeo-Christian understanding of one's own individualized consciousness, and is very much more of an Eastern or New Age concept. But it is an alternate theory to try to explain distant healing from prayer or what Dossey calls intentions.

In summary, Dr. Randolph Byrd has become a lighthouse of hope, pioneering a study to measure the efficacy of prayer. Even though there are some who do not believe such prayer results should be studied, what he found in his study is sure to be considered for many years to come.

Chapter 45
Dr. Nemeh on the Oz Show
A Healer in Cleveland

On June 14, 2011, a friend of mine e-mailed me, urging me to watch the Dr. Oz show on the ABC television network. The e-mail told me that it had something to do with healing and I just had to see it.

Dr. Oz is the physician who was brought to fame because of Oprah Winfrey. America came to trust Dr. Oz and today he has his own television show that airs daily on the ABC network.

So I turned on the television, only to learn that the Dr. Oz show had already aired earlier in the day on the West Coast where I live. I had missed it. So I went looking for a website for the Dr. Oz show. I found it. To my surprise and delight, the show was available in three on-line video segments. I watched the Oz show videos and learned about a healer in Cleveland named Dr. Issam Nemeh. What follows is a summary of how Dr. Oz presented the work of this extraordinary healer. The book written about Dr. Nemeh, entitled Miracles Everyday is also a source for this chapter.

If you go to the Dr. Nemeh website you can watch the Dr. Oz show as it was broadcast, and many interviews with Dr. Nemeh. There are also testimonials and stories of healing. When you get to this page, on the right hand side are some other popular TV episodes. You can also go to his home page and look at the bottom for a list of his prayer events around the country.

Dr. Oz began his broadcast by telling his TV audience that this was going to be the most unusual show he had ever televised. He said, "I want to open the door today." What he meant was that he was going to take a look at prayer for healing and the laying on of hands, a controversial topic among physicians and lay public alike.

But Dr. Oz bravely decided to place this under the microscope of scientific and medical scrutiny. He was about to not only present the diagnostic files of patients in his audience who had been treated by Dr. Nemeh. He was also going to interview patients and also have other medical professionals weigh-in as to their opinion about what was going on.

A man, says Dr. Oz, had come to his attention, a physician, from Cleveland, Ohio, who was a board certified anesthesiologist. What this physician was doing was not only using his medical training to heal people but he was also healing people through prayer and the laying on of hands.

Dr. Oz decided to check out this physician and to examine the claims made about him. Dr. Oz described how he sent his staff to Cleveland to investigate the medical authenticity of the claims. He told his audience that he was going to share with them what he had learned after doing a thorough investigation of the claims of those healed.

Then he picked up a pile of medical files and said that he was holding the diagnostic tests that showed each patients' illness. He then said that many of these people were in his studio audience. He said that the medical files showed these people as having no more symptoms and indeed appear cured. Dr. Oz was indeed "opening a door" to a dialogue between patients, physicians and researchers. Could faith have an impact on healing? Did Dr. Nemah have some special power? Why were his patients reporting miracle cures?

During the show Dr. Oz interviews several different patients. He is very respectful towards them, listening carefully to their stories of healing. These patients are very well-informed about their medical status. They are sophisticated about terminology and details of their medical conditions. They each give witness to the extraordinary changes in their medical status after seeing Dr. Nemeh. Dr. Oz gently probes and questions various aspects of each one's healing. It is clear that Dr. Oz believes something is happening. But it is difficult for him, as it is for many physicians, to believe that prayer or laying on of hands brings about a cure.

At one point during the program Dr. Oz brings up the topic of "spontaneous healing" which is the medical community's label for miraculous changes seen among patients. He brings in a medical expert and asks him what he thinks is going on. The expert says that clearly something is going on, and that faith may be a factor as well as prayer. Dr. Oz asks him if these could be "spontaneous healings." The guest physician says that "spontaneous healing" is the label the medical profession uses when they don't understand what's going on. Dr. Oz laughs and agrees.

Eventually in the program they bring out Dr. Issam Nemeh. He is an older man, quiet and humble. Dr. Oz asks him why he changed his medical practice and began to use prayer and laying hands on his patients. Dr. Nemeh describes a vision he had from God asking him to change his practice. He intimates that he was just following God's command. He says that he was quite surprised when so many of his patients began to get well.

The story is told how a television station in Cleveland aired a brief profile on the medical practice of Dr. Nemeh, and how the Catholic Church decided to have Dr. Nemeh available on a Saturday for anyone who wanted to come for healing prayer. They estimated and planned for about 500 attendees. What happened was astounding! Instead of 500 attendees, 10,000 people showed up to hear Dr. Nemeh and to have him touch them and pray for them. After this event, Dr. Nemeh became very well known in the Cleveland area and was often sought out for healing.

A friend of mine, Rev. Ken Frese, a former campus pastor in California, and later a chaplain at a senior living facility in Cleveland, says that they invited Dr. Nemeh over to their facility in Cleveland. He says that in his opinion, Dr. Nemeh is the "real deal." He was very impressed with Dr. Nemeh's humility and belief that he is but a conduit of God's love for people, expressed as healing.

Dr. Nemeh's own explanation for what is happening, which he shared with Dr. Oz in the televised program, is that he is not the energy source, but that he focuses on loving and really connecting with people. He spoke about being connected to those who sought out his help. He said that he offers free healing services to anyone who is suffering. He said he often feels the things that are happening in the body of the person who comes to see him. He prays for them, lays hands on them, and waits to see what happens. In one case he told a woman he touched who began to breathe rapidly, "save some oxygen for me." His warmth and personal style of care and concern radiates out from him.

Hearing Dr. Nemeh speak on the show about loving people and doing what he can for them, knowing that not everyone will receive healing, reminds me of the conversation I had years earlier with Francis MacNutt. MacNutt told me in his office in Florida that not everyone for whom he prays is cured immediately, and some apparently do not appear to receive any healing whatsoever. While Dr. Nemeh did not say as much, reading between the lines you could see that not everyone touched or prayed for by Dr. Nemeh receives an obvious healing. But that does not prevent either of these men of God from doing what they do through prayer and the laying on of hands.

In both cases, these men feel called by God and compelled by love to pray for and lay hands upon those in need. In both cases, it is clear that healing does take place. Sometimes that healing is immediate and in some cases the healing is gradual. In some cases it doesn't look like anything has happened at all. But neither of them is discouraged by this. They are filled with love for the "other" and prayer for them is a central focus.

Sometimes the medical community has another way of explaining, and perhaps in some cases, even dismissing the notion of healing prayer, and that is the concept of "placebo effect." That is the situation where a patient "believes" that the medicine they are receiving has curative properties, and that belief is what actually "cures" them. This is well documented in situations in which a patient has been given a sugar pill instead of real medicine for a certain condition, and the patient gets better or even completely cured. It isn't the actual medicine that cures but the person's belief in the medicine or belief in what the physician has told the person about the medication.

Many in the medical profession believe they see the same phenomena with healing prayer and the laying on of hands. These medical professionals do not believe there is any healing power intrinsic to the prayers or the laying on of hands. They see this as "placebo effect" meaning the patient improves because of their belief in the curative and miraculous healings possible through these practices. The medical community feels way more comfortable with concepts of "spontaneous healing" or "placebo effect" which have more to do with a person's mind and belief systems, rather than belief in God or spiritual explanations for what is happening.

If you, dear reader, want to learn more about Dr. Nemeh's life and work as a healer, you will want to read Miracles Everyday which chronicles many of his cases and presents his philosophy of God's love for all people. Dr. Nemeh is clearly a Christian who believes in using his medical training and spiritual resources to bear on illness. Many give testimony as to his influence in their lives. It is not unusual to hear people say that "Dr. Nemeh saved my life."

He is a healer in Cleveland. He embodies God's deep love for those sick and infirmed. It is remarkable that Dr. Oz brought Dr. Nemeh to a larger audience through his TV program. For those still skeptical about miracles happening in this day and age, reading Dr. Nemeh's story and seeing what Dr. Oz thinks about him will challenge one's skepticism.

Miracles do happen everyday. Dr. Oz has opened a door. The discussion will continue. You may want to attend one of Dr. Nemeh's healing services near you.

Dr. Nemeh is an important lighthouse of hope for thousands.

* * *

Shortly after writing the above, I learned that Dr. Nemeh had been traveling throughout the United States giving inspirational presentations, and then laying on of hands for healing to anyone who came to his conferences. So I decided to travel to nearby Arizona, to Phoenix, to attend a session with Dr. Nemeh.

On February 29, 2012, I flew into Sky Harbor Airport in Phoenix, Arizona. I caught the hotel shuttle which departed for the hotel where Dr. Nemeh was holding his conference. When the bus arrived, I got off, and entered the lobby of the hotel and got directions to the small section of ballroom where people were gathering. I presented my ticket I'd purchased online to the receptionist at the table outside the ballroom. I told her that if there was any possibility that Dr. Nemeh might have a few minutes after the conference, I would enjoy asking him a few questions for my book. She said she would see if that were possible. Another staff person traveling with Dr. Nemeh said, "I'm sure he would be happy to speak with you. Go on in and I will pass your request onto Dr. Nemeh." I thanked both of them and went to find a seat in the room.

I sat at the end of a row next to two women. I introduced myself to both of them. They had traveled from the midwest to attend this conference. As I was to learn later, each of them had what are considered life-threatening diseases and one of them was not doing well at all. I was chatting with them when someone tapped me on the shoulder and said, "Please come with me." I excused myself, got up from my chair and followed. I was taken back out of the room to the registration desk where I had presented my ticket. Imagine my surprise, when there, waiting for me, was Dr. Nemeh. With a wonderful smile, he put out his hand and said a heartfelt "Hello, I'm Dr. Nemeh. I'm so glad you have come to the conference." I shook his hand and asked him if he would consider a brief interview after the presentation, or perhaps I might call him later for a phone interview. He smiled and said, "Why a phone interview when we are both here? Yes let's meet following the presentation." I agreed and said I would meet him after the healing session. I turned and went back into the ballroom and took my seat again next to the two women.

The conference began with a brief introduction of Dr. Nemeh. Then he came out and began by asking if people in the audience like science. He then proceeded to speak about the growing body of scientific evidence for healing. He outlined some of the work that former NASA scientists are doing to understand what is going on scientifically with healing as Dr. Nemeh practices it. Among one of the more mysterious findings is that when Dr. Nemeh uses Skype (a technology which allows for face to face communication over the internet), a strange hum is heard. This tone varies in pitch dependent on each person he is working with. This sound is reported not to be a part of the Skype transmission. Dr. Nemeh, if I understood correctly, believes his is a transmission sound of the healing process going through the Internet. I was not sure if he meant this was a healing force that made such a tone, or perhaps it was evidence in sound of the healing power of the Holy Spirit. He reported that Skype looked into this phenomena, and that it does not exist within their broadcast bandwidth, and that apparently, it only occurs when Dr. Nemeh is healing those whom he works with through Skype.

What is clear is that Dr. Nemeh is not your usual "faith-healer." He is attempting to establish healing as a verifiable scientific phenomena. A number of creative experiments are being tested, and it is clear that this scientific investigation is embryonic. Something is definitely going on that is happening on two levels: one spiritual and one scientific. He sees this healing process as holistic, that is, it involves healing energies, faith responses, and scientifically verifiable realities. His presentation on these matters were highly engaging, and during the question and answer period following his talk, many in the audience asked follow-up questions to further understand details of his scientific quest in search for answers about the healing process.

Dr. Nemeh clearly feels called by God to reach out across the country to heal people of their many conditions, manifested physically and psychologically. He is very empathetic with those who have come for the healing that he offers.

Following his talk, all of us in the audience received instructions on how to come up for the healing portion of the session. The first group came up to receive the healing from Dr. Nemeh. About 10 persons at a time, faced forward, and Dr. Nemeh took time with each person laying hands on them, and speaking prayers for healing. I watched how his hands moved to touch each person where there was pain or a disorder. He would often place his hands on the head of the person for whom he was praying. Soft music played throughout the event and led to a most relaxing atmosphere.

Dr. Nemeh did not rush from one person to another. He took his time with each participant, sometimes spending as much as five minutes on someone who was terminal or near terminal. His focus on each person showed his deep respect and unconditional love for each he prayed for or touched. When I finally had my time for healing, he placed his hands on me and prayed for me. I could feel heat in his hands, and a powerful presence around me. His hands moved to where I needed healing. I felt relief as he prayed for me. I was aware of his incredible spiritually and deeply caring heart. I felt tears well up in my eyes in deep appreciation for his gift which he was sharing with me and hundreds of others also present.

The session was to last about two hours. But it took much longer for Dr. Nemeh to serve each person who came forward for healing prayer. When the final person in the room had been served, Dr. Nemeh then went out into the lobby and prayed for others who had come late. After nearly three and a half hours he was looking very tired and exhausted. One of his staff came over to me to say that Dr. Nemeh regretfully would not be able to honor his commitment to me for an interview. I said I completely understood, and I made eye contact with Dr. Nemeh as his staff led him away for much needed rest. I then made my way out through the lobby to board the shuttle bus back to the airport.
As I was just boarding the shuttle bus, I heard my name called. It was Mrs. Nemeh. She had come out to apologize that her husband was too fatigued for an interview. She thanked me for coming, and said that a telephone interview would be better after they returned to Cleveland. I thanked her and told her I very much looked forward to it. She told me how to reach them, and I said I would do so.
When I returned home, I sent a thank you email to Mrs. Nemeh requesting a possible time in the future for a telephone interview. After a week or so of no reply I wrote again. Unfortunately I never received a reply.
I do know that Dr. Nemeh had a very energetic schedule in the weeks ahead as he continued to meet with people all across the country. If you Google for Dr. Nemeh you will find a number of websites and online videos about him and his work. He is, without doubt, a lighthouse of hope to many.

SECTION IV
Other Voices of Healing

Chapter 46
Guided Imagery and the Healing Mind

The work of Martin L. Rossman, David E. Bresler, Belleruth Naparstek, and others.

I have used the metaphor of "lighthouses of hope" to describe healers and healing practices which bring hope to people. As I have shared in the last couple of chapters, Christian healing is of great importance. But it is not the only understanding of healing that exists today. One of the more important of those is known as "guided imagery" and speaks of a "healing mind." In this chapter I will touch upon a few practitioners of forms of guided imagery. While these men and women are not religious and are not Christian, they do seem to have uncovered some important avenues to healing.

As I said in Chapter One of this book, I first heard of the use of imagery for healing from Betty Lareva, the wife of my pastor friend, Jim, while Betty was struggling in her battle with cancer. Using guided imagery, Betty was improving in her battle and wanted me to learn about this new healing "technology." I promised her I would.

That led me as I described to the Academy of Guided Imagery and the work of Dr. Martin L. Rossman and his colleague, Dr. David E. Bresler.

In 1987 Dr. Martin Rossman wrote a wonderful book entitled Healing Yourself. The first chapter is called Faith Healing, Placebo Effects and Imagery. Rossman begins with a fascinating story about his second year of practice in a county medical clinic where he came into contact with a middle-aged female patient who had a precancerous condition. She refused over and over to have biopsies taken. When Marty asked her why she was placing herself at risk by refusing these tests, she replied that Jesus would heal her and that she didn't need any surgery. Marty, being the quality physician that he is, asked the woman how she communicated with Jesus. Her reply was that she sees him when she prays and that Jesus communicated with her just like she was talking with Marty. Then Marty told her about how he and the other doctors were concerned about her health, and he also told her that he had no doubt that Jesus could heal her if He wanted to but he wondered how long it would take. He then surprised this patient by asking her if she would be willing to get in touch with Jesus and ask him if he'd agree to heal her in the next six weeks. Marty writes: "She closed her eyes, and after a few minutes smiled and nodded her head. 'Yes, he says he can and will heal me in six weeks.' She agreed to have another pelvis exam in six weeks and Pap smear at that time and also agreed to have a cone biopsy if the Pap smear was still abnormal. 'But it wont be,' she said, 'I know that now.'"

Marty was glad to have gotten a commitment from this patient to have a biopsy if prayer proved ineffective.

Six weeks later the woman returned. She allowed her cervix to be examined and it looked normal. Her Pap smear report came back three days later and was perfectly normal.

Marty's conclusion: This woman's story doesn't mean that you can forgo Pap smears, nor does it mean you have to believe in Jesus. But, in Marty's opinion, this woman's story points to the "potent healing effects of faith and belief."

Marty goes on to describe the power of positive expectant faith, that is, the power of belief. An example Marty gives is of patients being given water injections for pain while telling these patients that they were being given a powerful pain medication. As Marty points out, and as many other physicians have noticed, this "water injection" could relieve pain as effectively as if it had been morphine in many cases. There are literally hundreds of examples of the effectiveness of what is called The Placebo Effect.

Marty makes an important statement: "To call a response a 'placebo' does not mean the response isn't real. It simply means the results stem from the belief of a patient in the therapy, rather than from the therapy itself. The important thing about the placebo response is that it demonstrates beyond doubt that thoughts can trigger the body's own self-healing abilities."

I shared Marty's above thought with a friend of mine. This initiated a spirited discussion of placebo effect. He asked me, "Do you think the placebo effect was given by God?" I thought about it and answered, "Yes... that makes sense to me." He then asked me, "Does prayer function as a placebo?" That stopped me in my tracks for a moment. If a placebo effect results from the belief of a patient in the therapy, rather than the therapy itself, it could be that if one believes in the power of prayer, the placebo effect would come from belief in that prayer, not necessarily in the actual effectiveness of the prayer. He went on to ask, "Couldn't the placebo effect harness the mental energy of belief, and that brings about healing?" Following Marty's statement in the above paragraph, it might mean that thoughts that prayer can heal may trigger the body's own self-healing abilities. Just as the woman in the example above, believed her Jesus would heal her. Marty is saying that her thought (belief) in that could trigger her body's own self-healing abilities. On the other hand, the woman believes that Jesus did heal her. I decided to think about this further.

Marty traces his own introduction to imagery to when he met and studied with Dr. Irving Oyle in 1972. Oyle's method of treatment would be to have his patients relax and then visualize themselves healing or having a conversation with a wise figure who could tell them "why they were sick and what they could do about it." Later on Marty heard Dr. Carl Simonton and his wife at that time, Stephanie Matthews-Simonton, talking about how they were using visualization techniques with cancer patients. If you read Getting Well Again by Simonton or go up to his website (simontoncenter.com) you can learn more about Simonton's ongoing writing and working with cancer patients using visualization techniques.

Marty and his colleague David Bresler were, of course, not the only ones discovering the powerful use of guided imagery. However, they managed to put their teachings into a training program that was easy to learn and easily duplicated, so that thousands of therapists and medical doctors, nurses, and other health professionals trained with Rossman and Bresler for the benefit of their patients. I am very grateful for all that these two men taught, and to the mentors who served under them who taught me so much about interactive guided imagery.

I encourage you to read Marty's original book, Healing Yourself. The revision of this book carries a new title: Guided Imagery for Self-Healing: An Essential Resource for Anyone Seeking Wellness. This new revision, unfortunately, does not carry the story above about the female patient who believes Jesus will heal her, but it is an outstanding book which describes how imagery works, how you can use imagery for your own self healing, and if you wish, you can contact the Academy for Guided Imagery to find an imagery practitioner.

During my sabbatical reading I also came across an excellent compendium of articles in a book entitled Healers on Healing edited by Richard Carlson, Ph.D. and Benjamin Shield. Some of the best and well-known healers of today write about the essence of healing. Some of these healers whose work is included are: Bernie Siegel, Hugh Prather, Serge Kahili King, O. Carl Simonton, Norman Cousins, Rachel Naomi Remen, Rollo May, Emmett E. Miller, Delores Krieger, Elizabeth Kubler Ross, Larry Dossey, Harold Bloomfield, Joan Borysenko, Martin L. Rossman, and many others.

For those of you who only wish to read Christian writers, the above mentioned book is made up of many authors who are spiritual but are not practicing Christians. However, much of what they write is informative and useful.

Marty's contribution in Healers on Healing was to write a chapter called, Illness as an Opportunity for Healing. He describes some of his techniques briefly in this article, including, "listening to your symptom" in which he describes how to focus on a symptom, "allowing an image to represent it, and then engaging the image of the symptom in dialogue in order to find out why it is there, what it wants, and how you can meet the needs it represents."

The goal of healing through imagery is to reestablish a healthy balance. Whether you work with an imagery practitioner or some other healer, almost all of them are on the same page: the goal is balance. As Marty puts it, "Clearly, the more knowledge and self-awareness you have, the more able you will be to support the process of reestablishing a healthy balance."

I have turned to Marty's colleague, David Bresler for support to reestablish balance in my own life. Several years ago I went through a horrible experience with vertigo which debilitated me for several weeks. Through David's support using acupuncture and imagery I was able to reestablish that balance. Of course, I also used other medicine. I also set aside a greater number of hours for sleep and exercise, and changed my diet to aid in reestablishing the balance I needed. All of these, including the imagery, helped me find out more about why I was going through this difficulty. Imagery allowed me to ask why this symptom was in my life, what it wanted, and how I could meet the need it represented.

I have used imagery with many of my clients as well. One woman, a pastor's wife, had a terrible headache coming into one of her sessions. Through the use of interactive guided imagery, she was able to relieve the symptoms, even to have them go away during the session. In her case, the image that came up was of a giant who was using a sledge hammer to pound on an anvil. Each time the anvil was struck by the giant, her headache throbbed. She asked him why he was there, what he wanted, and she got messages that were helpful to her. She invited the giant to relax for a moment, offered him some cold lemonade (he had worked up a sweat striking the anvil over and over). He thanked her and said he didn't like his work. He hated causing people pain. They dialoged within this image for awhile. He thanked her again for the lemonade and asked her if it was OK with her if he took a break. She replied, "Of course." He got up and walked away. This became the end of her imagery. When I invited her to begin coming out of the imagery and "back into the room," she reported her headache gone.

Another example is when I was invited to present how imagery might be used within a pastoral counseling setting. I made my presentation on the use of interactive guided imagery at the American Association of Pastoral Counselor's western regional meeting in Fresno. I was surprised when a woman in the back of the room asked if she could work with me a little bit on some pain she was having. I shared that I had never done a public demonstration of the use of interactive guided imagery before, but if she wished she could come forward and I would do what I could.

She and I sat in front of the pastoral counselors assembled for this workshop. I invited her to become relaxed. She closed her eyes and allowed an image to come to her that represented her "pain". Her image was of a sword that went into the right side of her shoulder and pierced through her body and exited her left shoulder. As taught by the Academy of Guided Imagery, I "guided" her through the imagery process which enabled her to see more clearly what this image was. I used the technique called "listening to your symptom" and not only did she "get" what this pain was all about during our demonstration session together, but her pain completely disappeared. After her imagery experience concluded, she thanked me and said she was going to make an appointment with her own therapist to follow up on what she learned from the imagery. I asked her if she might be willing to also answer any questions from the audience. She agreed to do so. Prior to doing the "demo" in front of the group, one therapist in the room announced that he did not believe in this type of technique. He was quite vocal about his negativity. Afterwards, he told the group that he was amazed at what he had just seen transpire in a 20 minute imagery session. He said something like, "I think I could have spent five or six sessions of talking therapy with her and still not have gotten as much as you did in 20 minutes." He apologized for his negativity, and I thanked him for sharing with all of us his shift in viewpoint. The woman also shared that she too was amazed at how quickly her pain had disappeared and that she was able to finally get in touch with what this was all about.

I know that imagery works. We know that there is no technique that works all of the time in healing modalities. As Marty says in Healers on Healing:

"None of them works all the time. We don't know why. Yet, even in terminal situations, healing can take place, even though it is not physical. Deep emotional and spiritual healing can accompany fatal illness as well as recovery, and we can learn to be a friend to that as well."

Marty and David, of course, are not the only experts of imagery practice. But they have trained thousands of imagery practitioners throughout the United States (in fact I just referred a pastor friend to an imagery practitioner in Ohio). The Academy's approach to interactive guided imagery is very helpful. It is also non-invasive, non-toxic and very respectful of each person's unique process.

One more comment about the work of Dr. Martin L. Rossman and Dr. David E. Bresler. There have been some evangelical Christians who have attacked their work, and truthfully, they are misguided in their attacks. They operate from a fundamentalist position that says that all imagery is from the Devil. They also assume that anything psychological from any teachers who are not Christians is of the "Enemy." This is simply not true. There are many things about God's creation, including our brains and our minds that are just now beginning to be understood. Going "inward" through the use of imagery can be greatly beneficial to Christians and non-Christians alike. I thank my friend Betty for introducing this form of healing to me.

Another good example of the use of imagery for healing and wellness is The Healing Presence: Spiritual Exercises for Healing, Wellness, and Recovery by Thomas A. Droege. A friend of mine, Rev. Frank Janzow, who is a Lutheran pastor in the Evangelical Lutheran Church of America (ELCA), introduced me to this wonderful book which can easily be used on retreats or for personal use. Droege, most recently with the Carter Center in Atlanta, is a former teacher at Valparaiso University in Indiana. He has also written a book using imagery in grief work.

The Healing Presence shows how imagery can be greatly beneficial, not only for healing, but also for strengthening one's walk with God. Each chapter of the book uses the same pattern. First there is a Biblical story with a brief commentary on the story. Then there is a healing transcript that can be read silently to oneself, or in a retreat setting, allowing persons to see this event in their imagination which invites them into the experience. This is a very effective use of imagery for Christians, to deepen faith, help them deal with unresolved issues, and bring God into their hearts in a more profound way.

Rev. Art Umbach, Mission and Ministry Facilitator of the Southeastern District of the Lutheran Church - Missouri Synod has used prayer imagery to deepen a person's walk with God. During the prayer, Pastor Umbach invites people to 'imagine' that they are in the story enabling them to notice in a different way how God comes to them, talks with them, speaks to their soul. People often tell Art how this has brought them closer to their Lord. Recently, Art has begun to expand his teachings on prayer, and has developed an entire curriculum on prayer forms. I have listened to him make this presentation twice and the response to him has been deeply appreciated. He introduces his audience to ancient prayer forms, with personal examples from his own prayer life. (See the chapter about Arthur Umbach on the many forms of prayer.)

Another form of imagery being used in a therapeutic way is called Theophostic, used by a number of evangelical Christian counselors. Theo stands for God, and Phostic stands for Light. During the counseling, the counselor helps the client retell the difficult story or event that has traumatized them or injured them. At the most intense moment of this retelling, the Christian counselor has the client invite Jesus into this situation. The client then sees Jesus there. The counselor asks the client to ask Jesus what he wants to say to the client. The client listens to what Jesus says or watches what He does. This often brings comfort and support to the client.

While I am not really sure if the originators of Theophostic would agree that this is another use of imagery (I think they would say this is indeed Jesus Christ Himself with the client), it does fit the criteria in some ways of being what I think of as an "inner advisor" technique or "inner wisdom figure" similar to that which Dr. Rossman has spoken of on numerous occasions. I know that the power of belief is very powerful and if a Christian doing this kind of work believes this is Jesus, then indeed it IS Jesus for them. It is similar to the story that Dr. Rossman shared in his book where the patient closed her eyes and spoke with Jesus and listened to what he said to her before she agreed with Dr. Rossman's suggestion. The Theophostic form of therapy has drawn some criticism and is controversial in its style, but there have been reports of it being highly effective with some clients. I personally know several Christian mental health practitioners who use it with good results. However, I am not an endorser of this technique. I have some questions about the possibility of someone being re-traumatized during the "imagery" session, and in the hands of a lesser skilled clinician, I think this technique could be dangerous. However, I do not have sufficient exposure or experience to comment very much on the Theophostic form of healing.

But there are still other ways that imagery can be helpful and healing. Jeanne Achterberg, a non-Christian therapist, has written a couple of books on imagery and healing that extensively cover a wide range of issues. She does not write from a religious perspective but she does share how imagery can indeed help in very powerful ways. Her books, Rituals of Healing: Using Imagery for Health and Wellness, and Imagery in Healing: Shamanism and Modern Medicine, provide significant insights into how the mind and body interact with each other. Jeanne Achterberg has also written a deeply personal account of her battle with cancer entitled Lightning at the Gate, of which Joan Borysenko (author of Minding the Body, Mending the Mind) said, "It is far and away the best book about healing that I have ever read."

Another very creative imagery practitioner is Belleruth Naparstek. The first book of hers that I read and used is entitled Staying Well with Guided Imagery. Her work is very useful along a wide range of illness issues. One of the things I most liked about her work is her discussion about how and why imagery works and the different kinds of imagery that exist. She then presents imagery scripts that help strengthen the immune system, improve cardiovascular system function, help improve emotional well-being, provide relief for such common complaints such as feeling sluggish, having headaches, overcoming insomnia, and what to do about allergies. This book is endorsed by Larry Dossey, and was also featured as a Doubleday Health Book and an alternative selection of Prevention Book Club.

In addition to her writings, she has also recorded a number of audiotapes and CDs of meditations on such health issues as diabetes, weight loss, healthful sleep, rheumatoid arthritis, lupus, handling stress, depression, relaxation and wellness, and self confidence. Again, she is another resource in the field of mind/body imagery.

There are also the techniques of visualization that first came to the public awareness in the early 1970's by O. Carl Simonton mentioned above. In his book Getting Well Again, a number of different visualization approaches were promoted, including some of a more aggressive nature where cancer cells were being attacked. Some of these healing techniques have had their critics or have had alternative techniques developed by other practitioners. I recall seeing a videotape featuring Dr. Andrew Weil, the well known physician from Tuscon, who has argued strongly that the future of medical care in the United States should be an "integrative approach." He spoke somewhat negatively on the use of aggressive images, or warlike images, where one visualizes cancer cells being attacked like in a PacMan or Ms. PacMan kind of way. However, sometimes these types of images do work. On the other hand, in the case of one person I know, whose battle with cancer was reported earlier in this book, she imagined cancer cells rising up like bubbles in a champagne bottle as they rose from her shoulders and lifted away into the sky. I know of another patient who imagined her cancer cells as flowers needing special love and care and she believes she "loved" her cancer into remission and eventually was "cured" of her cancer through these loving thoughts and images.

As I will say throughout this book, there are many different pathways to healing and even cure. No one system works all of the time, and honestly I don't think we often understand how or why it works when it does.

Those healers who have had the opportunity to travel the world (e.g. Andrew Weil who shares that he spent eleven years studying shamans, Native-American medicine, osteopaths, etc) to study many types of healing methodologies, conclude that there are anecdotal stories telling of the healings of persons within each culture.

Dr. Herbert Benson of Harvard University says that most of these healing systems elicit a "relaxation response" that is part of the healing mechanism that enables the body-mind to be placed in its most healing posture. In other words, there are many ways that the mind and body are one in the healing process.

My friend and former trainer with the Academy for Guided Imagery, Roxanne Whitelight, approached me some years ago, suggesting that we do a workshop for the Academy for Guided Imagery. We eventually did just that, and this is how it came about. I had heard Roxanne do a spirituality and imagery workshop at one of AGI's national conferences on Maui, Hawaii. Afterwards, I came up to her and told her what a magnificent presentation she did, thanking her for the way in which she brought spirituality to the conference through the use of imagery. I did not know Roxanne at the time, but she said something to me that I will never forget. She said, "I think some time you and I will do something together on spirituality and imagery." Well, that opportunity presented itself as she and I worked up a training session we called "Imagery and the Christian Client." One of our concerns was about the biases and prejudices that secular therapists, and in this case, imagery practitioners, might bring to sessions where they were working with Christian clients. In order to get at the deep prejudices that may be in the subconscious of imagery practitioners, we designed an introduction set of four images that we shared with those who attended our workshop.

Suffice it to say that the four images we created were of religious figures who presented themselves for healing. We designed images of a Native-American shaman, a priest, a rabbi and a protestant minister. As we had our imagery colleagues close their eyes and imagine each of these figures one by one, we were hoping each figure would bring up some thoughts or feelings in the workshop attendees which were previously not conscious. When we brought them out of the images and debriefed this introductory session in our workshop, everyone had one or more biases or old concepts creep into their images. During the debriefing we learned how some of our colleagues had been wounded by the church or had had negative experiences with someone of the "cloth." Some got in touch with issues that they would have to set aside if they were going to be effective with religious clients. The surprise was that some of our colleagues actually found these images healing of some of their own wounds. I remember one person, a woman who said she had been the wife of a minister, found that this exercise empowered her to speak more about her own use of imagery with Christian clients. Over the multi-hour workshop, Roxanne and I presented many of the images that religious people find "grounding" and "sacred" and "highly important," such as a cross or a rosary or a prayer shawl. I felt good about this presentation to our peers because it gave us an opportunity to sensitize them to the need for respect and openness to traditions that either they knew nothing about or perhaps had abandoned out of some wounded part of themselves. It was one of the highest rated workshops offered by the Academy at that time. I was proud to have worked with Roxanne, and I hope that someday we can do something together again.

I thank God for people like Marty and David and the other imagery practitioners who have been trained in this method or similar methods. Imagery is a tool like so many other healing tools, and when used in the hands of an ethical and sensitive practitioner, the changes that can come about are amazing. I still thank David for his healing treatments when I battled Durcam's Disease. The acupuncture and imagery, and the music from the album entitled Land of Merlin brought about great pain relief and renewed hope. Another time when I battled labyrinthitus, David once again became a life saver, and through his healing practice I was able to return to work and to function once again. Remember, imagery is one tool that works for many people. Perhaps not everyone can gain from it. But many can. That is true of so much in medicine. If you were not aware of it before, at least you now know that guided imagery methods for healing, both interactive and directive, are another lighthouse of hope. I know I have benefited from its usage as have many.

Chapter 47
Molecules of Emotion
The Body-Mind Matrix

Towards the end of my sabbatical I felt as though I had learned a great deal about prayer and healing, but was still lacking a good understanding of "psychoneuroimmunology," that field of study whose phrase was coined by Dr. Robert Ader.

Then a wonderful thing happened. I was talking with someone about this frustration and he asked me, "Have you ever read Molecules of Emotion by Candace Pert?" I said I had not, nor had I ever heard of her. He said that he thought her book would be perfect reading for my sabbatical topic. So I got a copy and read it.

It was like reading something that made all of the pieces of the puzzle fall into place. For me it was the missing piece of my sabbatical. Certainly prayer involved emotions, and so did healing. But I had never thought of emotions as being... molecular. The implications of this finding are far-reaching. It brought me back to my high school physics class in the early 60's when I learned that light is made up of both a wave and particles. Light was both. While my mind could not comprehend it, it was clearly demonstrated scientifically (and it too has had far reaching implications within the field of science, particularly, astrophysics). Now here was another of those things that made no sense to me. How could an emotion... like the four basic forms of sad, mad, glad and scared... be comprised of physical things called molecules? If that were true, then time and space as we think about it in a Newtonian world were not at all what it is in a quantum or post-quantum world. Perhaps laughter then could indeed change a person's physiology. Prayer could change a person's very being. There really would be what Candace Pert has gone on to call "a body-mind matrix."

I've had the opportunity to hear Candace speak at an annual conference of the Academy for Guided Imagery which was held up at the Asilomar Conference Center, in Pacific Grove, near the town of Monterrey, California. I also had a chance to speak with her one-on-one during a break at the conference. The ten minutes

I had alone with her were wonderful as I explored a number of questions with her. Her thinking is cutting edge, and she is a down-to-earth, humorous speaker as she brings to her presentations wonderful stories about her own humanity and frailty. She puts a smile on your face as you identify with her explorations, mistakes, and foibles even as a great researcher. She does not take herself too seriously, and enjoys poking fun at herself. She was such a delight to hear as her creative mind set my own to thinking about new realities of time and space, and particularly about how the mind and body are a Oneness.

At this particular conference she admitted to sneaking a candy bar into her briefcase so that her husband would not know she had it with her (she has a bit of a weight problem). What she didn't realize is that a paper she was to deliver to a national conference of researchers and scientists was underneath that candy bar in her briefcase! The candy bar melted all over that paper she was to present at the conference. She was so embarrassed when her husband caught her with the candy bar, and even more chagrined that the paper she was to deliver was now covered with chocolate! She easily endeared herself to all of us in the audience. She was revealing how human she is. We all chuckled at her story because we could all identify with it in some way. She is kind of a living legend but hearing that story made her very human indeed.

Molecules of Emotion is the story of Candace Pert's quest to find the receptor sites for the opiates (morphine, etc.). She was hired as a researcher and when asked what she wanted to study she replied that she wanted to discover the receptor sites for the opiates. She had fallen and injured her back and was in great pain as a young research assistant. She used morphine to handle the pain, found herself becoming addicted to morphine. So being asked what she wanted to focus on, she told her new boss that she wanted to find the brain's receptor site for the opiates. She was told that the only receptor site discovered so far was for insulin. So far, the receptor sites for drugs such as morphine remained elusive.

Through a number of ingenious tests she was eventually able to locate the receptor site for morphine, which meant that the human brain already had built into it a site for accepting morphine from outside of the body. She speculated on how that could be possible, unless the body created its own natural morphine. She set out to prove that this was so, and in the process discovered "endorphins" which is actually a made up name from two words: one of those words is "endogenous" which means "it's inside, already there," and the other word is "morphine" (the name of the powerful drug). Hence "endorphins" literally means "inside morphine."

In other words, the body is wired to receive morphine, the morphine manufactured naturally within the body. So naturally the body would also have built in receptor sites for morphine from outside the body as well as receptor sites for the natural morphine created within the body.

She began to speculate that emotions are in fact molecules. Or to turn it around, molecules can be emotions. Not just that emotions are carried in the body molecularly, but that emotions ARE molecules (like light is particles and wave).

When a person feels high on drugs, these emotions are sent out from the brain as "endorphins," real structures of chemicals which in turn make one feel pleasure. In an unusual experiment, she provided Petri dishes to friends and asked them to chew gum during sex. When they reached orgasm, they were to put those pieces of gum into the Petri dishes and send them to her. What she discovered is that the great pleasure released at the moment of orgasm in these women were found as endorphins inside the chewing gum. As her work continued, she discovered that the "mind" is everywhere in the body, not just in the brain. When the orgasmic release happened and the endorphins were released, every cell in the body knew what was taking place. She discovered molecules of emotion.

At first I struggled to comprehend this. Then I thought back to that science experiment I had in high school physics. The task before us was to determine if "light" were a particle or a wave. As I conceptualized this, particles were like tiny B-Bs, tiny round balls of steel. A "wave" on the other hand was something quite different. I had often played in waves at the sea shore of lakes and the ocean. This was a continuous fluid thing, these waves, not like tiny B-Bs at all.

When we did the experiment in high school, I saw light broken down into ball-like particles. Clearly light was a particle. But when another experiment was done, it showed clearly that light was a "wave."

Here was a dilemma for me. How could something be two different things at the same time? Light was clearly made of particles and clearly was made up of waves! Impossible, I thought! Yet that is exactly true of light. It is both particle matter and waves at the same time.

If this were the case with light, why couldn't emotions be molecular? Certainly this was not Newtonian science. This was in the camp of Quantum Physics. Somehow Candace Pert was finding parallels within the human body. Emotions are both something not matter, yet are matter.

This was a major finding around 1980. In fact, 1980 was a watershed year (and the years just prior to and after 1980) and the science of the mind was coming to the forefront. Today, looking back, its as if we take these discoveries for granted. By now, most people know about endorphins and their effects on human emotion. Most people know that sources of pleasure, regardless of where they are located, release endorphins, But Pert was saying "endorphins do not just carry emotions, rather, endorphins ARE emotions."

In the world of Newtonian physics this cannot be. But within the quantum field, this is most certainly the case.

The implications for these discoveries cannot be overestimated. If someone could, in fact, experience pleasure and well-being then perhaps that could effect the outcome of the healing process.

In fact that is exactly the case. Take the experiences of Norman Cousins for example. In his books, The Anatomy of an Illness and Head First, Cousins describes how he was able to laugh himself into healing. Cousins was editor of the Saturday Review and came down with a health condition that threatened to shorten his life, perhaps even kill him. All of the standard medical treatments seemed to fail. So he spoke to his doctor about a radical way of producing healing. He proposed to the doctor that he would watch a couple of hours of funny movies each day, and see if laughter had any effect on his illness.

Cousin's physician prescribed watching funny films. Watching funny movies made him laugh which in turn produced a healing process within the body. The old saying that "laughter is the best medicine" was coming true right before his eyes and the eyes of his physician. Within weeks, Norman Cousins was walking around healthy and well again. His experiment worked.

For Cousins it was the case of molecules of emotion. His body transformed laughter into endorphins which helped bring about healing. At least that is how it appears.

Now we can understand better the concept of psychoneuroimmunology. The human mind and psyche along with brain neurology can create immunology and transform immune processes to flow. This is the body-mind connection in which whatever one thinks in his or her mind has some kind of physical effect. The counter to that also seems likely. How one behaves can influence the mind. Healing of the mind and body comes about because they are "one" entity. Each co-influences the other but in the final analysis there is only one "body-mind." Prayer can cause positive effects within the mind and in the body resulting in healing.

There is what some have labelled "the new science." Its origins are in quantum theory. While Einstein was working on his theories about relativity (he was working on gravity and the space-time continuum), other scientists were working on other forces in the universe in a science called "quantum theory."

Of course there were attempts to reconcile these very different ways of understanding the universe, and over time there have been several attempts to create what is known as a "uniform field theory" that makes sense of all of the data. One of the most recent attempts to reconcile these huge differences in the theories has been what is called "string theory." But recently this theory has also begun to fall into disfavor for it cannot account for everything either.

Just one example of some of the "weird" discoveries within this non-Newtonian science. It has been discovered, and perhaps you have heard or read about it, that a particle can be at one place in the universe at the very same time it is in another place, at the very same time. This is impossible you say! I think like you do. How can something be in two "places" at the same time. In the world of Newtonian theory something cannot be in two places at once. My car cannot be in front of my house at the same time it is a couple of hundred miles away on a freeway. Either it is on the freeway out there or it is in front of my house here.

But at the sub-atomic level, a particle CAN be at two places at the very same time. Einstein, for example, theorized that as objects moved through space, these objects bent light. This in turn could alter time as we know it. Time travel became the stuff of comic books and science fiction. But some have gone on to demonstrate that Einstein's theories are not just theories. They have reality to them. Another example is that it is now known that a particle far distant from another one can influence it somehow through space and time. Again, in the Newtonian world this makes no sense. But in the world of Quantum it is reality.

Why am I sharing this? Because "reality" as we understand it from the world of mathematics (and Newton theory) is one kind of "reality" (for example, no matter how many times I drop an apple, it will fall to the ground). However, post-Newtonian science suggests that "reality" may be far different.

The work of Candace Pert and others shows us a "reality" that is new and different. Emotions are molecular. There are molecules of emotion.

We can say that light is of two natures, but it is just one "thing." What about emotions? Candace's research demonstrates that emotions are of two natures: one is non-physical and one physical. "Emotions" in common sense parley are not "things" like a chair or a desk or a car. We can see the "results" of emotions... tears, laughter, sadness, etc. But we don't normally speak of emotions as physical things. But in the new science, emotions also have a second nature: they are indeed physical structures within the blood stream.

This made me begin to speculate about other "things" which seem to be in some peoples' reality but not in others. For example, a friend of mine asked me if there are really (that is in "reality") alien beings visiting our planet. Some believe this is clearly the case, and speculate on how they get here, by what technology, and how they can travel at great speeds over great distances from other planets or galaxies. They clearly have "bodies." Yet what happens to their bodies as they travel through space and time? Are they like light? Do they function as both "solid things" (like the B-Bs of light) as well as "some other kind of thing" (like waves of light)?

For that matter (no pun intended), are there demonic forces which we cannot see but are "real" even though not in the "reality" that we are used to experiencing? Are some people so wired that they can catch glimpses of these demonic forces while others can not?

What then about other "entities" in the world? Are aliens able to come to our planet in ways we do not yet comprehend, via some other type of space-time continuum? Are there demonic forces, which we cannot see but are as "real" even though not in the "reality" that we are used to experiencing?

A friend of mine, for example, was asked to come to a house to give it "a blessing." When he got there he was informed that there is a room in this house, where something dark, very dark, indeed evil, lurked. My friend, being skeptical yet willing to see for himself, entered the room where this "darkness" was to be in existence. He was told that the "entity" was in the closet. My friend opened the closet and noticed immediately how extremely dark it was. More importantly, he felt something dark, cold, and evil come over him. He backed away quickly. He told members of the household what he felt and that they needed more help than he could give. When talking with my friend, it became apparent that whatever this "thing" was in the closet, it was "real" and it was frightening. Yet he will tell you that he really didn't "see" anything but he knew it was "real."

The Carl Sagans of the world would dismiss this notion. If it could not be photographed or seen in a test tube then it could not be real. Yet there are "realities" even in hard science that make one question "what exactly is reality?"

I am not writing very much in this book about demons or evil spirits as I have little working knowledge of them. However, writers such as the famous psychiatrist, M. Scott Peck (his final book is excellent called Glimpses of the Devil) tells of two complete exorcisms of evil realities that he waited to write about until he neared the end of his life. He waited to write of these "things," knowing, there would be skeptics. Or take someone like Francis MacNutt, who himself has never "seen" a disembodied spirit (such as a demon) yet he will do an exorcism when others who can "see" them point out where they are.

We are in the realm of mystery here. Reality at times truly is in the eyes of the beholder. What I may not be able to see with my own eyes (for example, a particle in two places at the same time) may still be true. I have speculated with friends and colleagues by saying to them, "How do we not know that, like bandwidth on the Internet, there is not a kind of bandwidth of reality... there is what I can see, touch, taste, smell, hear... but there is that which I cannot see, touch, taste, smell, hear... that is real as well." I know that dogs can hear higher pitches than I can and that there are lower tones that the human ear cannot detect. Those are still part of the Newtonian world. Yet at the subatomic world there are bits of matter we cannot see (photons, atoms, quarks to name a few) and that "matter" can act in strange and mysterious ways. There was just recently a new "reality" announced that it is speculated (believed) that there are particles that move faster than the speed of light. One scientist believes these particles slow down towards the speed of light.

In the first century, Jesus was casting out demons... and in the age of Enlightenment and post-Enlightenment, we don't see demons now... or do we? Some people do in fact see the demonic, or "sense" it. Some people even appear to become "infected" with the demonic, or parts of people seem to be "possessed." Perhaps these entities travel in other dimensions of reality.

All you have to do is read some of the writings of Michio Kaku or view his interviews on YouTube or other Internet places, to know that the scientific community is on the theoretical edge. His books such as Physics of the Impossible: A Scientific Exploration into the World of Phasers, Force Fields, Teleportation, and Time Travel or his book, Parallel Worlds: A Journey Through Creation, Higher Dimensions , and the Future of the Cosmos, give you a glimpse into the world where science explores what once was thought of as science fiction.

Who is Michio Kaku? He is a theoretical physicist specializing in string theory, and a believer in the strong possibility of multi-universes. He is a serious scientist (many consider him the heir apparent to Carl Sagan). His programs on the Discovery Channel are among the most popular and intriguing.

This past Easter my family and I went to the Hollywood Bowl for the Easter service. The choir was awesome, the orchestra was great, the praise band was terrific, and the soloists had wonderful voices. Then it was time for the preacher to deliver his message. When he spoke about the resurrection of Jesus Christ, he made reference to the new science. He said that friends of his at Cal-Tech and JPL tell him that Einstein was right, that space and time itself can bend. That the reality that we used to take for granted may no longer be the only reality.

That reminds me of when I visited the Griffith Observatory in Hollywood high above the Hollywood Hills some years ago, I attended a talk about the galaxies of the universe. In the planetarium, the lights were dimmed, and the "star field" was projected high above us in the dome of the planetarium. During this intriguing presentation, pictures of galaxies taken by the Hubble telescope were projected above the audience in the dome above. One slide showed what was called a "bar bell" galaxy... one end was a ball of millions of stars connected to another ball of millions of stars on the other end. What connected these two "balls" of star clusters was what appeared to be a long tube of more stars, so that the entire picture was in the shape of a bar bell like those wrestlers raised up over their heads in competitions.

But then the next slide also taken by the Hubble telescope was of a similar star cluster with a tube like gathering of stars with balls of stars on either end, like another bar bell. However, in this picture there was a third "ball" of star clusters out from the center of the bar bell. This cluster ball of stars was connected to the bar bell connecting tube by its own bar bell connecting tube. The commentator said, "Ladies and gentlemen... what you are seeing cannot be. It cannot exist. Yet you see it. In our understanding of physics, there is no known physics that can account for what we are seeing in the picture taken by the Hubble. From what we understand today, this formation with three ball clusters of stars connected by the two bars... would be blown apart, obliterated. Yet as you can clearly see, it is... at its very nature, different from what we can comprehend. Perhaps someday we shall have an explanation."

There are now a number of popular writers explaining the "new physics" to laypersons like myself. I didn't do all that well in High School math, so I cannot comprehend the math and science of the "new physics" so I am glad that there are writers who can make it understandable to the lay public.

What is clear to me can be summed up in that famous line from The Wizard of Oz... "we are not in Kansas anymore." We have now been lifted up like in a mighty cyclone and have been deposited in a strange new land. As that famous science fiction book was entitled Strangers in a Strange Land, so we find ourselves in a new frontier. Candace Pert is one of those pioneers and lighthouses of hope blazing a new trail for our understanding of the body and mind. Her term for it is matrix. It's a new understanding of Psychoneuroimmunology, a relatively new field of science with departments now in over 100 U.S. universities. Who knows what this new pathway will uncover or discover or how this new science will impact our mental or emotional or spiritual well-being.

This new matrix is the stuff of mystery and intrigue and it beckons scientists to explore strange new worlds. These scientists, like Candace Pert, stand like lighthouses high atop hills shining strong beams into the fog out there, guiding us to discover and uncover more secrets of the universe, both in outer-space and inner-space. We shall be surprised and we shall laugh like a child opening a special Christmas present on that special night of nights.

I thank God for all of these lighthouses who show us the marvelous creation our Creator has made.

Genesis 1: 1 "In the beginning God created the heavens and the earth." (NIV)

Psalm 139:14 "I praise you because I am fearfully and wonderfully made; your works are wonderful, I know that full well." (NIV)

Chapter 48
Non-Religious Forms of Healing
A Challenge

Perhaps the best place to begin our discussion on non-religious forms of healing is with the non-religious forms of treatment in medicine. The two broad categories of treatment procedures fall roughly into what are called "allopathic medicine" and "homeopathic medicine." If you look up the term allopathic on Wikipedia you will find this:

"Allopathic medicine refers to the practice of conventional medicine that uses pharmacologically active agents or physical interventions to treat or suppress symptoms or pathophysiologic processes of diseases or conditions. Allopathic medicine often refers to "the broad category of medical practice that is sometimes called Western medicine, bio-medicine, evidence-based medicine or modern medicine."

This is the world of seeing your doctor for a prescription, or going in for lab tests, or going in for surgery, or laser treatments. It is the world of television shows such as Grey's Anatomy, Private Practice, E. R., and the old show, St. Elsewhere.

If you look up the term homeopathic on Wikipedia you will find this:

"Homeopathy is a form of alternative medicine in which practitioners claim to treat patients with using highly diluted preparations that are believed to cause healthy people to exhibit symptoms that are similar to those exhibited by the patient. The basic principle of homeopathy, known as the 'law of similars,' is 'let like be cured by like.'"

This is the world of herbal remedies, exotic concoctions made from leaves and stems of plants, various salts and blends of organic material, and what are often called "home remedies" gleaned from folk wisdom down through generations of what cures common ailments.

Prior to the 19th century, medicine was often in the hands of what was known as an apothecary, a practitioner who offered advice and mixed elixirs for all sorts of ailments. These practitioners' shops, known as apothecary shops, date back into the 8th century. Chaucer wrote about them in the 14th century, and there is a reference to one in a Shakespeare play in the 16th century (a poor apothecary sells Romeo an elixir of death which later on Romeo drinks to commit suicide). But in the 19th century with the rise of what was known as "heroic medicine," the role of the apothecary eventually evolved into what we know today as: the pharmacist. The early apothecary became skilled in the art of homeopathic medicine. The pharmacist became skilled in the art of allopathic medicine.

While on my sabbatical, I visited the tiny village of Cluny, France, on my way to the Taize community. In Cluny, I saw a sign on a building that read "homeopathy" so I entered the professional building, found the door with the sign on it, and entered. I met a very pleasant man in a tweed jacket and matching pants. He asked if he could help me and I immediately noticed several walls of what looked like wood paneling with dozens and dozens of tiny boxes which pushed into the wall. Each small box drawer had a label on it. Most were titles of herbs and seeds and flowers and stems and all sorts of blends of natural materials. He asked me what ailment he could help me with, like depression or anxiety, and I explained about my study sabbatical, and wanted to understand more about homeopathic medicine. He was very kind and generous with his time, and briefly explained the history of homeopathic medicine in France. He told me that even today there are hundreds of practitioners of homeopathic medicine throughout France and Europe. He opened some drawers of his desk and showed me some of the blends he makes and uses for various conditions, and explained why even in Europe, many turn to homeopathic medicine over allopathic medicine because people believe it has such a beneficial effect and is far less expensive than allopathic treatments. He readily admitted that not all homeopathic solutions are the best for certain conditions, and that sometimes allopathic medicine has not done a good job at curing conditions. I explained to him that in the United States more and more people are seeking out alternative medicines in the wake of disillusionment with "managed care" and HMO's in America. He nodded in understanding.

So these two broad approaches to medicine, the allopathic way and the homeopathic way, are the treatment modalities which assist in the healing process. Prayer is not an allopathic or homeopathic treatment. It is a spiritual tool for healing. Religious people pray. Non-religions people pray. So we turn now to what is popularly known as the New Age and medicine. In the 80's and 90's so called "new age" medicine exploded. Websites, books, tapes, CDs, and many varied guru's claiming cures and improvements mushroomed throughout America. Some of these healings bore exotic names such as crystal healing, alchemy healing, moon healing, healing in the light, astrological healing, etc., which made main-stream medicine lift an eyebrow and assert that this was all rubbish, quackery, baloney, an even worse... unsafe, dangerous and in some cases, downright illegal, especially where healing practitioners claimed medical degrees which clearly they did not have.

Yet in spite of all the controversy, many people were drawn to these varied alternatives to healing processes. But in the midst of the marginal, also came new techniques and "new technology" based on new research. Some of these new techniques now have widespread endorsement because of their healing outcomes. Some of these are gaining greater acceptance such as Interactive Guided Imagery, and EMDR (Eye Movement Desensitization Reprocessing) which is used with great healing of those with PTSD, Post-Traumatic Stress Disorder.

Other new techniques do not yet have endorsements by mainstream mental health organizations (such as the American Psychological Association) and yet they are practiced in many parts of our country and around the world. One example would be Thought Field Therapy which is also known as the Callahan Techniques. TFT claims to heal a variety of mental and physical ailments through specialized "tapping" with the fingers at meridian points on the upper body and hands. (See [TFT at Wikipedia](#).) This would be an example of non-religious healing. But there are other non-religious healing techniques. One of these is known as Craniosacral Therapy (or CST). It is also sometimes spelled Cranial Sacral bodywork or treatment. If you look up the term Craniosacral Therapy on Wikipedia you will find this:

"A craniosacral therapy session involves the therapist placing their hands on the patient, which allows them to 'tune in to the craniosacral rhythm.'"

The website describes how the practitioner works with the skull or spine of the patient. It lists some of the "healers" who use the technique such as osteopaths, massage therapists, naturopaths, and chiropractors. There is also a brief list of the conditions most often used by craniosacral treatment. These include mental stress, neck and back pain, migraines, TMJ Syndrome, and chronic pain conditions such as Fibromyalgia. The page also indicates that there is little scientific support for the underlying theoretical model of this treatment.

In spite of the disclaimer in the final sentence in the above paragraph, my own experience with a craniosacral practitioner was extremely helpful. I did suffer from TMJ, and when I shared this over dinner in San Francisco with some fellow guided imagery practitioners, one of them had training in craniosacral healing treatment, and offered to use this technique for my TMJ. She told me this was one of the most effective things that CST was known for. At the time I had never heard of CST, but I knew the woman, and I was in a lot of pain. I granted her permission to work on me. So, right at the supper table in the fine San Francisco restaurant we were in, she pulled a chair up next to me. She placed my face in her hands and gently massaged my jaw and cheeks. She applied gentle pressure at strategic places. She worked on me for about 20 minutes. Following her work, I felt great. My pain was gone. I had an appointment with my dentist for two days later which included a follow-up consult on my TMJ. That day when I got into the dental chair, my dentist asked me about my TMJ. I told her, "It is gone." She raised her eyebrows. "Really?" she said. I nodded and told her about the CST session I had in San Francisco. She said she had heard of the technique but was doubtful about the scientific evidence behind it. I told her, "Whether or not there have been double-blind, evidence-based, clinical trials, I can assure you that what she did with CST not only worked, but I have been symptom-free for the past 48 hours." I can also report that it's been more than ten years since my single episode treatment, and my TMJ has never returned.

Again, the above healing treatment is a non-religious form of treatment that would likely be labeled as a "New Age" technique.

One of the greatest areas of non-religious forms of healing of the New Age is what is often called "energy healing." Energy healing basically believes that energy disorders (blocked energy, lack of energy, etc.) within the body (and mind) can be released, reconfigured, unblocked or enhanced for healing. Some of the various treatments of energy healing are Acupuncture, Energy (esotericism), Energy Medicine, Polarity Medicine, Reiki, and Therapeutic Touch, to name a few. (I would include the tapping at the meridians in Thought Field Therapy/Callahan method described above in this energy healing list). I will not describe each of the various treatments mentioned above. The reader can easily find each of them on the Web.

What is of importance is that energy healing usually deals with chi, a Chinese term and concept for "energy" or "life-force." It is often written as ch'i or qi. In Chinese culture the most used term is qi. Qi is frequently translated as life energy, life-force, or energy flow. You can find more on this by looking up Qi on Wikipedia.

The material on Energy (esotericism) at Wikipedia describes how energy is described in various cultures. It shares similarities and differences in the descriptions of energy, and the practices used to interact with this energy. In particular, there are links to the Chinese forms of this energy such as Qi in Taoism, Qigong, Jing Qi Shen, Internal alchemy, Meridian (in Chinese medicine), Acupuncture, and Shiatsu. All of these are healing practices used to balance the energy of the body, through balancing the energy, balancing the body-mind connection, improving energy flow, or increasing the life force at critical junctures within the body.

My own personal experience with acupuncture was very positive. I had been diagnosed with Meniere's disease, and so I saw my acupuncturist on and off for a year. When I went to see him, he would lay me onto a bed at his medical office, and dim the lights in the room. He would put on a music CD (he used In the Land of Merlin by Jon Land), and placed tiny needles along the edge of my ears. The needles did not hurt at all. I would go into a deep state of relaxation, never falling asleep, but often felt a sensation as if floating. The sessions lasted about a half hour. Afterwards, the wobbly, dizziness associated with my condition would disappear for weeks at a time. I found this procedure very helpful to me. I understood it as a re-balancing within my energy, and the outcome was indeed a re-balancing as I would not lose balance following the treatments.

I also had the opportunity to be introduced to Qigong. In my class, we were instructed to the purpose of this treatment and we were taught various standing postures. We would concentrate on holding these positions. I came away from this treatment much stronger, better balanced, well-grounded and was able to walk in a straight line with ease.

The scientific community (Western science) can find no evidence that Qi exists. Yet, the concept is more than 5,000 years old in Chinese medicine. For example, some forms of energy healing believes the body contains meridians. Here is just one website that maps and describes the meridians of acupuncture. A companion page describes a comprehensive acupuncture points database. It is believed that energy travels along these meridians and acupuncture is a way to change the energy flow for healing. Again, this is a non-religious form of healing.

Not only is energy (qi or ch'i) central to these healing therapies, but it is also important to be aware of the concept of chakras. The concept of chakras comes from Hindu and Buddhist teachings. Chakras are believed to be "force centers" within the body. These are considered to be focal points for the reception and transmission of energy. While there are a few different descriptions of the chakra system, probably the most well-known system in the West is that of the seven chakras. Wikipedia has a website on the chakras that differentiates the different chakra systems, and shows a colorful rendition of the chakras of the human body. Chakra 1 is the Crown Chakra at the top of the head. Chakra 2 is the Third Eye Chakra slightly above and between the eyes. Chakra 3 is the Throat Chakra located at the throat. Chakra 4 is the Heart Chakra, located in the center of the body at heart level. Chakra 5 is the Solar Plexus Chakra. Chakra 6 is the Sacral Chakra located in the lower abdominal area. Chakra 7 is the Base/Root Chakra. This is in the genital area.

Energy healers / practitioners who use the Chakra system, will work with the Chakra areas of the body to bring about greater flow of energy for the welfare of the patient. One of the physicians who compared Western medicine's understanding of key organs and their treatment with Eastern understanding of Chakra was Candace Pert (described elsewhere in this book). Candace ordered a transparency of the Seven Chakra System and overlaid it on the full-length map of the body which hangs in her office. She was amazed at how similar were the vital organs of the body described in Western medicine's view of the body when compared to chakras in Eastern medicine. She describes her surprise and wonderment in her book, Molecules of Emotion. Certainly the above named non-religious forms of healing are not an exhaustive list. Most of those I've indicated above come out of an Eastern medicine understanding of energy and healing. In the West we could also add to non-religious forms of healing such common things such as diet, exercise, sufficient sleep, weight management, stress-reduction to name a few. The point is this: God has created many forms of healing processes, both religious/spiritual as well as non-religious. My friend, Dr. David Bressler, uses the phrase "positive expectant faith" as a non-religious belief that a procedure will have salutary effect. We know that "placebo effect" is a well-documented positive outcome based on the belief and trust in a particular drug or procedure. In placebo effect, it is not the drug or procedure that heals, but the active ingredient in the healing process is a person's belief in the healing outcome. Again, this is a non-religious form of healing.

What makes all of this a challenge to religious people is that it comes from philosophies and teachings which have originated in the East, and for many Christian people, these philosophies and teachings are highly suspect. I have a colleague who absolutely believes that Buddhism is a darkness, and at its heart is something ugly and dangerous. He feels that anything which comes out of it should be avoided. A book entitled, The Seduction of Christianity, calls Dr. David Bresler (see the chapter on guided imagery) a shaman which in this book is a condemnation. This fundamentalist Christian book is designed to frighten readers and does not see the kinds of non-religious forms of healing I am describing in this chapter as something Christians can embrace. They actually believe these are tools of the devil designed to seduce Christians away from Jesus Christ, His healing and His gospel.

I certainly think it is always a good idea to gather data and to evaluate it before seeing any practitioner in the healing arts, whether from the West or the East. The Scriptures (the Bible) tell the reader to "test the spirits" and to "pray for discernment." This is a good thing to be done, certainly.

But I do not believe that all non-Christian forms of healing are to be avoided. When I go to see my dentist who has been trained in modern dental technology, I do not ask my dentist what her religious background is. What I am most concerned about as I sit in the dental chair is that she knows what she is doing, that she is confident and competent in dentistry. The same thing when I am prepared for surgery. I may have a Jewish surgeon or an atheist surgeon or a Protestant surgeon or an agnostic surgeon. I am most concerned that he has a medical degree, has experience in the procedure he is about to start, and that he understands what it will take to resolve the problem through surgery, so that complete healing occurs.

I am grateful to the woman who used her hands on my face to cure me of my TMJ. I am grateful to my acupuncturist who knew how to place those needles along the outside of my ears so that I could begin to function normally. I am grateful to all of the anesthesiologists and nurses and surgeons who were present at the surgeries I've had in my life. All of these have been non-religious forms of healing. Some of these forms have come from Western medicine, while others have come from Eastern medicine. Some are not fully understood and some have not been researched sufficiently to meet the standards of evidence-based medicine.

Yet I am thankful for those practitioners and their systems which have brought me to better health. Not all lighthouses of hope are religious or spiritual within the realm of healing. The pills and medications I buy over the counter or pick up as prescriptions are non-religious and they often bring about healing and wellness. Large pharmaceutical companies spend billions on research. While not all of the medications they produce are safe for everyone all of the time, I am glad that drugs exist. Insulin is the life giving liquid which keeps millions alive. Medications to remove plaque from arteries, and medications designed to prevent heart attacks and strokes are miracle drugs. They too are non-religious modalities to promote wellness and at times, healing.

More and more Americans are turning to alternative medicines and treatments as well as alternative medicine practitioners. While it is important to do your homework before seeking any of these medications or procedures, it is also important to understand that there are many lighthouses of hope out there. Some are religious. Some are non-religious. God has provided many pathways of healing. Evaluate them, discern them, and then decide if any of them are right for you. Sometimes this is an excellent time to take your concern/question to God in prayer. I wish you well.

Chapter 49
Psychoneuroimmunology Revisited

It's now 32 years since Dr. Robert Ader at the University of Rochester coined the phrase: psychoneuroimmunology. As I said earlier in this book (see chapter on Robert Ader), the word came out of psycho-somatic medicine, and was meant to cover mind-body immunology. It also sought to get physicians who specialized on one part of the body to begin talking with other specialists dealing with other parts of the body. As Dr. Ader put it, no one was talking to anyone else. The goal was to promote a more global view of the mind-body so that everyone would be learning from everyone else, sharing information, promoting more of a holistic approach to healing. So was that objective achieved? Is there now a more holistic approach to health and healing than 30 years ago? Some would say a definite yes, while others would give a qualified yes.

At a conference I attended, a speaker said that PNI (psychoneuroimmunology) studies were now being done at over 100 medical schools and universities. This statistic alone suggests the increasing interest in a more integrated approach to understanding the body-mind matrix. Certainly, the world of medicine is still dominated by specialists. That is where the money is, so that's why so many physicians specialize. However, even among specialists, there is more cross-fertilization, and exchange of information, between specialists. More physicians understand the impact of the body's disordering on the mind of the patient. Likewise, there is more information than ever before on how the mind impacts one's physiology and creates physical symptoms.

Today one of the greatest areas of research is of the human brain. Brain research dominates more and more as secrets of the body-mind matrix are discovered to reside in the human brain. From the work of Candace Pert and others, the brain is not the only intelligence in the body. As she writes in Molecules of Emotion, the mind is located throughout the body. This makes sense in particular with the disease of cancer. When my friend and colleague, Bill Dasch, spoke to physicians during his son's battle with leukemia, he asked why the cancer would disappear only to reappear weeks or months later during Tristen's medical treatment. One of the treating physicians said, "Cancer cells are smart... they know when the medicine is in the body and they literally run away from it, and hide... they are intelligent." So if this particular disease is smart, so are other cells of the body which seek to destroy these cancer cells. I also once heard a physician say that there really are "two brains" in the body. He went on to say that one of the brains is in our skull. The other brain is in our gut. He said that the intelligence within the upper and lower intestines and all of the organs associated with the "gut" were as smart at the brain in our heads.

I think that the picture is becoming more complex even as it is exciting. The human brain is an extremely complex organ. In many ways brain research is at an embryonic stage. When I was younger I used to wonder if the mind was located in the brain. I certainly thought so. Now scientists and physicians have postulated that "mind" is throughout the body. Certainly the brain governs a great deal of the body. Then along comes someone like Dr. Larry Dossey who believes in a "non-local" mind. This concept of mind is not bound by a human body.. But many consider Dossey's view as more science fiction than scientific fact. It has more to do with the metaphysical than the physical. Hard science continues to investigate the brain-body functions.

One of the most interesting discussions of the mind-body connection can be found on the website Mind Body Psychotherapy by Dr. Robin Roberts. Roberts discusses many features of the mind-body connection for the lay person. For example, she presents a nice simple graph of what is known as the Triune Brain. This concept of the brain was first presented to the world by physician and neuroscientist, Paul D. MacLean. Already back in the 1960's Maclean had postulated this concept but it became a popular way of thinking about the brain in his famous book, The Triune Brain in Evolution. Roberts, on her website, describes this model in simple to understand lay language.

The largest part of the Triune brain is the Neo-Cortex or "thinking brain" which governs by analyzing data, makes decisions, and holds values and core beliefs among many other functions. Then there is the Limbic System or Mammalian brain. This is known as the "feeling brain." This brain is the seat of feelings (glad, sad, mad, scared, bad, etc.), and is involved greatly with various immune functions. Finally there is what is called the Reptilian brain which is the "survival brain." Here is the seat of the fight or flight response as well as other automatic defense mechanisms which we share with other life forms. This model of the brain is very helpful in psychotherapy. In fact, Roberts calls her website Mind-Body Psychotherapy.

I first heard the Triune Brain described by my friend and colleague, Dr. Peter L. Steinke at a workshop for Healthy Congregations. After going into great detail as to how the Triune Brain functions in all its various parts, he made application to the church's function. Local congregations, for example, can use their thinking brain to describe mission statements, decide on priorities, evaluate programs and staffing needs, and become intentional about leadership. He then described how congregations are also emotional systems, and how members could become governed by their emotional reactivity. (See his book How Your Church Family Works: Understanding Congregations As Emotional Systems). His application of Bowen theory to congregational systems is excellent, and when one applies the Triune Brain model to such systems, it quickly becomes apparent that congregations can either build up or break down people, especially leadership. Steinke then went on to describe the Reptilian brain, and how certain issues within congregations trigger survival responses (flight, fight or freeze). Instead of thinking through issues, if members only come from the limbic system or are reduced to reptilian responses, the congregation begins to no longer function as a healthy congregation. Members attack their pastor or other leaders, and conflict in congregations can grow quickly. Speed Leas, a senior consultant at the Alban Institute, has written about the five phases of congregational conflict. Level 4 and 5 conflict is so out of control that it takes outside help and expertise to bring these emotional forces back into reasonable thinking.

But I digress. Back to Robert's website. Roberts agrees that the mind exists throughout the body. She writes:

"If you were asked to point to your mind, you would most likely point to your head, thinking that's where your brain is. However, you would be wrong to think that your mind is limited to your brain alone. The mind exists throughout the physical body, mediated by the neurons and biochemicals of the central nervous system and the hormones of the endocrine system."

That point was made clearly by Candace Pert through her research (see Molecules of Emotion). Today while brain research continues strong, the concept of psychoneuroimmunology includes much more than just the human brain. The entire brain-body is the focus, and "mind-body" is the landscape.

It is important to have a general overall understanding of what PNI is. Again, I point the reader to psychoneuroimmunology on Wikipedia. Here the work of Robert Ader and Nicolas Cohen at the University of Rochester is described in the early development of PNI. You can read about David Fenton's contributions to the field, and about how Ader, Cohen and Fenton published their ground-breaking book on Psychoneuroimmunology in 1981. The site goes on to briefly describe Candace Pert's discoveries in PNI research. Of note are the following sentences:

"The discovery by Pert et al. that neuropeptides and neurotransmitters act directly upon the immune system shows their close association with emotions and suggests mechanisms through which emotions and immunology are deeply interdependent. Showing that the immune and endocrine systems are modulated not only by the brain but also by the central nervous system itself has had an impact on the understanding of emotions, as well as of disease."

It is believed that emotions can and do have great impact on disease and healing. For example, studies have shown that breast cancer patients survive longer when they are in a breast cancer support group. Here it is believed that the emotional support somehow helps the breast cancer patient cope better. It may also retard the growth of cancer cells. It likely boosts the immune system so that it operates at a much higher function. This is an example of psycho (mind), neuro (body), immunology (healing). An excellent contribution to the understanding of psychoneuroimmunology and religion is the work by Harold

Koenig and Harvey Jay Cohen entitled The Link Between Religion and Health: Psychoneuroimmunology and the Faith Factor, published in 2002, about a year after I visited Harold Koenig in his home. We had briefly discussed the need for someone to write a book across the areas of prayer, healing and psychoneuroimmunology (my sabbatical study). Imagine my surprise and great delight to see Koenig's work come out on this topic.

This book, The Link Between Religion and Health, grew out of an extraordinary conference held at Duke University on July 12, 1999. This first of its kind conference "brought together twelve of the world's leading psychoneuroimmunologists, theologians, and physicians to review the effects of stress on the immune system, and to see how this knowledge might inform us about the religion-health relationship."

Koenig and Cohen's work covers the landscape of PNI. Chapter One describes the connection between PNI and Religion. In Chapter Two, the authors present the development and history of PNI. Chapter Three discusses how stress effects the physical body. It is authored by Bruce S. Rabin whom I also read during my sabbatical. Chapter Four and Five has the focus on stress and cancer. Chapter Six deals with stress and infection. Chapter Seven focuses on wound healing. Chapter Eight is on HIV/AIDS. Chapter Nine is on hostility and the endocrine system. Chapter Ten is on stress and the autoimmune diseases. Chapter Eleven brings together an understanding of immune, neuroendocrine and religious measures. Chapter Twelve looks at PNI and Eastern Religious Traditions. Chapter Thirteen is on PNI and Western Religious Traditions. Chapter Fourteen explores the implications for society of PNI and Religion. The book ends with avenues for further exploration and conclusions. What Koenig and Cohen are exploring is how the mind-body-immune system (PNI) is impacted by stress factors and disease processes as well as focusing on how religion and spirituality impact this complex wholeness. The enormous work done at Duke University clearly indicates how important religion is to health, and that the goal is optimal health of the complex integrated wholeness of the mind-body-immune system, which Candace Pert calls the "body-mind matrix." While Dr. Robert

Ader had said, rather tongue in cheek, that his three volume work was the best book on PNI, and that I would not be able to understand it (absolutely true, by the way), since his invention of the word PNI, researchers and authors now write works for the lay public, and many people are much more aware of the mind-body connections through articles in Reader's Digest, Time and Newsweek magazines, local newspaper articles, and special books online at Internet booksellers.

The research continues to expand. Each year I receive email notification of scholarships available at Duke University for further study in PNI and related fields. Medical research across the country at prestigious research centers and hospitals continue to make applications to various diseases and autoimmune dysfunctions directly coming out of PNI research projects. Lab technicians, endocrinologists, hemotologists, cardiologists, and a host of medical personnel are in this field, forwarding the knowledge base and sophistication in body-mind medicine.

This research is not confined to the United States. Canada and Europe are also involved in the study of psychoneuroimmunology. A nurse I know in Germany has shared with me how PNI studies have impacted patient care within her hospital unit. My stay at Burrswood, England, gave me insight into how the staff meetings on patient care involves looking at not only the physical problems of particular patients, but also focuses on the whole person– mentally, emotionally, physically, spiritually and how these impact the immune and coping systems of the body.

Does one's emotional state and belief systems impact recovery from cancer? Does one's emotional state and belief system relate to managing arthritis? Those who have studied Dr. Dean Ornish's work with cardiac patients, know that he was able to demonstrate the reversal of heart disease by applying a holistic approach to patient care including eating right, exercise, group therapy and meditation. Read Reversing Heart Disease by Dr. Dean Ornish for a greater appreciation of this body-mind recovery process.

As we re-visit psychoneuroimmunology, the lay public may not know this term, but many physicians, even specialists, have a greater "awareness" of a more holistic view of the body-mind matrix. Recently when I was diagnosed with prostate cancer, and a treatment plan was being considered, all of my physicians (primary care physician, urologist, oncologist, endocrinologist, neurologist) were all talking with each other on the phone and in e-mails to consider each other's opinions on various aspects of possible treatments. This was evidence of a much fuller holistic consideration of the patient. Several of the physicians asked about my mental health and relationships with family and friends as we moved toward a treatment plan. How would the treatment effect my work was raised by two doctors. These physicians entered into what I call a holistic view of care for me.

As the years move forward, we will be learning much from those involved in the field of PNI. As the ancient Hebrews "knew"... the mind and the body are one... holistic... inseparable. In the 21st century this will become even more greatly understood. We have a body-mind matrix. Intriguing, complex, adaptable, involving a multiplex of immune functions, we are as the psalmist says, "fearfully and wonderfully made." (Psalm 139:14)

Section V
Where Do We Go From Here?

Chapter 50
The Starting Place Matters

As we move deeper into the 21st century, more discoveries are being made in the interrelated fields of prayer, healing and body-mind medicine. Currently the focus is on how the human brain functions and how these functions impact health and healing. Questions are being asked about how prayer may impact the brain and in turn how the body translates that into possible healing. Another area under exploration is how one's attitude impacts healing and if a sense of "gratitude" opens one up to more possibilities for healing. The recent Oz show introduced a 21st century healer in Cleveland who is using prayer and his hands to bring about healing in his patients. This causes challenges to traditional medicine and the medical profession even interprets this type of healing in non-religious terms (placebo effect, or spontaneous healing).

So it becomes quickly apparent that the answer to the question, "Where do we go from here?" in terms of where the future study of prayer and healing may lead us is very important.

It seems to me that the starting place matters as we think about prayer, healing and the body-mind matrix. It not only matters but it is crucial, for where we start from may greatly influence where we may end up. Lawrence J. Peter is credited for saying, "If you don't know where you are going, you will probably end up someplace... else." I once entered a school room and that saying was reproduced on one of the walls in the following manner: Each word was written in a different colored box... "If" was on one box and "you" was printed on another box below the "if" box. The saying began at the top of the wall and box after box was on top of another box and so the boxes all went "If"... "you"... "don't"... "know"... "where"... "you"... "are"... "going"... "you"... "will"... "probably"..."end"... "up"... "someplace"... then a painted line went horizontal across the bottom of that wall... across the bottom of the next wall... all the way to the bottom of the next wall, ending at a box that read... "else."

Certainly as research continues it is quite possible to end up someplace else as the research may suddenly present surprises and phenomena which could not have been predicted or anticipated. This is common in research. As the saying goes, every system has its anomalies. If one looks at dictionary definitions of the word anomaly, one finds such definitions as "a deviation from the common rule, type, arrangement, or form" but an even better definition is "an odd, peculiar, or strange condition, situation, quality", and then there is always the definition of an anomaly being "an incongruity or inconsistency."

One has to be ready for the anomaly or anomalies in research results or new theoretical models or hypotheses. For me, Larry Dossey's concept of the "non-local mind" is one such unexpected hypothesis which seeks to explain distance healing. And this is precisely where one's "starting place" matters. For a Christian the starting place might be that one's prayer to God in Jesus' Name may account for distance healing meaning that the Christian's prayer is answered by God and God heals the beloved who lives elsewhere. On the other hand if one's "starting place" is non-religious as it appears from Dossey's writing, that there is a non-local Mind and that all of us are a part of that Mind, then there is no God or Jesus or theistic hypothesis. One's "starting place" matters.

I have many New Age friends and colleagues who believe healing is real. They do not, however, believe in Jesus nor do they think the phenomena of healing comes from God. For many of them, healing is a by-product of an evolutionary process within nature. Nature is not something from a Creator God, it is rather an outcome from the Big Bang theory.

My friend, Garth Ludwig, in his ground-breaking book, Order Restored, bears a subtitle of "A Biblical Interpretation of Health, Medicine, and Healing." For Ludwig, his starting point is the Biblical revelation of a Creator God whose good creation plunges into chaos as a result of sin. God in His wisdom sends His Son, Jesus Christ, to bring order and life into this chaos. For Ludwig, healing is what Jesus is about. Ludwig's "starting place" is not only theistic, it is Christocentric, meaning, restoration which includes healing, centered in Jesus Christ's healing activities culminating in His death and resurrection, with implications for all of creation.

In a similar way, Morton Kelsey's "starting place" is also Biblical. When he writes that for a Christian, healing starts with Jesus Christ, he means that Christians see healing in light of what Jesus did as a healer. With one-fifth of the New Testament being the healing actions of Christ, Kelsey points out how incredibly important healing was in the life of Jesus. When Jesus spoke of his ministry being three-fold, to preach, teach and heal, Christians see in Christ their hope for healing and in His resurrection their ultimate healing in heaven.

The "starting place" matters.

When I studied with Marty Rossman at the Academy for Guided Imagery, he would often ground participants in whatever power was above, or supported from beneath, to connect them to something greater than themselves. At times this seemed to be his starting place. But I knew that some of my imagery colleagues did not believe in a god or a higher power. They might believe in a oneness with an energy force, or follow Mindfulness (a perspective growing out of Buddhism but not religious), but for others it was quite difficult to know from where they began.

It appears to me that what one's world-view is informs the type of view you have about prayer and healing. If you believe there is a God who listens to prayers and responds to prayers (your world-view) then that is what informs your perspective. If on the other hand you do not believe in such a God, then healing will be seen from some other perspective. When Larry Dossey, for example, says that Christians do not have a monopoly on prayer, I think he means that "prayer" as "intentionality" is not the same as praying "to" a God who will hopefully make things better. No, for Dossey, my "intentionality" that things improve for you somehow impacts you and your situation because my mind and your mind are non-local. What I intend can make a difference for you no matter where you live since we are all part of this collective consciousness or Mind. He starts someplace else without a deity. He ends up someplace else without a deity.

There has always been tension between religion and science. As the scientific endeavor continues to uncover and discover new things about the human brain, the body, the mind, and new things about healing, the realm of "mystery" may indeed shrink. Certainly science can neither prove or disprove the existence of a Creator God, nor demonstrate that healing comes from Him. The belief in a God and His healing powers is a faith stance, a posture of trust. It falls within the realm of religion and metaphysics, not physics. Certainly spirituality and science can be compatible but not necessarily combatable. There are a growing number of astrophysicists and physicists who are now shifting over to greater spirituality and even religion. They have not given up an inch of the scientific realm, but they have begun to "see" that there may indeed be a greater force behind the universe as we understand it scientifically. John Polkinghorne (Quantum Physics and Theology: An Unexpected Kinship) is one such voice who has influenced the field of religion and science. There are others.

I certainly have great respect for those within the healing community who study the body-mind matrix who have a different "starting place" than my own. I have much to learn from them and value all of their insights, hypotheses, and worldviews. They often have alternative explanations which challenge my own thinking and beliefs, and I enjoy the dialogue in person or with the thoughts of a writer who presents something new to me that I have never considered. There is, in my opinion, a healthy tension between science and religion that brings about new understandings and hopefully, renewed tolerance for one another's endeavors to seek truth.

Where do we go from here? We go into the undiscovered country which lies before us. Each new discovery somehow raises new questions and pushes us further into the undiscovered country. We trust the process (as Marty Rossman would say) to see where it leads. Will someone discover a "uniform field theory" is yet to be seen. Will someone discover better ways of integrating science with religion is yet to be seen. Will someone discover definitively how prayer works in terms of healing is yet to be seen. Will there be new ground-breaking discoveries of the body-mind matrix is yet to be seen.

Recently there was an announcement in the news that the National Institutes of Health was going to curtail and perhaps defund future studies of prayer and healing. Whether this is for budgetary reasons or philosophical reasons I do not know. But if it is true, then the forward progress in this fascinating field of study may become something of the past. This will be most unfortunate.

Will science someday have "an answer" as to how Dr. Nemeh is able to heal so many? Will Dr. Oz someday understand? That is yet to be seen. Science so far has put forward the concepts of "placebo effect" and "spontaneous healing" to somehow explain the mysterious and the miraculous healings which occur. Their "starting place" informs their explanation for such phenomena just as surely as a religious person would counter with a quite different explanation for these mysterious and miraculous healings. They might not call them placebo effect or spontaneous healing, but rather they might say, "Look what God is doing! Praise God!"

My own thought is that there remain an openness to new possibilities as we move on from here. Healing comes down from both sacred and secular places. When Jesus healed the man at the Pool of Bethseda (John 5: 1-15) he came healing from the sacred framework. There were already healers in the land healing from a secular framework. Perhaps there will always be healing in the name of science and medicine and healing in the name of religion. These need not be incompatible. Clergy often say to their congregational members, "we are praying for you, and make sure you keep going to see your doctor." Both science and religion should be supportive of one another where possible in the healing enterprise. As Dr. Dale Matthews has said, it is a case of prayer AND Prozac.

As for my "starting place" I thank God for His healing presence and His healing actions in my life, the life of my family and friends, and in the lives of so many. When my adult daughter was 2 years old, she had a fall, and faced surgery for a double hematoma. The doctor was concerned about her future functioning, and there was a risk for permanent damage. I prayed for a miracle. I prayed for healing. And I also prayed for her surgeon and the surgery, and for the other physicians and nurses involved with the outcome uncertain. I praise God that the surgery was successful and that my daughter had no residual

effect from that horrible event, and that today she is in her early 30's, married and has an excellent job. I thank God for medicine and the science behind all that was done that day of surgery and during the recovery period. I believe in a God who cares and heals, who responds to prayers of gratitude and to prayers of request.
That's my starting place.
What is yours?

Chapter 51
What is this force?

Those who know me well, know I have always followed Star Trek starring William Shatner as Captain James T. Kirk and Leonard Nimoy as First Officer Spock. Years after the original series ended, a number of major motion pictures were made with the original series cast.

The motion picture Star Trek V: The Final Frontier is a story about how Spock's vulcan half-brother, Sybok, steals the Starship Enterprise in order to travel to where Sha Ka Ree is located. Kirk asks what Sha Ka Ree is, and is told that Sha Ka Ree is where a powerful entity called "God" exists, and that Sha Ka Ree is analogous to the Human Garden of Eden, the Klingon QuiTu or the Romulan Vota Vor. In other words there are many names for the same idyllic place... heaven, or in this case, known by the name of Sha Ka Ree. The story is about what happens on Sha Ka Ree when the crew of the Enterprise encounter "God" on Sha Ka Ree.

My point is that some things go by different names for the same entity or reality in various cultures. For example, you often hear people saying that "God" goes by many different names: Yahweh, Jesus Christ, Mohammad, Buddha, etc. People often do not make distinctions that differentiate these names and persons. It is not true, that all of these refer to the same God. As a Christian I could not possibly say that Muhammad or Buddha are the same God or point to the same God as that described in Judeo-Christian teaching and faith. But many do believe that regardless of what faith system one is in, that when they pray, they are all praying to the same god.

So this made me think about the question: What is this force for healing? Some call it healing energy, some call it Qui, some call it psychic energy, some call it Phrana, some call it the healing power of Jesus. Certainly there are many different people claiming to have healing power or a gift for healing. Some in psychology call themselves "energy healers" and seem to be able to control this energy for healing purposes. Shamans also make claims to have healing powers and direct healing energy. Some say they are "conduits" of special healing energy. Others claim that the healing ministry of Jesus exists today, and is available through prayer and the laying on of hands. There are Christians who believe that any healing apart from Jesus must come from the demonic, while others ask, "What purpose would it serve Satan and the demonic if Satan is healing and it gives glory to God?" They believe that God can even use non-Christian conduits for healing.

So what is this force for healing? I've thought a great deal about this. I have some thoughts I will share here. I haven't read anyone writing about it the way I think about it although I'm sure there may be some out there who have written eloquently on this topic and I just have no knowledge of them yet. I don't claim to have any special knowledge about this force. I may be completely wrong about it. What I will describe is pure speculation on my part and offered to the reader for consideration. Please do not label or brand me theologically as a bad guy for what, as Dr. Seuss calls, "The Thinks You Can Think." I haven't a clue if what I am thinking about (this force for healing) will bare the weight of scrutiny. But I'm going to speculate just the same. With various persons of different religions and psychologies not only claiming to channel this power, or even have this power, I have tried to find a "way" to think about it. So here are my thoughts.

I think that this force may be like electricity or gravity, in the sense, that it is invisible but we can see the effects of this force. My father was an electrician and I certainly felt the effects of electrical shocks even though I could never see electricity. I can also raise my pencil into the air, release it, and watch it fall to the ground. I cannot see gravity but I can see its effects. I also can not see the "healing force" but I can see, at times, the salutary (beneficial) effects of it through the prayers of others and in the unexplained healings in every culture.

We are pretty sure we "know" that sub-atomic particles exist although we cannot see them with the human eye. The secret work of the Manhattan Project during World War II brought together brilliant minds (Albert Einstein, Robert Openheimer and others) who brought about the "splitting of the atom" which resulted in the first atomic explosion in the Nevada desert. This was to bring in the nuclear age and demonstrated the reality of the sub-atomic "world" which led to nuclear proliferation of weapons of mass destruction. But in the year 1500 or 1700 or 1800, humans were not aware of this "world" of quantum. At the turn of the 20th century, science took gigantic steps forward in "discovering" the new realities previously unknown. Einstein's famous formula E=MC2 is just a summary of one of those discoveries.

Albert Einstein's life's work was an attempt to understand and describe the force of gravity as it operates throughout our known universe. He was single minded in his effort. One of the results of his research was his special theory of relativity. This grew out of his belief that the laws of classic mechanics could not be reconciled with the laws of the electromagnetic field. He also began thinking that a theory of relativity could be extended to gravitational fields. This led to his publication of the 1916 paper on a general theory of relativity. He continued to look into quantum mechanics and investigations of light and many more scientific endeavors. Much later, in 1950, he described his "uniform field theory," an attempt to harmonize various aspects of physics.

There are four fundamental forces known in the universe. These are: the strong nuclear force, electromagnetism, the weak nuclear force, and gravitation. Einstein continued to grow more isolated as he focused nearly all of his attention on gravity. The rest of physics concentrated on the other three forces. This has been the world of physics for the past 100 plus years. One of the latest theories in this field has been String Theory, an attempt once again to form a Uniform Field Theory. This was a very hot theory for perhaps five years or more, but as so often happens in the field of physics, there are things which the String Theory cannot account for and therefore the scientists move onto more new theories. (For an outstanding presentation of a scientific viewpoint of the cosmos, including Quantum Theory, String Theory and beyond, read Brian Greene's, The Fabric of the Cosmos: Space, Time and the Texture of Reality)

So is this "force" for healing something like those four fundamental forces named above or is this something more in the realm of "meta-physics?" For example, the concept of Chi, or energy, in Asian cultures, is believed to be a very real force in those cultures. Thousands of healers (energy healers, mystics, guru's, etc.) work with this concept. Yet there are physicians who do not believe Chi is real. But as alternative methods of healing grow in popularity in the West, more people turn to practitioners and healing arts which work with this fundamental notion of healing energy. Acupuncture is just one of these forms of healing which works with concepts of meridians and energy for healing. I know from my own personal experience, that the acupuncturist I worked with several times was able to bring healing when my doctors at Kaiser seemingly could do nothing. Both in outer space and inner space there are new discoveries all of the time. Layers upon layers of the unknown are peeled back and we "see" things we had never seen before. Yet mysteries still abound. What are "black holes" and what is "dark matter?" Is Michio Kaku (Physics of the Impossible: A Scientific Exploration into the World of Phasers, Force Fields, Teleportation, and Time Travel), the famous astrophysicist often seen on the Discovery Channel, right that instead of three or four or five dimensions of reality, there are multiple dimensions of reality that we just don't yet know enough about? (Some theorize that there are actually eleven dimensions while others say there are seventeen.)

What about the world of the para-normal? I've seen countless TV shows documenting all sorts of issues of the para-normal from ESP, Clairvoyance, and Remote Viewing to what are called "disembodied energies" or ghosts, to poltergeists, and alien visitations (the Greys and the Browns and other so called "beings"). Are these things real? And if they are real, how do they fit into our world view? And if they do not fit into our worldview, how do we develop a world-view that encompass them? Or do we simply dismiss them as fantasy and urban legend?

Is what I am calling the "force for healing" part of the normal unseen world we live in, or is it part of the paranormal? I'm going to side with those who believe it is part of our "normal" world. I believe it is something like gravity or electricity, or something like the four known forces of the universe (described above). I may be wrong.

There certainly is a theological point of view that believes God "breaks into our world" at various times to do what He chooses to do. Since the Judeo-Christian belief is that God created all things and all worlds and is beyond all worlds, He has the capacity to break in and create anything He so wishes. That means He can break in and cause healing in any given situation. He could, then, bring about healings as a result of one's praying that He would do so.

But I believe that God already has "built-in" to our very bodies and minds the capacity to heal, that is, that the "healing force" is already within us. When I fall and scrape my knee, I don't think about my knee and say "heal" to my knee. No, it just automatically gets a protective scab over it and it heals automatically. That "automatic" is the healing power already placed within our minds and bodies. It is the "natural" healing that God placed into His creation. Just as electricity was in the world before electricity was "discovered" and quarks were in the sub-atomic world before they were "discovered." I remember reading, a few years ago, about a Russian scientist who wrote a paper describing his belief that there is a speed greater than the speed of light. His article argued that there are "particles" moving greater than the speed of light that slow down as they decrease speed towards the speed of light. I've forgotten the name he gave to such particles, but perhaps he is right. Even Einstein would place X's into his mathematical formulas when he didn't know what was going on mathematically in various places of those formulas. When asked about those X's he simply said that they were a mystery but someday they might be known. Meantime, with those unknown X's he was able to complete formulas which still had to be "proven" in observable ways. Many of Einstein's formulas were not able to be verified until long after his death. I am told that some of them still have yet to be "proven" by experimental demonstration.

What I am speculating here is that this force for healing, while it remains a mystery in so many ways, may one day become revealed as a normal part of God's ordered creation. I remember Dr. Larry Dossey, in the film, The Power Within, saying that Christians do not have a monopoly on healing. By that he meant that while Christians do pray for healing, so do others who are not Christian and that healing is present for them as well. Dossey has theorized that not only is there healing in the mind, but that there is a "Healing Mind" (that may not be exactly how Dossey means it but that's how I understand him). His view is that I can have a healing intention for you as you live in New York City while I live here in Los Angeles, and that my healing intention for you here in L.A., has effect on you as you live in New York. When I first heard this my initial thought was "this is crazy." But then I remembered the story in my family of my grandmother on my mother's side. She was playing cards one night with family and friends when she suddenly gasped and dropped her cards and said with a shock on her face, "my brother just died!" No one around the card table knew quite what to do with this. But within the next half hour, the Sheriff in her town notified her of her brother's death. It was an incredible moment. It reminds me of the character, Spock, who suddenly looks up from his scanner, and announced to Kirk that he "knows" that a Vulcan ship has just been destroyed in another distant quadrant of the universe. Kirk asks him how he knows. Spock replies that he just "knows."

These two stories, the real one in my grandmother's life and the fictional one from the TV show Star Trek came to my mind when Dr. Dossey spoke about one's thoughts in one part of the country effecting the healing processes of a loved one 3,000 miles away. In the world of mystery there is the so-called "butterfly effect." It says that the beating of a butterfly's wings halfway around the world can effect the weather on the other side of the world. To my Western non-mystical mind this sounds preposterous. Yet perhaps it is true on some sub-atomic level. Every time I hear about the fact that the movement of one particle in the subatomic world can influence the effect of another similar particle in another part of the world, I cannot really wrap my mind around this fact. Yet it is a fact. How can this be? I don't know. I don't know if anyone knows. Those who specialize in particle physics report this as a fact. But what is the connection between these two different particles at a distance from each other which causes them to act the same.

So in the physical world, there are non-physical powers or "energies" which seem to be in operation. We all are familiar with the phrase "mind over matter." The non-corporeal "mind" can and does influence the corporeal "body." In extreme emergencies, for example, a person can bend down and lift a car up off of someone whereas if that person were asked to lift that car in a non-emergency time, they could not budge the car. Is this just the case of adrenaline and other chemicals making the person super strong in the crisis moment? Or is it something even beyond that?

We suspect that the body and the mind "talk" to each other, perhaps through the process of "symbols." There definitely is a unity between mind and body at times. For example, if you point out to me something that I am not aware of, I may feel embarrassed... a feeling in the mind... but there is also a body reaction... my face gets red, I feel flushed... as I feel the shame. John Bradshaw in the opening to his book Healing the Shame That Binds You describes how he is about to tape a PBS special and is walking up the side of the aisle when someone suddenly grabs his arm and he is suddenly startled not knowing what is going on. The intruder points to Bradshaw's crotch and tells him that his fly is open. Bradshaw suddenly turns red in the face, turns around, and zips up before going up on stage for the videotaping of his PBS special. He felt the feeling of embarrassment and his body responded in like manner.

These processes are out of our sight. We do not "see" what is going on in the mind-body but we may see their results. A shaman says words or administers herbs and there is healing. A kahuna healer does similar things and there is a healing result. A nurse places her hands over a patient's wound never touching it and the wound heals faster than if she had not laid hands over the patient. Prayer shifts the mind and impacts the body.

If what I am speculating is true, that there is a healing force in the universe, then what is it that Christians are claiming when they follow Jesus' ministry of healing? Is there anything special or unique about Christian healing if others seem to be able to heal as well?

Is Jesus Just One Among Many or Is He Unique?

There are those who do not believe Jesus was the Son of God. For that matter, there are those who do not believe there is a God.

There certainly are those who believe Jesus walked the earth, and they believe that much if not all of the New Testament is fabrication and was written to make claims about Jesus in order to "sell" the new religion. They do not believe that the Bible is inspired (or inerrant), and that the fictional writing about Jesus was basically written to promote the "Jesus sect" that was in competition with the "Essene sect," the "Zealot sect," the "Pharisee sect," the "Sadducee sect," and other Jewish subgroups of the early first century. To engage in any lengthy description of these sects is to go far beyond my book.

Suffice it to say that I am aware of those who have various interpretations of the Jesus material presented in what we call the "New" Testament. Many have written about the "quest for the historical Jesus" and the reader is commended to read that literature if he or she so desires.

For the purposes of my book, I believe that Jesus was real and that He was the Son of God. He was, as the ancient church creeds testify to, one with God and indeed was God incarnate (in the flesh). Since that is my starting place the question remains "was he a healer among healers, no different from the others," or was he in some sense a different kind of healer, "unique" in some ways. Or in other words, was Jesus just very good at harnessing the healing power better than anyone else, or does he really go above and beyond the healing practices of the first century. For example, Jesus was able to raise someone from the dead as documented in the New Testament. That would make Him unique. Others were healing, some in Jesus' name, and some not. Did they raise the dead as well? It doesn't appear to be the case. Later on some of Jesus' apostles raise people from the dead. The argument against these testimonials is what I've already shared, namely, there are those who believe these are fictional accounts.

Perhaps a quick look into Jesus' own perspective on this may be helpful. By the time of Jesus' life, the Greeks had already established a large cult around healing. There were special pools for a person to go to for healing. There were "physicians" to whom one could go. Most of us have heard of Hippocrates and the Hippocratic Oath that physicians even to this day live by... "do no harm" being part of that oath. Aescylus was the father of healing in the ancient world. So that by the time of Jesus' life and ministry, He knew of these healing traditions and healing cults.

I am quite certain that some saw Jesus as another healer of the age. In our terms they saw him as a "medicine man" who said words or touched others and they were healed. We know that one-fifth of the Gospels in the New Testament are dedicated to healings done by Jesus or in Jesus' Name. We know that Jesus himself said that the three things to be done were to preach and teach the Gospel and the third thing was to provide healing.

In one story Jesus approaches the man at the pool of Bethesda. This was one of those healing pools scattered around the ancient world. It is at this pool that Jesus heals a man.

Was Jesus simply using the force for healing as others may have been doing and still seem to do today?

Well, here again, is my speculation. I believe that Jesus knew all about the natural force for healing in the world. He doesn't knock healings done by others in his own time. He knows that healing comes in a variety of ways and from different sources. Yet He heals others, many others, giving all glory to God His Father, and also as a sign of the kingdom of God. I believe that Jesus has this force for healing either within himself (since He Is God as Christians affirm in the church's historical creeds, the Apostles Creed and Nicene Creed), or that he is the conduit of God's most powerful form of this healing power with God as the direct source for Jesus life and ministry. In John's Gospel Jesus speaks of He and the Father being one. At other times He speaks of glorifying His Father who is in heaven. Either way I view this, healing comes from Jesus to the one in need of healing.

Sometimes this healing is done remotely. Jesus isn't even present when the healing takes place. He just says the word and it is done. Sometimes it's as if His very being is of this healing force. There is the story about the woman who pushes her way through the crowds believing if only she could touch Him, she would be healed. When finally she drops down and reaches out and touches the hem of His garment, Jesus turns and acknowledges that some power has drained out of Him, and He wants to know who has touched Him. When He learns of this woman's great faith, He commends her to all of those around Him as an example of great faith.

Jesus is the Source of healing, and He is one with His Father in heaven. Jesus embodies, teaches and points to the true source of all healing... His Father in heaven.

That while Larry Dossey is probably right that Christians do not have a monopoly on healing, they do worship the One who is the creator of that healing, the true Source of all creation and who ultimately has the power to save people... which is our ultimate healing.

I was at a luncheon hosted by the California Association of Marriage and Family Therapists in which a speaker spoke about the benefits of medicine. He showed that the effectiveness of medicine is about 43% of the time. Then he asked "what is the effectiveness of mental health practice?" He showed that mental health counseling is effective about... ready?... about 43% of the time. Then he said "now hold on... look at this..." and he asked how effective the audience (made up of licensed marriage and family therapists) thought prayer was. His next slide gave the research and the statistic: prayer is effective 44% of the time! This showed that prayer was as effective as physical treatment or counseling. Can there be a uniform field therapy for healing? None of the three treatment's can account for all of the phenomena.

So what is this force? While I set out on my sabbatical study and spent ten years following that study pursuing the answer to what is healing... this... force for good... in our known universe... my answer comes up: it is a mystery. Obviously it is "there" and certain activities can trigger it... like prayer... or counseling... or surgery... or medications... or love. The work of Dean Ornish and Bernie Siegel (among many others) show that love heals. Within the religious world, the love of God heals... and saves. For the Christian, it is agape love... undeserved love... that ultimately heals through Jesus' actions on the cross. In popular language we hear "love can heal all things." In the New Testament, Chapter 13 of 1 Corinthians (sometimes referred to the love chapter) describes the healing properties of love. It ends by saying that three things abide: faith, hope and love and the greatest of these is love.

Is love a force in the universe? In the "metaphysics" of life, love is real. Love is eternal. Love reconciles (heals), forgives (heals), changes people (heals) and enables growth (like the love from a parent towards a child). I've even heard of some with cancer "loving" their cancer cells, and thereby creating healing.

We certainly can discuss this for a long, long time... the bottom line for me is that I believe there is a real force for healing... but it doesn't always work or perhaps it is not always effectively utilized, or perhaps there are ways to prevent it from working. Whatever it is, I continue to pray for it... pray for healing. From my own religious tradition, I pray that God will bring healing and wholeness where there is disease, discouragement, or disorder. That through healers the broken can be mended, and that there can be new life.

As Jesus said in John 10:10... he came that others might have life... abundant. That for me is healing. But perhaps even more telling is when Jesus was asked what are the greatest commandments to be kept. He replied, You should Love the Lord your God with all your heart, with all your soul, and with all your might... and you shall Love your neighbor as yourself. (Matthew 22:37)

Love your neighbor as yourself He said. Acts of mercy, forgiveness, unconditional positive regard for others, This love is healing. And when we look at the many healings Jesus did of strangers and friends, we have a window into the ultimate source and force of healing...a window into God who so loved the world that He gave His only begotten Son to this world... to heal it, save it and us... who became for us the ultimate healing presence. The Creator who made heaven and earth and all manner of forces whether gravitational, electromagnetic, thermonuclear, or healing forces, is still with us and "for us." Whatever this healing force turns out to be as it continues to be studied, its Source for me is well known. There is still mystery here of course. There are still many unanswered questions about this healing force. But we can use it for the well-being of others and that is another way of loving your neighbor as yourself.

I've told some colleagues that with the four known forces in the universe, I think I will call the force for healing, "the fifth force." It seems like a different kind of force than those others. It certainly is real. It can prolong life, bring back to life, and it can be life-giving. Energy healers seem to manipulate it for good. The body innately uses it to restore and renew. Faith healers often seem to be good conduits for it. Healing words and healing touch can make it happen before our eyes. We pray for it, we yearn for it, we can evaluate the results of it.

Like gravity which I can not see but I know it exists everywhere, and like electricity that is in many places even though I can not see it (but at times I can feel it), so this "fifth force" is something which I cannot see but it too seems to exist everywhere. It seems "natural" and it also can appear "supernatural" as when Jesus brings back someone from the dead in a show of extraordinary use of this healing force.

As a Christian, I believe that God raised Jesus from death. We celebrate that at Easter. We sing "He is Risen!" A Christian creed states, "on the third day He rose from the dead." Who has that power? Who can harness this force to make "alive" again? As a Christian I believe it is God who can do this, and that He is the author and creator of this Fifth Force. It is a gift to us to use and to cherish. Those of us in the "healing professions" learn all that we can in order to bring about the best outcomes from the use of this force.

Recently I had a major issue with the big toe of my left foot. I saw several specialists including two podiatrists, a vascular surgeon and a neurologist. One used a scraping tool, another used ointment and still another asked me to change my diet and to exercise more. The results were positive. The toe healed. This Fifth Force was well activated. The outcome was outstanding. I'm much better than I was. I say to family and friends, "it is healed."

What is this force? It is a mystery and it is a reality. I believe it has been given to us by a Creator because He loves us. It is a form of love for His children. I give Him gratitude and thanksgiving for this gift.

Chapter 52
Lighthouse of Hope

Healing prayer is real. I have seen it the lives of others, and I have experienced it myself. I have witnessed it on the West Coast, East Coast, Canada and in Europe. As the title of the book given to me by Rufus Womble says, "Yes, Virginia, there is a God who heals today!"

But I cannot prove it. I cannot prove that God exists even as I cannot prove that this God heals. It is from a position of faith that I come to this conclusion. It is also not only the religious community that is looking deeper into the power of prayer for healing, but even the National Institutes of Health has given large amounts of grant money for serious research into the study of prayer and its effectiveness. So has the Templeton Foundation among others. The pioneering work of Larson, Koenig, Levin, Matthews, Weaver and others, in the realm of religion and health, faith and prayer, has spurred a greater conversation among many researchers invested in knowing just what really is happening out there.

It has been my privilege as a lay person in this discussion to have met some of the big names in the field of prayer and healing and psychoneuroimmunology. To have experienced first-hand the relief from knee pain through the use of guided imagery was a breakthrough moment for me. To have a number of people lay hands on me over time and pray for my healing which ultimately led to the removal of all pain symptoms related to a disease I had was a remarkable and powerful encounter with God's healing presence.

As I reflect on the past 11 years of the selected experiences I had through the sabbatical and beyond, I have felt "led" to each new person, professional or lay, who has added one more piece to solving the puzzle of prayer and healing and the body-mind matrix.

On an airplane recently I sat next to a young high school girl and we began chatting. I learned she attends a boarding school in Ojai, California, a small quiet city just northwest of my own home. As we spoke, she told me she was on her way to Milan where she and some of her friends were gathering for three weeks near Lake Lugano, north of Milan. I told her I had been there and told her she would love the setting. Then she asked where I was going and I told her I was writing a book and I was going to a place where I could have some peace and quiet in order to concentrate on the writing. She asked me what I was writing about and I told her my book would be on prayer and healing and something called psychoneuroimmunology, a word for mind and body interaction. She nodded, then said, "I believe in healing." "Yes?" I replied. "Oh yes," she said, then continued, "My grandmother believed in healing and today my family gets together almost weekly to meditate on healing." I was rather shocked, so I asked, "Why do you do that?" She replied, "I am a Christian and so is my family. We are not part of any organized religion, but we believe in healing and so we gather together to meditate on God healing us." I asked if she knew of any healing stories in her family and she said yes and told me about some of the healing in her family and of healing of friends of her family. I asked her for permission to include her in my book. She smiled and said that would be very nice and we exchanged e-mail addresses and I told her I would contact her a bit later.

Over time, on planes and in restaurants, in many different places, people are willing to tell you about prayer and/or healing. Whenever I share with someone that I am writing on this topic, the person with whom I am talking almost always knows a healing story from their family, a friend of the family, a colleague or perhaps even themselves. At first it happened so often I was completely surprised. Now, it is rare that someone doesn't have something to share regarding prayer or healing. Some strangers I have met have been to healers or have gone into the study of some form of healing arts.

Many have discovered Reiki or one of the many other healing energy systems. Many who are on spiritual quests are looking into healing and what the human mind and/or body is capable of. Some of them are Christians, some are not religious, and some are self described spiritual seekers. As I indicated in an earlier chapter, there are healers all around the world, from Shamans and faith healers to eastern practitioners of energy healing to the western doctors who do allopathic medicine. The homeopathic doctor I spoke with in the village of Cluny, France, just outside of Taize, gave me a brief history of homeopathic medicine and said it is still a strong pathway to healing in Europe. A nurse I met in Europe told me that school medicine dismisses homeopathic medicine completely. As I learned, there are many branches to healing, and the Source of that healing is not always seen as God. The Wicca lady in England who pointed me to the Healing Tree would be one such example.

So what have I really learned from my brief study of this topic of prayer and healing? I have learned first and foremost that the field is much greater and complex than I had realized. I was surprised to find so many books on each topic taken separately: many books on prayer, many on healing, and a growing number on body-mind medicine. But I found surprisingly few books which crossed over all three areas. Most notably, the book by Harold Koenig (The Link between Religion and Health: Psychoneuroimmunology and the Faith Factor) focusing on psychoneuroimmunology did cross all three areas. I suspect that as time goes on and research deepens, that we will see more writers and researchers cross-pollinating through these three interrelated topics.

Does God heal? Yes, I believe so, strongly. I have seen it in the work of Rev. Bill Dasch. I have heard the testimonies of those from the Power Within movie. I have seen crutches hanging on walls at Chimayo and at the Basilica of the Fourteen Helpers which bear testimony to healing. Even the special medical board that convenes at Lourdes, France to try to discover the legitimacy of healings there, have authenticated at least 67 miraculous healings. The thick file of letters held by the priest in Augsburg, Germany are further testimony to the healing power of prayer.

As I reflect on this I am sad that I did not grow up within a denomination which took seriously the power of prayer for healing. In my seminary education, I regret never hearing one word about healing in today's world. Certainly the writings of Luther on healing which peppered the final years of his life were never shared in the seminary education. Had not the Anglicans and Roman Catholics preserved the deep traditions of prayer, and especially prayer for healing, I doubt I would have ever learned of these rich and profound teachings. The history of Christian healing through the ages from Christ to the present time, put together by Morton Kelsey after almost twenty-five years of careful research, is invaluable. In his book on Health and Healing in the Lutheran Tradition by historian Martin E. Marty, he reports that in the 60's, a blue ribbon panel of Lutherans from various Lutheran church bodies, made up of doctors, theologians, nurses, and other health care professionals, took the matter seriously and unanimously came to the conclusion that healing prayer was real and valid. However, they decided not to endorse it because they feared discouragement for those who may not be healed in spite of receiving healing prayer. At least that is the sense I get from Marty's book. To rephrase it, in my own words, it is as if the panel said, "...well it only works 43% of the time so we better not use it or promote it." On the one hand that makes sense if one considers that the FDA, Food and Drug Administration, will not bring a drug to the public until all of the clinical trials have been completed and the product is deemed safe. Would the FDA bring a drug to market if it only worked 43% of the time? Of course not. In a similar way, that blue ribbon panel may have been wise in withholding endorsement in congregational or even seminary circles. On the other hand, what if the healing prayer had been discussed openly with the research results of that blue ribbon panel endorsing it with reservations so that people would not be discouraged? One never will know what might have happened. (By the way, I am not suggesting healing prayer only works 43% of the time. I am referring to a study mentioned in a workshop I attended in which the speaker said that physical healing treatments and psychological treatments were only effective 43% of the time. He said that prayer seemed to work just as good, that is, it worked 44% of the time).

But perhaps it was not the right time. Now with solid research looking for answers, and a climate in which energy medicine is coming into its own, and with the failure of the HMOs to deliver on their promises of better health care (I have seen a statistic that more than 60% of Americans have turned to alternative medicine for help), that perhaps prayer and healing is a topic not only to be discussed and studied openly, but people are hungering for a closer relationship to God, and more open than ever before to experiencing God, especially through His healing power. With one-fifth of the Gospels being healing stories, certainly people of the Christian faith might ask the question, "Does God still heal today?" I believe that they will hear a resounding "YES!" to that question. Does it happen all the time to everyone? No, of course not. But for believers who believe that God does not let one prayer go unnoticed, His answers to our questions may not always be the ones we are looking for. Very often it lies within the realm of mystery. Simply said, we don't know why some are healed while others are not. We wish we knew why some are cured while others are not.

Physicians such as Dr. Andrew Weil believe that it is natural, spontaneous healing. We have all heard stories where a physician, after doing follow-up tests to an original diagnosis, comes back to the patient only to say, "It is astonishing. I have never seen this happen before. The disease is gone. It has just vanished. I have no medical explanation." We say it is a miracle. We say Praise God! Many ministers who have served a lifetime in prayer for healing remember the first time it happened: they prayed for someone with a catastrophic illness and the person prayed for indeed got well. They prayed for another patient at some time and they too got well. But not every patient for whom they offered healing prayer got well. Some worsened only to die. It was not like putting a key in the door lock, turning the key, and the door simply opened. Sometimes it was more like putting the key into the door lock, only to wonder if you had the right key at all, or if someone had secretly changed the locks on you. The "what" I have learned is simply this: it all still remains mostly a mystery. Medical science can sometimes tell you what they believe causes a disease or disorder and they can tell you what options you have for curing or arresting the disease/disorder. Very often they are right. But sometimes they are wrong. Sometimes they are as puzzled as we are.

I have heard criticism of televangelists, especially for raising false hopes among so many sick and desperate people. But sometimes, even these ministers of the TV tube may provide the occasion for healing. I know that sounds terrible to some readers. But I have always liked reading a passage from the final chapter of the novel called Just Shy of Harmony written by Philip Gulley. In it there is a minister whose name is Sam, who has a member of his congregation, named Sally, who is dying of leukemia. Sam has prayer with her, but she does not appear better. Meanwhile a televangelist comes to town. During his telecast he proclaims that he is sending healing power over the airwaves. He goes on to say that what is coming to him is that there is a woman out there named Sally who has leukemia. He declares her healed during the broadcast. One of Sam's parishioners, a woman named Bea, has been listening to the televangelist's broadcast and knows that it is her friend, Sally, that has now been healed! Later she is excited and tells Sam, the minister, who is quite skeptical. The next day after the television evangelist's declaration of the healing of Sally, doctors discover that her leukemia is gone! Members of the parish are so excited. But after an elders meeting, one of the women, named Mirium, asks the pastor whether he really believes Sally has been healed. He remains very skeptical that a healing could come from such a televangelist.

Sam says, "I'm reserving judgment. So far we have only the word of a television huckster that she's healed."

"You seem annoyed that she could be healed. What would be wrong with God using Johnny LaCosta to heal Sally?"

Sam sputtered. "First, God didn't use Johnny LaCosta to heal Sally. God doesn't use people like that."

"How do you know?"

"I just know, that's how."

"I think God can use anyone."

"You're entitled to your opinion."

"Sam Gardner, you are a mystery to me."

"How so?"

"Not six months ago you sat at this very table and told the elders how discouraged you were that God never seemed to do anything. Now it appears He might have done something and you're mad about it."

"That's not so."

"Forgive my impertinence, but I think it is. And what upsets you more than anything is that God might have used someone you don't care for."

Sam didn't say anything.

"I won't belabor the point," Miriam said. "But if God chose to heal Sally through this television preacher, shouldn't we be grateful? Would you have liked it better if God hadn't healed her?"

"Of course not."

"Then let's give thanks, Sam. It appears we might have a healing on our hands."

She smiled.

Sam smiled back. "I still think he's a Bozo."

"So do I. But apparently God uses Bozos too."

They laughed.

(the scene continues)

"Besides, Sam, Johnny LaCosta wasn't the only one praying for Sally. We had this church praying twenty-four hours a day. The Catholics were praying, and the Baptists. Fern and Bea and the Friendly Women and even Dale were praying for her all along. And let's not forget that a lot of doctors were working to make Sally better."

"That's right. It probably wasn't Johnny LaCosta after all."

"We'll never know, Sam, will we?"

"I guess not."

"Which means we shouldn't despise the prayers of any one person, should we?"

Sam didn't say anything.

Miriam gathered up her papers, and rose from her chair. "You take care, Sam."

"You do the same, Miriam." He paused. "Thank you."

"You're welcome, Sam."

(pages 240-241, Just Shy of Harmony)

I suppose I have come to the conclusion that healing is universal, given to us by a loving God who created the possibility of healing because He still loves mankind that He first created. The story of Adam and Eve is still, for me, a valid metaphor for humanity. What was once "ordered" in the words of Garth Ludwig, became "disordered," and in that disorder came pain and suffering and death. But God wished to restore the Order and sent His Son, Jesus Christ, to restore the broken, shore up the feint-hearted, and to bring about release to those who feel captive in their diseased bodies and/or broken spirits. This restorative power is not only in healing prayer. It comes in His Word and His sacraments and from the love of family and friends who love us unconditionally.

I have always loved the Gospel of John, Chapter 10, Verse 10 where we can read that Christ came that we may have life abundant in His Name. As a Christian I believe this. I believe that prayer for healing does positively impact our bodies and minds, even when we don't receive the cure which we so desperately want. As Father MacNutt told me, he does not know how many for whom he prays actually are "cured" of their disease, but he firmly believes that every time he prays for someone, something good comes of it, but not always in the way we might think of it.

Are there healers doing healings not in Christ's name? Of course. Do they actually heal? Sometimes they do indeed. Some Christian theologians and laity believe that all of that healing is from Satan; that the Devil mimics the goodness of God for his own devious ways.

I do not believe this. I believe that all healing comes from God. There may be other "conduits" of that healing power which do not give God the credit, or which may be conduits with which we are grossly uncomfortable. But God's love for all mankind is real. Perhaps we will, in time, learn that healing energy is much like gravity or electricity, and that Jesus Christ used that power to demonstrate God's love for humankind, and to point the way to His heavenly Father. Perhaps we will learn that this healing phenomena can be influenced for good or for harm, since it is more like an energy force than we now understand. Perhaps this is why Voodoo and Hoodoo work. Voodoo has the capacity to hex someone, even to death. Hoodoo is the positive side, where a shaman can do positive things through the manipulation of this power and energy.

Just as Jesus encountered those in the first century doing healings in his name, who seemingly could influence and control the power they had before them, it is clear that Jesus, in my opinion, said that yes, they could do these things, but that the true source of this power was God himself. We always see Jesus using the power of healing for good. Sometimes He heals just through His compassion for those who are ill. At other times He attaches a lesson to the healing or speaks of repentance and seeking God.

One thing is for certain: when one approaches prayer for healing and tries to understand the complexities of the mind and body connection, one can easily discover that science and religion meet here at a crossroads. There are those who like Robert Ader said, "There are no angels here." For him it is a matter of pure science. One does not need a god to understand how the body works or to consider placebo effect. Then there are those who shun the science and only take the religious pathway. Some religious persons refuse blood transfusions, for example, trusting only in God for healing. But the "prayer and Prozac" approach like that held by Christian physician, Dale Matthews, is the one I am most comfortable with. Here we see the best of faith and the best of science coming together for better health outcomes. The research of Koenig, et al, indicates better health outcomes for churchgoing people for a large variety of reasons. Religion and health do seem to correlate positively as so many research studies indicate. Prayer for healing is one aspect of this process, where prayer (one's "religion") seeks healing (one's "health" outcome), and not every healing appears to come from a placebo effect (example: the healings done by Dr. Issam Nemeh in Cleveland).

What would I recommend? That you keep praying and pray for healing. Not only will it bring you a deeper relationship with God, but it will have health benefits for years to come. Jesus said, "Come to me all ye who are burdened and heavy laden and I will give you rest." This is healing. This leads to greater health. As the old hymn puts it, "Take everything to God in prayer" (What A Friend We Have In Jesus).

May God heal you of all your infirmities and may you find peace in His Name. He is, after all, our greatest Lighthouse of Hope.

References:

Lighthouse Psalms: God's Gift of Hope and Direction by Terry Whalin, is my favorite book of hope featuring lighthouses and God's word

Chapter 53
2017 Post Script

"P.S. I love you."

That's the title of a famous Beatle's song which include the words, "treasure these few words til we're together...."

Those words popped into my mind as I sat down to write this post script to this new addition of Lighthouse of Hope. Many readers of the kindle version of my book asked for a paperback version, so here it is…finally.

I hope this book is a blessing to you. I hope you treasure these few words of post script as you finish reading and as you your thoughts deepen on prayer and healing.

Its hard to believe that my journey into prayer, healing and mind-body medicine began more than 20 years ago after meeting Adam Hall (Elliston Trevor) and Betty Larvae. I have been privileged to meet many healers and to be edified by their many words and concepts in their books on prayer and healing.

It's hard to believe its nearly 40 years ago since the revolutionary ideas for healing cancer using visualization techniques were first put forth by O. Carl Simonton (Getting Well Again). Around that same time Dr. Robert Ader was presenting his paper to an international gathering of physicians studying psychosomatic medicine where he introduced his brilliant phrase "psychoneuroimmunology," capturing an entire generation of doctors, researchers and healers to a holistic orientation towards health and well-being. Since those watershed years of the early to mid-1980s, when maverick thinkers and writers were pushing the boundaries of allopathic medicine, and as the fusion of Eastern and Western models of healing began to make in-roads into main-stream medicine, we have witnessed a major shift in America's openness to alternative healing. Licensed practitioners and guru's alike contend with each other in a smorgasbord of treatment techniques from which the public can choose. The quest for new treatment outcomes promotes a range of diverse viewpoints as to what constitutes legitimate medicine.

When I went to see a physician for a rare medical condition causing me excruciating physical pain (the condition I had is found on the list of exotic diseases at the Center for Disease Control), the physician offered me a list of 16 treatment options. Among the options offered were anti-depressant capsules with pain numbing properties. Also on the list were hypnotherapy, stress-management techniques, possible surgery and a dozen other treatments. He said all of them had risks involved and non of them were guaranteed to work. I paused as I looked down the list that he had handed to me, at all of the options. Then I looked up at him and said, "I see one medicine not on the list." He replied, what medicine are you thinking of?" I said, "Prayer. I don't see prayer on your list." He smiled and reached over and took the list from my hand. Then he wrote a number 17 on the sheet and wrote "prayer" next to it. He handed the list back to me and said, "You are right. Prayer is good medicine. I believe in the power of prayer. I've had patients with incurable diseases who used prayer to take away their disease. I support you in prayer. I need to add it to my list." I selected the anti-depressant pills for the moment, but they were not very effective and only dealt with the symptoms of my disease, and not the disease itself. In the end it was the power of healing prayer that took away the exotic disease and its symptoms.

I have become a believer in prayer for healing. I still visit my doctors and follow their advice but I have, like many people, considered other treatment options beyond allopathic medicine.

With the passage of time, we are losing many of the early pioneers I call "lighthouses of hope," many of them whose books I read and some I had the opportunity to meet. So before I close out this book, there are a few updates that I want to share with you as a sort of P.S. It feels right to send this off to you as a 2017 P.S.

Since I began my sabbatical, I have become much more aware of how many people are involved in healing today. The religious community, in particular, has caught fire with healing prayer ministries. Around the globe there are many reports of healings. The faith community of Catholics, Anglicans, Lutheran and non-denominational churches, especially Pentecostals, have witnessed a resurgence in the healings in the name of Jesus. The power of the Holy Spirit is seen as God's gift to the church for healing.

In Protestant circles the tremendous rise of the Pentecostal movement in Africa and Asia, is seen as the outpouring of the Holy Spirit who is the agent of healing. There are an estimated 400,000,000 Pentecostals in the world. Prayers for healing and the laying on of hands promotes the belief in God's grace and mercy. The heart of God is His love for people whom He desires to heal.

Even in the United States the charismatic/Pentecostal movement is growing. As people migrate from the Southern regions of the world, the so-called global south, they bring with them their beliefs in spiritual and physical healing given by God. People from Mexico, Central America, South America and Africa (for example, Ethiopians) have a rich tradition rooted in healing and miracles.

In Catholic circles, with the renewed emphasis on healing from Pope Francis and other Catholic leaders, the Church is once again placing healing ministries in the forefront of its care for people. Likewise, among Episcopalians in the U.S. and the world-wide Anglican community there are renewed signs of healing in the name of Christ. Lutherans are also catching fire with more trainings in healing prayer ministries.

So I want to briefly share with you some additional resources which I have come across in recent years.

In the religious faith community:

Lutherans

1. Bill Dasch Ministries: Rev. Bill Dasch, whom you met previously in this book, has retired from parish ministry and has gone full-time into healing ministry. He is doing prayer for healing workshops throughout the Southwest and does them upon request. He has an active prayer Team who works with him and they offer prayer for anyone who requests it from the internet or in person. His website teaches about healing prayer and offers and advice to those interested in prayer for healing. Go to his website to see what God is doing in the lives of people. www.billdasch.com

2. Paul Teske. Paul is a Lutheran minister who suffered a stroke in 2004 which disabled him profoundly during a lecture on Lutheran ethics. Unable to continue his presentation, he was rushed to the hospital where doctors were unable to reverse the effects from the stroke. For three weeks people from his congregation and many from the international community held him in prayer. His wife, Rivers, brought him to a Benny Hinn healing conference. Miraculously, his stroke was 100% healed at the conference, and Hinn anointed him to continue a healing ministry. Paul wrote a book about his recovery entitled Healing Today. His story is also included in the New York Times best seller, Miracles: What They Are, Why They Happen, and How They Can Change Your Life by author Eric Metaxas. Rev. Teske has a website and blog at http://paulteske.com

3. Rev. Ron Rehrer continues to lead workshops in Prayer for Healing, partnering with local clergy and their congregations throughout Southern California Arizona and southern Nevada.

4. If you type in "Lutherans in Healing Ministries" in your web browser, you will find many websites of churches and organizations dedicated to healing ministries. Two examples are

below:

4a. Lord of Life Lutheran Church, Maple Grove, Minnesota. Their website describes what healing prayer is for.
Healing prayer is for all people for any reason: addiction, general chronic and terminal illnesses, heart break, prayer before surgery, anxiety, mental illness, stress - healing prayer is for whatever may be affecting you, Healing from the Lord comes in many forms. It can be physical, emotional, spiritual, or psychological . Healing can also compass a feeling of love, peace, and comfort. www.lordoflife.org/healingministry

4b. St Stephens Lutheran Church Wilmington DE Pastor Dianne G. Loufman
office@ststeph.org
Their website states:
Hubert Humphrey, while hospitalized for the bladder cancer that ultimately claimed his life, reported in 1978 that for him it was "a spiritual experience" to receive word that congregations in churches and synagogues all over the world were praying for him: "I want to tell you, my friend, I could feel it, actually feel it. It came to me with a great surge of healing. I could feel it in my body, the warmth, the friendship, the prayers. It was really like a healing balm. I know it sounds almost irrational. I can't explain it, but I know something was happening to me and I was getting strength from it."
- June Bingham and Norman Tamarkin, M.D., The Pursuit of Health

Catholics

1. Healing: Bringing the Gift of God's Mercy to the World by Mary Healy,
published in 2015 by Our Sunday Visitor, Inc.
Mary Healy is a writer and associate professor of Scripture at Sacred Heart Major Seminary in Detroit and a member of the Pontifical Biblical Commission. This outstanding book introduces the reader to Jesus' words and works of healing and traces the history of Christian healing through its first several

hundred years of the Catholic Church right up to the writings of recent Popes, including the words of Pope Francis on healing. Ms. Healy's research is excellent and her Biblical knowledge is first-rate. Her nuanced text is a delight to read, and the power of God's Holy Spirit for healing is at the forefront of her understanding of healing. It is easy to read and gives the reader a very compact presentation of the essentials that will comfort Catholics and others as they turn to God for healing.

2. Deliverance from Evil Spirits: A Practical Manual by Francis MacNutt, kindle
edition, published in 2009.
Written in 1995, this new Kindle Version came out in 2009. Since that time there has been renewed interest in the phenomenon of possession, exorcism, evil spirits, and the like, Fueled in part by Hollywood movies but also from accounts of personal attacks from unknown sources in people's lives. Francis MacNutt's well-researched book is the most comprehensive in Christian literature. Its counterpart in Evangelical circles is "Unbound: A Practical Guide to Deliverance" by Neal Lozano (see below). MacNutt's presentation is called a "practical guide" and it is exactly that…practical. His appendix with sample prayers is very helpful. This is a book all priests, pastors, and ministers should have in there libraries.

3. If you put the phrase "Catholic healing ministries" into your web browser, you will find multiple websites describing healing and deliverance ministries. Here are some examples:

3a. Healing and Deliverance Ministries through the Archdiocese of St. Louis.
The website quotes the Gospel of St. Luke as the directive for its ministry:
"He summoned the Twelve and gave them power and authority over all demons and to cure diseases, and he sent them to proclaim the kingdom of God, and to heal the sick." (Lk. 9:1-2)
website: http://archstl.org/renewal/page/healing-deliverance-ministry

3b. Father Richard McAlear.
Internationally known as the healing priest, this website features many articles about his ministry of hope and healing; Thousands come to see him for prayer and healing. This is just one website that speaks about this ministry.
website: http://www.frmac.org/in-the-news.html

Evangelicals

1. Unbound: A Practical Guide to Deliverance by Heal Lozano, published by Chosen Books, Baker Publishing Group, 2003 and 2010.
This is an excellent follow-up to the Francis MacNutt book listed above. Lozano takes a very down to earth approach to the topic of allowing oneself to be overcome and captured by sin, its behaviors and addiction processes. Biblical throughout, he draws his reader into seeing themselves in the examples he gives and presents five keys to getting free of these evil entrapments. He sides with the Gospel in describing how to break free of anything which the devil and the dark powers and principalities for real, but instead of scaring the reader, he provides pathways for breaking free and becoming unbound. I highly recommend this book. It is a well researched, balanced. and thoughtful presentation on deliverance with practical recommendations to enable deliverance ministries.

~~~

So this is my brief update written on December 10, 2016. I pray that this new year will be one where you continue to be healed. If you need help in your life, I hope that you will reach out to one of the resources I have listed throughout the book.

I hope you will call upon God for healing when you need it. He wants to heal you and love you. Even if you are not a believer, he will not reject you. He says, in Psalm 50:15…
"Call upon me in the day of trouble, and I will rescue you" (some translations say "and I will deliver you,");

And God will say, "P.S....I love you"

(to give feedback or to contact Ron, go to ron@ronrehrer.com)

Appendices

Appendix A
List of Biblical Healings

The Gospel of Matthew:
4:23 Jesus heals the multitudes
8:2 Jesus heals a leper
8:5 Jesus heals the servant of a centurion
8:14 Jesus heals Peter's mother in-law
8:16 Jesus heals the multitudes
8:28 Jesus heals a demoniac from Gerasene
9:2 Jesus heals a man with palsy
9:18 Jesus heals the daughter of Jairus
9:20 Jesus heals a woman with a blood issue
9:27 Jesus heals two men who are blind
9:32 Jesus heals a demoniac who is dumb
9:35 Jesus heals the multitudes
11:4 Jesus heals the multitudes
12:9 Jesus heals a man with a withered hand
12:15 Jesus heals the multitudes
12:22 Jesus heals a demoniac who is blind and dumb
13:58 Jesus heals more people
14:14 Jesus heals the multitudes
14:34 Jesus heals the multitudes
15:22 Jesus heals the daughter of a Syrophoenician
15:30 Jesus heals great multitudes
19:2 Jesus heals multitudes
21:14 Jesus heals the blind and lame man in the Temple
The Gospel of Mark
1:23 Jesus heals a man with an unclean spirit
1:30 Jesus heals Peter's mother-in-law
1:32 Jesus heals multitudes
1:29 Jesus heals many demons
1:40 Jesus heals a leper
2:3 Jesus heals a man sick with palsy

3:1 Jesus heals a man with a withered hand
3:10 Jesus heals multitudes
5:1 Jesus heals a demoniac from Gerasene
5:22 Jesus heals the daughter of Jairus
5:25 Jesus heals a woman with a blood issue
6:5 Jesus heals a few more who are sick
6:55 Jesus heals multitudes
7:24 Jesus heals the daughter of a Syrophoenician
7:32 Jesus heals a deaf and dumb man
8:22 Jesus heals a bind man (gradual healing)
9:14 Jesus heals a child with an evil spirit
10:46 Jesus heals Bartimaeus who is blind

The Gospel of Luke

4:33 Jesus heals a man with an unclean spirit
4:38 Jesus heals Peter's mother-in-law
4:30 Jesus heals multitudes
4:46 Jesus heals the son of a nobleman
5:12 Jesus heals a leper
5:15 Jesus heals multitudes
5:17 Jesus heals a man sick with palsy
6:6 Jesus heals a man with a withered hand
6:17 Jesus heals the multitudes
7:2 Jesus heals the servant of a Centurion
7:11 Jesus heals a widow's son
7:21 Jesus heals the multitudes
8:2 Jesus heals Mary Magdelene and others
8:26 Jesus heals the demoniac from Gerasene
8:41 Jesus heals the daughter of Jairus
8:43 Jesus heals a woman with a blood issue
9:11 Jesus heals multitudes
9:38 Jesus heals a child with an evil spirit
11:14 Jesus heals a demoniac who is blind and dumb
13:10 Jesus heals a woman bound by Satan
13:32 Jesus heals various people
14:1 Jesus heals a man with dropsy
17:11 Jesus heals ten lepers
18:35 Jesus heals Bartimaeus who is blind
22:49 Jesus heals the ear of Malchus

The Gospel of John

5:2 Jesus heals an invalid man
9:1 Jesus heals a man born blind
111 Jesus raises Lazarus from the dead
Book of Acts
2:43 Many signs and wonders done by the apostles
3:1-11 Lame man healed by Peter and John
4:14 The religious leaders saw the one who was healed
4:30 The believers asked the Lord to heal.
5:12 Many signs and wonders by the apostles
5:15 Sick healed with shadow of Peter passing over them
5:16 Many sick brought to Jerusalem to be healed.
6:8 Stephen did great wonders and miracles
8:5-8 Philip did many miracles
8:13 Simon was amazed at the miracles and signs
9:17-18 Saul is healed by the laying on of hands by Ananias
9:33-35 Peter is healed by Aeneas
9:40-41 Peter restores Dorcas to life
14:3 Paul and Barnabas did many signs and wonders
14:8-10 Paul heals the crippled man at Lystra
16:16 Paul uses commands to rid a damsel of an evil spirit
19:10-12:20 Paul does many miracles
20:7-12 Paul is restored to life by Eutychus
28:1-6 Paul is unaffected by a viper's bite
28:8 Paul heals Publius' father
28:9 Paul heals many others on the island
Other New Testament References
1 Corinthians 12:9, 27-30 the gifts of healing are named
2 Corinthians 12:12 through signs and wonders the apostles are vindicated
Galatians 3:5 this is a reference to miracles by the one ministering
Ephesians 1:19; 3:7 the mighty power is working
1 Thessalonians 1:5 the gospel comes in power and not just in words
2 Thessalonians 1:11 the work of faith with power
Hebrews 6:2 the laying on of hands is a foundation of the church
James 5:14 anointing the sick
1 Peter 2: 24 by His stripes you are healed
3 John 1:2 a reference to being in health

Revelation 21:4 there is a wonderful final healing
Revelation 22:2 there is ultimately a healing of the nations

Appendix B
How To Set Up A Healing Ministry

Upon my return from my study sabbatical, I began receiving requests for information on how to set up healing ministries within congregations, specifically how to introduce prayer for healing into worship services. At the time of these requests I was not sure how to go about doing it. During my sabbatical I witnessed a number of healing services (more about those below), and brought back with me various models used in worship services. These ranged from special midweek or Saturday night worship services specifically focused on healing, to ways of using healing prayer in both communion and non-communion worship services on Sunday mornings.

I now believe there are several steps to be taken to successfully begin a healing ministry in the local congregation. I will share those steps and also describe various models of healing prayer in worship services. I will also suggest some study materials for healing prayer committees or prayer teams to deepen their awareness and understanding of the church's role in healing.

Steps To Take In Beginning A Healing Ministry

The first step is prayer. Those interested in beginning a healing ministry in their local church or congregation should begin praying about it. Is this what the Lord wants you to do at "St. Whatever by the Sea" congregation? Is this the right time to begin such a ministry? Is the Holy Spirit leading in this direction? Pray for wisdom and insight and listen for the Lord's response. Healing ministry is the work of God. Pray for direction and guidance as you consider beginning such a ministry.

The second step is to gather together a team or committee to study God's Word on healing. What does Scripture say about healing? How did Jesus heal and what motivated Him? What types of healings are described in the Holy Bible? What was the disciples' role in healing in the book of Acts? What does the book of James say about healing? Learn some historical perspective on how the early church in the first few centuries after Christ understood and practiced healing.

The third step is to enlist the blessing and support of the minister or pastor (or senior pastor) in healing ministry. Unless your minister/pastor is "on board" in this important ministry, it will likely fail. If he will become an active participant in the learning community about prayer and healing, then there is a very good chance that a healing ministry will begin well.

The fourth step is for the healing team or committee to obtain study materials from other congregations or ministries which have successfully launched a healing ministry. I have listed some resources below which you might consider using.

The fifth step is for the preparation of the congregation. Sunday School Bible studies should be aimed at educating a greater number of members into the Biblical accounts of healing. A series of sermons on aspects of healing and healing prayer should be given by the pastor. Some time for questions and feedback (even for the expression of resistance) should be scheduled so that questions and comments can be addressed. For example, when Pastor Bill Dasch and I did healing ministry workshops within our own denomination, we anticipated that some would be afraid if this were a charismatic approach to healing ministry (speaking in tongues, or other manifestations often attributed to healing ministry). We made it clear that we were not charismatics (not that there is anything wrong with being charismatic) but that we were presenting a middle of the road approach to prayer for healing ministries, grounded in Lutheran theology, and rooted in the historical witness of the church since the time of Jesus. We gave examples of Luther's writings on healings, and told the stories of Luther's own personal healing, and the prayers he said for the healing of others.

The sixth step is deciding what approach you will make to healing within your congregation. For example, many healing ministries consist solely of prayer. Others add the anointing with oil (see the Book of James) and the laying on of hands. Prayer teams are given training as to how to do healing prayer and they practice it until they are comfortable with it.

The seventh step is deciding whether or not you will use healing prayer in your worship services. If you decide to do this, what steps are to be taken to instruct the people in the pews about what will be taking place and how. For example, Canon Linda Nicholls worked with her leadership in Thornhill, Canada in how best to do healing prayer in Sunday worship. I was privileged to have her share that with me during my study sabbatical. I observed still another way of doing this while attending Burrswood in England. It is best to discuss this among church leadership so that everyone knows how it will be done and who will be responsible for it being done well.

The eighth step is doing it. Putting healing prayer into practice in worship and at other times is essential. At Pastor Bill Dasch's congregation in Mansfield, Texas, they know to "stop, drop and pray." What this means is that whenever someone needs healing prayer, the people stop what they are doing, drop whatever they have, and pray with that person needing prayer. St. John's Lutheran Church in Mansfield, Texas, has as their core value: prayer. It is the most important function in the congregation, and prayer teams have been developed and the elders have been trained as well as church staff, to stop, drop and pray whenever the request is made from a stranger or a parishioner.

Educational and Training Materials

One of the best materials comes from the "Reclaim! the Healing Ministry of Jesus" conference held in Texas in 2009. There is a study guide and leadership guide available which is ideal for training purposes. There is also a media guide with DVDs of all the presentations made, plenary and break-out groups. These can be ordered from St. John's Lutheran Church in Mansfield, Texas. This is a Lutheran approach to healing ministry, but can be easily adapted for any denominational group. It covers the history of Christian healing, practical suggestions and examples of healing prayer, and is thoroughly Biblical.

Another fine resource is the excellent book entitled Christian Healing: A Practical and Comprehensive Guide by Mark Pearson. This is an easy book to read. It presents the role of prayer in healing, the importance of healing ministry, and various approaches to healing practiced in orthodox Christianity. Another outstanding book, which some consider the best work on healing through prayer ever written, is Francis MacNutt's book entitled Healing. While he has written many books on healing, and has several training courses available through his organization called Christian Healing Ministries, his Healing book is really the best place to begin.

How To Pray For Healing

There are many approaches to this within Christianity. I want to share one way to pray for healing as taught during the Reclaim conference.

Your prayer should be simple and comes in three parts: Adoration, Request, Thanksgiving. Here is how you do it.

Ask the person, "What would you like Jesus to do for you today?" The person will tell you what they would like to have happen (they may ask for healing for a physical problem, or for a personal matter, or help in a difficult relationship issue). After they have shared this with you, repeat it to them in their own words so that you get confirmation that you have heard them correctly, and so that they know you will be praying specifically for their request. Use their language.

Next, ask them if it is okay to anoint them with oil. Usually they will say yes to this. Using an unscented oil (many prayer oils are online or at your local Bible bookstore), put some oil on your thumb or forefinger and place a small bit of oil on their forehead, making the sign of the cross with the oil. You may say, "In the name of the Father, Son and Holy Spirit" or simply say, "I anoint you with oil in the name of Jesus".

You may then wish to ask them if its okay to touch them or if it's alright to hold your hand over the place where there is need for physical healing (or place your hand on their head, or over their head, if you are praying for some non-physical healing as in healing or restoration of a relationship or praying for a family member with cancer or recovering from an accident).

Then begin your prayer with praise and adoration for God and all of the wonderful gifts He brings to us... For example, you might wish to begin, "Father, we approach your throne of grace today, giving you adoration and praise for all of the good gifts and blessings you have bestowed upon us... We have seen your creation and know that you love us, and we bow before you praising your Name and we adore You and all that you have done for us."

Then focus on the request brought to you. "Father, today, (name) is asking for... (name the request)..." Then tell the Lord what the petitioner needs, wants, wishes for, has requested. Use their words. For example, "Father, today Jeremy is asking that You help him in his relationship with Irene..." or "Father, Shirley is going to have surgery on Monday morning, and she is asking You to be with her doctors and nurses who will attend to her and she is also asking that You help her remain calm during the preparation for that surgery." (Again, you are using their language and praying only for what that person has asked for in prayer. Do not add or embellish what has been requested.)

Then after praying the petition (request), close the prayer with Thanksgiving. For example, "We thank you, Lord, for hearing Jeremy's request today. We thank you for the love and mercy you shower upon us. We give you thanks for life and love shown in your Son Jesus Christ." In other words, thank God in anyway you wish.

When you have finished praying the prayer, then you might say to the petitioner "God be with you," as he or she leaves.

Various Ways of Doing Healing Prayer

Below are some of the ways I saw healing prayer done in congregations during my study sabbatical. This may be helpful to you if you are thinking about how to set up and do healing prayer during or after worship.

The first prayer for healing I witnessed was during my study sabbatical in the Power Within video which I first viewed at the Anglican House of the Anglican Church headquarters in downtown Toronto, Ontario, Canada. In the video, one can see Canon Linda Nicholls resting her hands on a kneeling parishioner who has come to the altar rail for the Eucharist (Holy Communion) and healing prayer. When I spoke to Canon Nicholls about how they integrate it into their worship service, she explained that those who wish to receive the Sacrament (bread and wine), those persons come down the center aisle in their usual custom. But if in addition, a parishioner wishes to receive prayer for healing, or prayer for any reason, they first stand off to the side and then kneel to receive the laying on of hands and prayer. Following the healing prayer, they rise and join the group of people going up for the Eucharist. Linda says that she taught Bible classes on prayer in general, and then specifically on healing prayer as well as preached on this for about six months before they actually introduced it into the worship service. The first time it was done during the regular worship service, only a few people walked to the side for prayer. Slowly that number grew so that by the time I was interviewing her, Canon Nicholls said that perhaps half of the parishioners came for prayer prior to taking Holy Communion. She reported that this shifted their communion service to a more concentrated focus on prayer, and clearly linked healing with the Eucharist which was an ancient understanding of participation in the Sacrament, where God's power was present to heal and empower.

A second time I observed healing prayer was in a special service of prayer and healing set aside by Rev. Bruce Kelly, Pastor of St. Luke Lutheran Church on Harford Road in Baltimore, Maryland. This parish had set aside a special prayer and healing service for years, and was attended regularly by members of the parish as well as by people from the community. The night I attended, the order of service included hymn singing, confession, absolution, scripture reading, and the opportunity for people to come forward for prayer. They were invited to kneel before the pastor or one of the prayer team and state specifically what they wished to ask in prayer. Nearly everyone that night came forward for prayer. One older woman was introduced to me by the pastor following the prayer and healing service. I found her joyful and open, and the pastor said she had been coming to these services for years, and probably had never missed one. After we had chatted for a bit, I said, "Do you mind if I ask you a personal question?" She smiled and said, "No, not at all, go ahead!" So I asked her a sensitive question, "I notice you are in a wheelchair and your pastor said you cannot walk, and haven't been able to for years. Do you come each time, asking God to make your legs well, asking Him if He will miraculously heal you?" She smiled, looking up at me, and said, "Oh no, I don't pray for that. I know I am not going to walk again. I pray for healing of my spirit. I pray that God will forgive me of my shortcomings, and I pray that I will be able to forgive those who hurt me. I pray for my emotions." I was surprised by her honest and wonderful answer. I replied, "So you pray for what some would call 'inner healing.'" "Oh yes," she said, "That's more important than physical healing."

A third time I witnessed and participated in healing prayer was in Florida where Father Francis MacNutt and his wife Judith led the attendees of the Healing Trauma workshops in worship. At the end of the service, all were invited forward to have Francis or Judith lay hands on the heads or shoulders of those wishing healing prayer. In this case, no one knelt as in the previous two examples. Each of us stood in line, waiting our turn. When it was my turn I stood in front of Francis, he asked me what I wanted to pray for, and I told him. Then he placed his hands on my head and prayed exactly for what I had asked. Sometimes when a person lays their hands on you, you may feel heat from their hands. I did when Francis prayed for me. It was a gentle heat that seemed to radiate through my being.

I had the opportunity a few years later to attend a mid-week, daytime service led by Canon Linda Nicholls at her church in Thornhill, a suburb of Toronto. Nearly 60 or so elderly people came for the service. Linda preached one of the best sermons I have ever heard. Following her message, many of those in attendance came forward and either stood or knelt in the little chapel space off from the main sanctuary. There Canon Nicholls asked what the parishioner wished to pray for, then having heard the petition, laid her hands on the head or shoulders of the parishioner and prayed exactly for what was asked.

I have now given you four examples of what prayer for healing looks like. Let me give you a fifth example, where the healing prayer is offered immediately after the worship service. I observed this healing prayer ministry when Pastor Bill Dasch (mentioned earlier in this book) was pastor of a large Lutheran church in Houston, Texas. Following the worship service, Bill and others of his prayer teams, located themselves down in front, on either side of the front aisles. People were invited down to receive healing prayer. Prayer teams of three would surround the parishioner who came for healing prayer. One prayer team member would ask, "What would you like Jesus to do for you?" After the parishioner said what this was, then the prayer team leader would ask permission to place hands on the person. If the person gave consent, then the prayer team leader and sometimes other members of the prayer team would place a hand on a shoulder, or on the head or perhaps touch an arm, while the prayers were offered. Sometimes only the team leader would offer the prayer out loud. Sometimes each team leader would offer the prayer aloud. When only the team leader offered a verbal prayer aloud, all members of the team prayed silently. In this setting, the parishioner who came for prayer stood during the prayers.

When I attended Burrswood in England, I was given two different orders of healing services used in their midweek healing services. This healing service is led by the Chaplain and other members of the Burrswood staff. The service is open not only to in-patients and out-patients at Burrswood, but it is also open to anyone from the surrounding countryside. People come from various villages and small towns nearby as well as from London, about 45 minutes away. The Dorothy Kerin chapel is always full. The night I attended, sitting next to Michael, the executive director of Burrswood, everyone in the chapel went up for healing prayer. I would guess that the chapel seated perhaps 150 persons. Michael led the way for me. We stood in line moving from the left to the right. The chaplain, Steve, laid his hands on my head asking me what I would like to pray for. I told him, and he prayed for my concerns. It is a very pleasant and humbling experience to have someone lay hands upon you and pray exactly for what you have requested. When everyone had received prayer, the services concluded. It was a deeply reverent and moving experience.

I have attended a number of healing services in addition to those listed above. There are similarities in each, and the service can be created in any number of ways as per the tradition of the particular worship community. As one can easily see, the time for prayer for healing can be done during the service, after the service or as an adjunct to the service or as a special service at some other time, mid-week, Sunday night, day time or night time. As I have described above, the laying on of hands and the prayer itself is designed to use the petitioners own words of request. The prayer itself for the petitioners request can be a brief time or a longer period if time allows. There is also a special healing prayer called "soaking prayer" that can last an hour or more which is usually a specially designed prayer time outside of the worship setting, and is usually done as offered or upon request.

I like Canon Nicholls' approach to introducing healing prayer to a congregation through a variety of methods and after agreement by the church leadership. During the Sunday adult Bible study time, in thoughtful and reflective sermons, through Scripture readings on Jesus' ministry of healing, through connection with Baptism and Holy Communion in their most profound theological meaning with the ultimate healing of new life and resurrection and communion with the Living Lord, a gradual milieu of learning can be created so that people not only receive an introduction to the long history of healing in the Church, but also have an opportunity to learn about emotional and relational healing, not just the possibility of physical healing. There are many books, workbooks, CDs, and DVDs available to assist in the education of church leaders and members. In many communities, there are priests and ministers, and their prayer teams, available to speak with you about how they do it and why. Church denominations which have done the most in the prayer for healing tradition are the Anglican (Episcopal) and Roman Catholic communities. However, as pointed out above, Lutheran churches also offer healing prayer services. You can also find them in the Presbyterian church and other denominations. Another possibility is to search around to discover if any church offers the worship style from Taize.

Near where I live, a monthly Taize service is held in a large Methodist church on Sunday nights. While Taize is not strictly a prayer for healing service, its concept of prayer AS music is a soothing and deeply moving reverential experience. The songs are simple and healing. Between the music is silence and people are in meditation and prayer. The service usually lasts about an hour. At the service near where I live, a guitarist leads the singing accompanied by another singer. This simple approach is perfect for the music. During the service people are free to come forward to sit or stand in front of a simple cross which has been placed on the floor in front of the altar. In this case the cross is made of wood, just a bit taller than a six foot man, and is draped in white cloth. During one of the softer pieces sung by those in attendance, a young woman went and knelt beneath the cross. As she later rose, you could see tears streaming down her face. She took her place in the pew again and continued on in the singing. At Taize, France, these simple songs are sung together in the native language of each in attendance. It is a profound experience to hear the same song being sung in many different tongues at the same time.

Within the denominational region that I work, I've identified about a dozen Lutheran churches which do healing prayer. Some do it as a special Wednesday or Saturday night service. Others do it on the 5th Sunday of the month. Others do it once a year. Some do it weekly.

Some incorporate healing prayer during or after each regular worship service. Others write special healing services for special occasions. As you can readily see, there are many approaches to doing it.

The healing ministry can also go beyond healing prayer during or after worship services. Healing teams can be created, and may assist the pastor in visiting sick and shut-in persons. They may be included in hospital visitations or substitute for when the pastor cannot go. Sometimes this is connected to a congregation's telephone prayer chain. A prayer chain is made up of members of the church who when they hear of someone ill or in difficulty, they contact other members of the prayer chain and everyone prays for the person having difficulty.

A way one congregation set up a healing ministry is the way Gethsemane Lutheran Church of Tempe, Arizona did it. They enlisted the senior pastor and identified a group of mature members who had a heart for prayer. They ordered the Reclaim materials mentioned at the top of this chapter. Each member of the team had the assignment of one of the DVDs and would watch it and report on it back to the group. They also went through the participant's guide (one of them was designated as the leader and used the Leader's Guide). To kick off their very first meeting, they invited me over to talk a little about healing prayer, its history and its use today within the church. During our discussion together, I learned that many of them had some experience of personal healing or knew of someone who had been healed through prayer. Others knew very little but were very interested in learning how to do prayer for healing and knew of members of the congregation, relatives, neighbors or others they thought might appreciate healing prayer.

If you do set up a healing ministry, just know that you stand in a long historical tradition of Christians who have prayed for centuries for people in need. From Jesus Himself who taught His disciples how to pray, to the sending out of His followers (reported in the book of Acts in the New Testament), to the present time throughout the world, Christians still ask others what they would like Jesus to do for them. Then with humility and reverence they lift up the person in need to the throne of God, giving praises to God and offering thanksgiving for the healing presence of our Lord.

* * *

Before leaving this appendix on setting up a healing ministry, I thought it might be useful to the reader to actually "see" a worship service of healing in print. There are many examples which might serve as a model. What follows is just one example of what might be put together for a mid-week healing worship service, or in this case, what is being called "A Service of Spiritual Healing." This service was developed by Rev. Garth D. Ludwig referenced in other parts of this book. Following the reprinting of this service, I will also print out the description and rationale as to why the service has been presented in this way. Remember, this is just one of many approaches to healing services within the Christian church culture.

A Service of Spiritual Healing

(as used at Hope Lutheran Church, Upper St. Clair, PA)

Hymn

Salutation and Collect

Pastor: Grace to you and peace from God our Father and from the Lord Jesus Christ.

People: AND ALSO WITH YOU

Pastor: O God of Peace, Who has taught us that in finding our rest in You we shall be saved, and that in quietness and confidence You shall be our strength; by the might of your Spirit lift us, we pray, to Your Presence, where we may be still and know that You are God; through Jesus Christ, our Lord. Amen.

The Promises of God

Pastor: Listen to the promises of our Lord Jesus Christ: "Truly I say to you, if you have faith as a grain of mustard seed, you shall say to this mountain, be removed, and it shall remove, and nothing shall be impossible for you"
People: Lord, I believe; help my unbelief.
Pastor: Our Lord Jesus also said, "Heal the sick and say unto the people, the Kingdom of God is come near unto you."
People: Lord, I believe; help my unbelief.
Pastor: Listen to the words of St. James, the apostle of Christ, "Is there any among you sick? Let him call for the elders of the church, and let them pray over him, anointing him with oil in the Name of the Lord; and the prayer of faith shall save him who is sick. And the Lord shall raise him up and if he has committed sins, it shall be forgiven him. Confess therefore your sins to one another, that you may be healed."
People: Lord, I believe, help my unbelief.
Intercessions
Pastor: Seeing that we have a great High Priest, Jesus Christ, the Son of God, let us come boldly to the throne of Grace, that we may obtain mercy and find grace to help in time of need.
People: OUR FATHER WHO ART IN HEAVEN...
Pastor: Remembering that all of God's children are near and dear to Him, wherever they may be, let us first pray for those who desire our prayers, many of whom cannot be with us this day. (Here shall be named those who desire prayer to be made for them)
Pastor: Blessed Jesus, we bring unto your loving care and protection on the stretchers of our prayers, all those who are sick in mind, body or spirit. Take from them all fear and help them to put their trust in you, that they may feel beneath them and around them your strong and everlasting arms.
Cleanse them from all resentments, jealousy, self-pity, pride, or anything else that might block Your healing power. Fill them with a sense of Your loving presence, that they may experience the Kingdom of love in their whole being. And touch them with your divine power that they may be healed according to Your glory and for the building of Your Kingdom upon earth.
People: Amen

Pastor: Let us pray for ourselves, first putting ourselves - body, mind, spirit - in the healing presence of Christ.
(Then shall silence be kept for a time)
Affirmation
Pastor: O Lord, save your people
People: They that put their trust in You
Pastor: Send them your help
People: And always give them strength
Pastor: As I live in Christ I am supplied with all the spiritual resources required for my needs
People: As I live in Christ I am free from fear and have quietness and confidence within
Pastor: As I live in Christ I am at one with God and know the Peace of God which passes human understanding
People: I can do all things through Christ Who gives me strength
Pastor: Who shall separate us from the love of Christ? Shall tribulations or distress, or persecutions, or famine, or nakedness or peril?
People: No, in all these things we are more than conquerors through Him who loves us. For I am persuaded that neither death, nor life, not angels, nor principalities, nor powers, nor any other creature shall be able to separate us from the love of God which is in Christ Jesus our Lord.
Confession of Sins
Pastor: Let us humbly confess our sins to God.
In our confession let us think not only of gross sins but sins of disposition as well: bitterness, worry, hurt feelings, resentment, jealousy, spiritual pride, living in the past, self-love, self-pity.
People: Almighty God, Lord of all, we confess that we have sinned against You in thought, word and deed. Have mercy upon us, O God. According to Your great love do away with our offenses and forgive us all our sins, for the sake of Jesus Christ. Amen.
The Absolution
Pastor: The almighty, loving and merciful God now gives you absolution and remission of all your sins. I therefore proclaim His peace to you according to His Word.
People: AMEN
A HOMILY ON HEALING

Anointing and Laying on of Hands
Pastor: The Almighty Lord, who gives power and strength to all who put their trust in Him, is now and evermore your defender: may He instill in you an assurance that there is no other name but the name of Jesus Christ whereby you may receive health and salvation.
(Then shall the people come forward for the "laying on of hands" and prayers at the altar rail after which they will return to their places.)
Thanksgiving
Pastor: Lift up your hearts
People: We lift them up to the Lord
Pastor: Let us give thanks to the Lord our God
People: We do it because we love your Holy Name, O God.
Pastor: It is our grateful duty to give thanks to You, O Lord, who gives us health and salvation; whose Son came into the world that we might have life in abundance; Who in His love for all men ministered to their infirmities and gave both the power and command to His disciples to heal the sick. We give You thanks and praise that You have continued your healing work among us. May we never forget your faithful mercies, through Jesus Christ, Our Lord.
People: AMEN
Benediction
Pastor: May God our Father, God the Son, and God the Holy Spirit bless you in your departing, and may He preserve you in body, mind and spirit, until the last day.
People: AMEN

A Great Song for a Healing Service:
I highly recommend Healer of Our Every Ill composed by Marty Haugen. You can see this song being performed at the Cantus Mundi website, one of a church choir during a candle lighting ceremony and another by the handbell choir. You can also watch on YouTube a soloist at the piano performing this song.
* * *
The following was a published announcement about the hosting of this (above) "healing service." You may wish to publish

something similar before you begin a healing service in your congregation.

A SERVICE OF SPIRITUAL HEALING
Thursday, June 16, 8:00 p.m.

Hope Church will hold its first "Healing Service" this month and plans to continue them on a regular basis after the summer is over. This is a Service of Spiritual Healing with the emphasis on holistic healing – the total person (body, mind, spirit). All are invited, whether members of Hope congregation or not.

Our approach will be a liturgical, low-keyed, meditative type of service. It will emphasis the teaching ministry of healing with an equal accent on prayer and thanksgiving. It is a revival of the ancient ministry of the Church in which Christ told His disciples to preach the Kingdom of God and to heal the sick (Luke 9:2). It follows in the tradition of the early church in which pastors laid hands on the sick and anointed them with oil (James 5:14-16).

In a Healing Service, people come forward to the altar voluntarily for two reasons: (1) to have their own illness prayed for by the pastor (2) to be an intercessor for someone else who is ill. Such prayers at the altar are private, heard only by the person who requests the prayer. There is a laying-on-of-hands to symbolize the power of God to make people whole.

Bear in mind that we all need healing! Wholeness is not restricted to the physically healthy. If you have a domestic problem at home with your spouse or child, that indicates a need for healing in the mental dimension. If you are having problems with faith, spiritual healing is your urgent need. Remember the promises of God - "Praise the Lord my soul, and do not forget how kind He is. He forgives all my sins and heals all my diseases." (Psalm 103:2-3)

This Christian Ministry of Healing has been commended by our Board of Elders and by the Executive Council. More importantly it is commended by the LORD who gave this ministry to the Church two thousand years ago.

FELLOWSHIP OF ST. LUKE

A fellowship for those who would like to participate in the ministry of healing is being organized. It will involve visiting the sick and helping to bring wholeness to others. Contact Pastor Garth if you are willing to use this important spiritual gift.

Appendix C
Preaching on Healing: A Sermon by Garth Ludwig

On September 26, 2011, Jim Wright, a Lutheran who lives in Lake Havasu City, Arizona, sent me a few items from his files on healing. The first was a sermon by Garth Ludwig, preached on February 29, 1976 on Transfiguration Sunday, the Eighth Sunday after Epiphany, at Hope Lutheran Church, Upper St. Clair, Pennsylvania. When Jim Wright attended one of the Revive! the Healing Ministry of Jesus conferences put on by Rev. Bill Dasch and myself, Jim had shared with us that he knew of Garth's work in healing ministry way back in the 70's. I had known Garth when he was an anthropologist on the faculty of Concordia University, in Irvine, California in the 90's. But although he served with me on the Ministerial Health Advisory Board of the Pacific Southwest District of the Lutheran Church – Missouri Synod, I was not aware of his early work in healing. So it was a supremely nice surprise to receive Dr. Ludwig's sermon from when he was a younger man in parish ministry. His sermon is reprinted below. It is a good sermon for clergy looking for a model to preach on the topic of illness and healing.

* * *

"Fighting Back When You Become Ill"
Text for the sermon: Mark 1: 40-41
"A leper came to Him and pleaded on his knees, 'If you want to, you can cure me.' Feeling sorry for him, Jesus stretched out His hand and touched him. 'Of course I want to,' he said. 'Be cured.' And the leprosy left him at once and he was cured."

One of the things that really amazes me about the modern world is how we so casually seem to accept illness... almost as if it were a natural thing as the sun rising or the rain falling.

So a person has a temperature of 102 and he says to himself: "All I need are a couple of aspirins and some rest in bed, and I'll be all right. That's all there is to it."

Or another person has a problem with his stomach. He goes to a doctor and finds that he has a stomach ulcer. Which after the diagnosis he takes the treatment, makes the necessary adjustments in his diet, and then goes on trying to live as merrily as he did before.

And the thing that bothers me about all of this is not that people are seeking treatment and are trying to get well... but it is rather the question – "Where does God fit into the picture?"

Is God concerned about my physical and mental health? Does it really matter to God if I get a headache or if I wear glasses... or if I have a weak thyroid system... or if I am getting arthritis and neuralgia? DOES GOD CARE ABOUT ME AS A TOTAL PERSON?

This past month we have been talking about the fighting nature of our Christian Faith, but I wonder how many people associate the power of God with their own health... or indeed if they even think God has anything to do with their health and well-being. Never will I forget the time I called upon a man who was sick and I asked him if I could read the Scripture and pray for him. And he cut me off sharply by saying - "What's the matter? Do you think I am dying?"

And I think that man so typifies the state of the church today in which God is related only to a person's spiritual concerns... in which there is the old Greek belief which says that a person's body belongs to the "doctor" and the soul belongs to "God." And don't ever mix the two together. Of course if you get sick enough you may deign to call upon God to come to your rescue... but often this is motivated more from the fear of dying than it is from faith in the power of God to heal.

My message today is going to be a reaction against all of these distortions and mis-beliefs. I want to tell you what the Bible has to say about HEALING... and to share with you the Biblical picture of God who is concerned about our body and mind as well as our spirit... a God who tells me that illness is from the hand of the evil one... and that when I become ill I am to fight the good fight of faith.

I. The Healing Ministry of Jesus

Did you know that Jesus, when He preached the Good News of the Kingdom of God, healed people wherever He went? The Gospels of Matthew, Mark and Luke report a tremendous amount of healing activity in Jesus' ministry.

In Matthew 9:35 we are told - "So Jesus went around all the towns and villages teaching in their synagogues, announcing the Good News of the Kingdom, and curing every kind of ailment and disease."

Mark 3:10 says - "He cured so many that sick people of all kinds came crowding in upon Him to touch Him." There are, in fact, more miracles of healing in the first chapter of Mark than there are in the entire Old Testament put together.

One Sabbath Day in Capernaum Mark tells us that Jesus accomplished the following: He healed a man with a demon in the synagogue; then He went to Simon Peter's house and healed Simon's mother-in-law of a grave fever; and that night the whole town gathered at His door with the sick and the demon-possessed, all of whom He promptly healed. ALL OF THAT IN ONE DAY!

Jesus even had His disciples involved in the healing ministry. Look at Luke 9:2 - "He called the Twelve together and gave them power and authority to overcome all the devils and to cure diseases, and sent them to proclaim the Kingdom of God and to heal."

Nearly one-fifth of the entire Gospels is devoted to Jesus' healing. Out of the 3,779 verses of the four Gospels, 727 relate specifically to the healing of physical and mental diseases and the resurrection of the dead. In fact, there are very few cases of spiritual transformation reported in the Gospels, the stories of the conversion of Nicodemus, Zaccheus, and the woman at Jacob's well. But there are forty-one distinct instances of physical and mental healing recorded in the four Gospels... and add to that the sixteen cases of healing reported in the Book of Acts.

I think that the inference is inescapable. JESUS CAME TO HEAL AND TO MAKE PEOPLE WHOLE! It was part of His mission of redemption to the world, and it was the mission He gave to His church.

Remember the time a paralyzed man was let down through the roof by his four friends because they couldn't get through the front door? And Jesus said to the crowd - "What do you think is easier for me to do? To forgive this man's sins or to heal his body? But to show you I have power to forgive sins, I am also going to heal his body." Which He promptly did. He made the man whole.

WHOLE! To be complete. To be a total person in body, mind, and spirit. Jesus said that. Not me.

Was Jesus a faith healer? Perhaps not in the sense that we think of faith healers today... but it is very clear that His healing ministry was a sign that the KINGDOM OF GOD WAS breaking through. And that healing was a spiritual symbol of the new age that was dawning.

In fact, one day the disciples of John asked the question whether Jesus was the Messiah, promised of God, or not. And how does Jesus choose to answer the claims of His Messiahship? He says - "Go and tell John the things that you see and hear. The blind see, the lepers cleansed, the lame walk, the deaf hear, the dead are raised to life, and the poor have the Gospel preached unto them." The sign of the KINGDOM OF GOD. Great signs and wonders of the new rule of God for all to see. So does Jesus say that the Messiah has truly come. And so does the New Testament proclaim in passage after passage.

II. Why Did Jesus Heal?

Now, why did Jesus heal? I truly believe that this is the secret that the modern church has woefully distorted and for which reason we have forsaken the power of God in making people whole.

First of all, Jesus healed because He had care and compassion for people. This is so obvious we need not even labor the point. For example, in Mark 1:41 a leper comes up to Jesus and says, "If you want to, you can cure me." And the text tells us that, "Jesus was filled with compassion and reached out and touched him." But Jesus also healed because He was hostile to that what makes people sick. This is a feature we conveniently overlook... but time and time again the Gospels tell us that Jesus rebuked the illnesses of the sick who came to Him.

For instance, when he healed Simon Peter's mother-in-law of a grave fever, Luke states that Jesus rebuked it. That is, He commanded it to come out of her.

When He healed the epileptic boy, Jesus rebuked the unclean spirit. "Deaf and dumb spirit, I command you. Come out of him and never enter again." (Mark 9:25)

In other words, what comes across is an antagonism Jesus feels toward sickness and the power that is causing it. In the mind of Jesus some evil source, some destructive power - whether demons or Satan, the opposite of the Spirit of God - has gained power over the sick person. And Jesus, hostile to this evil power, rebukes it in anger and commands it to free its grip from the ill person.

Illness, therefore, is not from God. Illness is from Satan, whom C.S. Lewis calls a "parasite," and who is binding man by his destructive power.

Jesus says this so very clearly in the account reported in Luke 13: 16: "And this woman, a daughter of Abraham whom Satan has bound these eighteen years, was it not right to untie her bonds on the Sabbath Day?"

Or the case of the Pharisees claiming that Jesus was casting out demons through Beelzebub, the chief of the devils, in Matthew 12. But Jesus confounded their confused logic by saying that if He was helping Satan chase out demons, then Satan was working against himself. On the contrary, Jesus states that He was working against Satan by casting the demons out, attributing to Satan the cause of all such scourges.

III. Is Illness God's Will or Not?

Let me tell you something very personal. When this concept of a Healing God came home to me, I could only think of the hoax that has been perpetrated on the Christian Church these past 1700 years. Because the church has actually glorified sickness as something good. We have gone so far as to equate sickness with the will of God. We have told people that it is good for them to suffer and be in pain.

For years in my ministry I used to follow the line that if God wanted you to be sick, you couldn't do anything to change the situation. I used to talk to people in their sick beds about this being the will of God, and to bear up under in serenity and patience. I saw my own position as a clergyman to merely comfort, never to heal.

What changed my mind? By reading the Scriptures and seeing the healing ministry of Jesus for what it really was. That rather than it being God's will that I be sick, it was GOD'S WILL THAT I BE HEALTHY!

For why else would Jesus heal? Remember the leper who came pleading to Jesus, "Lord, if you want to, you can cure me?" What did Jesus say to him? "OF COURSE I WANT TO. BE CURED." Jesus didn't say - "No, I don't want to heal you. I think it's better for you to suffer as a leper; in fact, the more leprous you become, the more God is pleased." No, he said - "OF COURSE I WANT TO HEAL YOU." Read Mark 1:41 for yourself.

The question of God wanting us to be sick is so preposterous that we don't believe it in our own medical behavior. For if you really believed that it was God's will to be sick, you would never go to a doctor nor take any medicine... because that would be a deliberate act against the will of God.

Do you see the spiritual schizophrenia we've gotten ourselves into? We say that sickness is God's will and then we proceed to find the best doctor we can to get rid of the sickness. That doesn't make any sense.

I remember when one of our parishioners was being operated on for cancer, and I said to him - "Let's pray for your healing." And he said to me, "But what if this is God's will?" And I could only think to myself - "Then why are you fighting God by having an operation?"

Is it God's will that people die of polio – or is it God's will that Dr. Jonas Saulk discovered the vaccine for polio? Was it God's will that fifty years ago young mothers died so frequently in childbirth – or is it God's will that medical science has discovered the means today to preserve these mothers?

Jesus always looked upon healing as something that was good. In fact, He repeatedly broke the Sabbath Laws to bring this goodness to the ill. One day Jesus was in the synagogue when a man with a withered arm walked in – and the authorities watched carefully to see if Jesus would heal or not... But he said to them – "Is it against the Law on the Sabbath Day to do good or to do evil, to save life or to kill?" And then He proceeded to heal the man, the implication being that it was GOOD to heal. It was good for man and the Sabbath Day.

God is a healing God who desires our health and well-being. There is no other sense we can make out of the Scriptures. "Daughter, go thy way. Thy faith hath made thee WHOLE."

This was the message of Jesus Christ. And it was the ministry of the Early Church as well, who fervently believed in the healing power of God and did many great signs and wonders. In fact, there is documentation that the Church practiced the healing ministry until the third century after Christ – until Greek science came in to divide the body from the soul – and so it is divided even today. BUT IT NEED NOT BE SO! Not if we return to the healing ministry of Jesus Christ.

IV. Using The Healing Power Of God

Let me leave with you three vital truths about the healing power of God:

(1) First, know that when you become ill, you are being attacked. The power of evil is placing its grip upon you. That is when you must pray the prayer of faith. Pray that God will come to you in His power and love and rest His hand of healing upon you. Pray for the goodness of God to overwhelm the evil that would destroy and maim you.

But do not dictate to God how He will heal you! He may use medical science – or He may use the healing powers that are residual in your own body – or He may heal you spontaneously. I have seen miracles of healing with my own eyes that defy all description... and I have seen God heal through the skills of modern health delivery care. Who are we to dictate how God does His wonders – all manner of healing gives the glory to God. What matters not is how God heals you... but that He does heal you.

(2) Secondly, believe that a healing of some kind will come to you from God's hand of power. Perhaps it may not be within His providential purpose to deliver you from a physical malady at this particular time, but this does not mean that God is not healing you. He always heals in some way... especially does He touch the spirit of those who seek and hunger after Him.

I have talked to people who prayed to God for a physical healing and received instead a deep healing within their spirit. And they have told me that they would not trade their SPIRITUAL HEALING for any kind of physical healing. I have seen God heal people of bitterness, of hatred, of self-pity, and of guilt... just as I have seen healings of cancer, pneumonia, and club-foot. Who is to gainsay the God who touches us at the area of our deepest need? God always heals! The prayer of faith never returns empty.

(3) Thirdly, seek the Healer above the healing. The entire purpose of the healing ministry is to experience the redeeming power of Jesus Christ. And if through your prayer of faith you have come closer to His love and compassion... and the experience of His power in your life... blessed are you. For the Giver of the gift is always the greatest treasure. Just like the blind man whom Jesus healed. He said: "Once I was blind, but now I SEE."

And what He saw with his new eyes was JESUS, his Savior. Praise God who gives us the eyes of faith to see Him above all things.

– SOLI DEO GLORIA –

Rev. Garth D. Ludwig
Hope Lutheran Church
Upper St. Clair, Pennsylvania

* * *

Included in the packet which Jim Wright sent to me was a newspaper clipping from a newspaper, the Pittsburgh Post Gazette, April 24, 1977, which has the headline, "Pastor Studies Religion, Healing Link." The article talks about Garth Ludwig receiving his Ph.D in anthropology of man. It describes Garth's desire to study cultural anthropology in order the better understand the Hebrew culture in which the Bible was written. The article quotes Dr. Ludwig several times about religion and healing. One quotation is key. Dr. Ludwig says, "Western medicine is very, very passive. The patient is acted on by the physician. In primitive cultures and in the early Christian church, the person takes an active part – praying and meeting with a group to work out the problem."

He goes on to say that he believes medical science is beginning to move back in this direction. He also hoped that his doctorate will open up opportunities to discuss the church's role in healing with ministers. He also says that team work between minister and physician is essential in the healing process.

Appendix D
Additional Healing Stories and Poems

The Lighthouse
Once I was lost upon the sea
It seemed all hope was gone
My ship was drifting helplessly
Battered by the storms
But then I saw a brilliant light
Shining brighter than the day
It seemed to beckon come to me
I will light the way
Now my ship is in the harbor
Anchored firmly near the shore
In the shadow of the lighthouse
Safe forever more
Oftentimes I wonder
Just where that I would be
If my lighthouse- Jesus Christ the Lord
Had not rescued me
J. Morse 1997
* * *

The Lighthouse
The Lighthouse is a beautiful song written and performed by Ronnie Hinson.
It talks about a lighthouse whose light can be seen and shines out into the darkness of the sea. It thanks God for the lighthouse. Several webpages exist where you can view the words to this song.
Hear Ronnie describe how he came to write this poem and to hear him sing (YouTube)
* * *

Beautiful Lord
Beautiful Lord by Leeland is another great song which describes the storms at sea and how there is a light that shows the way to peace and calm. (YouTube)
The lyrics are by Leeland (Marc Byrd and Leeland Mooring.)

Another version called <u>Leeland Beautiful Lord - in New Song Cafe</u> (YouTube)
* * *
I'll Be Your Lighthouse by Craig L. Grimes
when you find
that you're lost
and your world
is crumbling down
and the sound
of emptiness
ever present,
the loneliest sound
hold this thought
in your heart
and what's lost
soon will be found
I'll be your lighthouse
and darkness comes down
when your days
are endless hours
and it seems
there's no hope at all
and every road
that you travel
on your journey is
blocked by a wall
hold this thought in your heart
and soon good fortune will call
I'll be your lighthouse
and darkness
starts to fall
if you need me
I'll be there
a guiding beacon of light
you know, I'll be your walls
in the cold of the night
when your dreams
all but shatter
and where you are

you've already been
and it seems
that all your troubles
keep comin' back again and again
hold this thought in your heart
and soon your heartaches will end
I'll be your lighthouse
when dark night begins
I'll be your lighthouse
when dark nights... begin
Copyright 1999 by Craig L. Grimes
From his album Craig L. Grimes
Reprinted here with permission of Craig L. Grimes
* * *

A Healing Story

The healing story below is real. It comes from a colleague of mine. It is what she and her husband went through in search of healing. I asked her to write up their story for my book. I thank her for taking the time to share it with you. – Ron Rehrer

My husband is a high school math teacher and has not missed a day of school for illness in 30 years. One of the most difficult journeys of our married life of 31 years started on April 24, Easter Sunday, 2011. Mark came down with flu-like symptoms - nausea, diarrhea, vomiting and general body aches. He was not running a fever. By the end of the day, he felt a little better. On Monday, he had planned to go with one of his buddies and his son to the local mountains for a few days of hiking and R and R. The few times that he called home during those three days he mentioned that he felt weak and still had flu-like symptoms, but was having a good time. By the end of that week, he had lost about 10 pounds, just not feeling well and keeping food down. The Monday of the following week he went back to school, still not feeling well, but able to teach. By the end of that second week of illness, he called his primary care physician (PCP) and scheduled an appointment. The appointment revealed nothing and the PCP referred Mark to a GI specialist. The Gastroenterologist saw Mark, ran some tests and ordered some additional testing (endoscopy and colonoscopy) to determine what was going on. These tests revealed some inflammation but nothing life threatening or serious. Medication was prescribed. Three more weeks passed, four more specialists were seen and their tests run, and Mark continued to lose weight. He also continued to complain of serious weakness and loss of "power" and strength.

At this point, I sent the following email to several friends who had many connections in the medical profession:

I would appreciate your prayers for Mark. He has been sick now for 7 weeks and has lost 27 pounds. He has extreme weakness and fatigue, but so far, no diagnosis. We have been to 6 specialists and he has had numerous tests run. We think it started perhaps as a flu virus the week after Easter, but he has gotten progressively worse, so maybe it was not the flu. They have ruled out some really bad things like cancer in his chest and abdomen, Lou Gehrig's, etc., but he continues to decline with no answers. If you know of any amazing doctors - like perhaps an internal medicine doctor, let me know! We are about ready to try anything even outside the insurance (which has been a royal pain!) We need someone who can look at the whole picture - everyone has their specialty, but no one is looking at the whole! His primary care is useless! Thanks in advance!

These friends did make several important connections for us at some very well-known and highly touted hospitals, and with prestigious and well-respected medical professionals, even with the head of physicians of a research hospital in our area that is considered one of the best in the country. Referrals continued to be made while we waited patiently (and sometimes impatiently!) for approval from our PCP and insurance to go to these medical specialists. By this time it was early July and Mark had lost 30 pounds with no diagnosis, 15 doctors seen and a myriad of prescription drugs - none providing an ounce of relief or help. At this point, I again reached out to the head of a major medical research hospital with the following email:

Thank you for the assistance you have provided to this point. Unfortunately, we continue to try to work within a system that is not providing answers and a diagnosis so treatment may begin for my husband. His condition continues to deteriorate. We are now in week 8 of this illness and he continues to lose weight (30 pounds now) and feels so sick. He has profound weakness and fatigue, and now is also experiencing tingling in his hands and arms the last day and a half. After seeing an acclaimed critical care doctor, he believes that my husband needs to be in a research hospital or facility to get the best team of doctors looking at him and at his condition. Yet, we are just getting referrals to additional doctors within the network of his insurance. This is not providing the answers and help that we need! We need the best doctors looking at him! And we need these medical professionals that can look at the whole picture - not just a system (according to their specialty). Certainly, specialists are needed, but they need to confer with each other! Your continued help is truly needed at this time!

During these weeks of illness, we continued to battle with the health insurance provider and with the network provider. It was truly a myriad of phone calls and referrals to other people to talk with - all without answers or a clear-cut direction. We spent hours on the phone almost every day.

On July 4th, he could withstand the discomfort, pain and uncertainty no longer, and asked that I take him to the Emergency Room of a major hospital in our area with a great reputation. I did so, and the ER doctor, upon hearing our story and the information about my husband's condition, admitted him to the hospital for more tests. We thought we were getting somewhere now! Each day my husband was in the hospital, his attending physician would come in and spend a little time with him, prescribe additional medication and run further tests including a PET scan. The good news was that all of the tests came back negative for cancer, MS, ALS, any infectious diseases, etc., but there were still no answers as to why he was so sick! The final day of his hospital stay, July 6, the doctor recommended that he see a psychologist or psychotherapist to discuss why he was so upset and had such high anxiety. He also prescribed an anti-depressant and anti-anxiety medicine! He took me aside and talked to me about my husband's anxiety and his state of mind, inferring that this was all in his head because there seemed to be nothing physically wrong with him! I was furious with this unreasonable and insensitive dialog!. In the 32+ years I have known my husband, he has always been very stable and healthy, emotionally and physically, and being a person of faith, he has always been strong spiritually as well! To hear this doctor's words of "diagnosis," inferring that he had a mental problem, angered me so intensely that I walked away from him as he was finishing up with me! My husband was discharged from the hospital the evening of July 6th with several prescriptions, but physically weaker and sicker than ever! By this time, he had lost almost 45 pounds.

That night we prayed for wisdom and guidance and we prayed for a healing miracle. On the morning of July 7th, after a sleepless night and a lot of discussion and searching the Internet and literature for any answer, we decided to take the recommendation of a dear friend of my husband's whose sister had been healed of a "mystery illness" by an acupuncture doctor. This acupuncturist was well known and respected in the community, having worked in the area for over 20 years. We had always thought that acupuncture and alternative medicine was not "real medicine" and shied away from any such association, but at this point we were desperate for answers - desperate for help and healing!

On July 8th, the acupuncture doctor fit my husband into her busy schedule and spent two hours with him, asking many questions, listening, touching, feeling, examining and finally offering treatment. The doctor's assessment in summary: his vital organs were shutting down due to an unknown illness, his energy channels (the chi) were blocked (thus the profound weakness) and his body was protecting the "core", thus the tingling in the extremities and coldness in his arms and legs (up to his thighs). On my husband's second visit to see her, the doctor stated to our son, "You almost lost your father. He had about a week to live before his organs would have stopped functioning altogether." Over the next two months, my husband saw the acupuncturist three times a week. During the first month, he saw the main acupuncturist, but during the second month, her brother came back to the U.S. from China and he saw both of these doctors - this brother/sister team, alternating each visit. Each of these doctors had extensive training in China and each also holds a medical degree from two prestigious medical schools in the United States.

During these two months, my husband experienced a new and very restrictive diet and had to drink a special "tea" that I brewed each morning for an hour. The tea was made up of many herbs and roots from China, and each week, an adjustment would be made to the portions and ingredients of the tea depending on his needs and his progress. It is important also to mention that from the first day my husband saw the acupuncturists, he stopped taking all of the prescription drugs, which were, by this time, almost too numerous to count!

Almost immediately upon receiving the acupuncture treatments and massage therapy, my husband began to feel better. As each week continued and his acupuncturist continued treatments, he started to gain weight, was regaining strength and energy slowly, and the pain and discomfort lessened. He was making steady gains each week and by the end of August, he had gained about twenty of the fifty total pounds he had lost and started teaching school again, although he taught the first couple of weeks from a stool in the front of the classroom!

In late September, seeing my husband's health restored significantly, both of the acupuncturists left to return to China for a year. At this point, he was strong enough to continue with his healthy diet (introducing several new foods each week), but he knew he needed additional treatments. Once again, we took the referral of a good friend to see a doctor who practices "alternative medicine" closer to work and home. He now sees this new doctor twice a week. He has now gained about 35 pounds back and is, as he describes, "about 85% healed." And although we have spent thousands of dollars for his treatments since July (insurance will not cover this alternative medicine), we know for certain that this was the route to take toward healing...this amazing, frustrating journey toward healing!

At this time, we still have no idea what caused my husband's critical illness, but we are grateful for the measure of healing received through some very unusual means of acupuncture, acupressure, massage therapy, Chinese medicinal herbs, roots, bark, etc., a very specific diet, vitamin and nutrient supplements, and prayer...lots and lots of prayer!

* * *

Another healing story comes from the Philippines. This story was told to me by my friend, Rev. Jim Johnson, who served as a missionary in the Philippines for twenty years. It is reprinted here with his permission. The story goes like this:

The young boy had an accident with a machete while harvesting cong-cong (water plant) in a field. Cut was deep and severe and got infected to the point that when the father took the boy to the ER, they were going to amputate the leg. Father picked up the boy, and left, saying, "You will not make a cripple of my son." He then took the boy to a herbaleria (herb doctor - female), who carefully cleaned out the wound, dressed it with herbs, some fresh and some in bottles she had. She then took a live chicken, killed it, cut it in half length-wise, and placed a half of the chicken on the top of the wound and a half on the bottom of the leg. She then bound it together with several long strips of cloth. She sent them home, telling the father to bring the boy back in seven days. [As you can well imagine, the smell got pretty rank during those days, given the heat and humidity of the Philippines].

When she removed the dead and decaying chicken from the wound on the seventh day, all the infection and poison from the wound and leg had been pulled into the decaying flesh and body of the chicken. The boy's leg was clean and clear of all infection. The boy (now man) is alive and well today. He has a scar, of course, on that leg, but does not even walk with a limp.

* * *

Don's Story (told with his permission). (I, Ron, was part of this healing event while in Texas, and I asked Don to write his personal healing story for my book).

During 2005 I was having headaches on a consistent basis. At Debbie's (my wife) urging I made a doctor's appointment to see if they could determine the cause. After an examination by my physician she could not determine any reason for the headaches. She suggested and scheduled for me to have a MRI done the next day. With some apprehension, since this was my first MRI, I went and had a MRI done.

The next morning at work Debbie called very upset. The MRI had shown a brain aneurism. The MRI had shown that it was 4cm long and the location in the brain. The doctor had called stating that I needed to get to a hospital in Arlington immediately to begin the process of registering to have an angiogram done. My first thoughts were that I was very busy at work and really did not have time for this. I drove to the hospital to satisfy Debbie's concern. At the hospital I was met by Pastor Dasch, Pastor Rehrer and Jerry Hayes DCE. I thought they were there to see someone else. I intended to say hello to them and if they asked to say I was there for a check-up of some kind. Then I realized these men were there on my account. Debbie had called my mother and mother had called Pastor Dasch and they had come. Pastor Dasch asked if there was some place we could sit and we found a place in the waiting area. After some discussion on what was happening Pastor Dasch asked if they could pray for me. I replied that was fine and I expected to fold our hands in prayer and pray. Pastor Dasch first asked what I wanted Jesus to do for me. I was caught off guard and replied somewhat sheepishly to heal me. After all, no Pastor had asked me what I wanted Jesus to do for me before. Didn't pastors already know what to pray for? Next he asked me if it was alright to lay hands on me. Again somewhat sheepishly I replied it was alright. Pastor Dasch then laid his hand on my head and the other 2 men laid their hands around me. My own ignorant thoughts were what ever happened to folding your hands. They all prayed for me to be filled with the Holy Spirit and for God to heal this aneurism. It was a humbling experience to be prayed for.

My angiogram was scheduled for the next morning and we all left the hospital. Pastor Dasch said he would be there in the morning before I had the procedure done. The next morning at the hospital Debbie and I was met by Pastor Dasch. In the pre-surgery room Pastor Dasch again asked me what I wanted Jesus to do for me and if he could lay hands on me. I replied it was alright (the ice had been broken the day before). Pastor Dasch prayed for the Holy Spirit to anoint me and for the aneurism to be gone. Afterwards he left and I was wheeled in to begin the angiogram.

The doctor performing the procedure began to inject the dye into my leg and to watch the monitor to determine more information on this aneurism. With this information they would determine how to treat it. I was awake and quietly watching the monitor to see what was going on as if I really understood this. The procedure seemed to last a long time when suddenly the doctor left. I thought where is he going. Afterwards the doctor returned and was seemingly upset but relieved for my sake. He stated that he had searched everywhere and had even gone and consulted another doctor. Their conclusion was that there wasn't any aneurism to be found. I was very stunned and relieved about all that had taken place. What was going on here?

Debbie and I remained for several hours in the pre-surgery room as a precaution since an artery in my leg had been cut where the dye had been injected. That evening we left and went to my mother's house. Later Pastor Dasch called and wanted to know what had happened. I told him that they could not find anything. The aneurism was gone. He asked me how I felt about this. I was very glad. But my mind was full of many questions about what had happened today.

First I had always been a rather private person and did not want to ask someone to pray for me. Prayers for myself should be done by me. I had thought a lot about this previously and realized this wasn't the way I should feel but could not determine a reason why. When Pastor asked what I wanted Jesus to do for me this knocked down all walls of self pride. To feel this way about someone praying for me was simply a matter of self pride and Jesus did humble me that day. God's healing is all about the glory of God and nothing about me. I realized that when I could not ask my fellow believers in Christ to pray for me I had not truly and honestly opened my heart to God. Thinking back it was a tremendous feeling knowing these men stood beside me on my behalf and prayed for me.

Secondly was Pastor asking if they could lay hands on me. My first thought was that this was very weird and I wonder what people were thinking. But there was nothing more personal and calming than these men praying for me and laying their hands on and around me. Later I found that many people had prayed for me that day and for their prayers I am very thankful. I am also thankful for the support and prayers from Debbie and my family. I thank Pastor Dasch, Pastor Rehrer and Jerry Hayes for praying for me that day. I am very thankful for my eyes to be opened to the healing by God. Healing is all about God and His glory and not about me.

* * *

While once visiting with my friend Diane and her husband, he had gone to work, and she and I were chatting in her living room. Down the hall there was a tiny alcove in which stood a bell. During our chat that bell suddenly rang. I stopped and asked Diane, if she had just heard something. She said, "Yes, the bell rang in that hallway." I nodded and said, "But there's no one else in the house. How could it ring?" Diane's reply was, "It's my Mom." We got up and walked down to where the bell was.
She picked it up, and rang it. It was the same identical sound we had both heard simultaneously. The rational mind says that is impossible. Yet we both heard it at the same time. Diane believed it was her Mom letting her know she was OK and safe in heaven. Below is an even stronger story she shared with me through email. Diane gave me permission to share the above story and the one below with you, the reader.
Ida's mom was diagnosed with lung cancer even though she had quit smoking several years before. She got progressively worse, and finally, when they knew she didn't have much longer, Ida and Nate and Ida's sisters all stayed with her until she died. I had talked to Ida on a regular basis and I knew that Marge didn't have much time left. I was getting ready for work the next morning and all of a sudden I felt the most peaceful feeling I had ever felt and I saw Marge in heaven with my Mom. Ida called about 10 minutes later and I said, "I know." I told her about what had happened to me - what I had seen and what I had felt. I wanted to share that peace with her. I have never had such a wonderful feeling as I did at that moment, and I will never forget it. Ida and I are very strongly connected, I just never realized how strong that connection was until that moment.

Appendix E
Rev. Paul Teske - Healed and Healing

In September of 2012, my friend, Rev. John Durkovic and myself flew to Geneva, Illinois, west of Chicago in order to observe and participate in a weekend of healing led by Rev. Paul Teske and his wife, Rivers.

John had invited me to this event. He knew I was interested in healing ministries, and so when he heard about this weekend, he approached me with the thought of going together.

The occasion was the 50th anniversary of Faith Lutheran Church in Geneva, Illinois. I told John I would love to go with him. I had heard about the healing ministry of Rev. Paul Teske from my friend Bill Dasch (featured earlier in this book). I had ordered Rev. Teske's book (<u>Healing for Today</u>) a year earlier but had not yet gotten around to reading it. So John and I made our plans, and flew to Chicago, rented a car, got an inexpensive hotel near the church location, and went to see and learn.

The schedule for the weekend began with a Friday evening praise and worship event with teaching on healing. On Saturday there would be further worship and singing. Then on Sunday morning, Rev. Teske would be preaching during the regular Sunday service.

When we arrived at the church on Friday night, we were warmly welcomed by church greeters. John went into the sanctuary and I sat just outside the glass doors and plugged in my laptop so that I could take notes on the teaching. I didn't want to sit in the sanctuary and bother anyone with the clicking of my keys on my laptop. So sitting next to the glass doors on the left side leading into the worship space, it was fairly easy to listen through the door

On that Friday night Rev. Paul Teske was introduced by the pastor of the church, Rev. Steven Okpisz. Then Paul welcomed everyone, gave a brief history of himself, and then told the story about how he suffered a major stroke while at a speaking engagement. He fell on stage and was rushed to the hospital. The result of this stroke is that it effected his walking so that he had to endure difficult physical therapy. He had to learn to walk with a brace, and the stroke made a major negative impact on him. However, Pastor Teske is a very strong believer in healing. He heard that Benny Hinn, a well-known television healer, was leading one of his major healing events within driving distance of the Teske home. So Paul and Rivers went to the Benny Hinn healing conference. It was to be the major turning point in his life and ministry.

At this point in his talk, Pastor Paul Teske showed a brief video of he and his wife, Rivers, going up on stage, as he sought to receive a healing from Benny Hinn. He told Hinn of his belief in healing. Hinn addressed the audience about this man's belief in healing. Then Hinn stretched out his arm, and Paul and Rivers flew backward on stage, as if hit by a huge surge of power.

The results were dramatic. Paul found his leg healed, completely. He then showed another brief video of he and Rivers going back up on stage in thanksgiving to God. Benny Hinn prayed for Paul and Rivers, told his large audience that this man was a pastor in the Lutheran Church – Missouri Synod, and that he believed Paul was going to lead a healing ministry. He then prayed for Paul and Rivers, and anointed them for healing ministry. For Paul, this was the turning point of his life. Not only had he been miraculously healed, he was now dedicated to the Lord for healing ministry. From that time on he has traveled to many places in the world doing healing ministries. His own congregation sets aside time and budget for him to be able to share the healing ministry of Christ with any who invite him. Paul is a humble man. He is warm and caring. He knows his Bible very well, and bases his ministry within Lutheran theology. He emphasizes the work of the Holy Spirit, and uses some of the language of what many refer to as the Charismatic Movement. But he is inviting and calm, and is completely convinced of the power of the Spirit to do anything.

On Saturday, Paul continued his teachings. The church building was filled with people eager to learn much. Like Friday night, the Saturday sessions began with some wonderful singing. Projected up on large screens were the words to the songs. They were not traditional hymns but rather they were contemporary songs rich with healing imagery about the mighty power of God.

While I knew very few of these songs, they were easy to sing, and while the "congregation" of people sang, clapped their hands, or raised their hands in praise to God, some women and young girls went to the open spaces to either side of the pew area, and using various colored flags, danced to the Lord. Some at times jumped up and down, while others spun or swayed back and forth. It was reverential and not showcasing. It was clear that these were alternative ways of giving non-verbal or non-singing tributes to the Lord.

I smiled at one point when a father and his daughter danced together in the large open space to my left. They were doing something like the "swing" and it reminded me of when I used to dance with my daughter when she was young. At my daughter's wedding reception, she danced with me in the daddy-daughter dance. We started out slow dancing to Lady In Red, then broke out into Rock-Around-the-Clock, doing the swing. I could imagine that father dancing with his daughter at a future wedding of his daughter.

But this was not a dance to rock-n-roll or to ballroom dancing. This was like liturgical dance, and again, was far off to the left so as to not disturb anyone. Obviously this was a tradition of this church and was very natural as both flag-wavers and dancers praised the Lord.

Then on Sunday, the worship service began with a half hour to forty minutes of singing a wide variety of praise songs of various content. The content of these songs projected on the screens gave praise to God, and also described thanksgiving to God as well as the broken condition of mankind needing the healing presence of Christ and the Holy Spirit. Pastor Paul did a teaching from the Scriptures on healing, and Holy Communion was celebrated at the altar in the front of the church.

Following this, many prayer teams came forward, and all were invited to come up for healing prayer with the anointing of oil. There was no time limit on this portion of the service. Pastor Teske announced previously that as many as came forward asking for prayer would receive prayer.

People came up one by one to each prayer team. They privately shared what they needed prayer for, and members of the prayer teams prayed for each person quietly and fervently. A choir, praise band, and piano played throughout this healing time. It was very well done.

My friend John has had some difficulty with his vision. We sat together in a pew, and he leaned over and said he was going up for prayer for his sight. He went over to the prayer team to our right. This prayer team consisted of two women. They asked John for what he needed prayer for, and after telling them, they spent a long time praying intensely for my friend. There was absolutely no rush, no hurry, no anxiety about how much time was needed for prayer. The women prayed and after some time, John returned to the pew and sat next to me, and bowed his head in prayer. Following the worship service, John told me that he could see very well for the first time in a long time.

Several weeks later after we returned in California, on my way down to Irvine, I pulled off the freeway at a prearranged offramp in order to give John a copy of Teske's book that I had purchased for him. He had told me to meet him at a strip mall nearby. When I pulled into the parking lot he was already waiting for me. I handed him the book and asked him about his vision. He smiled and said that it was amazing, that the restored vision he received at that healing conference in Geneva was still in place. He just smiled and was so happy. We talked a bit about the conference we had attended together. Then John told me he was thinking about offering a healing ministry at the church he attends. Just a week ago I saw John again and the healing ministry he said he was going to start had now begun. When people are healed they often begin healing ministries themselves. I pray that the healing ministry of Jesus which John has begun will be a blessing to many.

On Friday night, Pastor Teske began with Romans 6:23 from the Bible. This passage speaks about the wages of sin which is death, but the gift of God is eternal life in Christ Jesus. He also quoted Psalm 103:3 which speaks of the Lord who forgives all your sins and heals all of your diseases.

He also read 2 Corinthians 1: 3-5 which speaks of how we can comfort those needing comforting.

Then he shared some stories of people he knew who were healed. He spoke about a girl who cut herself, who no longer cuts herself. He described a pastor whose back pain was healed.

Then he went to the book in the New Testament, Matthew 4:23 which speaks about Jesus healing many. He spoke about how the church does much preaching and teaching but doesn't teach a lot about healing ministries. He describes how the church dropped the ball on this. He spoke about the many who know and believe Jesus has the power to heal brokenness.

But, he said, the church is now recovering the healing ministry of Jesus and is restoring it. He described how many mainline denominations are bringing back the power of God.

He then handed out an outline of everything he was going to cover. One of the key sections of his teaching was about the Person of Christ. He recounted that there are 23 healing accounts in the Gospels. He pointed to Matthew 4:22-24 Luke 4: 14, Matthew chapter 8, and to a passage in the Old Testament, namely Isaiah 61: 1-3.

Next he spoke about whom Jesus healed: both Jews and Gentiles. He addressed why Jesus did this: a) because people asked for it, b) out of compassion, and c) to glorify God. He then said "I did not volunteer for a stroke. God had to take me through this for God."

Then he described how Jesus healed. Jesus healed immediately (Luke 13: 10-13), and Jesus healed incrementally (Mark 8:22-25).

Pastor Teske also looked at Luke 9: 1-6 which describes how His followers are to be His surrogates. He also cited Luke 10: 1-17 where He sent out his followers in pairs to go and declare peace which breaks confusion and sets the mind. Teske makes it clear there is a battle for the mind.

It isn't possible for me to share all of what Pastor Teske and his wife, Rivers, taught and shared over that weekend.

What is important to note is how he sees the connection of Jesus to the power of the Holy Spirit to heal. He teaches that Jesus was conceived by the Holy Spirit, that this is part of his DNA. He quotes John chapter 10 where Jesus' empowerment came when He was baptized by spirit and water. Then at Pentecost the followers of Jesus received the power.

Through our own baptism, the power of God is within us, he teaches. The Holy Spirit needs a body to carry out his power. We are to respond, "Here I am Lord. Use me." He gives the analogy that you have a Ferrari in you, not a VW. He says the power "is in you to raise the dead." "You already have every gift of the Holy Spirit."

For Pastor Teske, the church (the followers of Jesus) received the Holy Spirit and His power as recorded in Acts chapter 2. Then in Acts 3 it is clear that the disciples have the name of Jesus. There is power in the name. When God shows up, He brings His power... which includes healing power. The member of Christ's body are charged to go out and baptize and that signs will follow.

He goes on to discus demons briefly. He says, "As a believer in Jesus Christ, you have power to cast out demons."

Then Pastor Teske charges the followers of Christ, to "have expectancy that God will use you."

He illustrates this by describing a girl diagnosed with cancer and her lung had collapsed. Hands were laid on her and she was anointed with oil. In the name of Jesus her lungs were healed. Her cancer went away.

He makes it clear that he no longer asks "why" questions like why is this person healed and another isn't. He has come to the position which says:

1. God is Good
2. God knows what He's doing
3. Trust God

Instead of asking "Why?", he has started asking "What do You want me to learn?"

Then using a baseball analogy he says, I throw the pitch and God hits the ball. God says "Throw the ball." Teske states, "God is good. He knows what He is doing."

If I understood Pastor Teske in his teaching, our job is to throw the ball, i.e., pray for healing and leave it up to God to do what He is going to do. In other words, "God hits the ball."

Teske continued "God can heal. I don't know why you are here and others are not. Keep throwing the ball."

At this point Pastor Teske asked people to share what types of issues they were dealing with. He asked, "any of you have head injury issues? Headache issues? Migraines or sinus? If you have any knee issues stand up... if you have any heart issues, stand up." When he asked for people with knee issues to stand, I counted eleven people stand up.

He went on to say you may have emotional issues or spiritual ones, or a relationship problem, or something psychological, or some other thing for which you need healing. Maybe you have stress, or ulcers, or you are trying to deal with spiritual roots. If you are not going to be here tomorrow or Sunday, I'll pray with you. If you feel God has called you into healing/deliverance ministry and you want me to anoint you, I will... so everyone who wants prayer, form a big line and we will pray for the impartation of the Holy Spirit."

Then Pastor Teske took time to pray for every single person in that big line.

I will close this out with just a little of Saturday's talk. In the morning he began by saying once again, "God is good."

Then he taught, "When people die they are getting their healing, they are getting their perfect body. Heaven is a great place. People who are going to heaven are not mourning. Everybody that dies in Christ is healed. But He also heals this side of the grave. God knows what He is doing."

He called for people to move in faith. To be positive, upbeat, and to declare that God is good.

I have not done justice to Pastor Teske's full and robust presentation over the weekend, but I've tried to give you, the reader, a little taste of his ministry. If you read his book you will get a much fuller sense of who he is and how he came to follow Jesus' invitation to do healing ministry.

It is clear that God has called Pastor Teske and his wife, Rivers, into healing and deliverance ministry. They are clearly lighthouses of hope to many.

Acknowledgments

I wish to thank so many for their contributions in making my sabbatical and this book possible. Without their input I would not have discovered the rich diversity of people and places dedicated to healing. Because of their suggestions, I was fortunate to interview both religious and secular professionals in the healing arts. It was also my privilege to visit a variety of locations where people have been healed. Those named here have been my own lighthouses of hope guiding my way.

At the top of my list are my long time therapist colleagues, Leila, Pieter and Richard. Richard Bingilli played a major role in suggesting that I interview Dr. David B. Larson, Dr. Harold Koenig and his best friend, Dr. Andrew Weaver, who opened the door to those contacts. Richard also shared his experiences at Taize, France and impressed upon me the importance of that praying community. Pieter Noomen shared his experiences at Bad Boll, Germany, where he attended a theological conference years ago on healing. His comments were the prelude to learning about the Blumhardts of Bad Boll. Leila's questions about healing led me to a greater search for answers and forced me to dig deeper into the mysteries of healing.

I wish to thank Rev. Lee Meyer for suggesting that I contact Dr. Francis MacNutt of Christian Healing Ministries in Florida. Lee's own family had benefited from Dr. MacNutt's healing ministry, and I will be eternally grateful to Lee for pointing me in that direction.

I thank my friend and colleague, Rev. Art Umbach, for hosting me in his home in Richmond, Virginia. Art personally took me to meet Rev. Ben Campbell, Director of Richmond Hill where prayer and healing are at the heart of their ministry. Art also took me to the home of Rev. Rufus Womble, one of the pioneers of the Order of St. Luke, an ecumenical nationwide group of Christians committed to healing ministries.

Thanks also go to my colleague Rich Brumfield for introducing me to Rev. Dr. Bill Dasch in Houston, Texas. Pastor Bill and I would grow a deep and everlasting friendship, and would later teach healing conferences together under the title "Reclaim!" as we helped people reclaim the healing ministry of Jesus. When Pastor Bill moved his family to Mansfield, Texas, to serve a new congregation, I watched as Bill and his wife, Sheila, prayed for healing for their son Tristen who battled leukemia. Tristen received his ultimate healing in heaven in August, 2010.

I must also thank Hillu Schleuter for her support in taking me to Bad Boll, Germany. Her translation of the many artifacts and books from German into English was so helpful to me. She was an excellent guide as we made our way through the spa building that houses the Blumhardt collection at Bad Boll. Still later, her translations as we made our way through a snow covered cemetery where the Blumhadt family rests was invaluable.

I thank the late Dr. Andrew Weaver for agreeing to meet me in Manhattan, New York City, where he did research for the hospital chaplaincy for his great assistance in setting up meetings with David Larson and Harold Koenig was spectacular. Andrew also shared with me much of his research on prayer as well as his co-publishing with Larson and Koenig. His brilliant mind, relentless research and gracious heart are deeply missed.

I thank Marlene Ludwig for sending me an early copy of Order Restored written by her late husband, Dr. Garth Ludwig, who was on the faculty of Concordia University in Irvine, California. Garth was an outstanding anthropologist, and his book, in my opinion, is the best of its kind from a Lutheran perspective on the theology of healing. Published by Concordia Academic Press, it is "must" reading.

I thank all of my colleagues from the Academy for Guided Imagery for their valuable input on healing. Certainly the co-founders of the Academy, Dr. Martin L. Rossman and Dr. David E. Bresler, added to my understanding of the healing process. It was my friend Roxanne Whitelight who told me about Glastonbury Tor in England, a mecca for healers from around the world. Another friend, Judith Westerfield, lead me to Art and Creativity for Healing in Laguna Nigel, California. The work of its director, Laurie Zagon, as well as the workshops led by Judith are among the most profound and moving in personal healing.

A special thanks to Rev. Ben Campbell, Episcopal priest and Executive Director of Richmond Hill for the invitation to attend the conference on Healing and Deliverance led by Francis and

Judith MacNutt. Not only did I learn a great deal about demonic forces and dark powers and principalities, but I also learned from Ben the profound healing that still continues since Colonial times and the Civil War in the aftermath of slavery and all of its darkness in Richmond, VA. Richmond Hill is a beacon for healing and reconciliation, unique in my experience.

Thanks also to Rev. Francis MacNutt for the invitation to visit him at Christian Healing Ministries in Florida. While there he showed me some of his work on video and he also gave me his personal copy of The Awakening which is a detailed account of the battle with the demonic encountered at Bad Boll in the 19th century which led to the healing of a young woman.

With deepest gratitude I thank Canon Linda Nicholls who welcomed me into her parish at Thornhill, Ontario, Canada, when she served as parish pastor there. Linda described the steps she took to introduce her parish to healing ministry. At the time she also served as the director of healing ministries under the Bishop's office for the national Anglican Church of Canada. I appreciated how she described their efforts to duplicate Burrswood in Ontario. She helped set up a private viewing of the film 'The Power Within' at the Anglican House in Toronto which featured her congregation at worship and the healing service incorporated into it. She also encouraged me to visit Burrswood near Tumbridge Wells, England, just outside London. At our second meeting a few years later in Canada, she invited me to worship with her senior members in a mid-week healing service. It was excellent. Subsequently she made a presentation on healing ministry at a university in Ontario, and sent me her PowerPoint slides. I thank her deeply for her insights and wisdom in healing ministry.

I would also like to thank Canon Linda Calhoun, also of Ontario, Canada, who invited me to become a member of the Order of St. Luke. Her telephone conversation with me was very inspiring.

I also wish to thank the Trappist monks at the Abbey of the Genessee in upstate New York (at Pifffard, N.Y.) for making me feel so warmly welcomed on two different visits with them. Their deep convictions about the work of prayer for the healing of the world is profound. I learned that Thomas Merton often visited there and that Henri Nouwen wrote about his nine month stay at the Abbey. The writings of Merton and Nouwen have made profound impact on millions of Christians throughout the world. They also make outstanding Monk's Bread at the Abbey which you can have shipped to you. I remember how excited I was when someone suggested that I visit this Abbey.

I thank Cathy Meadows for her constant encouragement and support as she recommended I join the Order of St. Luke. Cathy was a great cheer leader all along the way as she endorsed the work of Francis MacNutt, pointed me to friends of hers who had experienced healing, and shared her own infectious spirituality.

I am deeply grateful to two ministers who reached out to me while I was suffering and in need of my own healing. I thank Rev. Tom Rogers, pastor at Abiding Savior Lutheran Church in Lake Forest, California, who wrote a healing service for me, and invited his Board of Elders and leaders to lay hands on me and pray for my healing.

Also I thank Rev. Jess Knauft, pastor at Immanuel Lutheran Church, Redondo Beach, California, for taking me to <u>Father Robert Jepsen</u> for healing prayer. Jess and Father Jepsen, an Anglican priest, knelt with me at the altar of Grace Anglican Church of Oceanside, and there laid hands on me and lifted me up in healing prayer. My condition (adipose delarosa) never returned after this time of prayer. I also thank Jess for providing the many quotations from the early Church Fathers on healing in the first four centuries after Christ. Those quotations started me on the road of discovery of other early church fathers who gave testimony to early hearings in the young church after the outpouring of the Holy Spirit in the New Testament book of Acts.

I give a nod to Rev. Mason Okubo for his encouraging words to me to keep writing my book, and for his constant question, "when is it coming out? I want to read it!"

Another friend to thank is Iris Rudeseal for sending me texts of television broadcasts on healing, aired on her public television channel in Texas. I also thank another friend, Melissa Solomon, for the healing resources and reports she came across.

Thank you also to Evelyn Walz of Forchheim, Germany, who rented a room to me in Colmegna, above Lago Maggiore, Italy, and also drove me to Augsburg to translate my meeting with the healing priest in Augsburg.

A special thank you to my friend, Dr. Peter L. Steinke, for the articles on healing he also sent. Dr. Steinke's writings on healthy congregations from a family systems' perspective are extremely useful for healing brokenness in a congregational system. Also "must" reading.

I was so delighted to find Pearl Willemsson Hoffman, wife of the late Lutheran pastor, Bengt R. Hoffman, author of Luther and the Mystics. My corresponds with Pearl was marvelous. She edited her late husband's book which was republished under the title, Theology of the Heart. I profoundly thank her for permission to quote her husband. This is also another must read book.

Up near Sandusky, Ohio, there is a tiny island out in Lake Eerie called Kelly's Island. There in an old Victorian home is another Lutheran pastor whom I would especially like to thank. Rev. Bob Myer who allowed me to write at their Timothy House, and he also gave me his copy of Healing in the Lutheran Tradition by Martn E. Marty (famous church historian) which first brought me awareness of Martin Luther's healing prayers for Philip Melanchton. Marty's book also introduces the reader to the Blumhardts of Bad Boll. Bob's wife, Mary, was the perfect hostess and an outstanding cook! In their Victorian home there on Kelly's Island, when you step into the shower there is a sign that reads: "Remember Your Baptism."

I also thank Gary and Liz Norton for the use of their cabin up at Lake Arrowhead, California, in the San Bernardino mountains. It is such a peaceful, quiet and serene location, and enhanced my writing and prayer time.

Special gratitude goes to my friend, Rev. Paul Terhune, who told me the story he learned from his grandmother, about Luther's prayer for 'one of his friends who was near death." Paul described how this is a story which has come down through the generations of his family. Of course, the reference is to Martin Luther praying for the healing of his friend Philip Melanchton, Luther's partner during the Reformation.

I wish to thank Dr. Loren T. Kramer and Dr. Larry Stoterau, for their encouragement and support as I pursued my study sabbatical. Both of these church leaders know of the healing power of prayer and both of them provided ways for me to learn and share with many others. Loren approved the study sabbatical and Larry approved of the workshops co-led by Bill Dasch and myself. Without their confidence, support, and vision, this project would not have come to fruition. To God be the glory.

I would not have been able to complete this project without the help of close friends who volunteered to edit my manuscript. Barbara K. Stratton spent a Christmas vacation correcting errors (spelling punctuation, typos, etc.) and making suggestions to improve the manuscript. Thomas Gryn spent a considerable amount of time preparing the book from its original digital format to a print version.

Both Barbara and Tom offered their labor of love in the belief that this book needed a greater audience. I thank them for believing in me and for their hopes for healing others.

Last but not least, I thank my family for their love and support. Meg, my wife, patiently supported all of my reading and research time, as well as my travel. My adult children sent me emails of encouragement and were constantly interested in each new discovery that I made. There were also many friends who listened and asked careful questions. Each of these friends helped sustain me throughout my studies and writing.

Everywhere I went I heard stories of healing. It seemed at times as if everyone had one. Even I, along the way, experienced physical and emotional healing. I too now have a healing story. Thank you to all of those story tellers and for all of the many authors who have shared what they know about healing. I am indebted to you all.

Finally, I wish to thank my friend who created this book for publication, adding in the photos, editing the text, proof readings, doing research, etc. Without him this book would literally not exist. He wishes to remain anonymous. I honor that request. But I can not thank him enough. His fertile mind always asked insightful questions and his computer skills were awesome.

If you would like to contact me for any reason, I can be reached by e-mail: ron@ronrehrer.com

Made in the USA
Columbia, SC
16 August 2017